CALIBAN

Major Literary Characters

CHELSEA HOUSE PUBLISHERS

Major Literary Characters

DAVID COPPERFIELD
Charles Dickens, *David Copperfield*

ROBINSON CRUSOE
Daniel Defoe, *Robinson Crusoe*

DON JUAN
Molière, *Don Juan*
Lord Byron, *Don Juan*

HUCK FINN
Mark Twain, *The Adventures of
 Tom Sawyer, Adventures of
 Huckleberry Finn*

CLARISSA HARLOWE
Samuel Richardson, *Clarissa*

HEATHCLIFF
Emily Brontë, *Wuthering Heights*

ANNA KARENINA
Leo Tolstoy, *Anna Karenina*

MR. PICKWICK
Charles Dickens, *The Pickwick Papers*

HESTER PRYNNE
Nathaniel Hawthorne, *The Scarlet Letter*

BECKY SHARP
William Makepeace Thackeray, *Vanity Fair*

LAMBERT STRETHER
Henry James, *The Ambassadors*

EUSTACIA VYE
Thomas Hardy, *The Return of the Native*

TWENTIETH CENTURY

ÁNTONIA
Willa Cather, *My Ántonia*

BRETT ASHLEY
Ernest Hemingway, *The Sun Also Rises*

HANS CASTORP
Thomas Mann, *The Magic Mountain*

HOLDEN CAULFIELD
J. D. Salinger, *The Catcher in the Rye*

CADDY COMPSON
William Faulkner, *The Sound and the Fury*

JANIE CRAWFORD
Zora Neale Hurston, *Their Eyes Were
 Watching God*

CLARISSA DALLOWAY
Virginia Woolf, *Mrs. Dalloway*

DILSEY
William Faulkner, *The Sound and the Fury*

GATSBY
F. Scott Fitzgerald, *The Great Gatsby*

HERZOG
Saul Bellow, *Herzog*

JOAN OF ARC
William Shakespeare, *Henry VI*
George Bernard Shaw, *Saint Joan*

LOLITA
Vladimir Nabokov, *Lolita*

WILLY LOMAN
Arthur Miller, *Death of a Salesman*

MARLOW
Joseph Conrad, *Lord Jim, Heart of
 Darkness, Youth, Chance*

PORTNOY
Philip Roth, *Portnoy's Complaint*

BIGGER THOMAS
Richard Wright, *Native Son*

CHELSEA HOUSE PUBLISHERS

Major Literary Characters

CALIBAN

Edited and with an introduction by
HAROLD BLOOM

CHELSEA HOUSE PUBLISHERS
New York ◇ Philadelphia

Jacket illustration: Detail from *The Tempest* (c. 1735) by William Hogarth
(From the collection of Lord St. Oswald, Nostell Priory;
photographer Andrew Barton). *Inset:* First page of *The Tempest* from
the First Folio (1623) (With permission from the Folger Shakespeare Library).

Chelsea House Publishers

Editor-in-Chief   Remmel T. Nunn
Managing Editor   Karyn Gullen Browne
Picture Editor   Adrian G. Allen
Art Director   Maria Epes
Manufacturing Director   Gerald Levine

Major Literary Characters

Senior Editor   S. T. Joshi
Copy Chief   Richard Fumosa
Designer   Maria Epes

Staff for CALIBAN

Picture Researcher   Ellen Barrett
Assistant Art Director   Howard Brotman
Production Manager   Joseph Romano
Production Coordinator   Marie Claire Cebrián

First Printing

1   3   5   7   9   8   6   4   2

Library of Congress Cataloging-in-Publication Data

Caliban / edited and with an introduction by Harold Bloom.
p.   cm.—(Major literary characters)
Includes bibliographical references (p.   ) and index.
ISBN 0-7910-0914-9.—ISBN 0-7910-0969-6 (pbk.)
1. Shakespeare, William, 1564–1616. Tempest.   2. Browning, Robert, 1812–1889.
Caliban upon Setebos.   3. Auden, W. H. (Wystan Hugh), 1907–1973. Sea and
the mirror.   4. Shakespeare, William, 1564–1616—Characters—Caliban.
5. Shakespeare, William, 1564–1616—Influence.   6. Caliban (Fictitious
character).   I. Bloom, Harold.   II. Series.
PR2833.C3   1992
820.p'351—dc20
91-33570
CIP

CONTENTS

CONTENTS

THE ANALYSIS OF CHARACTER

Harold Bloom

"Character," according to our dictionaries, still has as a primary meaning a graphic symbol, such as a letter of the alphabet. This meaning reflects the word's apparent origin in the ancient Greek *charactēr*, a sharp stylus. *Charactēr* also meant the mark of the stylus' incisions. Recent fashions in literary criticism have reduced "character" in literature to a matter of marks upon a page. But our word "character" also has a very different meaning, matching that of the ancient Greek *ēthos*, "habitual way of life." Shall we say then that literary character is an imitation of human character, or is it just a grouping of marks? The issue is between a critic like Dr. Samuel Johnson, for whom words were as much like people as like things, and a critic like the late Roland Barthes, who told us that "the fact can only exist linguistically, as a term of discourse." Who is closer to our experience of reading literature, Johnson or Barthes? What difference does it make, if we side with one critic rather than the other?

Barthes is famous, like Foucault and other recent French theorists, for having added to Nietzsche's proclamation of the death of God a subsidiary demise, that of the literary author. If there are no authors, then there are no fictional personages, presumably because literature does not refer to a world outside language. Words indeed necessarily refer to other words in the first place, but the impact of words ultimately is drawn from a universe of fact. Stories, poems, and plays are recognizable as such because they are human utterances within traditions of utterances, and traditions, by achieving authority, become a kind of fact, or at least the sense of a fact. Our sense that literary characters, within the context of a fictive cosmos, indeed are fictional personages is also a kind of fact. The meaning and value of every character in a successful work of literary representation depend upon our ideas of persons in the factual reality of our lives.

Literary character is always an invention, and inventions generally are indebted to prior inventions. Shakespeare is the inventor of literary character as we know it; he reformed the universal human expectations for the verbal imitation of personality, and the reformation appears now to be permanent and uncannily inevitable. Remarkable as the Bible and Homer are at representing personages, their characters are relatively unchanging. They age within their stories, but their habitual modes of being do not develop. Jacob and Achilles unfold before us, but without metamorphoses. Lear and Macbeth, Hamlet and Othello severely modify themselves not only by their actions, but by their utterances, and most of all through *overhearing themselves,* whether they speak to themselves or to others. Pondering what they themselves have said, they will to change, and actually do change, sometimes extravagantly yet always persuasively. Or else they suffer change, without willing it, but in reaction not so much to their language as to their relation to that language.

I do not think it useful to say that Shakespeare successfully imitated elements in our characters. Rather, it could be argued that he compelled aspects of character to appear that previously were concealed, or not available to representation. This is not to say that Shakespeare is God, but to remind us that language is not God either. The mimesis of character in Shakespeare's dramas now seems to us normative, and indeed became the accepted mode almost immediately, as Ben Jonson shrewdly and somewhat grudgingly implied. And yet, Shakespearean representation has surprisingly little in common with the imitation of reality in Jonson or in Christopher Marlowe. The origins of Shakespeare's originality in the portrayal of men and women are to be found in the *Canterbury Tales* of Geoffrey Chaucer, insofar as they can be located anywhere before Shakespeare himself. Chaucer's savage and superb Pardoner overhears his own tale-telling, as well as his mocking rehearsal of his own spiel, and through this overhearing he is emboldened to forget himself, and enthusiastically urges all his fellow-pilgrims to come forward to be fleeced by him. His self-awareness, and apocalyptically rancid sense of spiritual fall, are preludes to the even grander abysses of the perverted will in Iago and in Edmund. What might be called the character trait of a negative charisma may be Chaucer's invention, but came to its perfection in Shakespearean mimesis.

The analysis of character is as much Shakespeare's invention as the representation of character is, since Iago and Edmund are adepts at analyzing both themselves and their victims. Hamlet, whose overwhelming charisma has many negative components, is certainly the most comprehensive of all literary characters, and so necessarily prophesies the labyrinthine complexities of the will in Iago and Edmund. Charisma, according to Max Weber, its first codifier, is primarily a natural endowment, and implies a primordial and idiosyncratic power over nature, and so finally over death. Hamlet's uncanniness is at its most suggestive in the scene of his long dying, where the audience, through the mediation of Horatio, itself is compelled to meditate upon suicide, if only because outliving the prince of Denmark scarcely seems an option.

Shakespearean representation has usurped not only our sense of literary character, but our sense of ourselves as characters, with Hamlet playing the part of the largest of these usurpations. Insofar as we have an idea of human disinterestedness, we tend to derive it from the Hamlet of Act V, whose quietism has about it a ghostly authority. Oscar Wilde, in his profound and profoundly witty dialogue, "The Decay of Lying," expressed a permanent insight when he insisted that art shaped every era, far more than any age formed art. Life imitates art, we imitate Shakespeare, because without Shakespeare we would perish for lack of images. Wilde's grandest audacity demystifies Shakespearean mimesis with a Shakespearean vivaciousness: "This unfortunate aphorism about art holding the mirror up to Nature is deliberately said by Hamlet in order to convince the bystanders of his absolute insanity in all art-matters." Of *Hamlet*'s influence upon the ages Wilde remarked that: "The world has grown sad because a puppet was once melancholy." "Puppet" is Wilde's own deconstruction, a brilliant reminder that Shakespeare's artistry of illusion has so mastered reality as to have changed reality, evidently forever.

The analysis of character, as a critical pursuit, seems to me as much a Shakespearean invention as literary character was, since much of what we know about how to analyze character necessarily follows Shakespearean procedures. His hero-villains, from Richard III through Iago, Edmund, and Macbeth, are shrewd and endless questers into their own self-motivations. If we could bear to see Hamlet, in his unwearied negations, as another hero-villain, then we would judge him the supreme analyst of the darker recalcitrances in the selfhood. Freud followed the pre-Socratic Empedocles, in arguing that character is fate, a frightening doctrine that maintains the fear that there are no accidents, that overdetermination rules us all of our lives. Hamlet assumes the same, yet adds to this argument the terrible passivity he manifests in Act V. Throughout Shakespeare's tragedies, the most interesting personages seem doom-eager, reminding us again that a Shakespearean reading of Freud would be more illuminating than a Freudian exegesis of Shakespeare. We learn more when we discover Hamlet in the Freudian Death Drive, than when we read *Beyond the Pleasure Principle* into *Hamlet*.

In Shakespearean comedy, character achieves its true literary apotheosis, which is the representation of the inner freedom that can be created by great wit alone. Rosalind and Falstaff, perhaps alone among Shakespeare's personages, match Hamlet in wit, though hardly in the metaphysics of consciousness. Whether in the comic or the modern mode, Shakespeare has set the standard of measurement in the balance between character and passion.

In Shakespeare the self is more dramatized than theatricalized, which is why a Shakespearean reading of Freud works out so well. Character-formation after the passing of the Oedipal stage takes the place of fetishistic fragmentings of the self. Critics who now call literary character into question, and who proclaim also the death of the author, invariably also regard all notions, literary and human, of a stable character as being mere reductions of deeper pre-Oedipal desires. It becomes clear that the fortunes of literary character rise and fall with the prestige of normative conceptions of the ego. Shakespeare's Iago, who wars against being, may be the first deconstructionist of the self, with his proclamation of "I am not what I am." This constitutes the necessary prologue to any view that would regard a fixed ego as a virtual abnormality. But deconstructions of the self are no more modern than Modernism is. Like literary modernism, the decentered ego came out of the Hellenistic culture of ancient Alexandria. The Gnostic heretics believed that the psyche, like the body, was a fallen entity, mechanically fashioned by the Demiurge or false creator. They held however that each of us possessed also a spark or pneuma, which was a fragment of the original Abyss or true, alien God. The soul or psyche within every one of us was thus at war with the self or pneuma, and only that sparklike self could be saved.

Shakespeare, following after Chaucer in this respect, was the first and remains still the greatest master of representing character both as a stable soul and a wavering self. There is a substance that endures in Shakespeare's figures, and there is also a quicksilver rendition of the unsettling sparks. Racine and Tolstoy, Balzac and Dickens, follow in Shakespeare's wake by giving us some sense of pre-Oedipal sparks or drives, and considerably more sense of post-Oedipal character and personality, stabilizations or sublimations of the fetish-seeking drives. Critics like Leo Bersani and René Girard argue eloquently against our taking this mimesis as the only proper work of literature. I would suggest that strong fictions of the self, from the Bible through Samuel Beckett, necessarily participate in both modes, the sublimation of desire, and the persistence of a primordial desire. The mystery of Hamlet or of Lear is intimately invested in the tangled mixture of the two modes of representation.

Psychic mobility is proposed by Bersani as the ideal to which deconstructions of the literary self may yet guide us. The ideal has its pathos, but the realities of literary representation seem to me very different, perhaps destructively so. When a novelist like D. H. Lawrence sought to reduce his characters to Eros and the Death Drive, he still had to persuade us of his authority at mimesis by lavishing upon the figures of *The Rainbow* and *Women in Love* all of the vivid stigmata of normative personality. Birkin and Ursula may represent antithetical and uncanny drives, but they develop and change as characters pondering their own pronouncements and reactions to self and others. The cost of a non-Shakespearean representation is enormous. Pynchon, in *The Crying of Lot 49* and *Gravity's Rainbow,* evades the burden of the normative by resorting to something like Christopher Marlowe's art of caricature in *The Jew of Malta.* Marlowe's Barabas is a marvelous rhetorician, yet he is a cartoon alongside the troublingly equivocal Shylock. Pynchon's personages are deliberate cartoons also, as flat as comic strips. Marlowe's achievement, and Pynchon's, are beyond dispute, yet they are like the prelude and the postlude to Shakespearean reality. They do not wish to engage with our hunger for the empirical world and so they enter the problematic cosmos of literary fantasy.

No writer, not even Shakespeare or Proust, alters the available stock that we agree to call reality, but Shakespeare, more than any other, does show us how much of reality we could encounter if only we retained adequate desire. The strong literary representation of character is already an analysis of character, and is part of the healing work of a literary culture, which implicitly seeks to cure violence through a normative mimesis of ego, *as if it were stable,* whether in actuality it is or is not. I do not believe that this is a social quest taken on by literary culture, but rather that we confront here the aesthetic essence of what makes a culture *literary,* rather than metaphysical or ethical or religious. A culture becomes literary when its conceptual modes have failed it, which means when religion, philosophy, and science have begun to lose their authority. If they cannot heal violence, then literature attempts to do so, which may be only a turning inside out of the critical arguments of Girard and Bersani.

I conclude by offering a particular instance or special case as a paradigm for the healing enterprise that is at once the representation and the analysis of literary character. Let us call it the aesthetics of being outraged, or rather of successfully representing the state of being outraged. W. C. Fields was one modern master of such representation, and Nathanael West was another, as was Faulkner before him. Here also the greatest master remains Shakespeare, whose Macbeth, himself a bloody outrage, yet retains our imaginative sympathy precisely because he grows increasingly outraged as he experiences the equivocation of the fiend that lies like truth. The double-natured promises and the prophecies of the weird sisters finally induce in Macbeth an apocalyptic version of the stage actor's anxiety at missing cues, the horror of a phantasmagoric stage fright of missing one's time, of always reacting too late. Macbeth, a veritable monster of solipsistic inwardness but no intellectual, counters his dilemma by fresh murders, that prolong him in time yet provoke him only to a perpetually freshened sense of being outraged, as all his expectations become still worse confounded. We are moved by Macbeth, however estrangedly, because his terrible inwardness is a paradigm for our own solipsism, but also because none of us can resist a strong and successful representation of the human in a state of being outraged.

The ultimate outrage is the necessity of dying, an outrage concealed in a multitude of masks, including the tyrannical ambitions of Macbeth. I suspect that our outrage at being outraged is the most difficult of all our affects for us to represent to ourselves, which is why we are so inclined to imaginative sympathy for a character who strongly conveys that affect to us. The Shrike of West's *Miss Lonely-hearts* or Faulkner's Joe Christmas of *Light in August* are crucial modern instances, but such figures can be located in many other works, since the ability to represent this extreme emotion is one of the tests that strong writers are driven to set for themselves.

However a reader seeks to reduce literary character to a question of marks on a page, she will come at last to the impasse constituted by the thought of death, her death, and before that to all the stations of being outraged that memorialize her own drive towards death. In reading, she quests for evidences that are strong representations, whether of her desire or her despair. Such questings constitute the necessary basis for the analysis of literary character, an enterprise that always will survive every vagary of critical fashion.

EDITOR'S NOTE

This volume gathers together a representative selection of the best criticism, old and new, that has been devoted to Caliban, the grotesque and pathetic slave of the magus Prospero in Shakespeare's late romance, *The Tempest,* in Robert Browning's remarkable dramatic monologue, "Caliban upon Setebos," and in W. H. Auden's poem, *The Sea and the Mirror.* I am indebted again to the skill and scholarly devotion of Richard Fumosa. The critical extracts, and then the critical essays, each are reprinted here in the chronological order of their original publication.

My introduction disputes the currently prevalent account of Caliban, who in the writings of New Historicists, Marxists, and other members of the School of Resentment becomes virtually a precursor of Nelson Mandela, rather than what he is, the weak and plangent sensibility that feels itself to have been betrayed by its former benefactor, Prospero.

The critical extracts begin with the distinguished triad of Dryden, Dr. Johnson, and Coleridge, and then proceed through modern critics such as Kermode, Empson, and Northrop Frye. Full-scale critical essays start with J. W. Draper's "Monster Caliban," which assembles the evidence that suggests Caliban's status as half-human, half-sea creature, rather than as the fully human slave of New Historicist fantasies. The focus shifts to Browning's "Caliban upon Setebos" with Barbara Melchiori, who finds in the poem a transition-point between the theories of Darwin and Freud.

We return to Shakespeare's monster of pathos with Mike Frank, whose Caliban is the principle of earth. James Smith defends Caliban as the victim of Prospero's extraordinarily vicious hatred, while Jacqueline Latham relates the poor slave to King James I's learned, demonological fancies. Lucy S. McDiarmid and John McDiarmid explore the use of artifice in W. H. Auden's *The Sea and the Mirror.*

G. Wilson Knight, one of the greatest of Shakespeare's critics, assimilates some of Caliban's imagery to that of the American Indians, after which Virginia Mason Vaughan traces the remarkably varied theatrical representations of Caliban, from monster to punkrocker.

The Calibans of Shakespeare and of Browning are closely contrasted by

Kenneth Maclean, while Meredith Anne Skura subtly analyzes the New Historical, "Colonialist" Caliban, and demonstrates cogently how inadequate the Marxist-Foucauldian reading is to the infantile elements in Caliban's nature. This book thus concludes by returning us to the vexed, quasi-familial relationship between Caliban and Prospero, which evokes more of the cosmos of Freud than of Marx.

INTRODUCTION

We are now in the age of Caliban rather than in the Time of Ariel or the Era of Prospero. Our archetypal, politically correct article on Shakespeare these days is likely to be called "Caliban and the Discourse of Colonialism," or else "Ariel and the Economy of Exploitation," or even "Prospero and Mercantilism." *The Tempest* is an uncanny play; nothing much happens after that opening storm that rather inappropriately gives the drama its title. Try to write a plot summary of *The Tempest,* and you will begin to grimace almost immediately. The last *Tempest* I saw in New York City pretended that there was a plot, with unhappy consequences for Frank Langella, who acted Prospero with an apologetic air, as if he wanted us to know how much happier (and better) he would be as Count Dracula. He was not helped much by an inscrutable Ariel, who seemed to want his freedom so as to escape from the stage to an appropriate dive, or by a hulking Caliban who assumed he was the mainstay of Steinbeck's *Of Mice and Men.* Shakespeare's mysterious Orphic drama is never easy to perform, and is more difficult to understand now than it ever was.

What is the genre of *The Tempest?* We have agreed to call it a romance, which is useful enough, since its protagonist is a magus, and his chief aide is a spirit, perhaps even an angel. Caliban, his slave, probably is not to be thought of as wholly human. There is something amphibian about him, something that suggests the sea-world. It is, after all, *his* island, as even the most politically incorrect among us would acknowledge. Shakespeare has so capacious an imagination of justice and of injustice that we scarcely comprehend why he does not conclude *The Tempest* with Caliban left alone upon the island, perhaps to await the female survivor of another shipwreck, with whom he could people the isle with Calibans. The possibility of Caliban being consigned to his native place is never entertained by anyone, Caliban included. It is as though the island, being magical, must cease to exist after Prospero renounces his art and leaves the theatre of his exile. More hurtful is a deeper matter; Prospero and Caliban have too intimate, too familial a relation for it to be dissolved. They loathe and fear one another; Caliban has plotted to murder Prospero; they have, in different ways, and from radically different perspectives, betrayed one another. Most profoundly, they have hurt one another intolerably; each suffers from the pride of wounded and abrogated affection. Each sees the other as having forsaken trust. Yet Prospero finally acknowledges Caliban as being his, almost as though Caliban was Adam to the magus's Yahweh. The attempted rape of Miranda was almost an incestuous offense, for in many respects Prospero and Caliban are father and son. If you are politically correct, you will see this very differently, and will dismiss the quasi-Oedipal complication as paternalistic colonialism. But Shakespeare is not politically correct, even if he is no more Prospero than he is Caliban. The art itself never becomes nature in *The Tempest.* Prospero is subdued, almost ruined, by his total victory; Caliban is merely subdued by his defeat, and is on the verge of a kind of victory through grace, just beyond the drama's conclusion. Of all Shakespeare's plays that are not tragedies, this one trails off in the subtlest and most intense of sadnesses.

Part of our difficulty in absorbing Caliban is his originality, even in Shakespeare's cosmos of characters. He is in the tradition of Shakespeare's displaced spirits, of figures who seem to have wandered in from the wrong play: Shylock, Barnardine, Lear's Fool, Malvolio. Yet to associate Caliban with displacement is a peculiar irony; only he, in the play, is where he belongs. A Hermetic sage is an absurd educator for Caliban; it is the education that constitutes the displacement. Everything that we like best in Caliban precedes his education. The aesthete in Caliban owes nothing to Prospero, whose music is never natural. Caliban before Prospero was the wordless poet of his own climate; after Prospero, Caliban knows language, largely to curse and to proclaim his sufferings, and his resentment. But not entirely:

> Be not afeard, the isle is full of noises,
> Sounds, and sweet airs, that give delight and hurt not.
> Sometimes a thousand twangling instruments
> Will hum about mine ears; and sometime voices,
> That if I then had wak'd after long sleep,
> Will make me sleep again, and then in dreaming,
> The clouds methought would open, and show riches
> Ready to drop upon me, that when I wak'd
> I cried to dream again.

The endowment for apprehending natural music is Caliban's, and the pathos is also his own, each by birthright. What is most moving is the opening signature: "Be not afeard," for the deformed Caliban is essentially timid, and scarcely partakes of the terrible nature of his late mother, the blue-eyed hag and sorceress, Sycorax. Caliban's father is never revealed; we have only Prospero's angry surmise: "got by the devil himself / Upon thy wicked dam." As a "freckled whelp," uniquely born upon an uninhabited island, Caliban is now a hero of our contemporary School of Resentment, who convert him into an anti-imperialist allegory. Here is the spokesperson for the New Historicism, Stephen Greenblatt, raising up Caliban as a beacon for Cultural Criticism:

Caliban, of course, does not triumph: it would take different artists from different cultures—the postcolonial Caribbean and African cultures of our own times—to rewrite Shakespeare's play and make good on Caliban's claim. But even within the powerful constraints of Shakespeare's Jacobean culture, the artist's imaginative mobility enables him to display cracks in the glacial front of princely power and to record a voice, the voice of the displaced and oppressed, that is heard scarcely anywhere else in his own time. If it is the task of cultural criticism to decipher the power of Prospero, it is its task to hear the accents of Caliban.

Confronted by this, I begin by murmuring that we have been hearing the accents of Caliban for some centuries now, and without the necessity of confusing them with the accents of Malcolm X. But then, the Cultural Critic Greenblatt deciphers the power of Prospero by telling us that: "As magician Prospero resembles no one in the play so much as Sycorax," a judgment that might have mystified Shakespeare himself, not to mention Ariel, or even Caliban.

Caliban, however you historicize him, is not going to turn into a classic object of the imperialistic drives of all the Dead White European Males, among whom Shakespeare reigns supreme. The pathos of Caliban centers his dramatic power, but it is not the pathos of victimage, as conveyed by Stephano-like cultural historicists.

It belongs instead to a greater pathos of displacement, which is one of Shakespeare's unique originalities. Like Shylock, Malvolio, and Lear's Fool, Caliban suffers an uncanny fate, in which the virtues of one mode of being are likely to become self-destructive when transferred to another context. Shylock, for all his dignity, becomes a hideous comic villain, and the devoted Malvolio becomes a grotesque comic butt. Lear's Fool, the damage already being done, does not rally the old king, but drives him on to madness. Caliban, not a natural man, but rather the natural child of an unnatural hag, has sustained three shocks before the play even commences: education by a magus; rejection after his attempted rape of Miranda; total powerlessness in relation to Prospero's domination over him. Alone on the island, Caliban would have become the island, without violating his own nature. Prospero's Hermetic art is white magic, and has nothing in common with the horrors of Sycorax. Prospero's true resemblance is to his favorite spirit, Ariel, who shares both Prospero's delighted pride in his art, and also Prospero's coldness. Caliban and Prospero are antithetical to one another, as they desperately discover. It is Caliban's island, but Prospero's play, and any critic who tries to displace Prospero will become only another Stephano. Poor Caliban follows Stephano, and lives to learn that freedom would not have ensued for him, even had Prospero been murdered.

No one is free in *The Tempest,* where only time triumphs, victor even over the Hermetic art of Prospero. Renunciation of his magic does not redeem Prospero from the harmonies and discords of time. The play does not idealize the magus, even as it refuses to idealize the only semi-human Caliban, who is a murderous coward, the most timorous of monsters. Earth and water together are only half of nature, or of imagination, even as air and fire together give us only the other half, Ariel. Shelley, as extreme a revolutionary as Trotsky, shrewdly identified with Ariel, a far better candidate for Marxist exaltation than the wretched Caliban can be. Like our contemporary academic lemmings, Caliban is an inauthentic rebel, a parody of the exploited, the insulted, the injured. In this again, he curiously shares with Shylock and with Malvolio. Yet they have no Prospero, who at last will confront the truth of relationship: "this thing of darkness I / Acknowledge mine." A failed teacher (rather than a cultural imperialist), Prospero asserts something well beyond ownership. Caliban's initial reaction is a hopeless misunderstanding: "I shall be pinched to death." But this is now the Prospero who will retire into mortality: "where / Every third thought shall be my grave." The rarer surprise comes from Caliban: "I'll be wise hereafter, / And seek for grace." Above all poets, even Ovid, Shakespeare's center is the representation of change. His great *topos* is changeability. Those who cannot change never can abide Shakespeare, even as they cannot survive in his scenes. Caliban can change, and will, though I am not certain that we fully understand how and why this can be.

I return, as I close, to the mutual bitterness between Caliban and Prospero, that begins to soften only as the drama ends. Prospero's failure as an educator takes its force only from the Orphic context of Renaissance Hermeticism: It is the failure of Ficino, Bruno and Pico della Mirandola, and not the failure of Shakespeare. Caliban's pragmatic refusal to transcend his own nature does not disturb us, even if we are politically incorrect to the highest degree. But for the great Hermeticist Prospero, it is the first intimation of those recalcitrances that at last will animate his rejection of his own art. As a redeemed Demiurge, Prospero has been as inadequate as Caliban's first maker. Adding to the pain of defeat is the poignance of Caliban's own sense of loss:

> When thou cam'st first,
> Thou strok'st me and made much of me, wouldst give me
> Water with berries in't, and teach me how
> To name the bigger light, and how the less,
> That burn by day and night; and then I lov'd thee . . .

I suppose that if you believe ideology is everything, and personal relations are nothing, then the accents you overhear in this are those of a native victim of paternalism and colonialism. But what, all too briefly, allied Caliban and Prospero was an absolutely personal relationship. The accents I hear are those of a mutually failed love, of an adoption slain, as William Blake would have said, upon the stems of generation.

—H. B.

CRITICAL EXTRACTS

JOHN DRYDEN

To return once more to *Shakespear;* no man ever drew so many characters, or generally distinguished 'em better from one another, excepting only *Johnson:* I will instance but in one, to show the copiousness of his Invention; 'tis that of *Caliban,* or the Monster in the *Tempest.* He seems there to have created a person which was not in Nature, a boldness which at first sight would appear intolerable: for he makes him a Species of himself, begotten by an Incubus on a Witch; but this as I have elsewhere prov'd, is not wholly beyond the bounds of credibility, at least the vulgar still believe it. We have the separated notions of a spirit, and of a Witch; (and Spirits according to *Plato,* are vested with a subtil body; according to some of his followers, have different Sexes) therefore as from the distinct apprehensions of a Horse, and of a Man, Imagination has form'd a *Centaur,* so from those of an Incubus and a Sorceress, *Shakespear* has produced his Monster. Whether or no his Generation can be defended, I leave to Philosophy; but of this I am certain, that the Poet has most judiciously furnish'd him with a person, a Language, and a character, which will suit him, both by Fathers and Mothers side: he has all the discontents, and malice of a Witch, and of a Devil; besides a convenient proportion of the deadly sins; Gluttony, Sloth, and Lust, are manifest; the dejectedness of a slave is likewise given him, and the ignorance of one bred up in a Desart Island. His person is monstrous, as he is the product of unnatural Lust; and his language is as hobgoblin as his person: in all things he is distinguish'd from other mortals.

—JOHN DRYDEN, "The Grounds of Criticism in Tragedy" (Preface to *Troilus and Cressida*) [1679], *The Works of John Dryden,* ed. Maximillian E. Novak (Berkeley: University of California Press, 1984), Vol. 13, pp. 239–40

SAMUEL JOHNSON

CALIBAN: As wicked dew, as e'er my mother brush'd
With raven's feather from unwholsom fen,
Drop on you both!

Whence these criticks derived the notion of a new language appropriated to Caliban I cannot find: They certainly mistook brutality of sentiment for uncouthness of words. Caliban had learned to speak of Prospero and his daughter, he had no names for the sun and moon before their arrival, and could not have invented a language of his own without more understanding than Shakespeare has thought it proper to bestow upon him. His diction is indeed somewhat clouded by the gloominess of his temper and the malignity of his purposes; but let any other being entertain the same thoughts and he will find them easily issue in the same expressions.

"As wicked dew." Wicked; having baneful qualities. So Spenser says "wicked weed," so, in opposition, we say herbs or medicines have "virtues." Bacon mentions "virtuous Bezoar," and Dryden "virtuous herbs."

—SAMUEL JOHNSON, *The Plays of William Shakespeare*
(London: J. & R. Tonson, 1768), Vol. I, p. 20

SAMUEL TAYLOR COLERIDGE

The appearance and characters of the super or ultra-natural servants are finely contrasted. Ariel has in every thing the airy tint which gives the name; and it is worthy of remark that Miranda is never directly brought into comparison with Ariel, lest the natural and human of the one and the supernatural of the other should tend to neutralize each other; Caliban, on the other hand, is all earth, all condensed and gross in feelings and images; he has the dawnings of understanding without reason or the moral sense, and in him, as in some brute animals, this advance to the intellectual faculties, without the moral sense, is marked by the appearance of vice. For it is in the primacy of the moral being only that man is truly human; in his intellectual powers he is certainly approached by the brutes, and, man's whole system duly considered, those powers cannot be considered other than means to an end, that is, to morality.

—SAMUEL TAYLOR COLERIDGE, "Notes on *The Tempest*" [1818],
Literary Remains, ed. Henry Nelson Coleridge (London:
William Pickering, 1836), Vol. 2, pp. 98–99

H. N. HUDSON

Caliban is among the standing wonders of Shakespear's genius. At once the antithesis and the supplement of the zephyr-like Ariel, Caliban has all the sense that the other wants, and wants all the soul that the other has: he is as supernatural a being as Ariel, though supernatural in the opposite direction; as if the material and spiritual elements of nature, instead of combining into a human being, had for once departed from the usual order, and shaped themselves into separate forms of life. All the finer elements of the place having been drawn off to fashion the exquisite soul of Ariel, Caliban, as his name imports, is altogether of the earth, earthy; as in the one we have, as it were, the topmost sparkling foam, so in the other we have merely the organized sediment and dregs of humanity. Yet both represent, after a sort, actual classes of men, though with bodies far more appropriate to and expressive of their dispositions than nature ever produces: for, were all men featured as they are minded; their bodies so made as to express, not conceal, their characters; were deformity of soul always accompanied with corresponding ugliness of person, we should either live in perpetual fright, or become incapable of fear: either the beauty of the good and the deformity of the bad would be mutually terrific and intolerable, or both would wax hard and insensible to all differences. It is worthy of note, that all the supportive mirthfulness of our nature is concentrated in Ariel, while Caliban is at once too muddy-souled to produce and too muddy-faced to express the sunshine of a smile: such is the malignity of his nature, that its proper music is to curse, its proper laughter is to rail. A mere human understanding without the reason or the moral sense, organized into an appropriate form; very much such a being as we might suppose the connecting link between man and brute would be, Caliban can use with tolerable skill the proper means, but cannot conceive the proper ends of human existence; has faculties corresponding to the material, but not to the moral world; can observe, compare, remember and classify facts, but has no emotions or perceptions of truth, or right, or beauty, or goodness; can apprehend the utility, but not the sacredness of justice, the rules, but not the principles of morality; is capable of knowledge, but not of wisdom, of prudence, but not of virtue, of rest, but not of peace, of regret, but not of remorse. Without any original ideas or innate sense of folly and wisdom, virtue and vice, of course a drunken sailor and the noble Prospero are just the same to him in themselves; and he learns to distinguish and choose between them only by experience of what they can do for him: accordingly, after experiencing the meanness and impotence of the one, he is glad enough to return to the service of the other.

Yet this strange, uncouth, malignant, yet marvellously life-like confusion of natures, part man, part demon, part brute, Prospero by his wonderful art and science has educated into a sort of poet. Instruction, however, has in no wise tamed, it has rather increased his radical malignity and crookedness of disposition: a slave "whom stripes may move, not kindness;" "who any print of goodness will not take;" and "on whose nature nurture can never stick;"

> his vile race,
> Though he did learn, had that in't which good natures
> Could not abide to be with;

and his chief profit of language is that "he knows how to curse" his teacher: even his poetry is made up of the fascinations of ugliness; a sort of inverted beauty; the poetry of dissonance and deformity. The dawnings of understanding in him, as in some animals and perhaps in some men, take the form of vicious propensities and vile cunning, so that he evinces his humanity chiefly by openness to its vices, and a readiness to become the foot-licker of whoever will feed his beastly appetites: the only celestial thing that he knows of, is the liquor that makes him drunk; his only god the man that gives it to him. Schlegel finely compares his mind to a dark cave, into which the light of knowledge falling neither illuminates nor warms it, but only serves to set in motion the poisonous vapours; wherein I probably need not say how numerous a kindred he seems to have in the human family. Before the instructions of Prospero, even his understanding was buried beneath his earthy grossness; for the mere understanding, disjoined from the supplementary powers of reason and conscience, has no spontaneous activity, can only be moved to action from without, and by one in whom those supplementary powers are awake and supreme. Perhaps the hero's greatest miracle is, that he "extracts sunbeams from this cucumber," teaching him how

> To name the bigger light, and how the less,
> That burn by day and night:—
>   I pitied thee,
> Took pains to make thee speak, taught thee each hour
> One thing or other; when thou didst not, savage,
> Know thy own meaning, but wouldst gabble like
> A thing most brutish, I endowed thy purposes
> With words to make them known.

Of course it is only by exhausting the resources of instruction on such a being that his innate and essential deficiency can be fairly shown: we cannot see what he wants until he develope all that he has. So that Prospero's having educated him into a sort of poet, without eliciting any sparks of genuine humanity, is the best possible proof what he is. That he has not the germs of a human soul, is equally evident from what education has done, and from what it has not done for him; so that I know not whether it be more wonderful, that Prospero should have made so much, as that he should have made no more out of him. High culture might indeed develope understanding in such a being, without the aid of human feelings, but it could not develope those feelings, because nature has not planted the seeds of them there. The magical world of spirits, it is true, has cast into the dark caverns of his brain a faint reflection of a better world; yet it is only in his dreaming, when sleep has in a manner relaxed the "muddy vesture of decay," which doth so "grossly close him in" that

> The clouds, methought, would open, and show riches
> Ready to drop upon me; that, when I waked,
> I cried to dream again.

In his waking moments all his thoughts, words, and images, though poetical in their way, seem, like his nature, to have been dug up out of the ground. It is as if human speech and understanding were given to a baboon, and the utmost power of culture brought to bear upon him; so that his poetry exemplifies at once the triumph of art over nature, and the triumph of nature over art.

—H. N. HUDSON, "Caliban," *Lectures on Shakespeare* (New York:
Baker & Scribner, 1848), Vol. 2, pp. 18–22

JOHN RUSKIN

The fact is that slavery is not a political institution at all, *but an inherent, natural, and eternal inheritance* of a large portion of the human race—to whom, the more you give of their own free will, the more slaves they will make themselves. In common parlance, we idly confuse captivity with slavery, and are always thinking of the difference between pine-trunks (Ariel in the pine), and cowslip-bells ("in the cowslip-bell I lie"), or between carrying wood and drinking (Caliban's slavery and freedom), instead of noting the far more serious differences between Ariel and Caliban themselves, and the means by which, practically, that difference may be brought about or diminished.

Plato's slave, in the *Polity,* who, well dressed and washed, aspires to the hand of his master's daughter, corresponds curiously to Caliban attacking Prospero's cell; and there is an undercurrent of meaning throughout, in the *Tempest* as well as in the *Merchant of Venice;* referring in this case to government, as in that to commerce. Miranda ("the wonderful," so addressed first by Ferdinand, "Oh, you wonder!") corresponds to Homer's Arete: Ariel and Caliban are respectively the spirits of faithful and imaginative labour, opposed to rebellious, hurtful, and slavish labour. Prospero ("for hope"), a true governor, is opposed to Sycorax, the mother of slavery, her name "Swine-raven" indicating at once brutality and deathfulness; hence the line—

As wicked dew as e'er my mother brushed
With *raven's feather,*—etc.

For all these dreams of Shakespeare, as those of true and strong men must be, are "φαντάσματα σεῖα, καὶ σκιαὶ τῶν ὄντων"—divine phantasms, and shadows of things that are. We hardly tell our children, willingly, a fable with no purport in it; yet we think God sends his best messengers only to sing fairy tales to us, fond and empty. The *Tempest* is just like a grotesque in a rich missal, "clasped where paynims pray." Ariel is the spirit of generous and free-hearted service, in early stages of human society oppressed by ignorance and wild tyranny: venting groans as fast as mill-wheels strike; in shipwreck of states, dreadful; so that "all but mariners plunge in the brine, and quit the vessel, then all afire with *me,*" yet having in itself the will and sweetness of truest peace, whence that is especially called "Ariel's" song, "Come unto these yellow sands, and there, *take hands,* courtesied when you have, and kissed, the wild waves whist:" (mind, it is "cortesia," not "curtsey,") and read "quiet" for "whist," if you want the full sense. Then you may indeed foot it featly, and sweet spirits bear the burden for you—with watch in the night, and call in early morning. The *vis viva* in elemental transformation follows—"Full fathom five thy father lies, of his bones are coral made." Then, giving rest *after* labour, it "fetches dew from the still vext Bermoöthes, and, with a charm joined to their suffered labour, leaves men asleep." Snatching away the feast of the cruel, it seems to them as a harpy; followed by the utterly vile, who cannot see it in any shape, but to whom it is the picture of nobody, it still gives shrill harmony to their false and mocking catch, "Thought is free;" but leads them into briars and foul places, and at last hollas the hounds upon them. Minister of fate against the great criminal, it joins itself with the "incensed seas and shores"—the sword that layeth at it cannot hold, and may "with bemocked-at stabs as soon kill the still-closing waters, as diminish one dowle that is in its plume." As the guide and aid of true love, it is always called by Prospero "fine" (the French "fine," not the English), or "delicate"—another long note would be needed to explain all the meaning in this word. Lastly, its work done, and war, it resolves itself into the elements. The intense significance of the last song, "Where the bee sucks," I will examine in its due place.

The types of slavery in Caliban are more palpable, and need not be dwelt on now: though I will notice them also, severally, in their proper places;—the heart of his slavery is in his worship: "That's a brave god, and bears celestial—liquor." But, in illustration of the sense in which the Latin "benignus" and "malignus" are to be coupled with Eleutheria and Douleia, note that Caliban's torment is always the physical reflection of his own nature—"cramps" and "side stitches that shall pen thy breath up; thou shalt be pinched, as thick as honeycombs:" the whole nature of slavery being one cramp and cretinous contraction. Fancy this of Ariel! You may fetter him, but you set no mark on him; you may put him to hard work and far journey, but you cannot give him a cramp.

—JOHN RUSKIN, "Government," *Munera Pulveris: Six Essays on the Elements of Political Economy* [1872] (New York: Charles E. Merrill, 1891), pp. 166–71

EDWARD DOWDEN

A thought which seems to run through the whole of *The Tempest,* appearing here and there like a coloured thread in some web, is the thought that the true freedom of man consists in service. Ariel, untouched by human feeling, is panting for his liberty; in the last words of Prospero are promised his enfranchisement and dismissal to the elements. Ariel reverences his great master, and serves him with bright alacrity; but he is bound by none of our human ties, strong and tender, and he will rejoice when Prospero is to him as though he never were. To Caliban, a land-fish, with the duller elements of earth and water in his composition, but no portion of the higher elements, air and fire, though he receives dim intimations of a higher world,—a musical humming, or a twangling, or a voice heard in sleep—to Caliban, service is slavery. He hates to bear his logs; he fears the incomprehensible power of Prospero, and obeys, and curses. The great master has usurped the rights of the brute-power Caliban. And when Stephano and Trinculo appear, ridiculously impoverished specimens of humanity, with their shallow understandings and vulgar greeds, this poor earth-monster is possessed by a sudden *schwärmerei,* a fanaticism for liberty!—

'Ban, 'ban, Ca'-Caliban,
Has a new master; get a new man.
Freedom, heydey! heydey, freedom! freedom! freedom! heyday freedom!

His new master also sings his impassioned hymn of liberty, the *Marseillaise* of the enchanted island:

Flout 'em and scout 'em,
And scout 'em and flout 'em;
    Thought is free.

The leaders of the revolution, escaped from the stench and foulness of the horse-pond, King Stephano and his prime minister Trinculo, like too many leaders of the people, bring to an end their great achievement on behalf of liberty by quarreling over booty,—the trumpery which the province of Prospero had placed in their way. Caliban, though scarce more truly wise or instructed than before, at least discovers his particular error of the day and hour:

        What a thrice-double ass
Was I, to take this drunkard for a god,
And worship this dull fool!

It must be admitted that Shakspere, if not, as Hartley Coleridge asserted, "a Tory and a gentleman," had within him some of the elements of English conservatism.

But while Ariel and Caliban, each in his own way, is impatient of service, the human actors, in whom we are chiefly interested, are entering into bonds—bonds of affection, bonds of duty, in which they find their truest freedom. Ferdinand and Miranda emulously contend in the task of bearing the burden which Prospero has imposed upon the prince:

        I am in my condition
A prince, Miranda; I do think, a king:
I would, not so! and would no more endure
This wooden slavery than to suffer
The flesh-fly blow my mouth. Hear my soul speak:
The very instant that I saw you, did
My heart fly to your service; there resides,
To make me slave to it; and for your sake
Am I this patient log-man.

And Miranda speaks with the sacred candour from which spring the nobler manners of a world more real and glad than the world of convention and proprieties and pruderies:

MIR.:   Hence, bashful cunning!
And prompt me, plain and holy innocence!
I am your wife, if you will marry me;
If not, I'll die your maid: to be your fellow
you may deny me, but I'll be your servant
Whether you will or no.
FER.:   My mistress, dearest;

And I thus humble ever.
MIR.:   My husband, then?
FER.:   Ay, with a heart as willing
As bondage e'er of freedom.

In an earlier part of the play, this chord which runs through it had been playfully struck in the description of Gonzalo's imaginary commonwealth, in which man is to be enfranchised from all the laborious necessities of life. Here is the ideal of notional liberty, Shakspere would say, and to attempt to realise it at once lands us in absurdities and self-contradictions:

GON.:   For no kind of traffic
Would I admit: no name of magistrate;
Letters should not be known: riches, poverty,
And use of service none; contract, succession,
Bourn, bound of land, tilth, vineyard, none;
No use of metal, corn, or wine, or oil;
No occupation; all men idle, all,
And women too, but innocent and pure;
No sovereignty.
SEB.:   Yet he would be king on't.

Finally, in the Epilogue, which was written perhaps by Shakspere, perhaps by some one acquainted with his thoughts, Prospero in his character of a man, no longer a potent enchanter, petitions the spectators of the theatre for two things, pardon and freedom. It would be straining matters to discover in this Epilogue profound significances. And yet in its playfulness it curiously falls in with the moral purport of the whole. Prospero, the pardoner, implores pardon. Shakspere was aware—whether such be the significance (aside—for the writer's mind) of this Epilogue or not—that no life is ever lived which does not need to receive as well as to render forgiveness. He knew that every energetic dealer with the world must seek a sincere and liberal pardon for many things. Forgiveness and freedom: these are keynotes of the play. When it was occupying the mind of Shakspere, he was passing from his service as artist to his service as English country gentleman. Had his mind been dwelling on the question of how he should employ his new freedom, and had he been enforcing upon himself the truth that the highest freedom lies in the bonds of duty?

It remains to notice of *The Tempest* that it has had the quality, as a work of art, of setting its critics to work as if it were an allegory; and forthwith it baffles them, and seems to mock them for supposing that they had power to "pluck out the heart of its mystery." A curious and interesting chapter in the history of Shaksperian criticism might be written if the various interpretations were brought together of the allegorical significances of Prospero, of Miranda, of Ariel, of Caliban. Caliban, says Kreyssig, is the People. He is Understanding apart from Imagination, declares Professor Lowell. He is the primitive man abandoned to himself, declares

M. Mézières; Shakspere would say to Utopian thinkers, predecessors of Jean Jacques Rousseau, "Your hero walks on four feet as well as on two." That Caliban is the missing link between man and brute (Shakspere anticipating Darwinian theories), has been elaborately demonstrated by Daniel Wilson. Caliban is one of the powers of nature over which the scientific intellect obtains command, another critic assures us, and Prospero is the founder of the Inductive Philosophy. Caliban is the colony of Virginia. Caliban is the untutored early drama of Marlowe. Such allegorical interpretations, however ingenious, we cannot set much store by. But the significance of a work of art like the character of a man is not to be discovered solely by investigation of its inward essence. Its dynamical qualities, so to speak, must be considered as well as its statical. It must be viewed in action; the atmosphere it effuses, its influence upon the minds of men must be noted. And it is certainly remarkable that this, the last or almost the last of Shakspere's plays, more than any other, has possessed this quality, of soliciting men to attempt the explanation of it, as of an enigma, and at the same time of baffling their enquiry.

If I were to allow my fancy to run out in play after such an attempted interpretation, I should describe Prospero as the man of genius, the great artist, lacking at first in practical gifts which lead to material success, and set adrift on the perilous sea of life, in which he finds his enchanted island, where he may achieve his works of wonder. He bears with him Art in its infancy,—the marvellous child, Miranda. The grosser passions and appetites—Caliban—he subdues to his service,

MIR.: 'Tis a villain, sir,
I do not love to look on.
PROS.: But as 'tis
We cannot miss him.

and he partially informs this servant-monster with intellect and imagination; for Caliban has dim affinities with the higher world of spirits. But these grosser passions and appetites attempt to violate the purity of art. Caliban would seize upon Miranda and people the island with Calibans; therefore his servitude must be strict.

—EDWARD DOWDEN, *Shakspere: A Critical Study of His Mind and Art*
(London: H. S. King, 1875), pp. 419–26

J. COTTER MORISON

It will be admitted that a poet endowed in the manner I have attempted to describe,—with an extraordinary gift, almost a passion, for analysis of character, with a dominant impulse towards humouristic portraiture,—was likely sooner or later, almost as a matter of course, to have his attention drawn to the strange figure of Caliban—one of the most singular creations of Shakspere's fancy. What an opportunity was offered by "the freckled whelp, hag-born," for subtle analysis and grotesque humour! "The poisonous slave got by the devil himself upon his wicked

dam" is a monster, indeed, but he has a human element within his monsterhood;
he can hate, fear, lie, curse, and grovel under the dominion of the basest lusts; but
he can also show the rudiments of pride, revenge, and love of power, foresight and
prudence too, on occasion, as when he urges Stephano to be quick in the murder
of Prospero. But there is nothing very complex and subtle in Shakspere's conception of Caliban. His physical form apart, he is little more than a depraved, brutish,
and malicious man. One cannot say that Shakspere has taken much pains with the
character; we see little more than the surface of such mind as he has: his sulky
anger, his fear of cramps and side-stitches "that shall pen his breath up," his vindictive rage against the enchanter. One might perhaps venture to say that Shakspere had placed his Caliban in a somewhat false and unfavorable position, in which
it was not possible for him to show his deeper nature and ultimate motives and
ideas. This deficiency has been supplied by Browning in the magnificent grotesque
work which we now have to contemplate ("Caliban upon Setebos"). Even after
taking account of all that Ruskin has written on the grotesque, we may doubt
whether its peculiar position and scope in Art have been fully explained. Its proper
province would seem to be, the exhibition of fanciful power by the artist; not
beauty or truth in the literal sense at all, but inventive affluence of unreal yet
absurdly comic forms, with just a flavour of the terrible added, to give a grim
dignity; and save from the triviality of caricature. Our best grotesques belong to the
art of the sculptor or the modeller, as in mediæval and Oriental work—griffins,
gargoyles, or Japanese and Chinese monsters. In literature, the grotesque does not
seem to rise with the same spontaneity: the tendency there is either to broad farce
or delicate comedy, in neither of which, as such, need the grotesque be present at
all. Browning, however, has produced a grotesque in language which is as solid and
sharp in outline as if by "Claus of Innsbruck cast in bronze for us."

Before going through the chief wonders of the poem, I should like to say a
word on its particular subject. The second title after "Caliban upon Setebos," or,
"Natural Theology in the Island," marks clearly enough the writer's intention. It is to
describe in a dramatic monologue the Natural Theology,—that is, the conception
of God,—likely, or rather certain, to occur to such a being as Caliban. And the
moral conveyed is plainly this: if Caliban, by appropriate reasoning, deduces from
his inner consciousness, feelings, and instincts, such a grotesque laughably hideous
theology as you see here, what right have philosophers of another order to
suppose that their deductions have any better success or foundation? I do not
approve of the attempt to turn Browning's works into an arsenal of agnostic
arguments. The poet is as much above the reasoner as the sun is above the earth.
It is not the poet's business to lead us to intellectual conclusions, which very inferior
men can do as well as he, but to give us living realities, creations organic and vital,
which take their place amid the works of nature as independent existences. A
character by Shakspere, a landscape by Wordsworth, are as much organic wholes
as their prototypes in the moral and physical world. But while I hold this view—that
it is beside the question, when considering the works of a great poet, to ask
whether his views as regards religion are orthodox or not, whether he holds or

rejects the current theology,—I by no means think we are called upon to shut our eyes to his obvious meaning in a given instance or poem. And I would ask those who may be disposed to take offense at the drift of "Caliban upon Setebos," whether they have any scruple in adopting and applauding the drift of another dramatic monologue of the poet, "The Soliloquy in a Spanish Cloister"? It is certainly not rash to say of that piece, that it was not inspired by an admiration of Monastic Institutions, at least in the form they recently took in Spain. On the contrary, the object evidently was to produce the most hideous and repulsive picture possible of the moral effects in some conditions of cloistered life. Now those who applaud this method in one case, when it suits or flatters their private opinions, cannot consistently reprove it when it happens to do the opposite, and cross their prejudices. The truth is, that "Caliban upon Setebos" is an indirect yet scathing satire of a rather painful class of reasoners who, while beginning with the admission that the nature of the Godhead is an inscrutable mystery, proceed to write long books to prove their special and minute knowledge of its character; which knowledge of theirs, you may by no means contradict or deny under penalties. "Very well," the poet seems to have said, "you complacently draw God after your own image—a flattering likeness no doubt—and you insist upon our accepting your picture as a facsimile of the original. But if your method is legitimate, you cannot pretend to a monopoly of it; other creatures, whether above or beneath you, have the same right to apply it with equal warranty. Here, for instance, is my Caliban, a sturdy reasoner after his own fashion. He looks within his bosom—just as you do—and this is what he finds, his conception of Setebos. You think it very unlovely, but what surety can you offer that your conception of the Eternal is not as repulsive to other beings who may be as much superior to you, as you are to Caliban? Nay, that it is not as repulsive to many of your fellow-men, who, by reason of a different education and studies, do not share your opinions?" Something like this may be supposed to have passed through the poet's mind. And now for a few glimpses at the work itself. What an opening!

> Will sprawl, now that the heat of day is past,
> Flat on his belly, in the pit's much mire,
> With elbows wide, fists clenched to prop his chin;
> And while he kicks both feet in the cool slush,
> And feels about his spine small eft things course,
> Run in and out each arm and make him laugh:
> . . . .
> He talks to his own self, howe'er he please,
> Touching that other, whom his dam called God.

Caliban, you see, has not risen to the consciousness of the Ego. He speaks of himself in the third person, and it is noticeable how much the device contributes to the presentation of the bestial, or rather non-human, character of the creature, assorting with his pleasure in slush and mire, and in being tickled by the small eft-things—lizards and centipedes we may suppose.

Caliban is not like those learned authors of whom Voltaire spoke, who never entered upon the proper subject of their work till the second volume. He is full of matter, and gives us his views of creation and its author with an exemplary absence of prolixity, worthy of imitation by other Natural Theologians.

Setebos, Setebos, and Setebos:—
Thinketh he dwelleth i' the cold o' the Moon.
. . . .
Thinketh, it came of being ill at ease:
He hated that he cannot change his cold,
Nor cure its ache. . . .
                    He made all these, and more,
Made all we see, and us, in *spite:* how else?
He could not, Himself, make a second self
To be his mate: as well have made himself.
. . . .
But did in envy, listlessness, or sport,
Make what Himself would fain in a manner, be—
Weaker in most points, stronger in a few,
Worthy, and yet mere playthings all the while
Things he admires, and mocks too—that is it.

Caliban's eloquence and insight wax stronger with the using; his confidence grows, and he sees the whole problem in a nut-shell:

Put case, unable to be what I wish,
I yet could make a live bird out of clay.
Would not I take clay, pinch my Caliban
Able to fly? . . .
There, and I will that he begin to live;
Fly to yon rock-top, nip me off the horns
Of grigs high up that make the merry din,
Saucy through their veined wings and mind me not:
In which feat, if his leg snapped, brittle clay
And he lay stupid-like—why I should laugh;
And if he, spying me, should fall to weep,
Beseech me to be good, repair his wrong,
Bid his poor leg smart less, or grow again,—
Well, as the chance were, this might take or else
Not take my fancy; I might hear his cry,
And give the mannikin three legs for his one,
Or pluck the other off, leave him like an egg,
And lessoned he was mine and merely clay.
Were this no pleasure, lying in the thyme,
Drinking the mash, with brain become alive,
Making and marring clay at will? So He.

This is a terrible passage, and cuts to the bone. It behoves those concerned with Theological matters to examine how far it is a free and spirited, but not less a faithful, translation, of much which passes for orthodox opinion. Even more incisive is what immediately follows:

> Thinketh, such shows nor right nor wrong in Him,
> Nor kind nor cruel: He is strong and Lord.
> 'Am strong myself compared to yonder crabs,
> That march now from the mountain to the sea;
> 'Let twenty pass and stone the twenty-first,
> Loving not, hating not, just choosing so.
> Say, the first straggler that boasts purple spots
> Shall join the file, one pincer twisted off;
> Say, This bruised fellow shall receive a worm,
> And two worms he whose nippers end in red;
> As it likes me each time, I do: So He.

Having shown triumphantly how Setebos had made all things and creatures not for themselves or their welfare, but out of a selfish and unscrupulous regard for his own exceeding power and glory, Caliban proceeds to dwell on the self-will of his Deity, his divine indifference to justice and mercy, his partiality, favouritism, and caprice. But Caliban has, moreover, the pleasing trait of being thoroughly candid; and his frankness is such, that we must conclude that he has had but an imperfect training in Theology. Unrelenting cruelty, he does not call loving mercy and great kindness, but bluntly says it is "Spite."

> Saith He is terrible: watch His feats in proof.
> One hurricane will spoil six good months' hope.
> He hath a spite against me, that I know,
> Just as He favours Prosper; who knows why?
> So it is, all the same, as well I find.
> 'Wove wattles all the winter, fenced them firm
> With stone and stake to stop she-Tortoises.
> Crawling to lay their eggs here: well, one wave,
> Feeling the foot of Him upon its neck,
> Gaped as a snake does, lolled out its large tongue,
> And licked the whole labour flat; so much for spite.

Caliban is a firm believer in the envy of his God; and hopes, with a subtle casuistry for which one would hardly have given him credit, to take the Deity in:

> Even so, would have Him misconceive, suppose
> This Caliban strives hard and ails no less,
> And always above all else, envies Him.
> Wherefore he mainly dances on dark nights.

(Is not this, by the way, quite marvellous in its fine irony?)

> Wherefore he mainly dances on dark nights,
> Moans in the Sun, gets under holes to laugh,
> And never speaks his mind save housed as now;
> Outside 'groans curses.

Still he has the fullest faith in painful sacrifice and mortification.

> If he caught me here
> O'erheard this speech, and asked "What chucklest at"?
> 'Would to appease Him cut a finger off,
> Or of my three kid yearlings burn the best,
> Or let the toothsome apples rot on tree,
> Or push my tame beast for the orc to taste;
> While myself lit a fire and made a song
> And sung it: *"What I hate, be consecrate*
> *To celebrate Thee and Thy state, no mate*
> *For Thee; what see for envy in poor me?"*

Poor Caliban! we may honestly pity him. His Theology is a torment to him, deepening the shadows already dark enough of his earthly home. Nature is hard, harsh, and destructive to any extent; but Nature is not cruel or spiteful: Setebos is. You can never be sure you have propitiated him aright:

> Never try the same way twice!
> Repeat what act has pleased, He may grow wroth.

Dreadful, he invents a God, an Almighty Frankenstein, which, unlike the "live bird out of clay" he wished to make, to be his abject slave, becomes his fierce master, and soaring away from him into the cold of the Moon, terrorises his life and every thought of it for ever.

No! I am wrong; not for ever. Caliban prudently refrains from making his Deity immortal. He cherishes a lurking hope that like other enemies and evils, Setebos may disappear just as

> Warts rub away, and sores are cured with slime;
> That some strange day, will either the Quiet catch
> And conquer Setebos, or likelier He
> Decrepit may doze, doze, as good as die.

But he cannot keep up this mood of hardy and profane scepticism. A sudden thunderstorm shatters it to pieces:

> What, what? A curtain o'er the world at once!
> Crickets stop hissing; not a bird:—or yes,
> There scuds His raven that hath told him all.
> It was fool's play, this prattling! Ha! the wind
> Shoulders the pillar'd dust: death's house o' the move
> And fast-invading fires begin! White blaze—

A tree's head snaps,—and there, there, there! there, there!
His thunder follows. Fool, to gibe at Him!

(Is there out of Browning a more daring, superb, and startling modulation than
this to be found in literature?—in Beethoven's and Wagner's music there may be,
but nowhere else.)

Lo! Lieth flat and loveth Setebos,
Maketh his teeth meet through his upper lip;
Wilt let those quails fly, wilt not eat this month
One little mess of whelks, so he may 'scape.

Onore a l'altisimo poeta!

—J. COTTER MORISON, " 'Caliban upon Setebos,' " *Papers of the Browning
Society*, Vol. I, No. 26 (April 25, 1884), pp. 493–98

SIR SIDNEY LEE

A strange fish!' exclaims Trinculo when he first catches sight of Caliban. *'Were I in
England now, as once I was, and had but this fish painted* [sc. outside a booth], *not
a holiday fool there but would give a piece of silver: there would this monster make
a man; any strange beast there makes a man. When they will not give a doit to
relieve a lame beggar, they will lay out ten to see a dead Indian.'* Trinculo bears
witness to a perennial phase of popular curiosity. A wild man from an unfamiliar
country will draw many doits from onlookers at any fair in the world. Shakespeare's
contemporaries were singularly eager for new experiences, and Trinculo does not
probably underrate Caliban's capacity to make a British showman's fortune.

But there was more literal substance in the jester-sailor's speech than students
of Shakespeare realise. Caliban was in a practical sense known in England not on the
stage alone. If in his own unique, dramatic shape he had not passed beyond the
boards of the theatre, near kindred of his had figured on the highways of English
life, and had excited much wild surmise among Shakespeare's contemporaries.
Caliban's creation may readily be traced to opportunities which Shakespeare and
his countrymen enjoyed in London of studying at first hand the aboriginal temperament. Verbal and written narratives of travel were rich in sketches of strange
human or semihuman inhabitants of distant lands. But 'wild' visitors were often in
England to supplement the teaching of books. It was a composite portrait which
issued in Caliban from Shakespeare's pen. There, detail, which was drawn from
very varied quarters, was fused together, at times somewhat capriciously, by his
imagination. The occasional presence in person of Caliban or his kindred on English
soil clearly whetted Shakespeare's interest in the riddle of uncivilised humanity. *The
Tempest* enshrines, within its vast bounds of life and poetry, memories of Englishmen's strange encounters at their own doors with wild men from the unmeasured
territories of the West. ⟨. . .⟩

America did not receive much notice from Elizabethan dramatists and poets. They viewed it as a Spanish treasury where the rivers rolled down golden sand, where mountains shone with priceless gems and the forests were fragrant with aromatic spices. Shakespeare, in his few direct allusions to the New World, does not travel beyond hints of the harvest of wealth which Spain was reaping there. To the New World belong 'the Armados of Spanish carracks ballasted with rubies, carbuncles, and sapphires,' of which mention is made in *The Comedy of Errors* (III. ii. 136–140). In the same vein Sir John Falstaff compares Mistress Ford to 'a region in Guiana, all gold and bounty' (*Merry Wives*, I. iii. 66–60).

About England's colonising experiments Shakespeare is silent. Fellow playwrights showed small respect for their countrymen's colonial ventures; they reckoned colonial settlements only fit for spendthrifts and ne'er-do-wells. But Shakespeare held aloof from the topic. His interests in the great discoveries which tempted colonial effort were mainly confined to the light which they shed on hitherto unknown forms of human nature and custom. The ritual of American sun worship he described in his earliest play. There, giving the word 'Ind' its common occidental significance, he gorgeously describes how:

A rude and savage man of Ind,
At the first opening of the gorgeous East,
  Bows low his vassal head and strucken blind
Kisses the base ground with obedient breast.

(Love's Labour's Lost, IV. iii. 222–5)

Few Elizabethan travellers had failed to notice the American Indian's daily obeisances to the solar deity, and Shakespeare proved by frequent allusions his curious interest in the pagan practice.

Not till the end of his career did the dramatist attempt in Caliban a full-length portrait of the aboriginal inhabitant of the New World. Caliban is no precise presentation of any identifiable native American. The dramatist more prudently attempts to reduce to one common denominator the aboriginal types, many of whom had wandered about London streets in his day. The practical interest which Shakespeare's patron, Lord Southampton, took in the native visitors doubtless facilitated the dramatist's personal intercourse with the strangers. But Elizabethan books of travel supplemented Shakespeare's first-hand observation. All sources of knowledge were laid under contribution. Shakespeare was not the only playwright of his era to bring the Indian on the stage, or to present him in his native garb. In more than one spectacular masque, actors assumed the rôle of Virginian chiefs, wearing feathered head-dress, feathered robes, and jewels on their faces, while they were armed with bows and arrows and smoked tobacco pipes as big as muskets. But Shakespeare stands alone in his endeavour to pass beyond the external features and to portray the essential significance of the native personality.

The main theme of *The Tempest* was obviously suggested by a recent episode in Anglo-American history, the casting away in a terrific storm on the rocky coast of Bermuda of an English ship bound for the new settlement at Jamestown. Prospero's realm is the little West-Indian island, the 'still vexed Bermoothes,' where shipwrecked English sailors, hopeless of rescue, had lately managed to live for ten long months. The mild beauty of the climate had proved a solace, but mysterious noises sorely tried them and led them to imagine that spirits and devils made the island their home. The scene of the play suggests new-discovered seas as clearly as new-discovered lands. The phantom blazes of fire which Ariel in the play scatters about the sinking ship are very literal reminiscences of startling phenomena which sailors imputed to Atlantic storms. Such is the setting into which the Indian native is introduced. Not the least intelligent playgoer could ignore the American source of the inspiration.

Shakespeare cast his net over a wide field of aboriginal life. He may well have spoken to Ralegh's tractable friends of Guiana (of the race known as Caribbean), to the more or less amiable Virginian visitors in London, and to the New Englanders who found a patron in Lord Southampton. But he also had heard vague rumors of monsters 'whose heads stood in their breasts,' and had read of the irredeemable savages, whether of the banks of the River Amazon, or of Patagonia to the extreme south of the Southern Continent. He sought the psychological import of the native temperament by welding together his varied pieces of observation and information. Montaigne, with whose philosophic point of view Shakespeare had much in common, had already been drawn by visits of American natives to France to pronounce on the quiddity of uncivilised humanity. But Shakespeare declined to acquiesce in Montaigne's complacent conclusion that American-Indians were living witnesses to the Utopian life of which a decadent Europe had lost the key. European civilisation had in Shakespeare's view advanced beyond the stage of American-Indian experience and was not likely to revert to it. To Shakespeare the western native was a human being endowed with live senses and appetites, with aptitudes for mechanical labour, with some veneration, knowledge and command of the resources of nature, but lacking moral sense, moral control, and ratiocination.

Caliban's name is clearly a modification of Cariban or Caribbean, the designation of the first American race which set eyes on Europeans. The Caribbeans, on the arrival of Columbus and his countrymen, fled from their homes in the West Indies to the South American mainland. There Ralegh met some of them in Guiana, and he offered them hospitality in England. The name was variously rendered in early reports of American adventures. The first syllable appears not only as 'Car-', but also as 'Cal-', and even as 'Can-'. Cannibal is one of the derivatives. But despite the significance commonly attached to that word, it was without authority that the imputation of man-eating propensities was cast in early reports on the 'gentle-kind' Carib. No such suspicion attaches to Caliban.

Caliban's nurture at times echoes the impressions of gentleness and trustfulness which Ralegh's Caribbean servants left on Elizabethan minds. Caliban almost always speaks in blank verse, and though his utterance is often of rough fibre, it rises now and again to levels of pathetic and tender eloquence. With fine imaginative serenity the savage seeks to quiet the fears which the mysterious noises of the island excite in the civilised ruffians, Trinculo and Stephano:

> Be not afeard: the isle is full of noises.
> Sounds and sweet airs, that give delight and hurt not.
> Sometimes a thousand twangling instruments
> Will hum about mine ears; and sometimes voices
> That, if I then had wak'd after long sleep,
> Will make me sleep again; and then, in dreaming,
> The clouds, methought, would open and show riches
> Ready to drop upon me, that when I wak'd
> I cry'd to dream again.   (III. ii. 130-8.)

All the relations of Caliban with the invaders of his island-home graphically embody, perhaps with a spice of irony, the experience of explorers among the natives of the new continent. When the wild man insists on detecting divine attributes in the brutish Trinculo, he recalls the reception of Sir Francis Drake as an emissary from heaven on the west coast of California. Pizarro had already faced the same ordeal in Peru, Cortes in Mexico, and Cartier in Canada. Often would a degraded explorer, after the manner of Trinculo, tempt the native with strong drink and find amusement in the creature's first experiences of drunkenness. Numberless pioneers of higher principles had also anticipated Prospero in seeking at an early meeting to win the savage's love by teaching him the true functions of sun, moon, and stars, and by warning him against his crude conception of nature's workings. On many a native Indian's ears there had fallen Prospero's words:

> When thou didst not, savage,
> Know thine own meaning, but wouldst gabble like
> A thing most brutish, I endowed thy purposes
> With words that made them known.   (I. ii. 355–8.)

The crabbed agglutinative dialects of the Indian moved many an English traveller to despair, and patient were the endeavours to familiarise the strange being with a speech which might prove intelligible to the English settler.

At the same time every would-be colonist sought much instruction from his aboriginal host. On him alone could the newcomer depend as Prospero relies on Caliban for knowledge of 'all the qualities' of the country, for guidance to the fresh-water springs and to the places where edible berries grew, and where good fish could be caught. The voice of history speaks in Caliban's promise, 'I'll show thee every fertile inch o' th' island,' with which the savage seeks to ingratiate himself with the stranger Trinculo.

Caliban's menial services of cutting and stacking firewood, of scraping trenchers and washing dishes, were those of all natives in the early American settlements. The Indians were the hewers of wood and drawers of water wherever Europeans set foot in America. Shakespeare offers especially precise testimony to the value attached by the early English settlers on the American continent to the industry and ingenuity of the natives as fishermen. More than once Caliban is made to boast of his prowess as a fisherman. 'I'll fish for thee,' he assures Trinculo, when offering his allegiance. But more illuminating is his exultant cry, 'No more dams I'll make for fish,' when he thinks that he has flung off Prospero's yoke. This threat, which commentators on Shakespeare pass over in silence, is a graphic allusion to a peculiar peril of which Englishmen in Virginia had made practical trial. The Virginians, like most Indians, caught their fish in their wide rivers by means of ingeniously constructed dams or weirs. A series of circular fences made of willow poles held together by wickerwork ran from the bank into the river bed, and suspended baskets within the fenced enclosures daily entrapped masses of fish. The secret of this Indian weir-construction was well kept by natives, and Europeans never learnt the art. On the natives' maintenance of the dams the early settlers chiefly depended for their sustenance, and when native disaffection put the dams out of working order, the lives of the colonists were at once in jeopardy.

In his comprehensive generalisation Shakespeare ascribes to Caliban some vague affinities with the most barbarous of all the American races, the Patagonians. These savages lived on the shores of the Magellan Straits, and strange rumours spread about them. Visits to their country were rare. The two Elizabethan circum-navigators of the globe, Drake and Cavendish, both touched Patagonian shores, but the native people declined intercourse with the English mariners. Drake echoes reports by earlier Spanish travellers of the savage worship, which the Patagonians offered their 'great devil Setebos.' Of this Patagonian deity Caliban twice makes mention, calling him 'my dam's god, Setebos' (I. ii. 373; V. i. 261). Despite his dissimilarity from the Patagonians in all other respects, he avows himself a votary of their 'great devil.'

In ascribing to Caliban a 'disproportioned' body and in likening him to 'a tortoise' or 'a freckled whelp,' Shakespeare departs from the strict letter of his authorities. There was nothing 'disproportioned' about any of the American-Indians whom Englishmen had seen. Their stature was invariably normal. Even a common allegation that the Patagonian was an ungainly giant, seven or eight feet high, was refuted by observers. Travellers brought back tales of monstrous distortions of the human shape lurking in distant recesses of the New World, but the evidence usually proved shadowy. Yet the misrepresentation on Shakespeare's part was no doubt deliberate and served both his dramatic and philosophic purpose. It was an act of involuntary homage to the Platonic idea, which Elizabethan thought assimilated, that the soul determines the form of the body. Shakespeare's seeing eye invested his 'rude and savage man of Ind' with a bearing and gait akin to his stunted intelligence and rudimentary sentiment. But the Elizabethan playgoer had followed strange Indians about London streets or had paid his doits to inspect their persons at close quarters in showmen's booths. The actor who created the part of Caliban was under no inducement to lay in his make-up any undue stress on the creature's physical deformities.

—SIR SIDNEY LEE, "Caliban's Visits to England," *Cornhill Magazine*
No. 201 (March 1913): 333, 341–45

ALLAN H. GILBERT

It has long been recognized that in *The Tempest* Shakespeare made use of Montaigne's essay "Of the Caniballes" as translated by Florio. The following description of an ideal commonwealth given by the old councillor Gonzalo is a paraphrase of a passage in Montaigne:

> I' the commonwealth I would by contraries
> Execute all things; for no kind of traffic
> Would I admit; no name of magistrate;
> Letters should not be known; riches, poverty,
> Bourn, bound of land, tilth, vineyard, none;
> No use of metal, corn, or wine, or oil;
> No occupation; all men idle, all;
> And women too, but innocent and pure;
> No sovereignty. (2.1.148–57)

The two speeches of Gonzalo immediately following are also related to Montaigne. Morton Luce, in his edition of *The Tempest* (Arden Shakespeare), after pointing out the parallels to the passages mentioned, quotes from "Of the Caniballes" as follows:

> Three of that nation, ignorant how deare the knowledge of our corruptions will one day cost their repose, securitie, and happinesse, and how their ruine shall proceed from this commerce, which I imagine is already well advanced—miserable as they are to have suffered themselves to be so cosened by a desire of new fangled novelties, etc.

This passage, he says, illustrates the ethical thought of the play, which is summed up in Caliban's speech:

> You taught me language; and my profit on't
> Is, I know how to curse: the red plague rid you,
> For learning me your language! (1.2.363–5)

He adds that many other resemblances to *The Tempest* may be found in the essay "Of the Caniballes," but gives no further examples; nor are any furnished by Mr. John M. Robertson in his work entitled *Montaigne and Shakespeare*. It may be of interest to suggest a few.

There are certain accidental resemblances that hardly need be regarded. Montaigne says that his servant who had been in Canada lived there 'ten or twelve years,' and twelve years is the time of Prospero's sojourn in the island. The passage:

> For more assurance that a living prince
> Does now speak to thee, I embrace thy body, (5.1.107–8)

a reminiscence of such scenes in classical literature as the attempt of Ulysses to embrace his mother in Hades, suggests Montaigne's 'We embrace all but we fasten nothing but wind'.

There is some likeness between the land of the cannibals and the island of Prospero. The island is, indeed, as in the Epilogue, usually spoken of as bare or desert, though speeches of Caliban (2.2.167ff., etc.) show it to be somewhat productive, but Gonzalo says of it: 'Here is everything advantageous to life' (2.1.48); a sentence that may be compared with the following in Montaigne: 'To this day they yet enjoy that natural uberite and fruitfulnesse, which without labouring toyle, doth in such plenteous abundance furnish them with all necessary things, that they need not enlarge their limits. . . . They neither want any necessary thing.' Adrian says of the island: 'It must needs be of a subtle, tender, and delicate temperance. . . . The air breathes upon us here most sweetly.' The cannibals 'live in a country of so exceeding pleasant and temperate situation, that as my testimonies have told me, it is verie rare to see a sicke body amongst them'.

The theme of Montaigne's essay is the contrast between the virtues of the savages and the vices of civilized men. In various ways he illustrates the thought:

> I finde there is nothing in that nation, that is either barbarous or savage, unlesse men call that barbarism which is not common to them. . . . They are even savage, as we call those fruits wilde, which nature of herself, and of her ordinarie progresse hath produced: whereas indeed, they are those which our selves have altered by our artificial devices, and diverted from our common order, we should rather term savage. In those are the true and most profitable vertues, and naturall properties most lively and vigorous.

The character of Caliban is sufficient evidence that Shakespeare did not believe in the perfect natural man, but rather in the blessings of education and civilization, aiding man toward a state of virtue. What is Prospero, the man so learned that he has gained control even over the phenomena of nature, so noble that he can forgive even his worst enemies, but the man who has in his search after wisdom been brought far toward the perfect state of humanity? Prospero's sentiments toward Caliban, the natural man 'whom stripes may move, not kindness', are like those of Wordsworth's Wanderer toward the American Indian:

> But that pure archetype of human greatness,
> I found him not. There, in his stead, appeared
> A creature, squalid, vengeful, and impure;
> Remorseless, and submissive to no law
> But superstitious fear, and abject sloth.   (*Excursion* 3.951–5)

None the less, between inhabitants of the island other than Caliban, and the civilized men shipwrecked there Shakespeare draws a contrast that suggests Montaigne. The latter says that the cannibals do not 'lack this great portion, to know how to enjoy their condition happily, and are content with what nature affordeth them', and that 'those that are much about one age, doe generally entercall one another brethren, and such as are younger, they call children, and the aged are esteemed as fathers to all the rest. These leave this full possession of goods in common, and without division, to their heires', and above all: 'There was never any opinion found so unnaturall and immodest, that would excuse treason, treacherie, disloyaltie, tyrannie, crueltie, and such like, which are our ordinary faults,' implying that such are not the faults of the cannibals. There is a similar contrast between the civilized man and the savage in the following lines, spoken when the strange shapes, helpers of Ariel, bring a banquet to the King of Naples and his companions:

> GONZALO: For, certes, these are people of the island,—
> Who, though they are of monstrous shape, yet, note,
> Their manners are more gentle-kind than of
> Our human generation you shall find
> Many, nay, almost any.
> PROSPERO: (*Aside.*) Honest lord,
> Thou hast said well; for some of you there present
> Are worse than devils.   (3.3.30–6)

Montaigne's civilized faults of 'treason, treacherie, disloyaltie,' in contrast to savage love of one's neighbor, are exemplified to the full in the men whom Prospero rightly calls 'worse than devils'; for, in addition to their older crime against Prospero, two of them have just been planning against their friends another crime for the sake of worldly gain.

Prospero has been the teacher of Caliban:

> PROSPERO: I pitied thee,
> Took pains to make thee speak, taught thee each hour
> One thing or other: when thou dids't not, savage,
> Know thine own meaning, but wouldst gabble like
> A thing most brutish, I endow'd thy purposes
> With words that made them known: but thy vile race,
> Though thou didst learn, had that in't which good natures
> Could not abide to be with.   (1.2.353–60)

Shakespeare represents Caliban as so corrupt that he cannot receive the good things Prospero endeavors to give him: quite different the thought of Montaigne, who (as appears in the passage mentioned in the quotation from Luce given above) fears that the knowledge of European corruptions will destroy the innocence of the savages. Speaking of a barbarous manner of execution learned by the cannibals from the Portugese, Montaigne comments:

> They supposed that these people of the other world (as they who had sowed the knowledge of many vices amongst their neighbours, and were much more cunning in all kinds of evils and mischiefs than they) undertooke not this manner of revenge without cause, and that consequently it was more smartfull and cruell than theirs, and thereupon began to leave their old fashion to follow this.

The readiness of Caliban, who could not profit by the wisdom of Prospero, to subject himself to so wretched a specimen of humanity as Stephano, even though the worst new vice he learns is drunkenness, is somewhat of a parallel. So far are Stephano and Trinculo from superiority to the native, Caliban, that they fall in with his worst vices, and plan to aid him in an attempt to murder Prospero—a deed that Caliban thinks will be possible for them, though impossible for himself. The admiration expressed by Caliban for the king and his companions—of whom he says: 'These be brave spirits, indeed' (5.1.261)—is full of irony, for some of them are in treachery and ingratitude worse than himself. Curiously similar to the admiration of Caliban is that of Miranda, who, when she exclaims at the sight of the newcomers:

> O brave new world,
> That has such people in't!   (5.1.183–4)

seems to act for the moment something of the part of the untutored savage first looking upon Europeans. Her words echo the phrase 'the other world' in a passage of Montaigne already quoted ('They suppose that these people of the other world' etc.). Her father answers in a speech that emphasizes her ignorance and his sad knowledge of the evil character of some of the nobly appearing men before her: 'New for you'.

Montaigne insists on the utter lack of covetousness among the savages, so much in contrast with the habits of Europeans, who make war for the sake of booty. The wars of the cannibals

> are noble and generous, and have as much excuse and beautie, as this humane infirmity may admit: they ayme at nought so much, and have no other foundation amongst them, but the mere jelousie of vertue. They contend not for the gaining of new lands, . . . else have they nothing to do with the goods and spoyles of the vanquished.

Shakespeare, in a scene none the less full of meaning for its humor, brings out the superiority in this respect of Caliban to Stephano and Trinculo. When, on their way to attack Prospero, the Europeans stop to seize the rich garments put out as a snare for them, Caliban cries out:

> Let 't alone, thou fool; it is but trash. . . .
> The dropsy drown this fool! what do you mean
> To dote thus on such luggage? Let's along, . . .
> I will have none on't: we shall lose our time.   (4.1.224–48)

It is sometimes said that Caliban is a poet; the following speech is especially remarkable:

> the isle is full of noises,
> Sounds and sweet airs, that give delight, and hurt not.
> Sometimes a thousand twangling instruments
> Will hum about mine ears; and sometime voices,
> That, if I then had wak'd after long sleep,

Will make me sleep again: and then, in dreaming,
The clouds methought would open and show riches
Ready to drop upon me; that, when I wak'd
I cried to dream again.   (3.2.141–9)

Montaigne praises the poetical gifts of the cannibals; quoting one of their warlike
songs, he remarks: 'An invention that hath no shew of barbarism'. Giving one of
their 'amorous canzonets' ('Adder stay, stay good adder, that my sister may by the
patterne of thy partie-coloured coat drawe the fashion and worke of a rich lace, for
me to give unto my love; so may thy beautie, thy nimblenesse or disposition be
ever preferred before all other serpents'), he comments: 'I am so conversant with
Poesie, that I may judge this invention hath no barbarisme at all in it, but is
altogether Anacreontike'.

How astonishing is Shakespeare's use of Montaigne's essay! The land of the
cannibals becomes the imaginary commonwealth of Gonzalo. By transposing letters
in Montaigne's title the poet transforms *cannibal* into Caliban, and to the creature
thus named he gives many traits not suggested in the essay. Though Caliban still
retains some of the excellencies of the virtuous native, he has also the vices of the
savage. The wickedness of civilized men is not less clear to Shakespeare than to
Montaigne; but the dramatist, remembering also their virtues, makes no sweeping
contrast between the evils of civilization and the blessings of savagery: in presenting
the vices of civilized men he contrasts his villains not merely with Caliban the savage,
or the supernatural people of the island, companions of Ariel, but also with the
charitable Gonzalo, the just and learned Prospero, and even the pure and lovely
Miranda herself.

—ALLAN H. GILBERT, "Montaigne and The Tempest," Romanic Review
5, No. 1 (January–March 1914): 357–63

COLIN STILL

Much has been written on the subject of Caliban. He may be said, in fact, to present
one of the most difficult problems of the Play. The proposition which I now submit
is that *in Caliban we have a personification on mythological lines of the Tempter
who is Desire.*

I have already dealt at some length with the aspect of the Tempter as Desire,
and also with the various forms in which he is represented. In the Genesis story the
Tempter is described simply as a Serpent. But the typical form which he assumes
in myth and legend is that of a monstrous Serpent or Dragon, as in the myths of
Cadmus, of Perseus, and of St. George. This creature is native to water, whence he
emerges to assail his victim. And since the conception of the Tempter, as Desire,
is entirely subjective in significance, the water whence the monster emerges must
be understood to be the emotional WATER in the human composition.

It is with the Tempter in his traditional form as a water-monster, more particularly as the Dragon, that I identify Caliban, basing the case upon a mass of textual evidence in the Play.

Now Caliban, like the mythical Dragon, is explicitly a monster and implicitly amphibious; for, although he lives upon the Island, he has the appearance of a fish:

> What have we here? A man or a fish? Dead or alive? A fish: he smells like a fish; a very ancient and fish-like smell.... A strange fish! Were I in England now (as once I was), and had but this fish painted, not a holiday fool there but would give a piece of silver; there would this monster make a man.... Legged like a man; and his fins like arms. Warm; o' my troth! I do now let loose my opinion; hold it no longer; this is no fish, but an islander.   (Act II., Scene 2.)

There is no mistaking Trinculo's first impression, which is strongly emphasised. Caliban certainly has a fish-like appearance; and, notwithstanding Trinculo's considered opinion that "this is no fish, but an islander," he subsequently makes the only compromise which he finds possible in the circumstances, for we find him exclaiming to Caliban:

> Why, thou deboshed fish thou ... Wilt thou tell a monstrous lie, *being but half a fish and half a monster?*   (Act III., Scene 2.)

We may also note the odd suggestion of Trinculo that Caliban has a *tail* (III. 2. 12–13).

The obvious implication of all this is that Caliban, like the Dragon, is a water-monster. And it is noteworthy that Antonio, when he has reached a state of clear reason at the end of the Play, has no doubts whatever as to the element to which Caliban properly belongs, for he remarks:

> One of them [Caliban]
> *Is a plain fish.*   (Act V., Scene I.)

Antonio, of course, is right. But Trinculo, being incapable of clear reason, is wrong when he "lets loose" his considered opinion. That Trinculo is right in his first impression of Caliban will hardly surprise the psycho-analyst.

Now, although Caliban is a water-monster, he does not reside in the water. Moreover, he is seemingly a *hybrid,* for he is "legged like a man, and his fins like arms," and he is described throughout the Play as a "monster." Furthermore, as I shall make abundantly clear, he plays in accurate detail the part of the Tempter.

Caliban has, therefore, four important points of resemblance to the Monsters of mythological tradition and initiation ritual; for—(a) he is native to water, (b) he resides, or is encountered, out of water, (c) he is of mixed species, and (d) he figures the Tempter. True to the tradition, he is met with by Stephano and Trinculo when, emerging from the water, they have wandered on the shore—that is to say, he is met with when in the course of the Reascent they have passed through WATER into MIST. This MIST is the Purgatorial Wilderness, the place of temptation and expiation. It is also, as we have seen, a place or state of darkness; so that Caliban is quite truly described by Prospero as—

> This thing of darkness . . .   (Act V., Scene I, line 275.)

This may be no more than a verbal coincidence. It is, perhaps, a remark that is conventionally moral rather than deliberately symbolical. In any case, the Tempter is pre-eminently a "thing of darkness." Indeed, he is the Prince of Darkness.

But, although Caliban has four important points of contact with all the mythical monsters, it is to the Tempter as the mythical Dragon that he conforms more particularly. We find him complaining to Prospero that—

> Here you sty me
> In this hard rock. . . .   (Act I., Scene 2.)

To which Prospero answers:

> I have used thee,
> Filth as thou art, with human care; lodged thee
> In mine own cell, till thou didst seek to violate
> The honour of my child.   (Ibid.)

These allusions have no bearing whatever upon the general action of the Play. Are they, like other side-strokes in the dialogue, introduced simply as clues for the sharp-witted reader? Let us see.

Now, until the very close of the Play, when the allegory has been completely set forth, no one is allowed to enter the Cell except Ferdinand after the Masque. The Court Party is invited only to "look in" when Prospero throws open the entrance. Moreover, the Cell is the abode of Prospero and of Miranda (the Celestial Bride). It therefore appears to be the "sanctum sanctorum"; in which case its archetype is Heaven. The expulsion of Caliban from the Cell is thus a version of the Fall of Satan from Heaven. In Revelation we are told that the great Dragon ("which is the Devil, and Satan") was cast out of Heaven for persecuting a woman there, and that he was shut up in the bottomless pit and a seal set upon him (xii. and xx.). In like manner was Caliban cast out of the Cell and shut up into the rock. And when he complains of this to Prospero, he is reminded of his persecution of Miranda and is told—

> Therefore wast thou
> Deservedly confined into this rock. . . .   (Ibid.)

According to Revelation xii., the Dragon ("which is the Devil, and Satan") was cast out of Heaven because he stood before a pregnant woman to devour her child when it was born. This offence attributed to Caliban (though different) is well adapted to the occasion, and accords with the traditional character of Satan, viz., presumptuous irreverence. Of Satan it is generally declared that he fell from Heaven through ambition. In Talmudic legend it is said that he attempted to learn the ultimate secrets behind the veil. Compare this with the cause of Caliban's expulsion from the Cell. Miranda is an allegorical figure. She is the Veiled Lady who is Wisdom, the Lady who unveils herself and "reveals her secrets" only to her tried and proved lover (the initiate). I have already dealt with the sexual allegory according to which Wisdom is the Bride of the initiate, to whom she unveils her "secrets" after the mystical marriage, the idea thus expressed being that of Revelation, as distinct from Inspiration. Caliban's attempt against Miranda represents the sin of Satan expressed in terms of this same sexual allegory. It is an attempt to rape the Veiled Lady—that is, to acquire the secrets that are veiled from all save the highest initiate. And it is doubtless in this sense that Dante describes Satan as "the first adulterer."

Let any critic who demurs to this interpretation, deeming it extravagant or fantastic, ask what conceivable reason germane to the ostensible purpose of the Play can be assigned for Caliban's attempt upon Miranda. It has no bearing whatever upon the immediate action of the Play; nor can Prospero's reference to it be defended as an explanatory "aside," for it explains nothing, save on my hypothesis that *The Tempest* is an allegory constructed on the lines of ancient mythology and ritual.

Many commentators make excuses for Caliban and contend that he is not without a certain crude nobility. One might with equal reason argue that the Devil of the Gospel myth is an amiable and generous fellow, and that Bunyan's Apollyon is a kindly patron. A lenient view of Caliban can be based only upon some of the speeches he addresses to Stephano and Trinculo; and, as I shall show in the succeeding section, throughout his association with these two men he plays the traditional part of the Tempter. No fair words he utters to them can, therefore, be held to his credit. Nor need we be surprised that it is Caliban, the water-monster, who makes the most sensuous speech to be found in the entire Play:

> The isle is full of noises,
> Sounds, and sweet airs, that give delight, and hurt not.
> Sometimes a thousand twangling instruments
> Will hum about mine ears; and sometime voices,
> That, if I then had waked after long sleep,
> Will make me sleep again: and then, in dreaming,
> The clouds, methought, would open, and show riches
> Ready to drop upon me, that when I waked
> I cried to dream again.   (Act III., Scene 3.)

It would be symbolically correct to say, in the common idiom, that at this moment Caliban is "in his native element." The speech seems out of place in the mouth of Caliban, until we realise (what my subsequent argument will confirm) that he is deliberately using the sweet seductive tones of the Tempter whose "native element" is the sensuous or passional WATER. Such speeches as this one are precisely what must be ignored in forming a judgment as to his real nature, which is wholly evil. And so long as commentators allow themselves to be beguiled in his favour by anything Caliban says while he is acting the part of the Tempter, they cannot lay claim to any greater measure of discretion and discernment than those two credulous fools whom he brings to disaster.

It is not strictly true that Caliban's more pleasing aspects are revealed only during his association with Stephano and Trinculo. There are two exceptions. Speaking to Prospero (I. 2), he protests that there was a time—before his attempt upon Miranda—when he loved his master. It is equally true that Satan was not always evil. He was among the Sons of God, being Lucifer the Light-Bringer; and he became maleficent only after his Fall from Heaven. And again, Caliban exclaims, when he is told that he may yet win Prospero's pardon:

> I'll be wise hereafter,
> And seek for grace. . . .   (Act V., Scene I.)

Well, there is a cynical saying that "when the Devil is sick, the Devil a monk would be." But the words of Caliban are, I think, intended in a better sense. Taken with Prospero's hint that pardon may yet be won, they seem to embody an important intimation. They convey that even for the monstrous Caliban, who represents the fallen Satan, there is (as he himself is aware) always the hope of salvation. They are a negation of the doctrine of eternal damnation. They reflect the teaching of the Kabbalah that even the agent of evil can and will one day be redeemed.

Caliban, it should be noticed, is met neither by the Court Party nor by Ferdinand until the end of the Play, when the initiation scheme has been wholly set forth. This is as the nature of the case imperatively requires. The temptation of the Court Party is figured by their encounter with the Strange Shapes. It is designed according to the Siren model, and the encounter with the Dragon is therefore unnecessary in the case of these men. Had the members of the Court Party met Caliban during their wanderings, they would have been obliged to fight with and vanquish him in order to achieve the Lesser Initiation. Such an incident would, perhaps, have made the purpose of the Play self-evident. As for Ferdinand, the phases of psychological experience represented by his adventures on the Island do not include the phase to which the traditional temptation belongs; hence he meets neither Caliban nor the Strange Shapes.

Thus far I have given only such part of the evidence in support of my view of Caliban as can be detached from the general scheme; and throughout the ensuing two sections a mass of further testimony will be forthcoming.

—COLIN STILL, "Caliban," *Shakespeare's Mystery Play: A Study of
The Tempest* (London: Palmer, 1921), pp. 170–77

LEVIN L. SCHÜCKING

The artistic counterpart of this figure ⟨Ariel⟩ in the play is Caliban. According to his appearance, Caliban—whose name is derived by means of metathesis from Canibal—is really a monster of the sea. His fantastic exterior is adumbrated by some hints contained in the text. His eyes lie deep in his head, he has long claws, is apparently covered with scales all over his body, has arms like fins, and he exhales a penetrating odour of fish. He was probably put by Shakespeare in the place of a less maritime demon who was the son of the witch Sycorax and the devil, and therein the poet was perhaps influenced by a piece of news which dated from about 1597 and mentioned a sea-monster having at its elbows large fins like a fish as the sole inhabitant of the Bermudas Islands. This figure was elaborated by Shakespeare with especial care. We learn that Caliban, while still young, was on good terms with the newcomer Prospero, consented to be received by the latter in his house and to be educated by him, in return for which he served him as guide on the island, until his beastly nature broke out and a vicious attack on Miranda opened his benevolent master's eyes and turned him into a severe ruler who has now become accustomed to enforce service by means of threats and violence. From that time a profound hatred of Prospero has taken hold of Caliban and fills his whole nature, all the more as it is not merely the vindictiveness of one who has been dispossessed, enchained, and, according to his own opinion, ill-treated, but also the deeply rooted opposition of the mean and base to the noble.

It is precisely this, however, that wins for Caliban a higher degree of psychological probability and a more specific personal attraction than the most finished Shakespearean villains. Like Shylock, he lives in a spiritual world of his own, with his own valuations and his own horizon. He has obscure ideas of a Setebos, his mother's god, clearly outlined legal conceptions of his title as rightful owner of the island, does not allow himself to be impressed by the wisdom of Prospero, but in a way finds out its weak point by scornfully turning up his nose at the dependence of the sorcerer upon his magic books, and rejoices at the reluctance with which the spirits serve him. He betrays his sub-human nature when he incites another person to *bite* his enemy *to death,* but on the other hand he reveals an inner life of his own by listening with rapture to music and telling of the beautiful dreams in which heaven rains down treasures upon him, and which upon awaking he yearns, with childish tears, to renew. There is hardly a touch of Shakespeare's art of characterization which has been applied with more consummate skill than this, which speaks of that peculiar sadness which usually accompanies spiritual deformity. But the slight touch of tragedy which lies in this loneliness, and which is still increased by the open defiance with which in the beginning he faces his master, is quickly lost in the subsequent comic situations. We see him fall into the hands of the half-drunk butler and the jester, who have saved from the shipwreck a cask of liquor which they are discussing. With a simplicity which, however, like the cowardice he shows on this occasion, does not quite agree with his behaviour at the beginning he goes down on his knees before the giver of the supernatural drink, worships him as a god, swears loyalty to him, and courts him with disgusting self-abasement and servility. What began almost like a tragedy now becomes a merry comedy, and we may be sure that nothing in *The Tempest* was so certain to please the audience as the drunken monster, the bawling fish-man, whose previous sulkiness turns under the influence of this heavenly draught to excessive merriment, as he joins the two boon companions from whom, with a quite groundless confidence, he hopes to receive his longed-for freedom. With a certain native shrewdness he feels that one of the two is brave, the other a coward—yet he enormously overrates them in considering them capable of carrying out the murder of his master to which he adroitly and perfidiously incites them. Only when they have promptly allowed themselves to be deflected from their boastfully announced purpose by the variety of glistening apparel which Prospero has intentionally hung up for them are his eyes opened to the stupidity of his adored protectors. Chased by the demon hounds of his angry master, he recognizes too late that he has deceived himself and failed. No comic part in all Shakespeare's works offers such a splendid opportunity to the actors. The self-destruction of the wicked, not always convincingly developed from the character itself in other cases, in this case, without any forcing, becomes an exceedingly fruitful theme of comic action.

—LEVIN L. SCHÜCKING, *Character Problems in Shakespeare's Plays*
(London: George G. Harrap, 1922), pp. 253–55

ELMER EDGAR STOLL

And Shakespeare also made Caliban—after the air the earth, or, as some say, alongside the spirit of poetry that of prose! But Caliban is as poetically conceived and expressed as Ariel, and as far beyond the reach of Shakespeare's experience and Goethe's imagination. He fits perfectly into the dramatic scheme as the creature of earth—both a parallel and a contrast with the spirit of the air—but not at all as the vulgar public. It is a state of nature—Prospero and Miranda as human figures coming in between—and what is drama, or the dramatic public either, doing there?

As we have seen, Caliban, like Ariel, the Ghosts, and the Weird Sisters, had, in his own day, the advantage with the audience (by the accepted interpretation now taken from him) of being somewhat familiar, a development out of a popular superstition. And from the familiar to the unfamiliar is the right dramatic and poetic procedure, particularly in dealing with the supernatural: it was followed by Milton when he peopled his hell, not with his own inventions, but with heathen divinities, such as Moloch and Mammon—followed by both Milton and Dante, indeed, when undertaking to present hell and heaven in the first place. With the mental image he began, but in his mind it budded and developed; and like many others of his, superstitious or not in origin, it seized and assimilated qualities of characters somewhat different but compatible and akin. Puck, merged with the "familiar spirit," becomes in *The Tempest* the spirit of the air. And Caliban is not only the offspring of witch and devil, but both a sea monster and a land monster, and also a native Indian or "man in the making," who, quaintly but decently, wears a gaberdine. As Luce (who thinks he is also a negro) has noticed, it is well-nigh impossible to visualize him: one half of his features seem to contradict the other half; and he belongs wholly to the poetical art, not the pictorial. But the contradictions in his inner make-up, still greater and more various—his lawlessness and his instinct to worship and obey, his affectionateness and his vindictiveness, his abusiveness and his murderousness and his craving and ready gratitude for human comfort and protection, his sensuality and his delight in the pleasures of imagination, that is, in dreaming and in listening to stories and music—all these nevertheless belong together, congruous in their incongruity, within the wide and elastic limits of the primitive mind. Unfamiliar, he is conceivable enough; for such, once upon a time, by ancestral proxy, were audience and author both, and, though with a shudder, they delight in the combination now.

This is only, so to speak, the structure or anatomy,—in Caliban it is more clearly indicated than in most of Shakespeare's characters—and the miracle of creation is yet to come. He is given a voice, his very own. As with the other great characters of Shakespeare the style (or accent) is the man, and here it is completely differentiated from that of any other in this play or its predecessors. Not that there is realism. What is more difficult, but therefore the finer, the dramatist keeps within the limits of metre and the established idiom: and does not let him take to Brooklyn wharf-rat jargon, like the Hairy Ape; or drop into baby-talk, like Kipling's Thy Servant the Dog; or revert to the third person, like the Caliban of Browning. He curses, and yet like the pirates in *Treasure Island* is not gross or blasphemous; he is lustful, and yet *un*like most of O'Neill's characters, not filthy or obscene. He is not a naked monster, happy in the mire; as Cleopatra is not a naked prostitute, Falstaff not a mere rogue nor Shallow and Silence mere bores, nor Iago a murderous beast. One and all they are clothed—in humor, thought, imagination, verbal music, and whatever else is woven into the magic mantle of poetry.

Prospero calls him, and by a felicitous stroke of stage-craft he bawls out before he enters: "There's wood enough within." The speech both sets the comic tone and gives at the outset the clew to his character. For him wood-carrying is his "cross," his tragic lot, as it still is, I fancy, for many a boy on the farm. It is continually on his mind, or so to speak, his conscience, and becomes a measure of his passions—fear or hatred, love or gratitude. Later, in dread of Trinculo and Stephano as spirits sent to punish him, he vows to bring his wood home faster; and when shifting allegiance to the new ruler, or god, who bears the celestial liquor, he not only will kiss his foot but "get thee wood enough." It is at once a comic device—a repeated *motif*—and a unifying and simplifying artifice in the presentation of the character.

Six lines are spoken—Ariel, for a contrast, meanwhile coming in and going out, and Prospero repeating his summons—before the mooncalf, cursing, lumbers in. All the malign and baleful operations of nature he can think of he now calls down upon the magician and his daughter, receiving threats in return. Scared by these, he thereupon takes to the defensive and to grumbling.

I must eat my dinner,

and it is a speech in the same vein as the first. Nothing irritates a servant like being interrupted at that sweet duty, and Caliban stands on his elementary rights. Others he remembers forthwith:

> This island's mine, by Sycorax my mother,
> Which thou tak'st from me,

—even as we now unconvincingly say of our Continent, though not born on it, to all new-comers. Then, by an illogical but delightfully natural transition, and in the same childish vein, he casts up to his master his kindness in the past and his own gratitude for it.

> When thou cam'st first
> Thou strok'dst me, and made much of me, would'st give me
> Water with berries in't, and teach me how
> To name the bigger light, and how the less
> That burn by day and night; and then I lov'd thee
> And show'd thee all the qualities of the isle,
> The fresh springs, brine-pits, barren place and fertile.
> Curs'd be I that did so.

And from out of the midst of this appealing whimper, he falls, despite his memories, to cursing Prospero anew. He must have release, as the saying now is; for has not yet developed "inhibitions." "His spirits hear me," he later confesses, "and yet I needs must curse." For only with time do punishments deter.

Never, I suppose, was by thought, word, and rhythm, as well as by mental process, a character so instantly created, and—for I have thus far omitted nothing—so perfectly preserved. Not a false note, anywhere. Caliban is the perfect brute, who would be petted, given food and drink, taught to talk and told stories, yet (with this given as the reason) turns vindictive when he isn't. And what follows is, though startling, as true. When he complains of being "stied in this hard rock," Prospero reminds him that he had lodged him in his own cell until he sought to violate his daughter. Then comes the one sexual touch that Shakespeare permits himself—imagine, with the opportunity, a Joyce or an O'Neill!—

> Oho, Oho! would't had been done!
> Thou didst prevent me: I had peopl'd else
> This isle with Calibans.

No doubt the picture would have been truer with the monster freely wallowing, and art is not morality. It is beauty, however.

After the sweet idyllic meeting of Miranda and Ferdinand, and the cynical but rather boresome conspiracy of Antonio and Sebastian, there comes—according to the delightful Shakespearean principle or practice of "vivid contrast between scene and scene swiftly succeeding each other," one of low life and comic relief—Caliban entering, amid thunder, bowed under the white man's burden, and with curses again pouring from his lips. His second entrance, though similar, is better than the first, and, as repeated *motif*, would instantly bring a laugh. This time we *see* the wood, cause of the cursing. And Trinculo the jester now appearing, he takes him, with his bad conscience, for a spirit dispatched to punish his sloth; and, like an oppossum or an ostrich (though not exactly), and Browning's Caliban seeking to escape Setebos' ire, he falls flat.

The scene which ensues is delectable. Trinculo, after due consideration of the ambiguous phenomenon (neither flesh nor fish) and of the unambiguous weather, arrives at the conclusion that it is an islander struck by a thunderbolt; and there being no other refuge hereabouts, crawls under his gaberdine. Then enters Stephano the butler, half-drunk, yet enriched with the drunken man's "double personality," trolling catches to his own disappointment, and if they were not of his choosing and singing, but, after each one, taking to his bottle for comfort. "Do not torment me, Oh!" cries the mooncalf . . . "Do not torment me, prithee; I'll bring my wood home faster." Stephano thinks him a devil, then a monster of the isle,—with four legs!—"who hath got, as I take it, an ague." "Where the devil should he learn our language?" he cries, with a start. But it is a point in common, a tie. "If it be but for *that,*" he will give him relief, such as he is enjoying. *Both* are having agues, and Caliban also—"you cannot tell who's your friend," quoth Stephano—takes the cure. Trinculo, meanwhile, should know that voice—"but *he* is drowned, and these are devils."—"Four legs and two voices," ponders Stephano, "a most delicate monster . . . If all the wine in my bottle will recover it (a test of charity indeed!) I will help his ague . . . I will pour some in thy other mouth." "Stephano!"—"Doth thy other mouth call me? Mercy, mercy!" The tie is a bit too close, and the butler now is one of a *second* shaking pair. "Stephano! If thou beest Stephano, touch me and speak to me; for I am Trinculo,—be not afeared—thy good friend Trinculo." In his fear, he would dissipate the fear that he causes, but is met by the sage and apposite reply: "If thou beest Trinculo, come forth." There are solemn and sacred reminiscences in these tremulous adjurations, and they have effect. "And art thou living, Stephano? O Stephano, two Neapolitans scap'd!" The stage business we divine.

Caliban, meanwhile, all innocence and gratitude—for this water has more than berries in it—looks on, and, with but a single misgiving, admires:

> These be fine things, an if they be not sprites:
> That's a brave god and bears celestial liquor.
> I will kneel to him.

The god is unworthily absorbed in Trinculo's story of his escape and his own tale of cask and bottle; but worship never demanded recognition, and the liquor works on within the mooncalf's veins and brains:

> Hast thou not dropp'd from heaven?
> STEPH. Out o' the moon, I do assure thee. I was the man i' the moon when time
> was.
> CAL. I have seen thee in her and I do adore thee.
> My mistress show'd me thee and thy dog and thy bush.

While his belly warms, his imagination expands; and as with most drinkers blest with this faculty, all his romantic dreams come true. It is so with Stephano as well; but himself being the dream rather than the dreamer, he would have the monster swear to his own unsettling words, kissing the book—pulling at the bottle—which in such fashion he does as to call forth the self-forgetful admiration of Trinculo. In his present state Caliban is not only generous but suggestive; and he will now kiss, not the butler's book, indeed, but his foot, and show him all his treasures and wonders, nay, work for him, though by nature so little inclined. Kindness conquers all; and I cannot think it true, though a great critic has said it, that he can only be controlled and made serviceable by terror. If that were so he would be far less of an artistic triumph.

> I'll show thee the best springs; I'll pluck thee berries;
> I'll fish for thee and get thee wood enough.
> A plague upon the tyrant that I serve!
> I'll bear him no more sticks, but follow thee,
> Thou wondrous man!

These final half-lines—"I will kneel to him," "And I will kiss thy foot," "Thou wondrous man"—are they not each equivalent to a genuflection or prostration? He is a right worshipper, with motives mingled—love with hatred, gratitude with desire—and it is a comic but (as with Shakespeare often) even well-nigh a pathetic situation as the poetical native worships the drunken white. Also he grows confiding and intimate:

> I prithee, let me bring thee where crabs grow;
> And I with my long nails will dig thee pig-nuts;
> Show thee a jay's nest and instruct thee how
> To snare the nimble marmoset. I'll bring thee
> To clust'ring filberts, and sometimes I'll get thee
> Young scamels from the rock. Wilt thou go with me?'

Who wouldn't? "Show thee a jay's nest!"—for there is only one, and Caliban's have been the only eyes to see it. Like Ariel, he loves nature, though after a different fashion; indeed, the two mythical beings alone betray any interest in the island. And now, seized by the spirit of rum and rebellion, and bidden by the newly chosen king, or Lord of Misrule, to lead the way, while Trinculo bears aloft, like mace or sceptre, the empty bottle—no empty symbol, however, for "we'll fill him by and by!"—the monster sings, howls, and dances his Declaration of Independence, to the tune, not of the Carmagnole, but of the can-can:

> Farewell, master; farewell, farewell.

> Ban, Ban, Ca-Caliban
> Has a new master, get a new man.
> Freedom, hey-day! hey-day, freedom! freedom, hey-day, freedom!

In throwing over his old master he has, like all primitive rebels, necessarily taken on another. Some critics, intruding not only their esthetics but also their latter-day ethics into the sacred text, declare that the play teaches the "beauty of service": in Caliban's case it is rather the necessity of it, as, though differently, in Ariel's and Ferdinand's. "Let *him* be Caesar," cries the rabble, after Brutus has justified Caesar's death.

—ELMER EDGAR STOLL, *"The Tempest,"* PMLA 47, No. 3 (September 1932): 711–16

HAROLD C. GODDARD

The Tempest has an unrivaled power to inspire in almost all sensitive readers a belief that it contains a secret meaning. Even those who make no attempt to search it out retain the feeling that it is there and that if it could only be found it would lead close not merely to the heart of Shakespeare's convictions about life but close to the heart of life itself. Naturally I have no reference here to the many minute and elaborate allegorical interpretations of the play that have been offered, which, even if they were convincing within their own limits, could have only a historical, bio-graphical, or other subpoetical interest. What I have in mind rather are more modest attempts to connect and elucidate the main themes and symbols around which the poem is obviously built and which seem to have in peculiar degree the power, in Keats's words, to "tease us out of thought as doth eternity." To set out to interpret *The Tempest* (which I do not intend to do) is one thing; to point out certain aspects of its symbolism and thematic structure with which any satisfactory interpretation must come to terms as a sort of minimum requirement is another and much less ambitious undertaking.

To begin with, this play is centrally concerned with the three things that Shakespeare had perhaps come to value most highly in life: liberty, love, and wonder—the identical trinity, by the way, that Hafiz, long before Shakespeare, had also chosen. Concerned with realities rather than with names, the poet not only gives examples of these things but, to make clear what they are in their purity, shows us what they are in their perversions: license is set over against liberty; lust against love; banality, but more particularly "wonders," against wonder.

And the play has also what might be called a biological theme. As has often been pointed out, the characters are arranged in a sort of evolutionary hierarchy from Caliban, who is a kind of demi-creature of water and earth, up through human strata of various stages of development to Ariel, who is all fire and air—though it is made clear that where human nature becomes degenerate it seems to sink to a level lower than that of Caliban.

Closely allied to this, yet distinct from it, is a psychological interest. The play is fairly saturated with references to sleep and waking—and to various states of consciousness and unconsciousness between the two, drowsiness, daydreaming, dreaming, trance, hallucination, and other hypnagogic conditions. Likewise *The Tempest* is filled from end to end with noises and music—from the thunder and roaring of the storm itself, the howling of beasts, through the sounds and sweet airs of the Enchanted Isle that could charm even Caliban, through every variety of human utterance from the cries and coarse ballads of drunkards to the voices of lovers, up finally to the songs of Ariel. And Shakespeare seems interested not only in these two things, sleep and music, but even more in the relation between them—in the relation, to put it more pedantically, between music and the unconscious mind. The voices of the isle could induce such sleep in Caliban that when he waked he cried to dream again. Miranda falls asleep on the entrance of Ariel and awakens on his exit. The same is true in some degree of the other good characters, but not of the baser ones, who become victims on at least one occasion of an evil form of waking hallucination. All these reactions turn on the receptivity of the unconscious mind.

These various themes and symbols are inextricably interwoven, and, seen from a slightly different angle, give us Shakespeare's final word on a subject that had engaged his attention from the beginning: the different kinds of power that men possess and are possessed by. Here the political and religious aspects of the story merge as we are carried all the way from the demonic tyranny of the witch Sycorax to the reign of pure goodness in old Gonzalo's ideal commonwealth. More specifically, we have within the main action of the play: the political and military power of Alonso and Antonio, the magical power of Prospero, the alcoholic power of Stephano, the unveiling power of love in Ferdinand and Miranda, and the musical power of Ariel. (Nor am I omitting, though I may seem to be, the religious power of forgiveness.)

The play culminates in three emancipations—of Caliban from the enthralment of the drunken Stephano, of Prospero from his magic, and of Ariel from the service of Prospero in the cause of that magic (not to mention the emancipation from moral bondage of Alonso and his companions). What might be called, grotesquely, the biography of Ariel gives at least an intimation of what these interrelated emancipations mean, though we must beware here not to fetter the play within any rigid allegory. For twelve years—"years" doubtless comparable to the "days" of creation in Genesis—Ariel was imprisoned in a cloven pine by the witch Sycorax because he was

> a spirit too delicate
> To act her earthy and abhorr'd commands.

This imprisonment, once imposed, Sycorax is powerless to undo and Prospero with his art must come to the rescue. What does this signify? Might it not mean that when imagination is enslaved by the senses superstition usurps its function—and the senses become powerless to release it? It must be set free by knowledge and reason. But that is not the end of the story. Out from under the domination of the senses, imagination now becomes the slave of the very intellect that rescued it. Prospero is now master and the delicate spirit he has set free from Sycorax is impressed into the service of his magic—even at one point at the threat of a second imprisonment, in a cloven oak, of like duration as the first, if he complains. Here, again, is a Prospero remote enough from anything we associate with Shakespeare.

⟨...⟩ Even in Caliban an Ariel slumbers. He loves the voices of the isle, and his moral awakening at the end—

What a thrice-double ass
Was I, to take this drunkard for a god
And worship this dull fool!

—though passed over swiftly is as hopeful a note as is struck in the entire play. Prospero was wrong in thinking that Caliban was impervious to education.

—HAROLD C. GODDARD, *"The Tempest," The Meaning of Shakespeare*
(Chicago: University of Chicago Press, 1951), pp. 666–68, 671

W. H. AUDEN

The Tempest, Shakespeare's last play, is a disquieting work. Like the other three comedies of his late period, *Pericles, Cymbeline* and *The Winter's Tale,* it is concerned with a wrong done, repentance, penance and reconciliation; but, whereas the others all end in a blaze of forgiveness and love—"Pardon's the word to all"—in *The Tempest* both the repentance of the guilty and the pardon of the injured seem more formal than real. Of the former, Alonso is the only one who seems genuinely sorry; the repentance of the rest, both the courtly characters, Antonio and Sebastian, and the low, Trinculo and Stephano, is more the prudent promise of the punished and frightened, "I won't do it again. It doesn't pay," than any change of heart: and Prospero's forgiving is more the contemptuous pardon of a man who knows that he has his enemies completely at his mercy than a heartfelt reconciliation. His attitude to all of them is expressed in his final words to Caliban:

as you look
To have my pardon trim it handsomely.

One must admire Prospero because of his talents and his strength; one cannot possibly like him. He has the coldness of someone who has come to the conclusion that human nature is not worth much, that human relations are, at their best, pretty sorry affairs. Even towards the innocent young lovers, Ferdinand and Miranda, and their "brave new world," his attitude is one of mistrust so that he has to preach them a sermon on the dangers of anticipating their marriage vows. One might excuse him if he included himself in his critical skepticism but he never does; it never occurs to him that he, too, might have erred and be in need of pardon. He says of Caliban:

born devil on whose nature
Nurture can never stick, on whom my pains,
Humanely taken, all, all lost, quite lost

but Shakespeare has written Caliban's part in such a way that, while we have to admit that Caliban is both brutal and corrupt, a "lying slave" who can be prevented from doing mischief only "by stripes not kindness," we cannot help feeling that Prospero is largely responsible for his corruption, and that, in the debate between them, Caliban has the best of the argument.

Before Prospero's arrival, Caliban had the island to himself, living there in a state of savage innocence. Prospero attempts to educate him, in return for which Caliban shows him all the qualities of the isle. The experiment is brought to a halt when Caliban tries to rape Miranda, and Prospero abandons any hope of educating him further. He does not, however, sever their relation and turn Caliban back to the forest; he changes its nature and, instead of trying to treat Caliban as a son, makes him a slave whom he rules by fear. This relation is profitable to Prospero:

> as it is
> We cannot miss him. He does make our fire,
> Fetch in our wood, and serve us in offices
> That profit us

but it is hard to see what profit, material or spiritual, Caliban gets out of it. He has lost his savage freedom:

> For I am all the subjects that you have
> Which first was mine own king

and he has lost his savage innocence:

> You taught me language and my profit on't
> Is, I know how to curse

so that he is vulnerable to further corruption when he comes into contact with the civilized vices of Trinculo and Stephano. He is hardly to be blamed, then, if he regards the virtues of civilization with hatred as responsible for his condition:

> Remember
> First to possess his books, for without them
> He's but a sot, as I am.

As a biological organism Man is a natural creature subject to the necessities of nature; as a being with consciousness and will, he is at the same time a historical person with the freedom of the spirit. *The Tempest* seems to me a manichean work, not because it shows the relation of Nature to Spirit as one of conflict and hostility, which in fallen man it is, but because it puts the blame for this upon Nature and makes the Spirit innocent. Such a view is the exact opposite of the view expressed by Dante:

> Lo naturale è sempre senza errore
> ma l'altro puote errar per male obbietto
> o per poco o per troppo di vigore.   (*Purgatorio* XVII.)

The natural can never desire too much or too little because the natural good is the mean—too much and too little are both painful to its natural well-being. The natural, conforming to necessity, cannot imagine possibility. The closest it can come to a relation with the possible is as a vague dream; without Prospero, Ariel can only be known to Caliban as "sounds and sweet airs that give delight and hurt not." The animals cannot fall because the words of the tempter, "Ye shall be as gods," are in the future tense, and the animals have no future tense, for the future tense implies the possibility of doing something that has not been done before, and this they cannot imagine.

Man can never know his "nature" because knowing is itself a spiritual and historical act; his physical sensations are always accompanied by conscious emotions. It is impossible to remember a physical sensation of pleasure or pain, the moment it ceases one cannot recall it, and all one remembers is the emotion of happiness or fear which accompanied it. On the other hand, a sensory stimulus can recall forgotten emotions associated with a previous occurrence of the same stimulus, as when Proust eats the cake.

It is unfortunate that the word "Flesh," set in contrast to "Spirit," is bound to suggest not what the Gospels and St. Paul intended it to mean, the whole physical-historical nature of fallen man, but his physical nature alone, a suggestion very welcome to our passion for reproving and improving others instead of examining our own consciences. For, the more "fleshy" a sin is, the more obviously public it is, and the easier to prevent by the application of a purely external discipline. Thus the sin of gluttony exists in acts of gluttony, in eating, drinking, smoking too much, etc. If a man restrains himself from such excess, or is restrained by others, he ceases to be a glutton; the phrase "gluttonous thoughts" apart from gluttonous acts is meaningless.

As Christ's comment on the commandment indicates, the sin of lust is already "unfleshly" to the degree that is possible to have lustful thoughts without lustful deeds, but the former are still "fleshly" in that the thinker cannot avoid knowing what they are; he may insist that his thoughts are not sinful but he cannot pretend that they are not lustful. Further, the relation between thought and act is still direct. The thought is the thought of a specific act. The lustful man cannot be a hypocrite to himself except through a symbolic transformation of his desires into images which are not consciously lustful. But the more "spiritual" the sin, the more indirect is the relationship between thought and act, and the easier it is to conceal the sin from others and oneself. I have only to watch a glutton at the dinner table to see that he is a glutton, but I may know someone for a very long time before I realize that he is an envious man, for there is no act which is in itself envious; there are only acts done in the spirit of envy, and there is often nothing about the acts themselves to show that they are done from envy and not from love. It is always possible, therefore, for the envious man to conceal from himself the fact he is envious and to believe that he is acting from the highest of motives. While in the case of the purely spiritual sin of pride there is no "fleshly" element of the concrete whatsoever, so that no man, however closely he observes others, however strictly he examines himself, can ever know if they or he are proud; if he finds traces of any of the other six capital sins, he can infer pride, because pride is fallen "Spirit-in-itself" and the source of all the other sins, but he cannot draw the reverse inference and, because he finds no traces of the other six, say categorically that he, or another, is not proud.

If man's physical nature could speak when his spirit rebukes it for its corruption, it would have every right to say, "Well, who taught me my bad habits?"; as it is, it has only one form of protest, sickness; in the end, all it can do is destroy itself in an attempt to murder its master.

Over against Caliban, the embodiment of the natural, stands the invisible spirit of imagination, Ariel. (In a stage production, Caliban should be as monstrously conspicuous as possible, and, indeed, suggest, as far as decency permits, the phallic. Ariel, on the other hand, except when he assumes a specific disguise at Prospero's order, e.g., when he appears as a harpy, should, ideally, be invisible, a disembodied voice, an ideal which, in these days of microphones and loud-speakers, should be realizable.)

Caliban was once innocent but has been corrupted; his initial love for Prospero has turned into hatred. The terms "innocent" and "corrupt" cannot be applied to Ariel because he is beyond good and evil; he can neither love nor hate, he can only play. It is not sinful of Eve to imagine the possibility of being as a god knowing good and evil: her sin lay in desiring to realize that possibility when she knew it was forbidden her, and her desire did not come from her imagination, for imagination is without desire and is, therefore, incapable of distinguishing between permitted and forbidden possibilities; it only knows that they are imaginatively possible. Similarly, imagination cannot distinguish the possible from the impossible; to it the impossible is a species of the genus possible, not another genus. I can perfectly well imagine that I might be a hundred feet high or a champion heavyweight boxer, and I do myself no harm in so doing, provided I do so playfully, without desire. I shall, however, come to grief if I take the possibility seriously, which I can do in two ways. Desiring to become a heavyweight boxer, I may deceive myself into thinking that the imaginative possibility is a real possibility and waste my life trying to become the boxer I never can become. Or, desiring to become a boxer, but realizing that it is, for me, impossible, I may refuse to relinquish the desire and turn on God and my neighbor in a passion of hatred and rejection because I cannot have what I want. So Richard III, to punish existence for his misfortune in being born a hunchback, decided to become a villain. Imagination is beyond good *and* evil. Without imagination I remain an innocent animal, unable to become anything but what I already am. In order to become what I should become, therefore, I have to put my imagination to work, and limit its playful activity to imagining those possibilities which, for me, are both permissible and real; if I allow it to be the master and play exactly as it likes, then I shall remain in a dreamlike state of imagining everything I might become, without getting round to ever becoming anything. But, once imagination has done its work for me, to the degree that, with its help, I have become what I should become, imagination has a right to demand its freedom to play without any limitations, for there is no longer any danger that I shall take its play seriously. Hence the relation between Prospero and Ariel is contractual, and, at the end of the drama, Ariel is released.

If *The Tempest* is overpessimistic and manichean, *The Magic Flute* is over-optimistic and pelagian. At the end of the opera a double wedding is celebrated; the representative of the spiritual, Tamino, finds his happiness in Pamina and has attained wisdom while the chorus sing:

> Es siegte die Stärke und krönet zum Lohn.
> Die Schönheit und Weisheit mit ewiger Kron

and, at the same time, the representative of the natural, Papageno is rewarded with Papagena, and they sing together:

> Erst einen kleinen Papageno
> Dann eine kleine Papagena
> Dann wieder einen Papageno
> Dann wieder eine Papagena

expressing in innocent humility the same attitude which Caliban expresses in guilty defiance when Prospero accuses him of having tried to rape Miranda,

> O ho, O ho! Would't had been done.
> Thou didst prevent me; I had peopled else
> This isle with Calibans.

Tamino obtains his reward because he had had the courage to risk his life under-going the trials of Fire and Water; Papageno obtains his because he has had the humility to refuse to risk his life even if the refusal will mean that he must remain single. It is as if Caliban, when Prospero offered to adopt him and educate him, had replied: "Thank you very much, but clothes and speech are not for me; It is better I stay in the jungle."

According to *The Magic Flute*, it is possible for nature and spirit to coexist in man harmoniously and without conflict, provided both keep to themselves and do not interfere with each other, and that, further, the natural has the freedom to refuse to be interfered with.

> —W. H. AUDEN, "Balaam and His Ass" [1954], *The Dyer's Hand and Other Essays* (New York: Random House, 1962), pp. 128–35

FRANK KERMODE

The last thing the "Names of the Actors" says about Caliban is that he is a slave. We have seen the readiness with which the white man took charge of the New World; Prospero arrived on his island "to be the lord on 't." If Aristotle was right in arguing that "men . . . who are as much inferior to others as the body is to the soul . . . are slaves by nature, and it is advantageous for them to be under government", and that "to find our governor we should . . . examine into a man who is most perfectly formed in soul and body . . . for in the depraved and vicious the body seems to rule rather than the soul, on account of their being corrupt and contrary to nature", then the black and mutilated cannibal must be the natural slave of the European gentleman, and, a *fortiori*, the salvage and deformed Caliban of the learned Prospero.

Caliban is, therefore, accurately described in the Folio "Names of the Actors". His origins and character are natural in the sense that they do not partake of grace, civility, and art; he is ugly in body, associated with an evil natural magic, and unqualified for rule or nurture. He exists at the simplest level of sensual pain and pleasure, fit for lechery because love is beyond his nature, and a natural slave of demons. He hears music with pleasure, as music can appeal to the beast who lacks reason; and indeed he resembles Aristotle's bestial man. He is a measure of the incredible superiority of the world of Art, but also a measure of its corruption. For the courtiers and their servants include the incontinent Stephano and the malicious Antonio. Caliban scorns the infirmity of purpose exhibited by the first, and knows better than Antonio that it is imprudent to resist grace, for which, he says, he will henceforth seek. Unlike the incontinent man, whose appetites subdue his will, and the malicious man, whose will is perverted to evil ends, "the bestial man has no sense of right and wrong, and therefore sees no difference between good and evil. His state is less guilty but more hopeless than those of incontinence and malice, since he cannot be improved." Men can abase their degree below the bestial; and there is possibly a hint, for which there is no support in Aristotle, that the bestial Caliban gains a new spiritual dimension from his glimpse of the "brave spirits." Whether or no this is true, he is an extraordinarily powerful and comprehensive type of Nature; an inverted pastoral hero, against whom civility and the Art which improves Nature may be measured.

I. *Buds of Nobler Race.* The civilized castaways of *The Tempest* are brought into close contact with a representative of Nature uncontrolled by Art. How do they differ from Caliban, and how is this difference expressed?

It is useful to compare Spenser's treatment of two salvage men in *The Faerie Queene*. The one who carries off Amoret in Book IV is an unamiable personification of greedy lust—"For he liv'd all on ravin and on rape." (IV. vii. 5). The full description leaves no doubt that this is the wild man of the entertainments, and that his are the "natural" activities of lust and cannibalism. The salvage man who treats Serena so gently in the sixth book is quite different; though he cannot speak he shows a tenderness which is, apparently, against his nature. The reason is, that "he was borne of noble blood" (VI. v. 2); we do not hear how he came to be languageless and salvage, but we know he owes his gentleness to his gentle birth.

> O what an easie thing is to descry
> The gentle bloud, how ever it be wrapt
> In sad misfortunes foule deformity
> And wretched sorrowes, which have often hapt!

For howsoever it may grow mis-shapt,
Like this wyld man being undisciplynd,
That to all virtue it may seeme unapt,
Yet will it shew some sparkes of gentle mynd,
And at the last breake forth in his owne proper kynd. (VI. v. l.)

That gentle birth predisposed a man to virtue, even if it was not absolutely necessary to virtue, was part of the lore of courtesy. *Fortes creantur fortibus* . . .—argument as to the mode of inheriting, and of cultivating, *nobilitas,* runs through the history of moral philosophy from Aristotle through Dante to the Renaissance. It is true that, with evidence to the contrary continually before their eyes, philosophers could not uniformly maintain that where there was high birth there was virtue, taking nobility to mean the *non vile,* "the perfection of its own nature in each thing" (Dante, *Convito*); and in Italy there was a growing tendency to judge of nobility by actual manners and merit, rather than by family. As early as the *Convito* the conditions of its development are described as much more complex than the racial theory of its provenance allows, but more commonplace thought constantly recurs to the biological analogy; *est in juvencis, est in equis, patrum Virtus*—as Polixenes conceived that there were "buds of nobler race".

The question is debated in the first book of Castiglione's *Courtier* by Canossa and Pallavicino. The arguments are conventional, but they serve to illustrate the theory of natural nobility which animates Spenser's portrait of the salvage man. Nature makes the work of greatness easier, and the penalties of failure heavier, for the high-born; "because nature in every thing hath deeply sowed that privie seed, which giveth a certaine force and propertie of her beginning, unto whatsoever springeth of it, and maketh it like unto herselfe. As we see by example . . . in trees, whose slippes and grafts alwaies for the most part are like unto the stock of the tree they cam from: and if at any time they grow out of kinde, the fault is in the husbandman"; which is to say, in the individual nobleman—a fault of nurture, not of nature. Thus Canossa, though not to the satisfaction of Pallavicino, accounts also for the Antonios of the world. He allows an important place to education, believing, with Prospero and against Socrates, that pedagogues could be found capable of nursing the seed:

> Therefore even as in the other artes, so also in the vertues, it is behofefull to have a teacher, that with lessons and good exhortations may stirre up and quicken in us those moral vertues, whereof wee have the seede inclosed and buried in the soule.

If the seed is not there (and here Prospero's experience confirms him) the husbandman loses his labour, and brings forth only "the briers and darnell of appetites" which he had desired to restrain. Canossa omits all the other factors which might be brought into consideration—"the complex nature of the seed", "the disposition of the dominant Heaven"—which Dante two centuries before had attempted to calculate, and takes account only of nature and of nurture. This leaves an opening for Pallavicino's reply, and Castiglione had, of course, to arrange matters to suit his dialectic scheme. But for Spenser moral virtues inhabit the simpler, the ideal, world of romance, and his salvage man differs from his kind in that he has the seed implanted by nature, though not husbanded by nurture.

There is a striking version of the theory of Edward Phillips, the nephew of Milton. Phillips, in a passage so much above his usual manner that critics have seen in it the hand of his uncle, identifies two forces which distinguish the better part of mankind from the more brutish:

> ... the first is the *Melior natura* which the Poet speaks of, with which whoever is amply indued, take that Man from his Infancy, throw him into the Desarts of *Arabia,* there let him converse some years with Tygers and Leopards, and at last bring him where civil society & conversation abides, and ye shall see how on a sudden, the scales and dross of his barbarity purging off by degrees, he will start up a Prince or Legislator, or some such illustrious Person: the other is that noble thing call'd *Education,* this is, that Harp of *Orpheus,* that lute of *Amphion,* so elegantly figur'd by the Poets to have wrought such Miracles among irrational and insensible Creatures, which raiseth beauty even out of deformity, order and regularity out of Chaos and confusion, and which, if thoroughly and rightly prosecuted, would be able to civilize the most savage natures, & root out barbarism and ignorance from off the face of the Earth: those who have either of these qualifications singly may justly be term'd *Men;* those who have both united in a happy conjunction, *more* than *Men;* those who have neither of them in any competent measure ... *less* than *Men* ...

Phillips here takes the view expressed by Dante, Pallavicino, and many others, that the want of nature can be partially supplied by Education, and in this respect differs from those who, like Canossa and, as we shall see, the romance-writers, held more rigidly to the notion of the seed without which all husbandry is not only wasted but even harmful, since it promotes the growth of undesirable weed-like qualities. The unknown poet's *melior natura* provides an excellent label for all the ideas associated with "buds of nobler race", and his "Education" enables us to see Prospero's "nurture" in its proper context. Miranda, as Prospero early informs us, is endowed not only with the *melior natura,* but with education:

> here
> Have I, thy schoolmaster, made thee more profit
> Than other princess' can, that have more time
> For vainer hours, and tutors not so careful.   (I. ii. 171–4.)

She has both these qualities of nobility "united in a happy conjunction". Caliban has neither, and there is in the structure of the play a carefully prepared parallel between the two characters to illustrate this point; Caliban's education was not only useless—on *his* nature, which is nature *tout court,* nurture would never stick—but harmful. He can only abuse the gift of speech; and by cultivating him Prospero brings forth in him "the briers and darnell of appetites"—lust for Miranda, discontent at his inferior position, ambition, intemperance of all kinds, including a disposition to enslave himself to the bottle of Stephano. And there is in his "vile race" that "which *good* natures Could not abide to be with"; in other words there is a repugnance between the raw, unreclaimed nature which he represents, and the courtier-stock with which he has to deal, endowed as it is with grace, and nurtured in refinement through the centuries, in the world of Art.

II. *Prospero's Art.* At the risk of introducing "distincts" where there is no "division" it may be said that Prospero's Art has two functions in *The Tempest*. The first is simple; as a mage he exercises the supernatural powers of the holy adept. His Art is here the disciplined exercise of virtuous knowledge, a "translation of merit into power" ⟨R. H. West⟩, the achievement of "an intellect pure and conjoined with the powers of the gods, without which we shall never happily ascend to the scrutiny of secret things, and to the power of wonderfull workings" ⟨Cornelius Agrippa⟩. This Art is contrasted with the natural power of Sycorax to exploit for evil purposes the universal sympathies. It is a technique for liberating the soul from the passions, from nature; the practical application of a discipline of which the primary requirements are learning and temperance, and of which the mode is contemplation. When Prospero achieves this necessary control over himself and nature he achieves his ends (reflected in the restoration of harmony at the human and political levels) and has no more need of the instrument, "rough magic".

The second function is symbolic. Prospero's Art controls Nature; it requires of the artist virtue and temperance if his experiment is to succeed; and it thus stands for the world of the better natures and its qualities. This is the world which is closed to Caliban (and Comus); the world of mind and the possibilities of liberating the soul, not the world of sense, whether that be represented as coarsely natural or charmingly voluptuous. Art is not only a beneficent magic in contrast to an evil one; it is the ordination of civility, the control of appetite, the transformation of nature by breeding and learning; it is even, in a sense, the means of Grace.

Prospero is, therefore, the representative of Art, as Caliban is of Nature. As a mage he controls nature; as a prince he conquers the passions which had excluded him from his kingdom and overthrown law; as a scholar he repairs his loss of Eden; as a man he learns to temper his passions, an achievement essential to success in any of the other activities.

Prospero describes his efforts to control his own passion in V. i. 25–7—

Though with their high wrongs I am struck to th' quick,
Yet with my nobler reason 'gainst my fury
Do I take part.

In an age when "natural" conduct was fashionably associated with sexual promiscuity, chastity alone could stand as the chief function of temperance, and there is considerable emphasis on this particular restraint in *The Tempest*. The practice of good magic required it; but in this it is again merely the practical application of civility. Prospero twice, and Juno again, warn Ferdinand of the absolute necessity for

it, and Ferdinand's ability to make pure beauty "abate the ardour of his liver" is in
the strongest possible contrast to Caliban's straightforward natural lust for it. The
unchaste designs of Stephano arouse Prospero's anger also; it is as if he were
conducting, with magically purified book and rod, the kind of experiment which
depended for its success on the absolute purity of all concerned; and indeed, in so
far as his airs were a dynastic marriage and the regeneration of the noble, this
was so.

This is the characteristic of the way in which the magic of Prospero translates
into more general terms. The self-discipline of the magician is the self-discipline of
the prince. It was the object of the good ruler to make his people good by his own
efforts; and that he might do so it was considered necessary for him to acquire
learning, and to rid himself "of those troublous affections that untemperate mindes
feele" (Castiglione). The personal requirements of mage and prince are the same,
and Prospero labours to regain a worldly as well as a heavenly power. Like James
I in the flattering description, he "standeth invested with that triplicitie which in great
veneration was ascribed to the ancient *Hermes,* the power and fortune of a *King,*
the knowledge and illumination of a Priest, and the Learning and universalitie of a
Philosopher" (James Cleland).

Learning is a major theme in the play; we learn that Miranda is capable of it
and Caliban not, and why this should be so; but we are also given a plan of the place
of learning in the dispositions of providence. Prospero, like Adam, fell from his
kingdom by an inordinate thirst for knowledge; but learning is a great aid to virtue,
the road by which we may love and imitate God, and "repair the ruins of our first
parents" (John Milton), and by its means he is enabled to return. The solicitude
which accompanied Adam and Eve when "the world was all before them" went
also with Prospero and Miranda when they set out in their "rotten carcass of a
butt".

> By foul play, as thou say'st, were we heave'd thence,
> But blessedly holp hither.   (I. ii. 62–3.)

They came ashore "by Providence divine"; and Gonzalo leaves us in no doubt that
Prospero's fault, like Adam's, was a happy one:

> Was Milan thrust from Milan, that his issue
> Should become kings of Naples? O rejoice
> Beyond a common joy! . . .   (V. i. 205–7.)

He had achieved the great object of Learning, and regained a richer heritage. But
he is not learned in only this rather abstract sense; he is the learned prince. Like
Boethius, he had been a natural philosopher, and had learnt from Philosophy that
"to hate the wicked were against reason." He clearly shared the view that "no wise
man had rather live in banishment, poverty, and ignominy, than prosper in his own
country . . . For in this manner is the office of wisdom performed with more credit
and renown, where the governors' happiness is participated by the people about

them." And Philosophy, though ambiguously, taught both Boethius and Prospero "the way by which thou mayest return to thy country".

There is nothing remarkable about Prospero's ambition to regain his own kingdom and strengthen his house by a royal marriage. To be studious and contemplative, but also to be able to translate knowledge into power in the active life, was the object of his discipline; the Renaissance venerated Scipio for his demonstration of this truth, and Marvell's Horatian Ode speaks of Cromwell in the same terms.

> The chiefe Use then in man of that he knowes,
> Is his paines taking for the good of all . . .
> Yet *Some seeke knowledge, merely but to know,*
> And idle Curiositie that is . . .

Prospero is not at all paradoxical in presenting himself at the climax as he was "sometime Milan". Yet he does not intend merely to look after his worldly affairs; every third thought is to be his grave. "The end of the active or doing life ought to be the beholding; as of war, peace, and as of paines, rest ⟨Castiglione⟩." The active and contemplative lives are complementary.

In all respects, then, Prospero expresses the qualities of the world of Art, of the *non vile*. These qualities become evident in the organized contrasts between his world and the world of the vile; between the worlds of Art and Nature.

—FRANK KERMODE, "Introduction" to *The Tempest* (Arden Edition)
(London: Methuen, 1954), pp. xli–li

DAVID I. MACHT

An interesting play on the Hebrew word for *earth* is found in Act 1, Scene 2, Line 314. The Hebrew for *adam,* or man, signifies earth, just as the word for earth is *adamah.* Note the epithet "thou earth" which Prospero applies to that extraordinary creature, Caliban, the personification of the vegetative brute, in contrast to homo sapiens. It certainly depicts the character concisely and epigrammatically.

In the same scene (Act 1, Scene 2, Lines 334 and 346) we have another direct and literal quotation from the Hebrew of Genesis, Chapter 1, Verse 16, describing the creation of the sun and moon:

> and teach me how
> To name the bigger light, and how the less
> That burn by day and night.

Caliban's work, the only one for which he was fitted, namely, to draw water and gather wood, is, of course, described in Joshua's dealings with the "Gibeonites" (Joshua, Chapter 9, Verse 21).

The Lines 70 and 71 Acts 3, in Scene 2,

I'll yield him thee asleep
Where thou mayst knock a nail into his head

are known by all to refer to Jael's slaying of Sisera in Judges IX, 21. What is not familiar to non-Jews is the justification for Jael's act. It was not merely a politically patriotic gesture, but, according to the Talmud, it was in defense of the Hebrew woman's honor. (See Macht, "Heart and Blood in the Bible," Balto. 1951, Page 10.)
      In Act 1, Scene 2, Lines 217–19, we read

Not a hair perished
On their sustaining garments; not a blemish
But fresher than before.

This description was undoubtedly suggested by Daniel, Chapter III, Verse 27, which recounts the tribulations of Shadrach, Meshach, and Abednego, who were cast into the burning furnace, but through Divine intervention escaped completely unharmed.
      Other passages suggesting their Biblical origin and idiom are as follows:
      In Act 2, Scene 1, Lines 22 and 43, the phrase

Subtle, tender, and delicate temperance.

echoes the idiomatic Hebrew of Deuteronomy XXVIII, Verse 56; and similarly in Act 2, Scene 1, line 160

No use of metal, corn, or wine, or oil

is reminiscent of Deuteronomy VII, Verse 13, and also Psalm IV, Verse 8.
      The Shakespearean couplet in Act 4, Scene 1, Lines 263–64,

more pinch-spotted make them
Than pard, or cat o'mountain,

are a paraphrase of Jeremiah XIII, Verse 23.
      Act 4, Scene 1, 156–158, has been the subject of hot dispute among most commentators.

We are such stuff as dreams are made on,
And our little life is rounded with a sleep.

Here Prospero discourses on life and immortality. Does "sleep" in this passage refer to eternal sleep and disintegration, or to a sleep which terminates with resurrection? Many parallel passages pondering on this theme are, of course, found in ancient literature. We read it in Pindar, *Pyth.* VIII, 99, and again in Aeschylus, *Prom.* 550, and Sophocles, *Aias* 126, and Aristophanes, *Aves* 686, and Euripides, *Aeol.* fr. 25. What was Shakespeare's philosophy on the theme? Knight mentioning Berkeley, the "no matter" bishop, wishes to convey that the Bard had the same views as Bishop Berkeley. *His* view, on the other hand, claims, Shakespeare did not take stock in spirituality at all, but was a materialist and atheist. So also Birch, in unequivocal and emphatic language, tries to prove from the above lines that the poet held the same materialistic ideas as those of Seneca and Cicero of old and those of modern materialists and atheists. It is astonishing to read of such inferences by Shakespearean scholars, who certainly knew of the dramatist's "small Latin and less Greek" on the one hand, and the widely read Bible translations appearing at the time, on the other. The above citation was most probably inspired by the famous soliloquy of Job XIV, 10, ff, in which he concludes by drawing an analogy from plant life, that the "sleep" of man on his departure from this vale of tears and sorrow must be only a temporary one. This philosophy of Job can be fully appreciated only from the original Hebrew version, which is rendered in an interrogative sense (compare Macht: *Bones and Verdure,* Balto. 1943, p. 49).

Perhaps the most interesting passage in *The Tempest* suggesting a Biblical origin, which has been entirely overlooked by all non-Jewish commentators, is Line 10, Act 3, Scene 2, which reads as follows:

thy eyes are almost set in thy head

The meaning of this sentence is difficult to surmise by one unacquainted with the "Old Testament." There in Ecclesiastes, Chapter II, Verse 14, we read:

"The wise man's eyes are in his head, but the fool walketh in darkness." A traditional Jewish interpretation is as follows: Why should the Bible state the obvious, that the eyes are in the head? The moral taught, however, is a profound one. The eyes are our chief organs of perception. The scientist employs this sense of vision to observe phenomena of nature, and these apperceptions are carried to the brain, there to be analyzed, weighed in the balance of calm judgment, resynthesized, and finally, if need be, converted into action. Not so the fool. He does not think, but when he gets an eyeful, his sensations are transmitted at once and directly by the shortest and easiest paths to the heart, viscera, glands, and muscles. A slave of his emotions, he is truly in darkness intellectually, and falls a prey to hasty and usually harmful reactions. Is not this a most appropriate epithet to apply to Caliban?

—DAVID I. MACHT, "Biblical Allusions in Shakespeare's *The Tempest*
in the Light of Hebrew Exegesis," *Jewish Forum* 38, No. 8 (August 1955):
118–19

JAN KOTT

Commentators on *The Tempest* concern themselves largely with opposing Ariel to Caliban. To my mind this approach is philosophically flat and theatrically vacuous. In terms of dramatic action Ariel is not Caliban's opposite number. He is visible only to Prospero and the audience. To all other characters he is just music or a voice.

Caliban is the main character next to Prospero. He is one of the greatest and most disturbing Shakespearean creations. He is unlike anybody or anything. He has a full individuality. He lives in the play, but also outside it, like Hamlet, Falstaff, and Iago. Unlike Ariel, he cannot be defined by one metaphor, or contained in one allegory. In the list of the *dramatis personae* he is described as "a salvage and deformed slave", Prospero calls him "devil", "earth", "tortoise", "a freckled whelp", "poisonous slave", and, most of all, monster. Trinculo calls him "fish". Caliban has legs like a man, but his arms are like fins. He chews something in his mouth all the time, snarls, walks on all fours.

Dürer has painted a pig with two heads, a bearded child, a rhinoceros looking like a monstrous elephant. Leonardo, in his *Treatise on Painting,* gives the following recipe for a dragon: "take the head of a mastiff, the eyes of a cat, the ears of a porcupine, the mouth of a hare, the brows of a lion, the temples of an old cock, and the neck of a tortoise." Scholars have found engravings dating from the beginning of the seventeenth century representing Caliban-like monsters; they have concluded that Shakespeare's description suggests most a certain mammal of the whale family living mainly in the Malay area. So Caliban would be a kind of huge cachalot.

But on the stage Caliban, like Ariel, is just an actor wearing a costume. He can be represented more like a fish, like an animal, or like a human. There has to be in him a kind of animal bestiality, and a reptile quality, otherwise the grotesque scenes with Stephano and Trinculo could not come off. But I would like to see him as human as possible. A metaphor of monstrosity expressed in words is something different from the concrete quality of gesture, mask and actor's make-up. Caliban is a man, not a monster. Caliban—as Allardyce Nicoll has rightly pointed out—speaks in verse. In Shakespeare's world prose is spoken only by grotesque and episodic characters; by those who are not part of the drama proper.

Caliban had been lord of the isle; after Prospero's departure he will again remain alone on it. Of all the characters of *The Tempest,* he is the most truly tragic. Perhaps he is the only one to change. All the other characters are drawn from the outside, as it were, shown in a few basic attitudes. This applies even to Prospero. Prospero's drama is purely intellectual. Ariel's drama, too, remains in the sphere of abstract concepts. Only to Caliban Shakespeare has given passion and a full life history.

Caliban had learned to speak. For let us remember that the island represents the history of the world. Caliban had been taught to speak by Miranda. She now reproaches him reminding him of it. Language distinguishes men from animals. Caliban is a symbol of Montaigne's good cannibals, but he is not a noble savage. This is not the island of Utopia, and the history of the world will be stripped on it of all illusions. The use of language can become a curse and only aggravate slavery. Language is then limited to curses. This is one of the most bitter scenes in the whole play:

> MIRANDA: . . . I pitied thee,
> Took pains to make thee speak, . . .
>   . . . When thou didst not, savage,
> Know thine own meaning, but wouldst gabble like
> A thing most brutish, I endow'd thy purposes
> With words that made them known. . . .

CALIBAN: You taught me language, and my profit on't
Is, I know how to curse. The red plague rid you
For learning me your language!   (I, 2)

To Miranda, Caliban is a man. When she sees Ferdinand for the first time, she will say: "This / Is the third man that e'er I saw". In the Shakespearean system of analogies and sudden confrontations Caliban is made Prospero's and Ferdinand's equal; Shakespeare stresses this point very clearly. A little later the same theme is taken up again by Prospero. He speaks to Miranda, referring to Ferdinand:

                                             . . . Foolish wench!
To th' most of men this is a Caliban,
And they to him are angels.   (I, 2)

Caliban is an unshapely monster, Ferdinand the handsomest of princes. But to Shakespeare beauty and ugliness are just a matter of what people look like to other people, in a place and part they have been asked to play.

The action develops on the island exactly as Prospero has planned it. The shipwrecked men have been scattered and brought to the point of madness. Fratricide, intercepted by Ariel at the last moment, has been meant as a warning and a trial. But the scenario devised by Prospero is spoilt by Caliban. Prospero has not foreseen his treason and the conspiracy plotted by Caliban together with Trinculo and Stephano. Caliban's treachery is a surprise to Prospero, and the only defeat he has suffered on the island. But it is the second defeat in Prospero's life. He had lost his dukedom as a result of his devotion to science and the arts; of the trust he had in his brother; in other words—because he had believed in the world's goodness. Caliban's treachery is a new failure as far as Prospero's educational methods are concerned. Again his staff has not proved all-powerful. Prospero wanted to perform on the island the history of the world to serve as warning to the shipwrecked, and to the audience. But the world's history turned out to be even more cruel than he had intended. It brought another bitter surprise, just at the moment when Prospero was solemnizing the betrothal of Ferdinand and Miranda, and evoking before their eyes a vision of the lost paradise.

A devil . . .

                                  . . . on whom my pains,
Humanely taken, all, all lost, quite lost!
And as with age his body uglier grows,
So his mind cankers. I will plague them all,
Even to roaring.   (IV, I)

This is one of the crucial sentences in *The Tempest,* and perhaps the most difficult to interpret. It is the climax of Prospero's tragedy. Only after this scene will he break and reject his magic wand. The very words used by Prospero are also most interesting in themselves:

                                  . . . on whom my pains,
Humanely taken, all, all lost, quite lost . . .

When Molière's Don Juan meets a beggar, he begins to sneer at heavenly justice. Then he offers him alms in return for a curse. But the beggar refuses. Don Juan eventually throws him a piece of gold saying: "I give it to you for the love of humanity." (*"Je te le donne pour l'amour de l'humanité".*) No other phrase written by Molière has been the subject of so many interpretations. Some commentators see in this sentence—unfamiliar in seventeenth-century French—only an equivalent to the standard "out of the goodness of my heart". Others see in it a rationalist inversion, or even parody, of the traditional form *"pour l'amour de Dieu"*. To others still, the word *"humanité"* in Don Juan's mouth is used already in the full sense of the eighteenth century's "Humanity", and Don Juan is a precursor of enlightened humanitarianism.

Shakespeare's words "humanely taken" are equally ambiguous. They can be understood in a very narrow sense and mean not much more than "undertaken in the goodness of heart". But we can also read in them the full sense of Renaissance *"humanitas".* To me, these two phrases: Molière's *"pour l'amour de l'humanité"* and Shakespeare's "humanely taken" show the same mark of genius.

If on Prospero's island the history of the world has been performed, then Caliban's history is a chapter from the history of mankind. With such a reading of *The Tempest,* three scenes acquire a special significance. The first of these occurs at the end of Act II. Stephano has already made Caliban drunk. The plot has been laid down. The "brave monster" will lead his new masters. It is then that Caliban sings for the first time. This drinking song ends with an unexpected refrain: "Freedom, high-day! high-day, freedom! freedom, high-day, freedom!"

In the first scene of the play it was Ariel who asked for freedom. Shakespeare now repeats the same situation with a cruel irony. And not just once; twice. In Act III, a drunkard, a clown, and a poor monster are ready for the coup. They are on their way to assassinate Prospero. Caliban asks for a song. This time Stephano will sing it:

Flout 'em and scout 'em
And scout 'em and flout 'em!
Thought is free.   (III, 2)

"Thought is free"—sings the drunkard. "Thought is free"—repeats the fool. Only Caliban notices that the tune has suddenly changed. At this point Ariel appeared with "a tabor and pipe", and mixed up the tune. "That's not the tune," cries Caliban. Caliban has heard Ariel.

This in essence is the Shakespearean tragi-grotesque, which by its barbarity terrified the classicists, and which the romantics hailed as the principle of a new drama. But they were unable to repeat Shakespearean tune. Instead of tragi-grotesque they wrote melodrama, like that of Victor Hugo. Grotesque and tragedy are mixed and intermingled in Shakespeare, like Stephano's and Trinculo's drunken song suddenly changing into Ariel's music.

Stephano and Trinculo are only grotesque characters, but Caliban is both grotesque and tragic. He is a ruler, a monster, and a man. He is grotesque in his blind, dark and naive revolt, in his desire for freedom, which to him still means just a quiet sleep and food. He is tragic, as he cannot be satisfied with his state, he does not want and cannot accept his fate—of a fool and a slave. Renan saw Demos in Caliban; in his continuation of *The Tempest* he took him to Milan and made him attempt another, victorious coup against Prospero. Guéhenno wrote an interpretation of Caliban as representing the People. Both these interpretations are flat and do not do justice to Shakespeare's Caliban.

In *The Tempest* there is Ariel's music and Caliban's music. There can be no performance of this play without a careful differentiation between them. But in *The Tempest* there is a moment when Caliban's music becomes close to Ariel's. That moment marks also a magnificent eruption of Shakespeare's poetry. Trinculo and Stephano are afraid of Ariel's music. Caliban hears it:

> Be not afeard. The isle is full of noises,
> Sounds and sweet airs that give delight and hurt not.
> Sometimes a thousand twangling instruments
> Will hum about mine ears; and sometime voices
> That, if I then had wak'd after long sleep,
> Will make me sleep again; and then, in dreaming,
> The clouds methought would open and show riches
> Ready to drop upon me, that, when I wak'd,
> I cried to dream again.   (III, 2)

To me this passage is a Shakespearean book of Genesis. The history of mankind begins. The same that has been performed on the island. Caliban has been deceived again. He has been defeated, just as Prospero has been defeated. Caliban has no magic wand, and no wizard's staff will help him. He has mistaken a drunkard for God. But he has entered the path trodden by Prospero. He has undergone a trial and has lost his illusions. He has to make a fresh start once more. Just as Prospero has to make a fresh start when he returns to Milan to become duke once more. "I'll be wise hereafter," says Caliban at the end. And, when Prospero is gone, he will slowly, on all fours, climb to reach the empty highest space at the top of Bosch's island, as Shakespeare presented it.

—JAN KOTT, "Prospero's Staff," *Shakespeare Our Contemporary,*
tr. Boleslaw Taborski (Garden City, NY: Doubleday, 1964), pp. 196–202

JAMES E. PHILLIPS

Caliban has been interpreted by commentators in different ways too numerous to be conveniently detailed here. All agree, however, that in Caliban Shakespeare intended to represent some form of life or activity below that of civilized man, whether it be the primitive savage encountered in England's colonial ventures, the monster frequently described in contemporary travel literature, the devil-daemon of black magic and medieval Christian tradition, or the cannibal, from which his name seems to be derived. Many critics see in Caliban a symbol of the brutish or animal element in human nature, a representation of the instincts and passions in man. John E. Hankins, for example, has argued that he is Aristotle's "bestial man", possessing the attributes of the sensible soul but not those of the intellectual.

If we regard only the history, the appearance, and the drunken, conspiratorial character of Caliban, each of these suggested interpretations appears plausible. But when we regard the function of Caliban on the island and his relationship to Prospero, his activities are remarkably like those attributed in the Renaissance not to the sensitive or animal soul, but instead to the vegetative or quickening power. Sir John Davies, it will be recalled, in describing the quickening power as it should function ideally, wrote:

> Her *quick'ning* power in euery liuing part,
>   Doth as a nurse, or as a mother serue;
>   And doth employ her *oeconomicke art,*
>   And busie care, her household to preserue.
>
> Here she *attracts,* and there she doth *retaine,*
>   There she *decocts,* and doth the food prepare;
>   There she *distributes* it to euery vaine,
>   There she expels what she may fitly spare.
>
> This power to *Martha* may compared be,
>   Which busie was, the *household-things* to doe;
>   Or to a *Dryas,* liuing in a tree:
>   For euen to trees this power is proper too.

Like the vegetative part of man's soul, Caliban is the "housekeeper" of the island. Only at the end, of course, does Caliban come to regard his duties with anything like an attitude that might be called "busie care". But from the beginning the activities expected of him are consistently similar to those assigned to the vegetative soul. Like this lowest power in man, Caliban is regarded as essential to simple existence on the island. When Miranda exclaims of him at the outset, " 'Tis a villain, sir, I do not love to look on", her father replies:

>   But, as 'tis,
> We cannot miss him: he does make our fire,
> Fetch in our wood, and serves in offices
> That profit us.   (I. ii. 311–315)

Soon these "offices" are more specifically indicated. It was Caliban, we learn, who first provided nourishment for Prospero and Miranda when they arrived on the island, showing them "all the qualities o'th'isle, / The fresh springs, brine-pits, barren place and fertile" (I.ii. 339–340). Later, Prospero commands him, "Fetch us in fuel, and be quick, thou'rt best, / To answer other business" (I.ii. 368–369). Even when he would change masters, Caliban speaks of his service function in terms of providing heat, drink, and nourishment. He promises Stephano:

I'll show thee the best springs; I'll pluck thee berries;
I'll fish for thee, and get thee wood enough.
A plague upon the tyrant that I serve!
I'll bear him no more sticks, but follow thee,
Thou wondrous man. . . .
I prithee, let me bring thee where crabs grow;
And I with my long nails will dig thee pig-nuts;
Show thee a jay's nest, and instruct thee how
To snare the nimble marmoset; I'll bring thee
To clustering filberts, and sometimes I'll get thee
Young scamels from the rock.   (II. ii. 160–172)

Caliban summarizes the housekeeping duties which he has performed for Prospero
(and will perform again) when he sings:

No more dams I'll make for fish;
    Nor fetch in firing
    At requiring;
Nor scrape trenchering, nor wash dish.   (II. ii. 193–196)

—JAMES E. PHILLIPS, "*The Tempest* and the Renaissance Idea of Man,"
Shakespeare Quarterly 15, No. 2 (Spring 1964): 150–51

WILLIAM EMPSON

As to the moralising which these religious critics naturally insert as part of their
programme, I have a different objection: I think their morals are bad. Just as there
isn't only one "religion", but a lot of religions, so there are many different ethical
beliefs and a man who is simply in favour of "religion and morality" is pretty sure
to include bad ones. The instincts of Derek Traversi keep him fairly straight, but his
principles might land him anywhere.

In *The Tempest,* Traversi invents a startling punishment for the clowns: "Stephano and Trinculo will be, in turn, left by Prospero on the island which he himself
abandons to return to the fullness of civilised life." Prospero says to his guests, when
the two sinful comics and Caliban shamble in at the end:

        two of these fellows you
Must know and own; this thing of darkness I
Acknowledge mine.

The "cell" needs getting ready to lodge the guests, and almost all Prospero says to
Caliban is:

Go, sirrah, to my cell:
Take with you your companions: as you look
To have my pardon, trim it handsomely.

The "owners" of the fellows are responsible for looking after them, and Caliban is given a strong hint that he will be pardoned. Marooning was naturally thought a terrible punishment, and the only drama in the play is that Prospero has brought himself to forgive his enemies. Traversi had no reason to expect marooning, except that he felt spiteful, and believed that this was a moral way to feel.

Caliban has also to be viewed gravely because in his case there is Symbolism at work. Sentimental critics have given Caliban credit for a poetical nature, but Traversi has an answer: "the poetry which we admire in Caliban was given him, at least in part, by Prospero" ("You taught me language; and my profit on 't / Is, I know how to curse"). We know that Caliban is beyond redemption because when boasting he threatens to inflict on Prospero "unrestrained physical cruelty"; whereas when Prospero makes Caliban scream with pain all night that is spiritual power. Indeed "Caliban is bound by his nature to service"; please notice that Traversi is expressing here the pure milk of the master-race doctrine, and it is presented with the usual glum sanctimoniousness as a traditional Christian moral, with no sign that it has ever been questioned. Before the first entry of Caliban, Miranda expresses distaste for him and Prospero answers:

> But, as 'tis,
> We cannot miss him: he does make our fire,
> Fetch in our wood; and serves in offices
> That profit us.

The kind of life that Prospero has established in his retreat assumes, in fact, the submission of Caliban as a necessary condition. That this submission requires an effort, indicates once more that the island is a reflection of the outer world.

It appears that, if you have to pinch Caliban black and blue as soon as he stops chopping wood, that is rather like keeping a vow of chastity. I must say, I wouldn't like to run into a Moral Critic on a dark night; there is something very shambling and subhuman about the whole movement.

Frank Kermode, whose edition of *The Tempest* came out the same year as *The Last Phase* (1954), realises that the tradition of "the Savage" was a very contradictory one: he appreciates the paradoxes of *The Faerie Queene* Book VI, and denies that the utopian fancy of Gonzalo is meant as satire upon the reflections in favour of savages by Montaigne. But he maintains that the description of Caliban in the List of Names as "a savage and deformed slave" means that Shakespeare considered him inherently a slave, much as Aristotle would have done. Well, Caliban simply *is* a slave of Prospero, who first addresses him as "slave!"; this is not in itself proof that Shakespeare approved of slavery. You might as well say that to write "a prostitute" in the dramatis personae would mean approval of prostitution. When Kermode assumes it he is accepting a formula: "Way back in early times they didn't have advanced ideas, like we have; they just had moral ideas, and that was much better." His own mind does not stop there, and I was not struck with the praise of slavery in reading the introduction to his edition; but then a student at Sheffield wrote an essay on it for me, and it was plain that her natural earnestness had been gravely misled. How *could* a prince be wicked, she wondered, when he has royal blood and a first class education too; it seemed to her a more painful difficulty than it does to Kermode; though she too brightened up at the thought that it illustrates the doctrine of Free Will. The first audiences of course could hardly feel the same surprise, because they seldom saw any play without a wicked prince in it. Surely it is an absurdly deluding education for the modern world, when it reaches the peak of this exquisite flowering confusion—how *can* a royal prince be bad at all? I don't think there can be much future in it.

—WILLIAM EMPSON, "Hunt the Symbol" [1964], *Essays on Shakespeare* (Cambridge: Cambridge University Press, 1986), pp. 238–40

HARRY BERGER, JR.

Caliban and Sycorax throw another kind of light on Prospero. The name *Sycorax* means, among other things, *hooped together:* "with age and envy grown into a hoop," as Prospero says. Turned in upon herself with envy, raven-black with malice, exiled for "mischiefs manifold and sorceries terrible," she appears to be Prospero's antithesis—the nightmare which complements his wish-fulfillment—and this contrast is emphasized by their parallel situations. Both owe their banishment to motives which lead them to the study or practice of magic. Though Sycorax is motivated by pure evil, and Prospero's motives by contrast seem very good, both are equally antisocial, both have withdrawn into themselves, have proved unfit for, or inadequate to, social and political existence. If Prospero withdrew for traditional reasons—extreme idealism and idyllism, contemplation and recreation—Sycorax embodies some of the features of a contrary though equally traditional form of withdrawal: the plaintive withdrawal of the have-not, those figures of envy and malice whose dissatisfaction with their lot produces hatred of self and others; who long for the beauty they lack and hate it in others; who spend their time trying to violate others either to possess their beauty and otherness, or simply for the temporary relief and communion gained by seeing them suffer.

Something of this disposition has been transmitted to Caliban. To the familiar etymological interpretations of his name—*cannibal* and *blackness* (Romany, *cauli-ban*, E. K. Chambers)—I would add *Kali* (beauty) + *ban* or *bane*, and I would translate it in two ways: first, and most simply, "the bane of beauty," which is the way Prospero comes to see him. The second translation is a little more complicated, and it refers to what *we*—as opposed to Prospero—see in Caliban: "banned from beauty, beauty is his bane." Many critics have observed that he has areas of feeling and sensitivity of which Prospero is unaware. Stephen Orgel remarks on his rich fantasy and his concrete sense of the island's natural resources. Clifford Leech notes that although there is "no moral good in him," "Caliban speaks throughout the play in blank verse: he is aware of beauty, whether in Miranda or in the fair features of the island or in the music or his dreams." But these awarenesses lead only to frustration. And since he is only, so to speak, a first-generation human being, his desire apprehends limited forms of beauty—money, wine, woman, and song; his impulses to love and worship are moved by brave and fine appearances when they are not moved by mere alcohol and lust.

The important point to be made about Caliban is that he can by no means be reduced to a figure of pure evil, the antithesis of Miranda or Ariel, the counterpart of Antonio. His baseness is shot through with gleams of aspiration, though the mixture is unstable and the diverse motives often undifferentiated. He displays the most transcendent, the most poignant, and the most natural urges of man as well as the most foolish and murderous and disloyal. Critics have noted the persistent parallels between Caliban and Miranda in regard to the nature-nurture theme, but there is no reason why they stopped there. Situational parallels exist to Ferdinand (the logbearing), to Antonio (the plot), and to Prospero (who supplanted him on the island). His longings appear modulated into ideal civilized form in Miranda's capacity for wonder and Ferdinand's for worshipful service; his visions of riches are sublimed in Prospero's insubstantial pageant and cloudcapped towers. Prospero's original openness and subsequent antipathy to Antonio are reflected by both himself and Caliban in their island relationship. Finally, though it may seem odd, Caliban is not unlike Gonzalo in his attitude toward the island, and in the way his simpleminded good will is abused by Stephano and Trinculo (as Gonzalo's by Sebastian and Antonio). Childlike in his fears and passions, ingenuous in the immediacy of his responses to nature and man, open in the expression of feeling, Caliban at his most evil and traitorous shows up as a mere puppy, a comic Vice, a crude conspirator in the pointed contrast to Antonio established in their plots.

He is thus a moonlight distortion not only of the villains but of all the figures who have come to the island from the daylight world of civilization. In this sense he *stands for* the world; a handy and compact symbol of human nature, not as we know it, but as we might have found it at the beginning of time, in the pre-history of civilization, when Carthage, Tunis and Troy were no more advanced than the Bermudas or Americas. We see in him all man's possibilities in their undeveloped form, and this means that we see the longing for brightness and beauty as no less real, no less rooted and persistent, than the tendency to darkness and evil. This is not what Prospero sees. Caliban is his epitome of human degradation: he is Milan without Prospero and Miranda; the cloven tree without Ariel; man as he really is and has become, rather than man as he could or should be—man, in short, as Antonio, spreading his poison from the top of civilized Italy down to its boot and root.

But Caliban in fact differs radically from his European counterpart. The difference is intimately bound up with the new world Prospero has created on the island, and to understand this we have to take very seriously Shakespeare's many efforts in the play to direct our glance backward to the history of the island before the play begins. This early history discloses an edifying transition from evil to good, and the emergence of a mythic or romance order. In his best of all possible worlds, Prospero sees himself as the new god who has displaced the old, therefore the hero and savior as well as the king of his island universe. The only ripple of disorder is caused by a difference between the old and new generations of evil. Sycorax, who died before Prospero reached the island, belongs to the archetypal past and is therefore an absolute or pure figure of evil. She may also be Prospero's archetype, his figment of evil, a relief from the various shades of human gray in Europe. She was, or would have been, easy to identify as the enemy. There would have been no such complicating factors as love, or trust, or kinship, or hypocrisy. She could have been dealt with by force alone, and Caliban comforts us on this point by suggesting that Prospero's magic is stronger than his mother's. Thus no problem about Prospero's dealings with Caliban could develop were Caliban identical in these respects with Sycorax. What initially confused Prospero was the ambivalence and instability, the mixture of human motives we have already seen in Caliban. Unlike his mother, he offered Prospero a chance to exercise his more humane gifts in the liberal arts. When this failed, Prospero consigned him to the category of pure evil, alongside Sycorax and Antonio. The interesting thing about this whole episode is its resemblance to the Milanese experience, of which it is a modified repetition. Caliban claims that the island was taken from him by Prospero, and Prospero complains in return that he tried to be kind to Caliban, that he lodged him in his cell and gave him lessons. Like Hamlet's "Mousetrap," the situation admits of a certain amount of role-switching: either character in the island drama can be seen as playing both parts, loser and winner, in the Milanese *coup*. Caliban is "all the subjects that he (Prospero) has," and in kicking him about, Prospero may continually, and securely, re-enact his failure in Milan. The analogy also points in the other direction: Prospero's ethical and symbolic reduction of Caliban to a figure of pure evil may suggest his share of guilt in encouraging Antonio to his crime; for unwittingly he did everything he could to cultivate whatever dram of evil his brother may have been heir to; in that sense, he—no less than Antonio—new-created the creatures that were his and gave them the occasion to say, with Caliban, "have a new master; get a new man."

The magic circle is a pastoral kingdom, a simplified and more controllable analogue of Prospero's former situation. To introduce some needless jargon, it is a version of what Erik Erikson calls the microsphere, "the small world of manageable toys" which the child establishes as a haven "to return to when he needs to overhaul his ego." There he constructs a model of his past painful experiences which will allow him to "play at doing something that was in reality done to him." In this way he "redeems his failures and strengthens his hopes." The actual demands of Caliban's role in the microsphere differentiate him from the civilized force of evil he symbolizes to Prospero. His value as a scapegoat exceeds his usefulness as a handyman. Continued in his helplessness, he stands as a token of his master's victory and power; continued in his boorish ingratitude, he is a constant reminder of Prospero's beneficence and patience. And to attenuate the tedium of the island's perfect bliss, his surliness no doubt gives Prospero a legitimate excuse for periodically venting his spleen and clearing his complexion. As a scapegoat and member of Prospero's microsphere, Caliban is bound by two basic conditions: First, he can always be controlled; this is of course guaranteed by the pleasant coupling of his general inefficiency with Prospero's magic. Second, so clearcut a case of villainy sets

Prospero's mind permanently at ease; there will be no deception, no misunderstanding of motives, no need to worry about Caliban's soul or conscience; he can be counted on to behave in a manner deserving only of righteous anger, discipline, and punishment. Poor Caliban is a platonist's black dream: Prospero feels he has only to lay eyes on his dark and disproportionate shape to know what Evil truly Is, and where.

In William Strachey's letter describing and commenting on the 1609 Bermuda shipwreck and the expedition's subsequent fortunes in Virginia, there is a passage which supplies a close analogue to Prospero's experience with Caliban. Sir Thomas Gates, one of the leaders of the expedition, and Lieutenant Governor of the colony, had sent a man out on a mission, and the man was killed by Indians. Strachey reports that "it did not a little trouble the Lieutenant Governour, who since first landing in the Countrey ... would not by any meanes be wrought to a violent proceeding against them, for all the practises of villany, with which they daily indangered our men; thinking it possible, by a more tractable course, to winne them to a better condition: but now being startled by this, he well perceived, how little a faire and noble intreatie workes upon a barbarous disposition, and therefore in some measure purposed to be revenged." Strachey's letter is dated 1610, and Shakespeare could have seen it in its unpublished form, but my interest is in something he could not have seen, a marginal comment in *Purchas His Pilgrimes* (1625), in which the letter was first published: "Can a Leopard change his spots? Can a Savage remayning a Savage be civill? Were not wee our selves made and not borne civill in our Progenitors dayes? and were not Caesars Britaines as brutish as Virginians? The Romane swords were best teachers of civilitie to this & other Countries neere us."

To this hard-headed historical perspective we may contrast another view of the—or a—New World, and a very different idea of the acquisition of civility. Imagine Prospero's delight were he to find himself translated to the island of Utopia where "the people are in general easygoing, good-tempered, ingenious, and leisure-loving. They patiently do their share of manual labor when occasion demands, though otherwise they are by no means fond of it. In their devotion to mental study they are unwearied. ... after a little progress, their diligence made us at once feel sure that our own diligence would not be bestowed in vain. They began so easily to imitate the shapes of the letters, so readily to pronounce the words, so quickly to learn by heart, and so faithfully to reproduce what they had learned that it was a perfect wonder to us." Here all things have been set in good order from the beginning. Within the scope of a single regime and lifetime, the first king "brought the rude and rustic people to such a perfection of culture and humanity as makes them now superior to all other mortals." In that island, which is Nowhere, Truth is not the daughter of Time. Time has no utility there, history no meaning. The hard-won accomplishments of western civilization have been handed to the Utopians in the Aldine edition, so that they can quickly and painlessly riffle through two thousand years of culture during study hour.

Shakespeare's image of unspoiled man lies somewhere between Prospero's view of him as a born devil and the vision Thomas More assigned to the professional traveller Raphael Hythloday (which means "well trained in nonsense"). But I think it is Hythloday's vision, rather than the more hard-headed attitude recorded by Purchas, which lurks behind Prospero's rejection. Prospero's phrase, "the dark backward and abysm of time," has a rich and profoundly resonant ring to us, but to him it signifies the space of twelve years, not the incredible vast of time which separates us from our progenitors. Shakespeare would have us remember that we cannot new-create Caliban from savagery to civility in twelve years, any more than we can new-create unregenerate Europeans in three hours, except in the world of romance. ⟨. . .⟩

⟨. . .⟩ For of all Shakespeare's human characters he ⟨Prospero⟩ is the only one to have become a god of power, to have attained to Hamlet's kingdom of infinite space in the nutshell of his microsphere, to have entered and passed through pure romance, to have achieved the dearest wish of hermetic sage or mage. His must therefore be the greatest disenchantment. He finds that magic cannot save souls, cannot even pinch the will. More than this, he finds that magic is the only effective policeman, and perhaps he comes to feel that there is very little to look forward to in a world without magic, the world to which he has committed himself to return. This mood has been well described in a recent study by Robert Hunter, who discussed the play's insistence on the inveteracy, the indestructibility of evil. "Only a rigid and unceasing control of the sort that Prospero had exercised over Caliban and . . . Antonio, can keep good in its . . . ascendancy." Prospero's pardoning of Antonio lacks any feeling, Hunter observes, because he knows that "to forgive unregenerate evil is safe only when . . . the good are in firm and undeceived control." But *control* here should be understood in a more restrictive sense than Hunter intends it; it is a control exerted nowhere but in the never-never land of magic and romance. This is why Prospero connects despair to his lack of "spirits to enforce, art to enchant," in the epilogue.

Caliban's role and function in this process are peculiar. As a model and scapegoat, everything that rendered him psychologically useful in the microsphere contributes to Prospero's disenchantment during the course of the play. The reduction of Caliban or man to a devil was the easier way out when Prospero wanted to resolve his mind, protect himself from humane attachments, maintain his psychic distance and mastery in his withdrawn world; but it is no help when he is preparing himself to return. Caliban's ineffectiveness now sets him apart from evil man and links him more closely to those ideal conditions of the microsphere which Prospero is about to renounce—there are, after all, no mooncalves in Milan. I can see no evidence for the view that Caliban is a real threat who keeps Prospero on edge, nor for the pietistic reading of the subplot as moral parody—e.g., the idea that Caliban's plot to murder Prospero as a comic analogue to the crimes of Alonso, Antonio and Sebastian reduces the pretensions of the latter by comparing their behavior "to the deformed and drunken idiocies of the clowns" (G. K. Hunter). On the contrary, the analogy stresses the difference between the unreal symbol and

what it represents—between the comic helplessness to which Prospero has reduced his symbol, and the insidious craft which would have succeeded anywhere
but on the island. It is only in respect to the rootedness of evil that symbol and
referent, Caliban and Antonio, coincide. And it is the awareness of this coincidence,
intensifying through the play since the murder attempt in the second act, which is
surely on Prospero's mind when Ariel tells him that the three drunkards are
"bending toward their project." "A devil," he exclaims, "a born devil, on whose
nature / Nurture can never stick: on whom my pains, / Humanely taken, all, all lost,
quite lost!" He is deeply troubled, as Ferdinand and Miranda had noticed, but this
has nothing to do with the external plot, the threat on his life, such as it is.

He is troubled because at this moment the meaning he has read into Caliban,
and the way represented by Caliban, become for him the meaning and the way of
reality. The series of reenactments of the same pattern of betrayal persuades him
to generalize and validate his disillusion as the one abiding truth of life. The radical
persistence of evil which he validates for himself at this moment is only the objective
consequence of another persistence—his idealistic separation of Ariel from Caliban; of Ariel from the cloven tree; of liberal arts from servile labor; of the vanished
age of gold which must be restored, from the present age of iron which must be
either repressively disciplined or willfully ignored. The implied validation of Caliban
as the real model of man is matched by the equally hasty act of generalization which
connects the dissolving masque, first to a dissolving culture, then to a dissolving
world. I think we are meant to note the suddenness, the violence and facility, with
which this reversal of his divided values takes place. What he feels this time, and for
the first time, is that everything golden, noble, beautiful and good—the works of
man, the liberal arts, the aspirations variously incarnated in towers, palaces, temples,
and theaters—that all these are insubstantial and unreal compared to the baseness
of man's old stock. And not merely as vanities; but as deceptions, fantasies which
lure the mind to escape from its true knowledge of darkness and which, dissolving,
leave it more exposed, more susceptible, more disenchanted than before.

Here and now, Caliban becomes most truly Prospero's bane of beauty, the
catalyst leading him, in his revels speech, to criticize as groundless the arts and
projects, the beliefs and hopes by which he had ordered his life. The crux of his
self-criticism lies in the phrase, "the baseless fabric of this vision," and especially in
the word *baseless. Baseless* means two things: insubstantial, not firmly based, without proper grounds; but also, not base, not evil, too purely beautiful, excluding the
dark substance of man; therefore, once again, without grounds. "We are such stuff /
As dreams are made on"—*on* as well as *of*: the evil matter or basis, the Calibanic
foundation on which our nobler works are built, which they deceptively cover over,
or from which they rise as in escape. Prospero would say, as Spenser said of the
golden House of Pride, "full great pittie, that so faire a mould / Did on so weake
foundation ever sit" (*The Faerie Queene*, I.iv.5). And man's works are dreams not
only in being vanities, fragile illusions, but also in being—as Freud called them—the
guardians of sleep protecting the mind in its denial of or flight from reality. Feeling
this, Prospero might well envy his actors for being spirits who can melt into thin air

after their performance. The best the vexed and aging mortal creature can hope for is to have his little life rounded—*crowned*—with sleep.

—HARRY BERGER, JR., "Miraculous Harp: A Reading of Shakespeare's *Tempest,*" *Shakespeare Studies* 5 (1969): 259–63, 269–71

LESLIE A. FIEDLER

To seek the past, the fable of his life signifies, is to leave action for books and to end up enisled with a nubile daughter in an ultimate travesty of the endogamous family, an incestuous *ménage à deux*. But in place of the East he dreams, the common source of Rome and Carthage and the "mouldy tale" of *Apollonius of Tyre,* he wakes to find the West, a beach more strange and fearful than the "still-vexed Bermoothes." Here rape and miscegenation threaten the daughter too dearly loved in an ultimate travesty of the exogamous family. And instead of himself—that is, the past—repeated in the child that daughter bears, he can look forward only to total strangers, monsters as grandchildren—that is, a future utterly alien to anything he knows.

The identification of incest with the riddle is traditional enough to seem convincing, even without the testimony of Claude Lévi-Strauss; but that of miscegenation-rape with the maze may seem at first arbitrary and implausible. Yet a moment's reflection on the myth of Crete reminds us that the latter identification, too, is rooted in ancient mythology; for at the center of the first of all mazes, the labyrinth, there lay in wait the Minotaur, bestial product of woman's lust to be possessed, without due rite or ceremony, by the horned beast, monstrously hung but bereft of human speech. And Caliban is, in effect, a New World Minotaur, inheritor by *Mutterrecht* of a little world which proves, therefore, a maze to all European castaways, even those who dream it Paradise regained. But Caliban exists in history as well as myth, or more properly, perhaps, represents myth in the process of becoming history: the Minotaur rediscovered in the Indian.

His very name is meant to indicate as much, since it is "cannibal" anagrammatized and "cannibal" is derived from "Carib," first tribal Indian name made known to Europe. Caliban seems to have been created, on his historical side, by a fusion in Shakespeare's imagination of Columbus's first New World savages with Montaigne's Brazilians, Somers's native Bermudans, and those Patagonian "giants" encountered by Pigafetta during his trip around the world with Magellan, strange creatures whose chief god was called, like Caliban's mother's, "Setebos." But to say that Caliban was for Shakespeare an Indian means that he was a problem, since the age had not been able to decide what in fact Indians were. And, in a certain sense, *The Tempest* must be understood as an attempt to answer that troubling question on the basis of both ancient preconceptions and new information about the inhabitants of the Americas.

That Caliban seems to be part fish has always troubled some readers of Shakespeare, though the characterization is apt enough for a native of the hemisphere which medieval scholars had believed to be all water. He is portrayed finally as a creature of the mud flats who has managed to climb onto land at long last, but has not yet acclimatized himself to the higher elements of air and fire. Humanoid without being quite human, though a step above what he himself describes as "apes / With foreheads villainous low," he is as the play draws to its close called more and more exclusively "monster": "servant-monster," "brave monster," "man-monster," or simply "monster" unqualified. And the point is to identify him with a kind of subhuman freak imagined in Europe even before the discovery of red men in America: the *homme sauvage* or "savage man," who, in the nightmares of Mediterranean humanists, had been endowed with sexual powers vastly in excess of their own. Such monstrous virility Shakespeare attributes to Caliban, associating him not with cannibalism, after all, but with unbridled lust, as Prospero reminds us when he answers Caliban's charges of exploitation and appropriation with the countercharge:

> I have used thee,
> Filth as thou art, with human care, and lodged thee
> In mine own cell till thou didst seek to violate
> The honor of my child.

And Caliban, glorying in the accusation, answers:

> Oh ho, oh ho! Would 't had been done!
> Thou didst prevent me. I had peopled else
> The isle with Calibans.

He becomes thus the first nonwhite rapist in white man's literature, ancestor of innumerable Indian warriors and skulking niggers who have threatened ever since in print, as well as on stage and screen, the fragile honor of their oppressors' daughters. And it is his unredeemable carnality which, as both Prospero and Miranda insist, condemns him to eternal slavery, since, incapable of being educated to virtue, he must be controlled by force. "A devil, a born devil, on whose nature / Nurture never can stick," the master of arts describes him. And his daughter, more explicitly racist, concurs: "But thy vile race, / Though thou didst learn, had that in't which good natures / Could not abide to be with."

This charge Caliban never directly answers, though with his usual generosity, Shakespeare permits him an eloquent plea on his own behalf, less relevant, perhaps, but quite as moving as Shylock's.

> This island's mine, by Sycorax my mother,
> Which thou takest from me. When thou camest first,
> Thou strokedst me, and madest much of me, wouldst give me
> Water with berries in 't. And teach me how
> To name the bigger light, and how the less,
> That burn by day and night. And then I loved thee,
> And showed thee all the qualities o' th' isle. . . .

Cursèd be I that did so!...
For I am all the subjects that you have,
Which first was mine own king. And here you sty me
In this hard rock whiles you keep from me
The rest o' th' island.

There is, moreover, a kind of music in Caliban's speech, one is tempted to say a "natural rhythm," quite remote from Shylock's tone; for the Jew is postulated as an enemy of all sweet sound, whereas the New World savage is a singer of songs and a maker of poems, especially when he remembers the virginal world he inhabited before the coming of patriarchal power.

Prospero thinks of his island kingdom as a place to be subdued, hewed, trimmed, and ordered, so that, indeed, the chief use of his slave is to chop down trees and pile logs for the fire. But Caliban remembers a world of unprofaned magic, a living nature, in which reality had not yet quite been separated from dream, nor waking from sleeping:

Be not afeared. The isle is full of noises,
Sounds and sweet airs that give delight and hurt not.
Sometimes a thousand twangling instruments
Will hum about my ears, and sometime voices,
That, if I then had waked after long sleep,
Will make me sleep again. And then, in dreaming,
The clouds methougtht would open and show riches
Ready to drop upon me, that when I waked,
I cried to dream again.

Once awakened from the long dream of primitive life, fallen out of the mother into the world of the father, there is no falling back into that intra-uterine sleep, only the hope for another kind of happiness, a new freedom on the farther side of slavery. Even drunk, Caliban remains a poet and visionary, singing that new freedom in a new kind of song.

No more dams I'll make for fish.
          Nor fetch in firing
          At requiring,
Nor scrape trencher, nor wash dish.
          'Ban, 'Ban, Cacaliban
          Has a new master.——Get a new man.
Freedom, heyday! Heyday, freedom! Freedom, heyday, freedom.

Particularly in its Whitmanian long last lines—howled, we are told by the two mocking European clowns who listen—he has created something new under the sun: the first American poem.

And what has this in common with the Old World pastoral elegance of the marriage masque, in which Prospero compels certain more "temperate" spirits to speak for the top of his mind, even as the rebellious Caliban does for the depths of his soul.

> You nymphs, called Naiads, of the windring brooks,
> With your sedged crowns and ever-harmless looks,
> Leave your crisp channels, and on this green land
> Answer your summons. Juno does command.
> Come, temperate nymphs. . . .

They simply cannot see eye to eye, the bookman and the logman, for while one is planning marriage, the other is plotting rape, since the savage (as even Gonzalo seems to know, providing that "Letters should not be known. . . ." in his commonwealth) prefers freedom to culture and would rather breed new Americans in passion than himself become a new European in cold blood. But against Prospero's "art" he is powerless and must abide, therefore, enslaved and desexed until some outside deliverer comes to his rescue.

That outside deliverer turns out to be, alas, the team of Stephano and Trinculo, the scum of the Old World promising themselves unaccustomed glory in the New and attempting to use against their old masters the New World savage, converted by whisky to their cause. But a drunken revolution is a comic one, and joining the clowns who would be kings, Caliban turns drunken, too, which is to say, becomes a clown himself. Indeed, the subject of drunkenness haunts *The Tempest* early and late as compulsively as it does *Macbeth* or *Othello*. But it has lost its tragic implications, providing only occasions for jokes, from the first scene, with its sodden sailors, to the last, from which Stephano and Trinculo exit "reeling ripe" and prophesying that they will remain "pickled forever." "What a thrice-double ass / Was I," Caliban comments toward the play's close, "to take this drunkard for a god." And we remember how only a little while before, he had cried, "That's a brave god, and bears celestial liquor," thus preparing to become the first drunken Indian in Western literature.

Together with Stephano and Trinculo, in any case, he had plotted a slave's revolt against what Shakespeare believed to be proper authority. Caliban, in fact, was the tactician of this fool's rebellion, suggesting, out of his fantasies of revenge, means to destroy their common enemy: "with a log / Batter his skull, or paunch him with a stake, / Or cut his weasand with thy knife." But especially he insists that they must first take from the master of arts the instruments which give him a fatal advantage over them all: his books, which is to say, those symbols of a literate technology with which the ruling classes of Europe controlled the subliterates of two worlds. The theme recurs almost obsessively in his speeches: "Having first seized his books. . . . Remember / First to possess his books, for without them / He's but a sot. . . . Burn but his books." Yet the revolt is foredoomed because Stephano and Trinculo prove interested only in the trashy insignia of power, while Caliban is dreaming not just the substitution of one master for another but the annihilation of all authority and all culture, a world eternally without slaves and clowns. ⟨. . .⟩

Thus fallen into history, however, has Shakespeare not also fallen out of his own myth, for what, after all, has America to do with *Apollonius of Tyre,* the guilt of expropriating ex-Europeans with that of incestuous fathers? It is easy enough to perceive on the literal level of his fable common images which betrayed Shakespeare from legend to chronicle: the sea voyage itself, for instance, along with the attendant circumstances of storm and shipwreck and miraculous salvation. In the most general sense, moreover, both the Old World of Apollonius and the New World of Caliban are worlds inhabited by terrifying and hostile strangers or, conversely, ones in which the castaway European feels himself a stranger in a strange land. Indeed, the word "strange" appears everywhere in *The Tempest,* not only in the speeches of the shipwrecked Neapolitans but in the stage directions as well: "strange drowsiness," "strange beast," *"strange music," "strange Shapes,"* "strange stare," "strange story"—all climaxing in Alonso's description of Caliban: "This is a strange thing as e'er I looked on."

These last words are only spoken, however, after Prospero's unknotting of the web he has woven; before, it is themselves and their plight which the displaced Europeans find superlatively "strange." And this sense of total alienation stirs in them not only "wonder, and amazement" but "trouble" and "torment," too, which is to say, the pangs of guilt. It is not merely that all of them are in fact guilty of treachery and usurpation in respect to each other but that having entered so alien a realm, however inadvertently, they become also guilty, on the metaphorical level, of rape and miscegenation. They are all, in short, Calibans, for America was at once virgin and someone else's before they came—and this they dimly surmise.

The figure of Caliban, at any rate, casts its shadow upon two utopian visions at once: that of Montaigne-Gonzalo, on the one hand, and that of Shakespeare-Prospero, on the other, the dream of a political utopia and the vision of sexuality redeemed. Inside the skin of every free man, Mark Twain was to observe three centuries later, there is a slave; and Shakespeare has concurred in advance, adding, And a monster as well! But all this Prospero has somehow temporarily forgotten, as the play which Shakespeare let him write moves—inexorably, it seems—toward its intended happy endings. ⟨. . .⟩

And there is a sense in which Caliban has, since Prospero's abdication, taken over the island and the play. Being, that is (like Joan and Shylock), a truly mythical character, less invented than discovered, he has continued to live on in the public domain, becoming, in spite of Shakespeare, the hero, not the villain of the piece. Especially as black writers have learned in the last decades to invert the racist mythology of their former masters, he has been remade in fiction and drama into a central symbol both for their old indignities and the possibility of revolt against them. The exponents of *négritude* tend to read *The Tempest* as a kind of prefiguration of Melville's *Benito Cereno:* a parable of slave trade and slave rebellion and the fatal link which joins Europe, Africa, and America in guilt and terror.

Aimé Césaire, for instance—in a play less well known in the West than in Eastern Europe, Africa itself, and Asia—has rewritten Shakespeare's fable so that what disrupts Prospero's classicizing masque is not just the drunken plot of a slave and two clowns but the epiphany of a Congolese god, a dark divinity which the master of arts had failed to take into account. Such rewritings of *The Tempest* are true enough to a part of what moved Shakespeare at his prophetic unconscious depths. But they leave out, on the one hand, what is specifically Indian rather than African in Caliban; and on the other, they ignore the sense in which he represents not merely the oppressed nonwhite minorities in America but *all* America insofar as that country remains Europe's bad nigger.

This D. H. Lawrence knew, and writers for the popular European press dare not forget even now, the mythological identification coming to the surface without reflection whenever they are most moved to rage against a culture they know to be an extension of their own, but long to believe to be totally alien. So, for example, an English journalist commenting in retrospect on the assassination of John F. Kennedy was moved to write that "the murder of the President" held up "a mirror to America which reflects such a Caliban image of brutishness and corruption that her enemies can only view it with glee...."

In Shakespeare's conclusion to *The Tempest*, however, the total complexity is preserved. At first, it appears as if he is willing to grant the "savage and deformed slave" no future at all, as Prospero, in what seems more an exorcism than a proper farewell, first cries impatiently, "Go, sirrah, to my cell," then, ignoring Caliban's promise to reform, "Go to, away!" And Caliban, exiting on the line, seems rather to disappear than leave the stage. Yet we have the sense somehow that he will dog Prospero's footsteps until his death, the distorted shadow, which lay before him in the morning, following after in the evening of his life. Prospero has, in fact, implied as much, declaring, just after Ariel enters for the last time, *"driving in* CALIBAN, STEPHANO, *and* TRINCULO, *in their stolen apparel"*:

> Two of these fellows you
> Must know and own, this thing of darkness I
> Acknowledge mine.

The "I" and "you" suspended in brief hiatus at the endings of the run-on lines define two kinds of man: the one remade in the New World, whatever its origin, and resolved now to return; the other unchanged, though chastened by its voyage into the unknown. There is special ambiguity, however, in the phrase "this thing of darkness I," which seems for a moment completely to identify the occultist Duke with the "savage and deformed slave"; but it is qualified by the sentence's end, "acknowledge mine." Yet there is a ritual ring to the formula, all the same: *"This thing of darkness I / Acknowledge mine,"* as if, through Prospero, all Europe were accepting responsibility for what was to remain forever malign in the America just then being created by conquest and enslavement.

But he speaks on a psychological level, too, as indeed he must, since, in general, the oppression of minorities always implies the repression of certain elements in the psyche of the oppressors with which those minorities are identified. And more particularly, the Anglo-Saxon "plantation" of the New World was somehow early linked, by analogy at least, with the puritan rejection of "cakes and ale" and unbridled sexuality—clearing the woods and subduing the savage, being metaphors for ascetic control. Such early English ventures into the New World as Roanoke and the Bermudas and even Jamestown were, to be sure, cavalier in spirit and motivation and sometimes carried with them actual magicians and poets. But as those settlements moved northward, eschewing slavery for a few in favor of work for all, it was the Malvolios who began to set the tone, not the Duke Orsinos, in love with love, or the masters of arts, like Prospero.

Yet Prospero could have warned such *émigrés* that even the noblest of puritan dreams, the making of marriage into a myth as potent as courtly adultery, was doomed unless the Caliban principle was given its due. But this means that the patriarchal consciousness must acknowledge the dark motivations, the maternal residue, which, even when they do not write the plots we live, mar those which our best magic strives to make come true. It is Prospero's own residual lust which has broken the spell of the marriage masque; and confessing this, he knows himself checkmate once more.

> —LESLIE A. FIEDLER, "The New World Savage as Stranger; or, ' 'Tis New to Thee,' " *The Stranger in Shakespeare* (New York: Stein & Day, 1972), pp. 232–40, 247–50

TERENCE HAWKES

Caliban, it seems clear, must rank less as Prospero's opposite, than as the other side of the same coin. He stands as far removed from involvement in talking and listening as Prospero originally did, and his barbarity, although the opposite of Prospero's condition, thus represents perhaps a sophisticated enough comment on his master's and Gonzalo's Milanese 'civilization', in the spirit of Montaigne's trenchant views on cultural relativity given in his essay on cannibals.

It has been pointed out that the Elizabethan-Jacobean civilization had a clear-cut view of the nature and function of the spoken language in social life. The prime, and most forcefully expressed notion was of speech as a unifying and civilizing force amongst men. In the *Leviathan,* Hobbes argues that language actually *confers* manhood, and keeps bestiality at bay. Without it '. . . there had been amongst men neither Commonwealth, nor Society, nor Contract, nor Peace, no more than amongst Lyons, Bears and Wolves.' Earlier writers concurred. George Puttenham, for instance, was in no doubt that

> Utterance also and language is given by nature to man for perswasion of others, and aid of them selves, I meane the first abilite to speake.

Such ends were helped by an intensification of language's essential characteristics in the 'artificiall' form of Poesie, the 'profession and use' of which can be traced back

> . . . before any civil society was among men. For it is written, that Poesie was th' originall cause and occasion of their first assemblies, when before the

people remained in the woods and mountains, vagrant and dispersed like the wild beasts, lawlesse and naked, or verie ill clad, and of all good and necessarie provision for harbour or sustenance utterly unfurnished: so as they little differed for their maner of life, from the very brute beasts of the field.

Certainly, in the concern of those who wrote of language at the time, the voice of Cicero and Isocrates is plain to hear. Thomas Wilson sees in language the basis of man's construction of social forms:

Where as Menne lived Brutyshlye in open feldes, having neither house to shroude them in, nor attyre to clothe their backes, nor yet any regarde to seeke their best auayle: these appoynted of God called them together by vtterance of speache, and perswaded with them what was good, what was badde, and what was gainefull for mankynde.

In fact writers of the sixteenth century often cite Orpheus, son of Apollo (the god of speech), as a major example of language's creative power as a persuasive to civilized life. Just as his song tamed wild beasts, so (the analogy went) by the power of his language he was able to charm men from bestiality to civilization, and to persuade them to form human communities. In this, he was also sometimes identified with Christ, in Puttenham's words

implying thereby, how by his discreete and wholesome lessons . . . he brought the rude and savage people to a more civill and orderly life.

Orpheus's descent into Hades, like Christ's harrowing of Hell, ranks as a standard metaphor of language's power, even over death.

The later sixteenth century in England stresses this 'Orphic' view of language, with its Christian analogues, as an educational ideal. For example, Stephen Guazzo's widely read *Civile Conversation* (1586), bases its precepts for behaviour wholly on the social art of speech, and the concept of 'civil conversation' as the ultimate goal of language amongst men seems to develop naturally from such a view.

Of course 'civil conversation' is exactly what the unredeemed Caliban lacks. The dimension of reciprocity essential to the act of conversing is entirely absent from his speech. He never 'Yields us kind answer' (I, ii, 307) and, animal-like, has rejected those attempts to 'civilize' him which, notably, have taken the predominant form of teaching him language. In Miranda's words,

. . . I pitied thee,

Took pains to make thee speak, taught thee each hour
One thing or other. When thou didst not, savage,
Know thine own meaning, but wouldst gabble like
A thing most brutish, I endowed thy purposes
With words that made them known. But thy vile race,
Though thou didst learn, had that in 't which good natures
Could not abide to be with.   (I, ii, 354–61)

The biological analogue of linguistic interchange might be said to be the act of sex. The word 'intercourse' legitimately applies to both activities, and both clearly have a fundamental role to play in the structure of any society. The analogical relationship between conversing and coupling was lightheartedly explored, it was noticed, in *Love's Labour's Lost*. There, linguistic intercourse was seen to precede and prefigure its sexual counterpart, the 'fruitfulness' of both being necessary to the preservation of a healthy community.

Marriage traditionally stands as one of the manifest signs of 'civilized' human society in European terms. Men and women are said to be redeemed from bestiality, indeed to *become* fully men and women by its means. The Elizabethan horror of sexual licence, and the felt need to contain its drive by means of the institution of marriage needs no exposition. Absence of marriage, or its abrogation, seemed a sure sign of savagery, of decline from human status. The linguistic ana- logue of 'married' sex might thus be said to be 'civil' conversation. Both act as a socially sanctioned means of fruitful intercourse between humans, on which the health and future of society depends.

An interesting link between Caliban and Prospero, which again emphasizes that they represent not opposites, so much as differing degrees of the same situation, lies in their deficiencies in these fundamentally related respects. Caliban's resistance to language constitutes a basic part of his wholly unredeemed nature which 'any print of goodness wilt not take' (I, ii, 353). His reply to Miranda is explicit:

> You taught me language, and my profit on 't
> Is, I know how to curse. The red plague rid you
> For learning me your language!   (I, ii, 363–5)

Appropriately, and analogously, his sexual interest in Miranda proves equally unre- deemed. The institution of marriage never enters into it. Nor does the sense of the fruitful generation of those 'civilized' human beings on which successful colonization (and potentially disastrous under-population at home) depends. On the contrary, Caliban's lust concerns only himself, and his own gratification. Miranda is reduced in his eyes to an object by whose means he might have 'peopled. . . . This isle with Calibans' (I, ii, 350–1). The absence of reciprocity, of the ability to venture beyond himself noticed in his language, thus also characterizes him on this level, and serves to define his lust, and to distinguish it—in our eyes perhaps no less than in those of the Elizabethans—from its opposite, love.

In the case of Prospero we are confronted not by sexual, but by a kind of intellectual lust, manifested in his earlier, almost narcotic dependency upon books. The printed page naturally tends to generate, not a sense of community, of others and their needs, and their existence, but a mirror-image of the self. Books do not converse. And they may feed a self-concerned, self-obsessed abstraction from reality. In fact Prospero recognizes this as the cause of his own deposition. He has peopled his Milanese kingdom with Prosperos.

True love, true reciprocity, true humanity, finds its aptest representation in the play in the relationship between Ferdinand and Miranda. The innate nobility of each will, we are told, result in the breeding of noble (i.e., 'non-vile') offspring which will guarantee the future of the race (and the colony). Of course, this can only take place within the institution of marriage, and the virtues of restraint and chastity— the opposite of the qualities represented by the unredeemed Caliban and Prospero—are frequently enjoined upon the lovers, and readily acceded to by them (IV, i, 16ff.: 52ff.). The game of chess at which Prospero later 'discovers' them (V, i, 171ff.) traditionally symbolizes a sexual or linguistic encounter. The *formality* of the game, and its insistence on carefully defined interrelationships, and the prohibition of 'false' play are emphasized. Fittingly

>   All sanctimonious ceremonies . . .
>   With full and holy rite   (IV, i, 17–18)

will, we are told, constitute the appropriate 'civile' stamp on this 'conversation'. And so it is not without significance that at their first meeting Ferdinand responds traditionally to the unmistakable sign of common humanity that Miranda gives him. He asks

>   My prime request
>   Which I do last pronounce, is—O you wonder!—
>   If you be maid or no?

She replies, confirming the virginity that both manifests her restrained and 'civilized' status, and links her with the innocent newness, and promise, of the colonial Eden named for England's virgin Queen,

>   No wonder, sir,
>   But certainly a maid.

—and he responds

>   My language? Heavens!   (I, ii, 425ff.)

She speaks his language, she is human, like him.

We may contrast Ferdinand's surprise that Miranda speaks his language, with that of Stephano when confronted by Caliban:

>   This is some monster of the isle with four legs, who hath got, as I take it, an
>   ague. Where the devil should he learn our language?   (II, ii, 64–6)

However, it quickly becomes clear that Caliban's command of the language may easily be overcome—and by a traditional colonial stratagem: the use of alcohol. Significantly, the drink given to Caliban to 'humanize' him

>   Open your mouth. Here is that which will give language to you. . . .
>   (II, ii, 81–2)

acquires the metaphorical dimension of the written version of the language;

STEPHANO: Here, kiss the book *(He gives him wine)*   (II, ii, 127)

The 'kissing' of this 'book', far from affirming Caliban's human status, serves only to make him the besotted slave of Stephano and Trinculo. As literally in the case of Prospero, so metaphorically in the case of Caliban, 'books' constitute a means of alienation and subjugation. Caliban's role as the duped aboriginal here excites our sympathy, and perhaps sorts oddly with his function elsewhere in the play. It serves, none the less, to link him significantly with Prospero in the capacity of one whose language and humanity are sapped by contact with a corrupting, though apparently 'civilizing' force. Wine becomes to Caliban what books were to Prospero: a drug.

—TERENCE HAWKES, "*The Tempest:* Speaking Your Language," *Shakespeare's Talking Animals: Language and Drama in Society* (London: Edward Arnold, 1973), pp. 203–9

STEPHEN J. GREENBLATT

The link between *The Tempest* and the New World has often been noted, most recently by Terence Hawkes who suggests, in his book *Shakespeare's Talking Animals,* that in creating Prospero, the playwright's imagination was fired by the resemblance he perceived between himself and a colonist. "A colonist," writes Hawkes,

> acts essentially as a dramatist. He imposes the 'shape' of his own culture, *embodied in his speech,* on the new world, and makes that world recognizable, habitable, 'natural,' able to speak his language.

Conversely,

> the dramatist is metaphorically a colonist. His art penetrates new areas of experience, his language expands the boundaries of our culture, and makes the new territory over in its own image. His 'raids on the inarticulate' open up new worlds for the imagination.

To read such glowing tribute, one would never know that there had been a single doubt whispered in the twentieth century about the virtues of European colonialism. More important, one would never know that Prospero and the other Europeans leave the island at the end of the play. If *The Tempest* is holding up a mirror to colonialism, Shakespeare is far more ambivalent than Terence Hawkes about the reflected image.

Caliban enters in Act I, cursing Prospero and protesting bitterly: "This island's mine, by Sycorax my mother, / Which thou tak'st from me" (I. ii. 333–334). When he first arrived, Prospero made much of Caliban, and Caliban, in turn, showed Prospero "all the qualities o'th'isle." But now, Caliban complains, "I am all the subjects that you have, / Which first was mine own King." Prospero replies angrily that he had treated Caliban "with human care" until he tried to rape Miranda, a charge Caliban does not deny. At this point, Miranda herself chimes in, with a speech Dryden and others have found disturbingly indelicate:

> Abhorred slave,
> Which any print of goodness wilt not take,
> Being capable of all ill! I pitied thee,
> Took pains to make thee speak, taught thee each hour
> One thing or other: when thou didst not, savage,
> Know thine own meaning, but wouldst gabble like
> A thing most brutish, I endow'd thy purposes
> With words that made them known. But thy vile race,
> Though thou didst learn, had that in't which good natures
> Could not abide to be with; therefore wast thou
> Deservedly confin'd into this rock,
> Who hadst deserv'd more than a prison.

To this, Caliban replies:

> You taught me language; and my profit on't
> Is, I know how to curse. The red plague rid you
> For learning me your language! (I. ii. 353–367)

Caliban's retort might be taken as self-indictment: even with the gift of language, his nature is so debased that he can only learn to curse. But the lines refuse to mean this; what we experience instead is a sense of their devastating justness. Ugly, rude, savage, Caliban nevertheless achieves for an instant an absolute, if intolerably bitter, moral victory. There is no reply; only Prospero's command: "Hag-seed, hence! / Fetch us in fuel," coupled with an ugly threat:

> If thou neglect'st, or dost unwillingly
> What I command, I'll rack thee with old cramps,
> Fill all thy bones with aches, make thee roar,
> That beasts shall tremble at thy din. (I. ii. 370–373)

What makes this exchange so powerful, I think, is that Caliban is anything but a Noble Savage. Shakespeare does not shrink from the darkest European fantasies about the Wild Man; indeed he exaggerates them: Caliban is deformed, lecherous, evil-smelling, idle, treacherous, naive, drunken, rebellious, violent, and devil-worshipping. According to Prospero, he is not even human: a "born devil," "got by the devil himself / Upon thy wicked dam" (I. ii. 321–322). *The Tempest* utterly rejects the uniformitarian view of the human race, the view that would later triumph in the Enlightenment and prevail in the West to this day. All men, the play seems to suggest, are *not* alike; strip away the adornments of culture and you will *not* reach a single human essence. If anything, *The Tempest* seems closer in spirit to the attitude of the present-day inhabitants of Java who, according to Clifford Geertz, quite flatly say, "To be human is to be Javanese."

And yet out of the midst of this attitude Caliban wins a momentary victory that is, quite simply, an assertion of inconsolable human pain and bitterness. And out of the midst of this attitude Prospero comes, at the end of the play, to say of Caliban, "this thing of darkness I / Acknowledge mine" (V. i. 275–276). Like Caliban's earlier reply, Prospero's words are ambiguous; they might be taken as a bare statement that the strange "demi-devil" is one of Prospero's party as opposed to Alonso's, or even that Caliban is Prospero's slave. But again the lines refuse to mean this: they acknowledge a deep, if entirely unsentimental, bond. By no means is Caliban accepted into the family of man; rather, he is claimed as Philoctetes might claim his own festering wound. Perhaps, too, the word "acknowledge" implies some moral responsibility, as when the Lord, in the King James translation of Jeremiah, exhorts men to "acknowledge thine iniquity, that thou hast transgressed against the Lord thy God" (3:13). Certainly the Caliban of Act V is in a very real sense Prospero's creature, and the bitter justness of his retort early in the play still casts a shadow at its close. With Prospero restored to his dukedom, the match of Ferdinand and Miranda blessed, Ariel freed to the elements, and even the wind and tides of the return voyage settled, Shakespeare leaves Caliban's fate naggingly unclear. Prospero has acknowledged a bond; that is all.

⟨...⟩ Shakespeare, in *The Tempest,* experiments with an extreme version of this problem, placing Caliban at the outer limits of difference only to insist upon a mysterious measure of resemblance. It is as if he were testing our capacity to sustain a metaphor. And in this instance only, the audience achieves a fullness of understanding before Prospero does, an understanding that Prospero is only groping toward at the play's close. In the poisoned relationship between master and slave, Caliban can only curse; but we know that Caliban's conscience is not simply a warped negation of Prospero's:

> I prithee, let me bring thee where crabs grow;
> And I with my long nails will dig thee pig-nuts;
> Show thee a jay's nest, and instruct thee how
> To snare the nimble marmoset; I'll bring thee
> To clustering filberts, and sometimes I'll get thee
> Young scamels from the rock.   (II. ii. 167–172)

The rich, irreducible concreteness of the verse compels us to acknowledge the independence and integrity of Caliban's construction of reality. We do not sentimentalize this construction—indeed the play insists that we judge it and that we prefer another—but we cannot make it vanish into silence. Caliban's world has what we may call *opacity,* and the perfect emblem of that opacity is the fact that we do not to this day know the meaning of the word "scamel."

—STEPHEN J. GREENBLATT, "Learning to Curse: Aspects of Linguistic Colonialism in the Sixteenth Century," *First Images of America: The Impact of the New World on the Old,* ed. Fredi Chiappelli et al. (Berkeley: University of California Press, 1976), Vol. 2, pp. 568–71, 575

ERROL G. HILL

When the establishment theatre slowly began to overcome its opposition to interracial casting in Shakespeare, Caliban was one of the first nonblack roles offered to black actors. The occasion was the 1944 production by Margaret Webster which opened at the Alvin Theatre in New York on January 25, 1945, after short tryout runs in Philadelphia and Boston. In the cast were Arnold Moss as Prospero, Canada Lee as Caliban, and the ballerina Vera Zorina as Ariel. Webster had, a few years earlier, created a breakthrough of sorts by casting Paul Robeson as Othello in the record-breaking Theatre Guild production of that play and now she was building on that success. The February 1945 issue of *Theatre Arts* defended her choice of Canada Lee for the role of Caliban:

> In picking the Negro actor for the role, Miss Webster made it clear that she meant to exploit his particular intensity, his power to come to grips with character, and not the pigmentation of his skin. "I do not intend," she insists, "to make Caliban a parable of the current state of the American Negro." Yet her willing eyes discover a ready parallel.

Webster may not have intended it, but she was setting a dangerous precedent. In his first night review of the production, one of the major New York critics observed that "Caliban is a perfect role for a Negro." The production ran for one hundred performances at the Alvin Theatre and was revived later that year at City Center, New York, for a further three weeks.

Now it is true that to the medieval and Elizabethan mind, blackness was associated with evil and hence with the devil who is "the prince of darkness" and personifies evil. Caliban, we are told in the play, was fathered by the devil and is referred to by Prospero as "a devil, a born devil" and "a thing of darkness." It can therefore be argued that he ought originally to have been played black. However, to my knowledge, there is no tradition of playing the role in blackface or of using a black actor prior to Webster's production, and certainly from a modern viewpoint there is no logical justification for casting a black actor as Caliban when the counterpart role of Ariel is given to a sylphlike white actor or, quite often, actress. If anything, the reverse is more appropriate.

Caliban's mother, we recall, was a foul blue-eyed witch called Sycorax who, pregnant with him, had been banished from Algiers to the island. She was either European or Mediterannean in origin and her misshapen son who, Shakespeare tells us, is freckled, must have shared his mother's ethnic pedigree. The delicate Ariel, on the other hand, was found on the island by Sycorax and imprisoned in a pine tree until freed by Prospero who promptly enslaved him as his personal genie. Though unhuman and free of the elements, Ariel inhabited the island prior to the arrival of foreigners and is presumably indigenous to the Caribbean—in any case hardly European. These considerations have been generally ignored in filling the roles. Instead Ariel, the creature of air and native to the Caribbean, is white. Caliban, the savage monster and would-be rapist from the Mediterranean, is black.

It is beauty and the beast all over again, with white equating beauty and black bestiality.

—ERROL G. HILL, "Caliban and Ariel: A Study in Black and White in
American Productions of *The Tempest* from 1945–1981,"
Theatre History Studies 4 (1984): 2–4

NORTHROP FRYE

In writing this play, Shakespeare read some pamphlets about voyages to Bermuda, and some other works on the New World. We know that he read them, because of specific phrases incorporated into the play. Because they are definite source material, every editor of the play has to include them in his introduction, where they seem to do little but confuse the reader. Why would Shakespeare be using such material (some of it still unpublished, and read in manuscript) for a play that never moves out of the Mediterranean? The only clue is that practically all the material used has to do with Caliban. It seems clear that these accounts of the New World are to be connected with Montaigne's essay on the cannibals, which is the source of Gonzalo's reverie about his ideal commonwealth and probably of the character Caliban as well. Caliban, though not technically a "cannibal," and if not quite "the thing itself" like Poor Tom, deprived of all the amenities of specifically human life, is still a kind of "natural man": an example, as Prospero says, of nature without nurture, the much neater phrase that Shakespeare's time used for heredity and environment.

Montaigne's essay touches on the question so intensely discussed a century later, of whether a "natural society" was possible; that is, a society that lived in harmony with nature, as social animals do up to a point, and had much less, if any, need of the cultural envelope of religion, law, morality and education. We notice that there is a very clear moral classification in the society of *The Tempest,* but that there is no alteration of any social ranks at the end of the play. Antonio and Sebastian can still regard themselves as gentlemen compared to Stephano and Trinculo, and Sebastian can still twit them with stealing Prospero's clothes, forgetting that a few hours back he was plotting with Antonio to steal his own brother's life and crown. Prospero is never under any doubt that he is king of his island, or that Stephano's plot against him is a rebellion, or that Caliban is a slave. Caliban is to comedy what Swift's Yahoos are to satire: evidence that the animal aspect of man, when isolated by itself, is both repulsive and incompetent.

And yet the paradox in Montaigne's essay remains unanswered. We have no doubts about the superiority of our way of life to that of the "cannibals." But in what does the superiority consist? In torturing other people to death for trifling deviations in religious belief? The "cannibals" don't do that, nor is there anything unnatural in being healthy and physically vigorous, or even in getting along without most of our class distinctions. They don't have a lot of our worst vices: perhaps we could do with some of their virtues.

—NORTHROP FRYE, *"The Tempest," Northrop Frye on Shakespeare*
(New Haven: Yale University Press, 1986), pp. 180–81, 184–85

STEPHEN ORGEL

Caliban has generally been seen as a foil to Ariel—the airy spirit, the earthy monster—and Prospero confirms his servant's place in an elementary hierarchy by referring to him as 'earth' (1.2.314). Both long for freedom, and, while only Ariel is offered the hope of obtaining it, in fact both Prospero's servants receive it at the same time, when Prospero resumes his dukedom at the play's end. In contrast to Caliban's elemental sameness, Ariel is volatile and metamorphic. He is male, the asexual boy to Caliban's libidinous man, but (in keeping with his status as a boy actor) all the roles he plays at Prospero's command are female: sea nymph, harpy, Ceres. Though his relation to his master includes a good deal of obvious affection, he is no more a willing servant than Caliban, and Prospero keeps him in bondage only by a mixture of promises, threats, and appeals to his gratitude.

In the dramatic structure of the play, Caliban is even more significantly contrasted with Miranda. The two children have been educated together on the island, the objects of Prospero's devoted care; Miranda has developed into a wonder of civilized grace, Caliban into a surly, malicious and—what is most upsetting to Prospero—a lustful monster. Prospero concludes that Caliban, therefore, is monstrous by nature; but once again the issue is complicated by Prospero's and Miranda's claim that they have taught Caliban everything he knows, and by the clear parallel in Prospero's mind between Caliban and the other wicked child for whose education he claims responsibility, his younger brother Antonio. Prospero acknowledges (indeed, insists on) his complicity in the events that led to his overthrow in Milan. The gesture is symbolically repeated in his final acceptance of Caliban as his own.

Caliban, like Sycorax, does in fact embody a whole range of qualities that we see in Prospero, but that he consistently denies in himself: rage, passion, vindictiveness; perhaps deepest and most disruptive, sexuality. Theatrically and critically, the most troublesome aspects of the magician's character have been those relating to libidinous energy. Prospero's charge of ingratitude against Caliban, and Miranda's startling denunciation of him, are provoked by the recollection of an attempt by Caliban to rape Miranda. Caliban compounds the offence by acting both unrepentant and retrospectively lecherous:

> O ho! O ho! Would't had been done!
> Thou didst prevent me—I had peopled else
> This isle with Calibans.   (1.2.348–50)

Caliban's, however, is not the only dangerous sexuality to be feared in the play. Prospero's repeated warnings to Ferdinand against pre-marital sex are not prompted by anything we see of Ferdinand's behaviour. Caliban, in this context, is any man who takes an interest in Miranda, even the suitor of Prospero's choice. The ambivalence towards Ferdinand is expressed, too, in the tasks Prospero sets for him (3.1.9–11), which are, explicitly, Caliban's tasks. Prospero later apologizes for 'too austerely' punishing Ferdinand (4.1.1), but leaves the young man's offence unexplained. Nor is Caliban the only criminal Prospero sees in his prospective son-in-law:

> ... Thou dost here usurp
> The name thou ow'st not, and hast put thyself
> Upon this island as a spy, to win it
> From me, the lord on't. . . .
> Speak not you for him: he's a traitor. (1.2.454–61)

The crimes Prospero charges Ferdinand with in this strange moment are those of his brother Antonio: usurpation and treason.

And in fact, Prospero *has* installed another usurper in his kingdom. To provide a husband for Miranda is to acknowledge his own age and declining powers. Reconciliation and restoration involve yet another withdrawal from the world of action, in which 'Every third thought shall be my grave' (5.1.311).

—STEPHEN ORGEL, "Introduction" to *The Tempest* (The Oxford Shakespeare) (Oxford: Clarendon Press, 1987), pp. 26–29

JOHN D. COX

In comparison to what Shakespeare does with Prospero, other qualifications of power in *The Tempest* are relatively unimportant, but they serve nonetheless to clarify how Shakespeare turned to the medieval dramaturgy of power in his late plays. At the opposite end of the social scale from Prospero is Caliban, the universally despised native of the desert isle. Caliban can hardly be said to enact *potentia humilitatis*, for he is rebellious, sullen, and vengeful. But like many lower-class characters in medieval drama and in Shakespeare's romantic comedies, Caliban is graced with unexpected dignity (as in his lyrical appreciation of the island's beauty and profusion), and more important, he eventually demonstrates a characteristic in common with Prospero and Alonso: the ability to come to the end of himself in acquiring moral wisdom:

> I'll be wise hereafter,
> And seek for grace. What a thrice-double ass
> Was I to take this drunkard for a god
> And worship this dull fool! (5.1.298–301)

No "grounded" character, in Jonson's phrase, Caliban is thus embraced within human society by the play's most important criterion for belonging to it. To be sure, Caliban's repentance is offensive to liberal humanitarian sentiment, for his moral insight does nothing to ameliorate his social situation: he is still Prospero's slave, only now more willing than before. To see this as the play's definitive moral stroke against Prospero, however, is to render meaningless the wisdom Prospero has acquired and to ignore the dignified humanity that Prospero and Caliban come to share. The point is not that Shakespeare sows the seeds of imperial exploitation in *The Tempest*, but that he implicitly denies the Renaissance assumption that virtue is reserved for those at the top of the social scale.

As qualifications of Jacobean ruling taste, what Prospero and Caliban have in common is complemented by what is shared between Stephano and Antonio. For the first two are paradoxically humbled and ennobled by a growing awareness of their limitations and the acquiring of wisdom, while the second two put themselves beyond the human pale by their grounded resistance to moral improvement of any kind. The fact that Antonio is brother to a duke also negates the Renaissance tendency to associate virtue with nobility, for Antonio's viciousness is what he shares with a drunken butler. In the first place, both are willfully myopic about the extraordinary beauty of the island on which they have been shipwrecked. Antonio sneers at Adrian's and Gonzalo's exclamations of wonder (2.1), and Stephano has an interest only in wine, no matter where he finds himself, or in what circumstances: the same butt of sack on which he escaped the shipwreck (2.2.120–22) is the source of his constant inebriation on the island. Caliban's intense longing for the island's beauty thus makes him naturally superior to Antonio and Stephano, even though he falls ready prey to the latter's alcohol in a distressing enactment of European corruption in the New World. Second, Stephano and Antonio are instinctive exploiters of what they find in their new environment. Stephano sees economic profit in Caliban the minute he perceives that this "monster of the isle" is a creature with language, and his purpose in making Caliban drunk is to capture him and present him to a European emperor—presumably in exchange for court preferment (2.2.68–79). Trinculo's thoughts run in the same vein, with more pointed significance for a Jacobean audience:

> Were I in England now, as once I was, and had but this fish painted, not a holiday fool there but would give a piece of silver. There would this monster make a man; any strange beast there makes a man. When they will not give a doit to relieve a lame beggar, they will lay out ten to see a dead Indian.
> (2.2.28–33)

What occurs to a butler and a jester also occurs immediately to Prospero's brother when he first sees Caliban. In response to Sebastian's question whether "money will buy" the three clowns in their stolen apparel, Antonio calculatingly replies: "Very like. One of them / Is a plain fish, and no doubt marketable" (5.1.268–69). These are Antonio's last words in the play, and they therefore indicate that he, not Caliban, is one whose nature "any print of goodness [will] not take, / Being capable of all ill" (1.2.354–55). His cold estimate of Caliban's marketability is a foil to Prospero's treatment of the islander, for Prospero's first instinct was kindly and well intended (1.2.334–50). Whatever retrospective ambiguities may haunt Prospero's response to Caliban, they always need to be considered in conjunction with Antonio's response.

Third, Antonio and Stephano are alike in their common *libido dominandi,* the principal characteristic of tyrants great and small in the mystery plays. The absurdity of Antonio's lust for power is manifest in his tempting Sebastian to join him in assassinating Alonso at the first opportunity after their arrival on the island (2.1.197ff.). Even in the desperate exigency of being shipwrecked, Antonio's sense of mutual support is so deficient that he can think of nothing but his own political advantage among a community of six castaways. In this characteristic, too, Antonio contrasts with his brother, who is capable of renouncing his power when it is at its height. But Antonio has a kindred soul in Stephano, who quickly thinks of inheriting the island (2.2.713), though as far as he knows, it has only five inhabitants: Caliban, Trinculo, Prospero, Miranda, and himself. With a little information and encouragement from Caliban, Stephano quickly sinks to Antonio's level, planning an assassination attempt on the lord of the island: "Monster, I will kill this man. His daughter and I will be king and queen—save our Graces!—and Trinculo and thyself shall be viceroys" (3.2.107–9).

In sum, while Shakespeare's debt to the medieval dramatic heritage in *The Tempest* is general, it is also distinctive and definitive. A king and duke, like Shakespeare's tragic heroes, are most noble when their human fragility is most apparent, and the dramatic model for this paradox is not the royal apotheosis of the court masque but the afflicted peasant in medieval passion plays, who, like Lear, is every inch a king when he smells strongest of mortality. The same model, moreover, applies to the strange case of Caliban, a subhuman monster despised by everyone, who is yet surprisingly ennobled, as his social superiors are, by his repentance. "An heroical spirit," Daniel Dyke maintains, consists not in "a word and a blow, a lie and a stab" but in repentance, which "is a far greater argument of a noble and generous spirit than to pursue so eagerly the revenge of every petty injury." If this concept of heroism is a characteristic of Shakespeare's romances that looks forward to Milton, it is not because Shakespeare was a radical Puritan but because Milton schooled himself in the same theological tradition that gave rise to the archaic dramaturgy Shakespeare turned to as a means of qualifying Jacobean social privilege in his late plays.

—JOHN D. COX, "Ruling Taste and the Late Plays," *Shakespeare and the Dramaturgy of Power* (Princeton: Princeton University Press, 1989), pp. 204–7

MICHAEL DOBSON

So thoroughgoing is *The Enchanted Island* in its emphasis on gender that it virtually occludes Caliban altogether: in Davenant and Dryden's adaptation he gets drunk so thoroughly during his first encounter with the sailors that so far from leading an attempted coup against Prospero he neglects even to alert his new comrades to the Duke of Milan's existence. He is in effect rewritten as a potentially unruly woman by the provision of a sister, Sycorax, over the possession of whom Trinculo and Stephano struggle in a deliberate reiteration of the Hippolito / Ferdinand duel of the romantic subplot. Thomas Duffett's illuminating travesty of *The Enchanted Island, The Mock-Tempest* (1674), which transfers the action of the play to contemporary London low-life, is similarly uninterested in colonialism, translating Caliban perfunctorily into class terms (he features, briefly, as a lower-class hired bully, Hectoro), and preferring to gloss, in a strikingly Foucauldian fashion, Davenant and Dryden's overriding concern with gender politics by casting Prospero as the keeper of the Bridewell prison, the state's official punisher of prostitutes. Discussing Caliban in the preface to his subsequent adaptation *Troilus and Cressida; or, Truth Found Too Late* Dryden simply mystifies him as an example of the supernatural grotesque rather than a dispossessed native ([Shakespeare] *there seems to have created a person who was not in Nature'),* and this neglect of the racial issues raised by Shakespeare's 'salvage and deformed Slave' seems to have persisted in the early eighteenth-century theatre, one production of *The Enchanted Island* at Drury Lane in 1729 having apparently omitted Caliban altogether. ⟨. . .⟩

If the identification of Shakespeare with Prospero serves here to claim *The Tempest* for what may look like a form of Little Englandism, it also presses it more strenuously than ever into the service of imperialism. Garrick's own version of *The Tempest,* an operatic abbreviation which ran for only six performances in 1756, was staged at the height of the Seven Years War, as Britain vied with France for control over vast colonized territories in India, the Far East, and the Americas: eschewing the interpolated pleasures of the Dorinda/Hippolito scenes, and cutting Sycorax, this adaptation restores the rebellion and punishment of Caliban to prominence in the subplot, and is additionally prefaced by a prologue which cites English opera as an ideal patriotic stimulus to its audience to commit deeds of valour against the French. ⟨. . .⟩

Both *The Enchanted Island* and Garrick's operatic *Tempest* had by 1769 long been laid aside in the theatres in favour of Shakespeare's original text, and that this shift away from the adaptations, contemporary with the definitive appropriation of Shakespeare/Prospero as a figurehead for imperial expansion, is also a shift away from a gender-oriented and towards a race-orientated reading of *The Tempest* is perhaps suggested by the sole illustration of the play in performance which survives from this period. The frontispiece to the play in Bell's acting edition of 1774 ignores Miranda, Ariel, Ferdinand, and indeed Prospero to illustrate the moment in Act 2 when Trinculo and Stephano force the newly-drunk Caliban to swear allegiance—a primal scene of colonialism if ever there was one, and significantly the actor playing the kneeling Caliban is made up not as Dryden's supernatural freak but, perfectly representationally, as a Negro. Garrick, too, chooses this scene as the central moment of the play in the procession of Shakespearian characters which marks the climax of *The Jubilee,* having Prospero, preceded by Ariel 'with a wand, raising a tempest' and a model 'ship in distress sailing down the stage', march triumphantly downstage ahead of Miranda, and Caliban 'with a wooden bottle and 2 Sailors all drunk': contemporary engravings depicting this procession similarly record Caliban's representation as a black slave. Prospero here serves as a living emblem of the proper jurisdiction of Englishmen over not only women and the incipiently mutinous lower classes (as he certainly does in *The Enchanted Island*) but also over the subject races newly compelled to pledge allegiance to the Empire.

—MICHAEL DOBSON, " 'Remember / First to Possess His Books':
The Appropriation of *The Tempest,* 1700–1800," *Shakespeare Survey* 43
(1991): 101, 104–5

RENÉ GIRARD

For all his physical and moral ugliness, Caliban is an authentic poet; the critics never fail to observe that some of the most beautiful lines in the play belong to him:

Be not afeard; the isle is full of noises,
Sounds and sweet airs, that give delight and hurt not.
Sometimes a thousand twangling instruments
Will hum about mine ears, and sometimes voices
That, if I then had waked after long sleep,
Will make me sleep again . . .   (III, ii, 135–40)

Caliban symbolizes uneducated poetic feeling, poetry before language, formless, amoral, even immoral, dangerous therefore and possibly reprehensible, but real poetry nevertheless. Prospero teaching Caliban how to speak is Shakespeare himself transforming into actual poems and plays the still nonverbal poetic inspiration that he owes to Caliban. The monster represents a literary mode of which the later Shakespeare disapproves, while acknowledging the crucial role that it played in his career.

Caliban symbolizes that portion of Shakespeare's own works that, being full of monsters, may be viewed as somewhat monstrous itself. Shakespeare does not deny the poetic quality of his past works but detects in them a principle of disorder, bitterness, violence, and moral confusion that he retrospectively condemns as "monstrous." The allegory would be obvious if we did not mistake Caliban for a nineteenth-century monster in the style of Frankenstein or, at best, Victor Hugo's Quasimodo, the hunchback of Notre-Dame. Our ignorance of mythical monsters turns Caliban into a mere freak.

It is significant that, in his major epiphany as a monster, Caliban is not Caliban alone but someone else as well; he is combined with Stephano. The two are huddled together under some kind of blanket. When a drunken Trinculo comes upon this bizarre assemblage, he mistakes it for a single monstrous creature of which he himself tends to become a part, as he proceeds with a tumultuous exploration of it.

In connection with *A Midsummer Night's Dream,* we defined a mythical monster as a mixture of creatures or of parts thereof that, at the height of some sacrificial crisis, seem to lose their distinctiveness. This is what we have here. Caliban is both the product, the mythical monster, and the process that produces it—our mimetic process, of course. We can see this as soon as interpersonal relations come into play. Caliban is so impressed with the wine offered by Trinculo that he asks this poor drunkard to be his god:

> That's a brave god, and bears celestial liquor.
> I will kneel to him. . . .
> . . . .
> I'll show thee every fertile inch o' th' island;
> And I will kiss thy foot. I prithee be my god.   (II, ii, 117–18; 148–49)

Caliban's idolatrous propensity is more important than his physical ugliness; the former can account for the latter, whereas the reverse is not true. Caliban is a monster because he worships Trinculo, not the other way around. We can see this immediately if we remember the midsummer night. Caliban speaks of Trinculo just as Helena speaks of Hermia and Demetrius. To assert that Helena worships these friends because she is a horrible beast would be ridiculous. Helena feels like a horrible beast because she foolishly worships mere human beings.

Idolatrous desire is not a gratuitously comic touch that could be removed from the play without changing its nature. If we separate the monster from his mimetic crisis, he makes no more sense as a monster. Trinculo's wine is the object in a triangle in which Trinculo himself and Caliban occupy the other angles. This wine is the counterpart of Eros with the four lovers, or of theatrical impersonation with the craftsmen.

As he selects Trinculo for his mediator, Caliban makes him the same offer as to Prospero earlier; he wants to show his new god his beautiful island. When the mimetic illness intensifies, its victims tend to exchange their mediators faster and faster. As these substitutions multiply, their destabilizing effect worsens, generating the violent confusion conducive to the proliferation of monsters. For giving up his cult of Prospero, Caliban would deserve our applause, if he did not immediately turn to the even less divine Trinculo.

When Caliban discovers Trinculo's wretchedness, he understands his error; he has the flash of insight typical of all hypermimetic characters when the sacred prestige of their current idol crumbles:

> What a thrice double-ass
> Was I, to take this drunkard for a god
> And worship this dull fool!   (V, i, 295–97)

We must not conclude from this that Caliban has really learned his lesson and that he will never relapse into idolatry. Caliban embodies the paradoxical combination of blindness and insight that characterizes the lower regions of conflictual mimesis. At times he seems so stupid that we doubt his humanity; at other times he seems more intelligent than anyone else in the play.

—RENÉ GIRARD, "They'll Take Suggestion as a Cat Laps Milk: Self-Satire
in *The Tempest*," *A Theater of Envy: William Shakespeare* (New York:
Oxford University Press, 1991), pp. 344–46

John W. Draper

MONSTER CALIBAN

Sometimes Shakespeare, like Chaucer,[1] notes some detail of a character's physique in order to reinforce or explain an associated mental trait or humoral tendency; but, without such psychological purpose, the dramatist seldom gives physical description merely for itself: Falstaff's mountain belly expresses his easy-going, phlegmatic humor; Sir Andrew's straight, flaxen hair implies his arrant stupidity;[2] and Macbeth's cyclopean strength that could cleave a man "from the nave to the chaps" sets off in contrast his infirmity in purpose. Even these bits of description, Shakespeare uses sparingly, for an actor of different build might take the role at a revival of the play; and, furthermore, basic disagreements among writers on physiognomy show that in the Renaissance this pseudo-science was uncertain of its essentials, and so would be subject to misunderstanding by the audience.

Of all the characters in Shakespeare, Caliban is the most fully and repeatedly described, though not always consistently; and his bodily parts seem to show little relation to his humor or his character except that both are monstrous. Monsters were popular; and, as Trinculo remarks, any "holiday fool" in England would pay out "silver" for the sight of one. Caliban's monstrosity, however, out-Herods Herod, with enough conflict of incongruity to make one wonder how Shakespeare came to portray him thus, and how the actors could have set him forth upon the boards. Indeed, one might well search the text to find out just how he was supposed to appear. Producers of the play and illustrators of its editions should be grateful for any light that can be thrown on this perplexing matter. Just what did Caliban look like; and what was the source of this subhuman anomaly?

Scholars, though they discuss Caliban's actions and his mental and moral shortcomings, have generally scanted this subject, and leave him, as the text repeatedly calls him, merely a "Monster". Since *The Tempest* is a sort of Fletcherian romance, its plot directed by Prospero's magic and two of its chief characters beyond the pale of normal humanity, the Romantic critics of the nineteenth century—Coleridge, Hazlitt, Schlegel and the rest—quite naturally took Caliban as the product of

From *Revue de Littérature Comparée* 40, No. 4 (October–December 1966): 599–605.

Shakespeare's pure imagination. Verplanck even says that he is without "parallel in poetic invention." Intellectually and morally, his status is clear enough—no Noble Savage but a low primitive, whom even Prospero cannot teach to read; and, before the play began, he had tried to violate Miranda. McCloskey, however, like a modern social theorist, excuses all this on the basis of his environment and "limited experience".[3] Hankins, on the other hand, with a more historical approach, takes him as the "offspring of an incubus" and therefore "deformed in shape as in mind," and thinks that Shakespeare, as Trinculo suggests, may have derived him "from some freak of nature brought back or described by returning voyagers"—indeed, a "Bestial Man".[4] Goldsmith remarks that the wild man was common on the Elizabethan stage and "often took on a monstrous shape, adopted cannibalism [cf. the name Caliban], and became a cruel ravisher of ladies." He furthermore suggests that the conception of Caliban owes something to the "medieval wodewose", who was likewise lecherous and cruel;[5] but this conception seems to have little in common with Caliban's personal appearance. Neuhof, answering Meissner, shows that though Shakespeare took the name of Caliban's god, Setebos, from Magellan's account of an incident off the coast of Patagonia, yet Caliban was not modelled on the Patagonians, who were large, well-made men of a "frolicksome disposition."[6] Nor, one might add, is Caliban's like among the monsters described in Pliny's *Natural History* nor does Gesner picture such a creature; nor is he an alluring siren;[7] nor is the Salvage Man in Book VI of the *Faerie Queene* his archetype. The nearest parallel seems to be Giles Fletcher's reference, cited by Rogers and Beazley,[8] of a "fish, with head, eyes, nose, mouth, hands, feet and other members utterly human in shape." Such a being appears in Assyrian and Neo-Hittite art (which Shakespeare could not have known), and came into Greece as Triton.[9] Indeed, Shakespeare knew of Triton and mentions him in *Coriolanus*;[10] but Caliban is no marine demigod. Scholars, in short, have not treated systematically Caliban's physical appearance and its possible sources.

The Monster has a speaking part in each of the five acts, and is also described at length by other characters. Prospero in Acts I and V explains "this thing of darkness" as being the bastard of a witch begotten by a devil, and so a creature of "vile race". He is a "slave", a "villain", a "savage", a "misshapen knave" and a "demi-devil"; but his master has taught him to speak and to obey, and so he seems a human being, though "disproportion'd". He wears some clothing, for he tries to hide from the storm under his "gabardine". In Act I, Scene ii and Act III, Scene ii, Trinculo and Stephano are less certain of his human status; and the former on first observing him before he has tasted Stephano's wine cries out, "What have we here? a man or a fish?" The creature has "fins like arms", but later Caliban walks about and carries wood; and, when he lies down under the gabardine, his two legs protrude. He has "long nails" attached to hands; and he has a mouth that speaks and sings or howls and swallows sack. Even so, Trinculo and Stephano remain doubtful. More than a score of times, they call him "monster", "scurvy monster", "ridiculous monster", "abominable monster", "brave monster", "ignorant monster" and the like. To be sure, Alonso in Act V says that Stephano is "drunken" and Trinculo "reeling ripe"; but both speak clearly enough to know their minds.

The nature of Caliban's monstrosity is several times suggested in the play, especially in connection with certain animals. In Elizabethan drama, the initial appearance of a character generally strikes a fundamental keynote in his nature; and Caliban is first shown as unwilling to obey his master: "Come forth, I say!" Prospero commands, "Come, thou tortoise! when?" Does "tortoise" refer only to his slowness, or does it also imply that, as an expression of his alchemical element, the earth, he crawls along the ground and so resembles this humble animal? Hunter suggests the latter explanation, and even takes Caliban as a depiction of the Philistine fish-god Dagon, a theory supported by Trinculo's thinking him a sort of fish; but is Caliban a god? Likewise "puppy-headed" may refer not only to his stupidity but perhaps also to his appearance:[11] is he supposed to have a protruding jaw and a receding forehead like pre-historic man? This would fit Stephano's calling him a "cat"; but this may be a mere term of opprobrium, for Shakespeare does not seem to have liked cats. Trinculo, furthermore, suggests that he has a "tail": is Trinculo only trying to be witty, or is it an actual tail like that commonly portrayed on his devil-father, or more probably, a sort of fish-tail, for certainly the upper part of his body is not fish-like? Of the three illustrations that portray him in the Rolfe edition, one (p. 54) suggests such a tail, and the head seems to show a dog-like shape, and his sprawling on the ground under his gabardine has the appearance of a tortoise. The literal meaning of some of these details may be open to question; but some part of his body—and it must be the lower part—certainly suggests a fish. Indeed, Trinculo at first declares him "A fish: he smells like a fish; a very ancient and fish-like smell; a kind of, not of the newest, Poor John. A strange fish! . . . and his fins are like arms!" but later he decides, "This is no fish but an islander, that hath lately suffered by a thunderbolt." Trinculo, however, remains uncertain; and, when a bit tipsy in Act III, he declares Caliban a "deboshed fish" and then "half a fish and half monster." On this matter, the best evidence is that of Antonio, who, on first seeing the creature in Act V, declares him at once "a plain fish, and no doubt marketable." The only part of his body that could be fish-like is the tail, for the rest of him is described as more or less human. This strange assemblage of members apparently arose not only from his parentage but also from his being a "moon-calf", a being begotten under evil lunar influence and so fated by the stars to evil.

Caliban's body is indeed an aggregation of odd parts, half man, half fish, with fins like arms with long, sharp fingernails for digging, perhaps with a receding forehead like a puppy or a cat and the earthbound appearance of a tortoise. His mental and moral shortcomings noted by most critics are mere matters of stupidity and vice attributable to many primitives and so of little help in determining whence Shakespeare took him; but the physical details are vividly distinctive, and so may serve as a criterion for seeking his origin.

Why, indeed, does the dramatist confuse his description by making Caliban part fish? The plot requires nothing of the sort. Caliban is earth-bound to agree with his alchemical type. In contrast, Ariel rides on the whirlwind and directs the storm; whereas the Monster grovels on the ground under his gabardine to escape even the rainwater. Prospero first addresses him as "Thou earth", being "not honored with / A human shape": why then does Caliban look so like a sea-creature that Trinculo and even Antonio first take him for a fish? In this piscine guise, Caliban contributes less than nothing to the plot. Indeed, could fin-like arms carry wood? The half-human Caliban, who curses and howls and plots against his master, is necessary to the comedy; but why this needless and inconsistent half-fish Caliban? How did he happen to get into the play—unless he be a holdover from Shakespeare's source?

The plot of *The Tempest* requires a setting on a small island somewhere in the Mediterranean between Tunis and Naples; but a number of references in the text imply that Shakespeare used American voyage-material for local color. This is not surprising since the play seems to have been written to encourage emigration to Bermuda, which the London Company that settled Virginia had recently acquired by royal grant. Indeed, evidence exists that the playwright had access to the Company's papers for propaganda purposes.[12] Ariel's reference to the "Still vex'd Bermoothes", which were thought to be islands of enchantment, fits nicely with the magic of the comedy. From Patagonia, some thousands of miles to the south, Shakespeare took Setebos, the god worshipped by Sycorax and her misshapen son; but Caliban is no Patagonian, as Magellan's description of them shows. A less often noted American reference is "Poor John" mentioned in a passage quoted above. It was a cant term for the dried codfish from Newfoundland commonly fed to sailors.[13] Probably also American is the allusion to "savages and men of Ind"; for Englishmen after the foundation of the East India Company in 1600 must have known that the people of southern Asia and its islands were not "savages"; and at that time *India* might also refer to America. Indeed, Prospero's island has been termed "clearly West Indian".[14] Shakespeare, in short, took at least some of his local color from directly across the Atlantic: the Mediterranean was too well known to supply enchanted islands with misshapen savages; and one might ask whether the physical conception of Caliban may not be American.

The trading companies of the different nations, especially Spain and Portugal, regarded the information that their navigators brought home—climate, harbors, flora and fauna, trade-goods, and especially the people and their customs—all these as highly secret, for fear that some interloper might profit by their hard-earned knowledge. They tried to exclude all foreigners, particularly merchants, from their colonies; and their later experience with the Dutch and the English confirmed their fears. By degrees, however, detailed reports of these quasi-mercantile explorations got into the hands of rivals, and some were given to the world, notably in the collections of Hakluyt and Pruchas and later compilers such as John Harris. Sometimes the date and authorship of a "voyage" is uncertain, especially when the editor has brought together data from different sources to make a general conspectus of a whole region.

Harris has two surveys of coastal Brazil,[15] one by Anthony Knivet, which can be dated in the 1590's when he spent some years in the region northeast of Rio sometimes with the natives, sometimes as a slave of the Portuguese, and one compiled from the reports of an unidentified Portuguese[16] and of a Frenchman, Jean de Léry (Lerius), both of whom "had liv'd there a great while." In 1591, Knivet had been left to die with some other stricken shipmates by the mouth of a river. The "Wild Men" in the tribes that he later came to know can hardly be prototypes of Caliban, for he describes them as well-formed and "of good stature" like Magellan's Patagonian. Soon after he was put ashore, however, "a terrible sort of Creature came out of the River, and marched directly toward him; its back was all cover'd with Scales, it had great ugly Claws, and a long Tail ... and opening his Mouth thrust out a long Tongue ..." Knivet stood his ground, and the monster went away. Later he describes "Serpents" that have "four Legs and a long Tail like a Crocodile and are preying, ravenous creatures" that kill their victims with "a couple of sharp fins from the fore quarters ..." These "Serpents" (perhaps alligators) might have given Shakespeare the hint for Caliban's claws, tail and fins; but they are not even sub-human—purely sea-beasts that could not carry wood and cannot speak, and according to Knivet do not even cry or howl. One doubts, furthermore, whether they drank sack and grew tipsy.

A closer parallel appears in the *Histoire d'un Voyage en la Terre du Brazil* by the Huguenot Jean de Léry.[17] The Bibliothèque Nationale has a copy dated Geneva, 1578, and several later editions including one in Latin that the compiler in Harris seems to have used. The work, therefore, must have had a considerable sale; and, since a Huguenot author such as Du Bartas was highly regarded in England so that even Milton apparently used him, a Huguenot description of Brazil was likely to be taken seriously there. During this period, the Huguenots, like the English Puritans somewhat later, were seeking an escape in the New World from religious persecution, and so took a practical interest in regions that they might colonize. In 1555, the French had founded Rio de Janeiro with a promise of toleration, which was not kept; and, some ten years later, the Portuguese had ousted them; and, even as late as 1711, France was still hoping to plant a colony in that region.

Since Léry agrees with Knivet that the natives of Brazil were generally well formed, they could hardly have been prototypes of Caliban. More significantly, however, Léry supplies an anecdote told by a native of a Brazilian man-fish. It is "un gros poisson", which grasped the side of the boat as if to overturn it. The native with a boathook cut off its hand, which fell into the boat and had "cinq doits, comme celle d'vn homme"; and the pain that this "poisson sentit, montrant hors de l'eau une teste qui semblablement forme humaine, il ietta vn petit cry." Léry then mentions Triton and the sirens as similar beings; and, since like them its head and hands are human, its fish-like appearance must have been in the tail as in the case of Caliban. Léry's book classifies this creature among the fishes; and, though he never saw one, he apparently accepted the incident as fact; and his strict Huguenot conscience would make him seem to contemporary Englishmen a scrupulous reporter.

In short, Léry, even more than Knivet, could well have suggested to Shakespeare most of the details of "Monster" Caliban: his fish-like appearance and tail: his arms like fins and claw-like fingers and his sub-human head with a mouth that can sing or howl. Fletcher's fish, mentioned by Rogers and Beazley, had, to be sure, most of these characteristics; but Fletcher may well have read Léry. Caliban then is no figment of Shakespeare's romantic imagination. He is founded on accepted fact; and, as the retention of his fish-like appearance shows, the dramatist intended to portray his physique with full and authentic realism, as he did with so many of his other characters. If, as some think, *The Tempest* was written especially to please Prince Henry, who is supposed, like his royal father, to have taken a particular interest in the supernatural, this authenticity of Caliban's appearance would follow the pattern of Shakespeare's depiction of the Witches in *Macbeth*, who are clearly modeled on the King's beliefs.[18] The Monster's role in the play required the addition of some human elements such as speech; but, as far as he could, Shakespeare protected himself against criticism by the use of condign authority.

The Tempest is supposed to take place on an island somewhere between Tunis and Naples; but the references to Bermuda, to the Indies, to the Patagonian Setebos and to the dried cod from Newfoundland, suggest trans-Atlantic connections; and, if Caliban has a Brazilian origin, the American local color is even more enhanced. Shakespeare, indeed, could hardly find an enchanted isle with an authentic monster in the central Mediterranean, a region well known to Elizabethans; and so he turned to Léry for his Caliban as he turned to Magellan for Caliban's deity. Perhaps then one might call Ariel and Caliban Shakespeare's two Americans, the former apparently of native stock; the latter, a second generation immigrant. This notion, however, may have too much of fantasy; but at least Caliban as the portrait of an American can hardly be ascribed to the wishful thinking of the present writer.

NOTES

[1] W. C. Curry, *Chaucer and the Mediaeval Sciences*, New York, 1960.

[2] J. W. Draper, The Twelfth Night *of Shakespeare's Audience*, Stanford U. P. [copr., 1950], pp. 50–51.

[3] J. C. McCloskey, "Caliban, Savage Clown", *College English*, I (1940), 354–57.

[4] J. E. Hankins, "Caliban the Bestial Man", *P.M.L.A.*, LXII (1947), 793–801.

[5] R. H. Goldsmith, "The Wild Man on the English Stage", *Modern Language Review*, LIII (1958), 481–91.

[6] H. Neuhof, "Die Calibangestalt in Shakespeares Sturm", *Germ.-roman. Monat.*, XXIII (1935), 116–28.

[7] The matter of sex rather precludes Caliban's being a sort of siren. On the siren's many forms, see N. Douglas, *Siren Land*, Chap. I.

[8] J. D. Rogers (revised by C. R. Beazley), "Voyages and Exploration" in *Shakespeare's England*, ed. Lee, Oxford, 1917, I, 182.

[9] J. Boardman, *The Greeks Overseas*, Baltimore, [copr. 1964], p. 97.

[10] *Coriolanus*, III, i, 89.

[11] Cf. Rogers, pp. 182 and 186–7.

[12] D. G. Nuzum, "The London Company and *The Tempest*", *West Virginia University Philological Papers*, XII (1959), 12–23.

[13] A. S. Cook, *Modern Language Notes*, XXI (1904), 50–51.

[14] Rogers, p. 195.

[15] J. Harris, *Navigantium atque Itinerantium Bibliotheca*, London, 1705, I, 698–710 and 720–38.

[16] Harris also describes an "Oxfish … all cover'd with yellow Hair"; it has two arms and hands "with five Fingers a-piece and on each a nail like that of a Man's." There is also a "Merman … entirely human" in shape. These are presumably taken from the Portuguese account. The anecdote he includes is dated 1682; and so one judges that this material is too late for Shakespeare's use.

[17] Ed. 1594, p. 169, the only one of its copies that the New York Public Library allows to be reproduced. I wish to express my thanks to my friend and former student, N. S. Evans Esq., for obtaining the necessary photostats. Unfortunately, Léry gives no illustration of the monster described.

[18] J. W. Draper, "*Macbeth* as a Compliment to James I", *Englische Studien*, LXXII (1938), 207–220.

Barbara Melchiori

UPON ''CALIBAN UPON SETEBOS''

Wilde, when he declared that what fascinated Browning was not thought itself but rather the processes by which thought moves,[1] gave us a key to Browning's work which has since been too much neglected. The ultimate dissatisfaction one feels with so many of the critical books on Browning lies, I believe, in just this—that they are occupied too exclusively with Browning's thought, even with Browning's philosophy, while this early pointer of Wilde's has been too little followed. That Browning was a fine psychologist has always been noted in relation to the dramatic monologues, and to *The Ring and the Book*, but the extent to which he was discovering and applying psychoanalytical processes still remains to be investigated.[2] F. R. G. Duckworth, who set out to examine Browning thoroughly, came to the conclusion that "Browning, in spite of all appearances, does not as a rule probe deep", and adds "nor has he much to say of the part played by the unconscious in the working of the mind", although "a trace may be found, here and there".[3] This reasoned conclusion to a book which shows considerable understanding of both Browning's background and his poetry is hard indeed to understand, especially because Duckworth knew and quoted Swinburne's opinion that Browning had "an unique and incomparable genius for analysis". This much, indeed, Duckworth accepts, and even goes on to criticise Browning for the use he made of this gift:

> but he represents his characters as analysing themselves and expressing the results of their analysis with an insight and a delicacy and a thoroughness of which they were incapable.[4]

Browning's "Caliban upon Setebos; or, Natural Theology in the Island", written between 1859 and 1864, seems to lie open to this last criticism as no other poem, for the speaker of the monologue is a primitive man. This Caliban is the vehicle through which the complex and conflicting ideas of the thought of Browning's own time are filtered to us. C. R. Tracy has shown that the poem contains "an expression of Browning's own opinion on certain religious questions of considerable

From *Browning's Poetry of Reticence* (Edinburgh: Oliver & Boyd, 1968), pp. 140–57.

importance"[5] and that it reflects closely the ideas of the Unitarian, Theodore Parker: yet Caliban, as Paul de Reul wrote, "parle de lui-même à la troisième personne, comme un vrai sauvage".[6]

This "savage", none the less, comes to us already laden with a chain of literary associations; it is the Caliban of *The Tempest*,[7] the educated savage whose teacher was the mage Prospero himself. Prospero comments that his pains have all been lost, quite lost, and this, on a moral level, is true. Browning nevertheless has solved one of the major problems which his choice of subject raised: he has selected a primitive creature with a Shakespearian gift for expression and use of language. There is therefore no difficulty in communicating his thought in rich, even poetical words. It is when we consider the nature of his thought that we stand amazed at Browning's vision into the working of man's mind.

Two facts must be clearly remembered before we can fully appreciate this. "Caliban upon Setebos" was written when the publication of Darwin's *Origin of Species* was already giving rise to wide discussion, and some forty years before Freud's psycho-analytical work began. Stewart W. Holmes declares (italics mine) that Browning

> *never understood the theories behind Darwin's evolutionary hypothesis, apparently*, he was more interested in looking backward to certain people of importance in their day—who could not argue with him and who used terms in that good, old, easy, intentional, generalized way. He contorted [could this be a curious misprint for consorted?] with phantoms, human and linguistic.[8]

I wish to show in the following pages that "Caliban upon Setebos" was at least an inquiry into these theories of Darwin's, an attempt on Browning's part to understand and apply them, and that the short clear statement attributed to Huxley is the right interpretation of the poem: that Browning's aim was to present "a truly scientific representation of the development of religious ideas in primitive man".[9]

For Caliban is a primitive man—he has been defined as the "missing link"—who asks himself about the nature of God (Setebos). The poem is an examination of the thought-processes of this creature: Browning was using the poem to bring Darwin's theory of evolution to the test. The scientific evidence he accepts, the newt is there "turned to stone, shut up inside a stone" as part of the geological-historical evidence on which Darwin's theory is so largely based. But how, Browning asks himself, could thought grow and develop in evolved creatures? The question which the poem is debating is not, as has often been argued, as to whether Darwin's theory denies the existence of God. Browning asks instead: how did God evolve? And he answers the question by showing the thought processes by which a concept of God could, or would, come into being.

This does not mean that Browning accepts Darwin's theory, any more than he accepts Caliban's God:[10] as so often elsewhere, he begs the question by vague references to an over-God, called "the Quiet", which clearly covers a highly evolved concept, far beyond the Jehovah of the Old Testament and beyond any literal interpretation of the Trinity of the New, a name suggestive of philosophical meditation and a non-anthropomorphic deity, in no way concerned with the running of human affairs.

The starting-point of the poem is a text taken from Psalm L. 21: "Thou thoughtest that I was altogether such a one as thyself". This is the key Browning himself gives, and we should do well to read the Psalm. The stress throughout Psalm L is on the power of God. It opens with the words "the mighty God" and continues, in the second verse:

Our God shall come, and shall not keep silence:[11]

a fire shall devour before him,
and it shall be very tempestuous round about him.

The God of the Old Testament, the Jehovah, who was, after all, the God of a fairly primitive people whose existence was largely tribal, is equated with Setebos coming in vengeance and tempest at the end of the poem. The last lines of the poem include two other references to a clearly Old Testament god—"His raven that has told Him all!", from the story of Elijah and the raven,[12] and the pillar of dust (in the Old Testament the pillar of cloud or fire meant God—here it is a pillar of dust, implying death).

More is taken from the psalm, as Browning meant his readers to realise when he affixed the motto, deliberately putting into our hands a key since grown rusty. Caliban thinks to appease Setebos with burnt offerings:

Or of my three kid yearlings burn the best.[13]

But in Psalm L. 8 God refuses burnt offerings:

I will not reprove thee for thy sacrifices
    or thy burnt offerings, to have been continually before me.
I will take no bullock out of thy house,
    nor he goats out of thy fold.

The Old Testament God, that is to say, had evolved from the more primitive carnivorous God who accepted Abel's burnt offerings of flesh and refused Cain's garden produce at the very beginning of the story of creation. What the God at the time of King David requires in the place of burnt offerings (as Psalm L tells us) is "thanksgiving and vows"; he wants man to "call upon me in the day of trouble: I will deliver thee and thou shalt glorify me". That Browning remembered this is shown by his echo of it in Caliban's creation of a clay creature:

I might hear his cry,
And give the mankin three sound legs for one,
Or pluck the other off, leave him like an egg,
And lessoned he was mine and merely clay.[14]

The simile "like an egg" came to mind because it embodied the theory of Darwin as opposed to the theory of creation, for which the potter and the "clay" is a favourite Old Testament image. Even the concept of a god who breaks legs as well as making them is reflected from the psalm immediately following:

> Make me to hear joy and gladness,
>   that the bones that thou hast broken may rejoice.[15]

The God evolved in the mind of Caliban, that is to say, is not such an improbable being—he is the counterpart of the God evolved by the Jews at a certain stage of their development as a race—the God later adopted and adapted by the Christians. Browning is not afraid to face the inconsistencies in the figure of this creator-god which have puzzled so many orthodox Christians and Bible-readers, and he is attempting, in the light of Darwin's theory, to explain them.

Caliban, the primitive man, continues to see his god as primitive, and to try to appease him with offerings and sacrifices. Threatened by the vengeance of Setebos at the end of the poem, he grovels—

> 'Lieth flat and loveth Setebos!'[16]

and makes the unwanted sacrifices—

> Will let those quails fly, will not eat this month
> One little mess of whelks, so he may 'scape![17]

The whole concept of sacrifice, so basic in primitive religions, is here raised—and we must remember that Browning was writing not only long before Freud, but long before Frazer's *Golden Bough*.[18] He had, that is, to solve the problems they were later to raise by doing his own field-work. If he argued at times too freely from analogy, yet he brought a retentive memory and a fine power of observation to bear. A further quality he shared with the scientists was his ability to look contrary evidence in the face and to attempt to explain it within his theory. As his theories were at times untenable, this led him to perform dialectic somersaults, often so spectacular as to draw all attention away from the serious groundwork he was doing.

Biblical quotation, as always in Browning's work, is used with a sense of the implications of the context. The psalm from which the motto is taken offers an interpretation of the poem as a whole which links up with its literary source in *The Tempest* and with Browning's own dilemma as a poet. The closing words of Psalm L are: "To him that ordereth his conversation aright will I show the salvation of God". The point of Browning's poem, both at the beginning and the end, is that it is Caliban's *speech*, rather than his actions, which vexes Setebos. At the beginning Caliban goes into hiding, in his grotto, for the express purpose of saying what he thinks:

> And talks to his own self, howe'er he please,
> Touching that other, whom his dam called God.
> Because to talk about Him, vexes—ha,
> Could He but know! . . .
> Letting the rank tongue blossom into speech.[19]

This last line recalls Shakespeare's "You taught me language, and my profit on't/Is, I know how to curse". At the end of the poem Browning's Caliban returns to the theme of forbidden speech:

> If He caught me here,
> O'erheard this speech, . . .
> It was fool's play, this prattling! . . .
> Fool to gibe at Him![20]

Caliban ends, crouching flat before the storm which bears the anger of his god, and the line

> 'Maketh his teeth meet through his upper lip[21]

shows how determined he is to hold his mouth firmly shut, to speak no more.

So the *sin* of Caliban against Setebos, as Browning sees it (and he finds support for this interpretation both in *The Tempest* and in Psalm L) lies in his speech. To this extent Browning is dealing with a personal problem. As a writer he was concerned with speech, and he must often have asked himself whether he was not offending God by some of the ideas he expressed. In Caliban's case the offence is followed by swift punishment, showing that what Browning unconsciously feared was divine wrath and the punishment of Hell.[22] As a child he had been taught to believe in this, and what his conscious reasoning could and did refute, his whole mind always dreaded. The introduction of Caliban's "dam" is significant here, for the teaching of this primitive creature has come from his mother

> Touching that other, whom his dam called God

and

> His dam held that the Quiet made all things
> Which Setebos vexed only. [Caliban] 'holds not so.[23]

In creating Caliban Browning had to search back into his own early or primitive experience, and what he found there was his own mother's early teaching, and his own first questioning of it, in the " 'holds not so!" What is striking is that in both the above quotations the child's god is shown as a creature who must not be "vexed" (the very word is childish), showing how closely the idea of punishment was connected with the simplest concept of a god. Later study has shown the general application of this, but it is remarkable to find Browning examining thought-processes so accurately as to observe and record the same phenomenon, realising its significance. Like Caliban he felt at the same time that such thoughts were dangerous, and could only be uttered in safety hidden away in a cave, and that even there God's raven might be eavesdropping. This poet's fear of offending God by his speech is, I think, the simplest reading of "Caliban upon Setebos", to which the opening quotation from the Psalms gives a clue.

The words of the quotation, of which so far we have only examined the background, "Thou thoughtest that I was altogether such a one as thyself", raise the question of the nature of God. Darwin's newly discovered theories had opened up a whole new interpretation of creation, it had become possible to conceive of God as imaginary, made by man in his own image. C. R. Tracy has shown how probable it is that Browning should have derived this idea from Theodore Parker, quoting Parker's own words:

> This is anthropomorphism. It is well in its place. Some rude men seem to require it. They must paint to themselves a deity with a form—the ancient of days; a venerable monarch seated on a throne, surrounded by troops of followers. But it must be remembered all this is poetry; this personal and anthropomorphic conception is a phantom of the brain that has no existence independent of ourselves.[24]

And again Tracy points out another passage from Parker which may well have struck Browning and gone into Caliban's conception of Setebos:

> A man rude in spirit must have a rude conception of God. He thinks the deity like himself. If a buffalo had a religion, his conception of deity would probably be a buffalo, fairer limbed, stronger, and swifter than himself, grazing in the fairest meadows of heaven.[25]

At a certain stage of man's development (which Browning equates with the period of history related in the early books of the Old Testament, where Jehovah seemed unjustly to favour certain of his creatures, or to torment others) God would be Setebos. So Setebos favours Prosper—"who knows why?"—and torments Caliban, which is probably a protest of the poet's. Throughout the poem Prosper and Miranda are asleep. Again there may be sociological comment—they, the masters, sleep while others work for them. But they have little importance for the beast-man, whose relations are directly with Setebos. True, Caliban imitates them, blinds a sea-creature to be his Caliban, dresses up in the skin of a wild animal to resemble Prosper, etc., but nothing much comes of it. His real personal concern is with his God.

The body of the poem is concerned with Caliban's fantasy of himself as a god, as the Lord of Creation, and the analogies he draws between his own casual behaviour in awarding rewards and punishments, and that of Setebos. How would such a creature reason, how would he interpret the actions of his god? This is the question before Browning, and his answers are sometimes startling. It should be remembered that Darwin's theory was based on the physical life cycle: creation through procreation. The poem is chock-full of sexual symbolism, much of which Browning uses elsewhere, but much also new. The fullest possible use is made of plants and animals—images which would come naturally to Caliban, but at the same time which are relevant also to Darwin. And reading the symbolism we find that the reason given for Setebos' creation of both men and animals is simply so that they can supply the faculty of reproduction which the god does not possess.

Caliban argues by analogy. He wishes that he had been born a bird:

> Put case, unable to be what I wish,
> I yet could make a live bird out of clay:
> Would not I take clay, pinch my Caliban
> Able to fly?—for, there, see, he hath wings,[26]

therefore, if he creates a clay Caliban, he will fashion it with wings. Leaving aside the Freudian symbolism of wings in this context, I suggest we follow Caliban's own argument:

> He, [Setebos] could not, Himself, make a second self
> To be His mate ...
> But did, in envy, listlessness or sport,
> Make what Himself would fain, in a manner, be—
> Weaker in most points, stronger in a few....[27]

Having so created them, Setebos envies and plagues them:

> And envieth that, so helped, such things do more
> Than He who made them.[28]

The power given by Setebos to his creatures, the power he envies them for, is just the power of procreation on which the theory of evolution depends. For Setebos lacks this "warmth"[29]—the power with which the Greeks and Romans so generously endowed their gods:

> it came of being ill at ease:
> He hated that He cannot change His cold,
> Nor cure its ache.[30]

To explain what this "ache" was, Caliban has recourse to a simile of a fresh-water fish attracted and repulsed by the warm sea-water, a simile which would have little meaning were it not for the strongly marked sexual symbolism it contains. The icy fish attempting to

> thaw herself within the lukewarm brine
> O' the lazy sea her stream thrusts far amid,
> A crystal spike 'twixt two warm walls of wave,...[31]

but who

> ever sickened, found repulse ...
> Flounced back from bliss she was not born to breathe,[32]

reflects the despair of Setebos at his physical limitations. So, as Caliban makes his image with wings, Setebos endows *his* with the powers of reproduction:

> Weaker in most points, stronger in a few.

Over and over again the symbolism of the poem echoes this theme of sexual potency. In the second sentence we have "a flower drops with a bee inside";[33]

Calibar. makes himself drunk with a "gourd-fruit" to which he adds "honeycomb and pods" which "bite like finches when they bill and kiss", the "froth rises bladdery", and Caliban says he will

> throw me on my back i' the seeded thyme,
And wanton.[34]

What Browning is openly describing in these lines is the effect of drink, but the words chosen ("bill and kiss", "bladdery", "seeded", "wanton") indicate the further meaning of the passage. This meaning is more basic to the sense than Caliban's drunkenness, which is a literary echo from Shakespeare. The preoccupation with the process of reproduction is further hinted at in the introduction of the swimming creatures,

> Yon otter, sleek-wet, black, lithe`as a leech,[35]

and the badger, and again by

> the pie with the long tongue
That pricks deep into oakwarts for a worm. . . .[36]

The creatures themselves betray the underlying theme: they are poetic symbols, not scientific specimens, and are far from being engaged in overt sexual activities. The primly Victorian billing and kissing of the finches is indeed the nearest approach to anything of the kind.

The underlying concern with the processes of reproduction is offset by another series of images, all concerned with mutilation, in the castration symbolism Browning had used elsewhere,[37] and which emphasise the predicament of Setebos. The first victims are the grass-hoppers, for the Caliban bird is commanded to begin to live and to

> Fly to yon rock-top, nip me off the horns
Of grigs high up that make the merry din. . . .[38]

The bird, however, soon falls a victim himself with

> His leg snapped, brittle clay,[39]

and his Caliban creator amuses himself either with removing the remaining leg or in giving him four. This may contain a passing reference to the evolutionary process with its development through sports and rejects. Soon after, we have the line of crabs, and the one with purple spots gets "one pincer twisted off". After this we have the odd image of the broken pipe, which is used later in *Fifine* to suggest impotence. This pipe is a thing "created" by Caliban as a bird-whistle, but should the pipe declare

> I make the cry my maker cannot make
With his great round mouth; he must blow through mine![40]

then, Caliban declares

Would not I smash it with my foot? So He [Setebos].[41]

Once again the god is seen as jealous of his creature's powers of reproduction, and the punishment implied by the imagery is castration. These mutilations, occurring to the various creatures in the poem, are nevertheless symbolic of the central situation of the god who creates but does not procreate. The worst vengeance, the final impotence, awaits Darwin's newt, a creature Setebos

> may have envied once
> And turned to stone, shut up inside a stone.[42]

The newt is a central symbol here and its presence has an interesting history. For even before being Darwin's, the newt was Browning's own. In a letter written to Elizabeth on 5 January 1846, a letter she describes as "all alive as it is with crawling buzzing wriggling cold-blooded warm-blooded creatures", he writes of Horne's question to him "for what do you know about newts?" Browning, as he proceeds to show, has spent a long time in observation of newts or water-efts:

> What a fine fellow our English water-eft is; "Triton paludis Linnaei"—e come guizza (that you can't say in any other language; cannot preserve the little in-and-out motion along with the straightforwardness!)—I always loved all those wild creatures God "sets up for themselves" so independently of us, so successfully. . . .[43]

But what is more interesting is the way in which he relates the creature to Elizabeth herself, and the suppressed eroticism of his final invocation. His injunction to her to "walk, move, guizza, anima mia dolce" shows the stress of these months when he was trying to convince her to find the strength to escape with him, and using every means in his power:

> "I may change"—too true; yet, you see, as an eft was to me at the beginning so it continues—I may take up stones and pelt the next I see—but—do you much fear that?—Now, walk, move, guizza, anima mia dolce. Shall I not know one day how far your mouth will be from mine as we walk?[44]

That the newt so full of life here is the same newt we find imprisoned in the fossil is shown by the repetition in the poem of the argument of the letter, the idea that he may take up stones and pelt the next he sees. Caliban, speaking of the crabs, says he will

> Let twenty pass, and stone the twenty-first,
> Loving not, hating not, just choosing so.[45]

Browning, that is to say, when he was writing "Caliban upon Setebos" recalled the letter written to Elizabeth some four to eight years earlier, or perhaps rather than the letter itself he recalled the mood and suppressed emotions which lay behind. A personal emotional state, which had left a deep mark on him, has entered, utterly transmuted, into the material of the poem. This assertion finds further support from another passage in the same letter, which contains mutilation imagery of exactly the same sort we find in the poem:

> But never try and catch a speckled gray lizard when we are in Italy, love, and you see his tail hang out of the chink of a wall, his winter-house—because the strange tail will snap off, drop from him and stay in your fingers—and though you afterwards learn that there is more desperation in it and glorious deter- mination to be free, than positive pain (so people say who have no tails to be twisted off)—and though, moreover, the tail grows again after a sort—yet . . . don't do it, for it will give you a thrill![46]

Browning was writing here with a frankness few lovers would risk today. The "thrill" he speaks of can only be related to a situation which he outlines in an earlier letter of 18 September 1845:

> . . . for at, and after the writing of *that first letter*, on my first visit, I believed— through some silly or misapprehended talk, collected at second hand too— that your complaint was of quite another nature—a spinal injury irremediable in the nature of it. Had it been *so*—now speak for *me*, for what you hope I am, and say how *that* should affect or neutralize what you *were*, what I wished to associate with myself in you?[47]

The extraordinary situation of a man who for a time was uninformed as to the "nature" of the complaint of the woman he wished to marry, his ignorance con- fessedly extending to an uncertainty as to whether physical union would at any time be possible, explains his unusual preoccupation with mutilations and impotence, a preoccupation noticeable in many of his poems, but nowhere more than in "Caliban upon Setebos".

That this interpretation of the thought-processes of Caliban, who sees god as jealous of his creatures, and furnishes this odd explanation of the cause of his jealousy, is not fantastical, is further shown by the nonsense song in which Caliban from his hiding place dares to taunt the god:

> What I hate, be consecrate
> To celebrate Thee and Thy state, no mate
> For Thee; what see for envy in poor me?[48]

Like Antiochus' riddle in *Pericles,* the nonsense song is used by Caliban for the purpose of concealing-revealing the truth which cannot openly be uttered. It is the clue to the whole poem. For in it Caliban dares, from his hiding place, to mock at Setebos. He consecrates to him only what he hates, and mocks him for being without a mate, for being forced to envy his own creature, even such a creature as Caliban knows himself to be.

Yet the god hears him; or rather hears through his messenger the raven, and the punishment begins, with the storm and the moving pillar of dust. And here we have a further echo from the Old Testament. The last lines of the poem, where Caliban offers a sacrifice of appeasement

Will let those quails fly, will not eat this month
One little mess of whelks, so he may 'scape![49]

echoes Numbers XI. 29–35, which is a description of God's punishment on the Israelites because they lusted after flesh. The wrath of the Lord was kindled, and

there went forth a wind from the Lord and brought quails from the sea and let them fall by the camp.

The surfeit of quails is too much for the Israelites, weary of their diet of manna, and "there they buried the people that lusted ..."

Caliban, seeing the approaching storm, first rebukes himself

Fool to gibe at Him[50]

(so the song *was* intended in mockery), then tries the old line of appeasement

Lo! 'Lieth flat and loveth Setebos![51]

This failing in effect, he makes what amounts to a vow of abstinence, hoping thereby to appease the "envious" god. The flesh after which the Israelites lusted had for Browning, I believe, a further meaning more in keeping with the New Testament teaching of St. Paul:

This I say then, Walk in Spirit, and ye shall not fulfill the lust of the flesh[52]

which links, in turn, back to the underlying concept of the poem, the physical pleasure in reproduction, arousing the jealousy of a god deprived of the capacity enjoyed by his creatures. A daring thought, but Browning's mind was often daring.

Darwin's theory of evolution seemed to undermine the whole of Christianity or of any other theology. What need for a creator god if man was self-created or evolved? For this reason many theologians simply refused to consider Darwin's evidence, and it was only later that some Churches came to terms with evolution as the "method" of creation employed by God, or more often settled down in an uneasy truce until the scientists should find all the missing links. To many thinking people Darwin's discovery seemed to strike right at the heart of accepted beliefs, and Browning, who was always interested in ideas, and who had already written "An Epistle Containing the Strange Medical Experiences of Karshish", inevitably turned them over in his mind. Postulating, in order to work out Darwin's theory in full, the idea of a god *evolved* in the mind of man, Browning has to explain the relationship between "creator" and "creature". Taking the fairly primitive concept of god as exemplified in the Jehovah of the early books of the Old Testament, he struggles to find a convincing psychological explanation of why a primitive man should conceive of a creator and how he would motivate the creator's interest in him. The solution he finds, that of an impotent god deriving a somewhat vicarious satisfaction by creating creatures capable of physical reproduction, and then provoked to petty acts of spite and vengeance through jealousy, is a subtle attempt to penetrate primitive thought-processes, documented as best he might with the material that lay closest at hand, the early history of the Jews as recounted in the Old Testament, and his own childish reasoning. His exposition is not scientific, but poetic; nevertheless it is a poem in which he was attempting to work in full conscious control of his material and to allow his character to express himself through psychologically convincing images[53]—the gift Shakespeare possessed so supremely, in which Browning from time to time reached up to touch him.

"Caliban upon Setebos" is neither an acceptance nor a refutation of Darwin's theory of evolution: it is an experiment in the application and development of new ideas. "Thou thoughtest I was altogether such a one as thyself" is a clear statement of this approach to the subject, and Browning's own theological beliefs are quite outside this discussion, fluctuating between his early training, which left the idea of Heaven and Hell indelibly printed on his mind, and the more philosophical, more evolved concept of "the Quiet". What remains most striking in this poem is, not so much the rather doubtful conclusion reached concerning the hypothetical reasoning of primitive man, but rather the modernity of Browning's approach: that almost immediately after the publication of *The Origin of Species* he grasped that it opened the way to great discoveries in the field of psychoanalysis and that such study should go hand in hand with anthropological research. His investigation in 1864 of natural theology in the island was pioneer work in research which only the twentieth century was to see developed. That it is also poetry is greatly to his credit. However complex and even confused the ideas discussed, even a cursory reading leaves us with the newt

> turned to stone, shut up inside a stone[54]

—a symbol as beautiful and significant in its way as was Keats's Grecian urn, and no less durable.

NOTES

[1] Oscar Wilde, "The Critic as an Artist", in *Selected Works*, ed. R. Aldington, London 1947, p. 69.

[2] Stewart W. Holmes, "Browning: Semantic Stutterer", in *PMLA*, LX (1945), pp. 231–55, attempts this approach to Browning. His examination of the inchoate constructions in the early poems is interesting, but his thesis that Browning cured himself is hardly tenable in view of later poems such as *Fifine*.

[3] F. R. G. Duckworth, *Browning: Background and Conflict*, London 1931, p. 124.

[4] F. R. G. Duckworth, op. cit., p. 52.

[5] C. R. Tracy, " 'Caliban upon Setebos' ", in *Studies in Philology*, XXXV (1938), pp. 487–99.

[6] Paul de Reul, *L'Art et la pensée de Robert Browning*, Brussels 1929, p. 165. I find this simpler explanation more convincing than that given by E. K. Brown in "The First Person in 'Caliban upon Setebos' " in *Modern Language Notes* (1951), pp. 392–5, which sets out to prove that "the shifts to the first person and back to the third enrich the characterization and heighten the drama." It would be interesting in this connexion to compare Caliban's monument of chalk and turf (ll. 192–9) with the Druid monument in *Fifine at the Fair*.

[7] See John Howard, "Caliban's Mind", in *Victorian Poetry*, I (1963), pp. 249–57, for a study of the characteristics of Caliban which Browning may have found in *The Tempest*.

[8] S. W. Holmes, "Browning: Semantic Stutterer", p. 251.

[9] Quoted by Arthur W. Symons, *An Introduction to the Study of Browning*, new edn., London 1906, p. 125.

[10] In a late poem, "Reverie", Browning definitely and characteristically refused to pronounce on the subject: "Do I seek how star, earth, beast,/Bird, worm, fly, gained their dower/For life's use, most and least?/Back from the search I cower".

[11] As such he is the opposite of "the Quiet".

[12] The raven is at the same time an attempt to find a Scriptural equivalent for Ariel, for in Shakespeare's *Tempest* it is Prospero and not Setebos who is the "god" with the supernatural powers of punishment.

[13] "Caliban upon Setebos", 272.

[14] Op. cit., 91–4.

[15] Psalm LI. 8.

[16] "Caliban upon Setebos", 292.

[17] Op. cit., 294–5.

[18] This point has been noted by Leonard Burrows, in *Browning: An Introductory Essay*, Perth (Australia) 1952, p. 58: "Remembering that Browning wrote without the benefit of anthropology, one may find (as I do) that *Caliban* is persuasively plausible as a re-creation of a limited, earth-bound, egocentric anthropomorphism".

[19] "Caliban upon Setebos", 15–18, 23.

[20] Op. cit., 269–70, 287, 291.

[21] Op. cit., 293.

[22] C. R. Tracy, " 'Caliban upon Setebos' ", p. 494, writes: "His scorn of Calvinism remains, and also his rejection of the doctrine of eternal punishment". This refutation was conscious, but traces of the effect of this early teaching on his unconscious mind are frequent in his poems, especially "The Heretic's Tragedy" and *The Ring and the Book*.

[23] "Caliban upon Setebos", 16, 170–1.

[24] Theodore Parker, *A Discourse of Matters pertaining to Religion*, Boston 1907, pp. 146–7, quoted by C. R. Tracy, " 'Caliban upon Setebos' ", p. 496.

[25] T. Parker, op. cit., pp. 120–1, quoted by C. R. Tracy, " 'Caliban upon Setebos' ", p. 497.

[26] "Caliban upon Setebos", 75–8.

[27] Op. cit., 57–8, 61–3.

[28] Op. cit., 113–14.

[29] In *The Ring and the Book*, VII, 792–3, "warmth" is used with a sexual connotation in lines spoken by the Archbishop commanding Pompilia to yield her virginity to Guido: "The earth requires that warmth reach everywhere:/What, must your patch of snow be saved forsooth?" The same connotation was current as early as Dryden's *Absalom and Achitophel*, 7–9: "Then, Israel's Monarch, after Heaven's own heart,/His vigorous warmth did, variously impart/To Wives and Slaves . . ."

[30] "Caliban upon Setebos", 31–3.

[31] Op. cit., 35–7.

[32] Op. cit., 38, 41.

[33] Op. cit., 10. Browning often uses the same symbol of the flower and the bee with sexual overtones. The most obvious examples are in "Women and Roses" and "Popularity", but in "Porphyria's Lover" and *The Ring and the Book* the sexual implication of the symbol, although not openly stated, is none the less present, as I believe it to be in the above lines from "Caliban upon Setebos".

[34] "Caliban upon Setebos", 73–4.

[35] Op. cit., 46.

[36] Op. cit., 50–1.

[37] See his letters to Elizabeth, some of *The Ring and the Book*, *Fifine at the Fair*, and above all, *Red Cotton Night-Cap Country*.

[38] "Caliban upon Setebos", 82–3.

[39] Op. cit., 85.

[40] Op. cit., 124–5.

[41] Op. cit., 126.

[42] Op. cit., 214–15.

[43] Robert to Elizabeth, postmarked 5 Jan. 1846, in *The Letters of Robert Browning and Elizabeth Barrett Barrett, 1845–1846*, London 1899.

[44] Ibid.

[45] "Caliban upon Setebos", 103–4.

[46] Robert to Elizabeth, postmarked 5 Jan. 1846, in *The Letters of Robert Browning and Elizabeth Barrett Barrett, 1845–1846*.

[47] Robert to Elizabeth, 18 Sep. 1845, op. cit.

[48] "Caliban upon Setebos", 276–8.
[49] Op. cit., 294–5.
[50] Op. cit., 291.
[51] Op. cit., 292.
[52] Galatians, V. 16.
[53] An even better example of this psychological realism is the use of torture imagery by the condemned Guido in *The Ring and the Book*.
[54] "Caliban upon Setebos", 215.

Mike Frank

SHAKESPEARE'S
EXISTENTIAL COMEDY

When, in *King Lear*, the old king violates the divine and social order of things the entire universe is thrown into upheaval, reminding us of one of the conventional ideas of Shakespearean criticism, namely that there is a moral order in the universe, and that any human violation of that order must lead to a more general chaos; nature itself is disturbed by human malice or folly. Similarly, in *Macbeth* the agonies of the tragic protagonist are reflected by the world around him, while in *Hamlet* the prince's dilemma is seen as an expression of the time itself being out of joint. But it is hard to see how this same bit of conventional Shakespearean wisdom, so appropriate to the great tragedies, relates to *The Tempest*. The striking differences between the world of the tragedies and the world of *The Tempest* is perhaps best seen in a comparison of the situations out of which *Hamlet* and *The Tempest* grow. In both cases there has been a usurpation of power, a transgression against the proper order of things. In *Hamlet* a force outside of the lives of the characters themselves, the ghost, appears and instigates the dramatic action; it is as though nature—the universe itself—is not content to rest until matters have been set right. But a similar usurpation in *The Tempest* elicits no comparable response from external forces. In the twelve years that have elapsed between the treachery of Antonio and the opening of the play nothing of especial note has happened either to Antonio himself or to the Milan which he now rules. And when a storm at sea leads to the righting of old wrongs the very storm itself is the handiwork of human agency.

The crucial difference between these two sets of circumstances is in the extent to which nature has ceased playing a providential role in the later play. Nature—by which I mean everything in the universe except human action and human will, everything except what we might call the human spirit—nature, which in the tragedies is an active agent bent on correcting the general disorder resulting from human folly, is in *The Tempest* quite neutral. The view of nature in *The Tempest*

From *Shakespeare's Late Plays: Essays in Honor of Charles Crow*, edited by Richard C. Tobias and Paul G. Zolbrod (Athens: Ohio University Press, 1974), pp. 142–65.

is, then, not very different from the modern view: it is an inescapable force which can be exploited for human good—Prospero *does* use the storm as a way of reestablishing a disrupted moral order—but which in and of itself is neither good nor evil. In a curious essay—wonderfully perceptive in many ways and yet based on a fundamental misconception of the world of the play—Robert Langbaum argues that the "profoundest statement" of *The Tempest* is "that life, when we see through it, is tragicomically gay—that the evil, the violence, the tragedy are all part of a providential design."[1] He is surely right in insisting on the tragicomical gaiety. But surely he makes what must be a fundamental mistake in seeing that gaiety as the result of providence. For isn't the point of Prospero's actions that there is no providential design, that man must forge his own moral order? Jan Kott, I think, is much closer to the truth when he speaks of the world of *The Tempest* as one "in which nature and history, royal power and morality, have for the first time been deprived of theological meaning."[2]

Indeed if one may speak of *The Tempest* as having a thematic nexus, as being about—and thus defining—a particular idea, that idea is nature, and the way nature must be dealt with in a world deprived of theological meaning. The word *nature*, and the idea it represents, is as central to the play as *nothing* is to the opening of *King Lear*. Miranda sees Ferdinand as unnatural (I, ii, 420–422); Prospero calls Antonio "unnatural" (V, i, 79); and Alonso realizes that the events on the island involve "more than nature" (V, i, 243). Behind these specific references, of course, is the question of art—or magic—versus nature and, most important, the setting of the action on an apparently natural island, a setting which allows for the reexploration of the notion of a pastoral utopia and the relative advantages of nature and civilization. In a brilliant essay Leo Marx relates *The Tempest* to the explorations of the new world with which it was contemporary, and shows that early reports from the West Indies alternately extolled the virtues of the islands as arcadian paradises and condemned them as hideous, fearful, and barbaric.[3] Clearly these early reports influenced the writing of the play—the opening of Act II is a comic rehearsal of the debate about the virtues of unspoiled nature; and one of the underlying purposes of the play is to deal with this problem, to arrive at a coherent view of nature.[4]

The vision of nature in *The Tempest* is likely best suggested—in very different ways—by Gonzalo and by Caliban; the former holds a persistently myopic view of nature, while the latter seems an incarnation of nature's real potential and its role in human affairs. It is generally agreed that Shakespeare mocks Gonzalo's notion of the island as a pastoral utopia, and it is often felt that the cynical comments of Sebastian and Antonio which surround Gonzalo's observations fatally undermine them. As Marx says, "It is impossible to miss the skepticism that Shakespeare places, like a frame, around the old man's speech" (p. 49). But surely there are other elements in the play which show the fatuousness of Gonzalo's views; after all, the comments of Sebastian and Antonio are surely not reliable guides. As it happens, in Act II, scene 1, we do realize that Gonzalo is wrong and the evil courtiers right, but this is only because Shakespeare has carefully led up to this scene by showing, first, that nature is not benevolent, and second, that Gonzalo is a somewhat dotty old man. Both of these purposes are accomplished in the very open-ing scene where we see the awesome power of nature and Gonzalo's inability to come to terms with it. In that scene we immediately encounter the insolent meanness of Antonio and Sebastian, but even they seem more aware of the need to defer to the boatswain than is Gonzalo, who, while the storm is raging, urges the boatswain to "be patient" (I, i, 15). Gonzalo is clearly a "good" man, his heart is in the right place, as Prospero makes very clear in Acts Four and Five. But in the face of the fury of nature, goodness is not enough. In his excessive benevolence Gonzalo is a first cousin to Polonius and perhaps even to Glouces-ter, all of whom deserve affection, perhaps, but surely not respect.

There are any number of obvious fallacies involved in Gonzalo's utopian vision, the most evident being the one pointed out by Sebastian, that he would be king of a commonwealth without sovereignty. We must also keep in mind that Gonzalo is so enthusiastic about the virtues of unspoiled nature not more than a few moments after he has faced a storm which seemed for the time to promise death to him and his party. But there is one further feature of Gonzalo's utopian dream that is less immediately striking and yet may be of even more fundamental importance. Gonzalo would abolish not only government, poverty, labor, treason, and impurity, but "letters" as well (II, i, 146); that is to say Gonzalo would dispense with learning, or, to take a somewhat broader view, with civilization itself. In short, Gonzalo seems to favor a reversion to a state of noble savagery. Now, whatever credence one gives to such an idea, it must be extremely suspect in a play whose very meaning depends on the learning of the protagonist. Prospero's original mis-take may have been one of excessive devotion to learning—and the concomitant handing over of the reins of government to his brother—but it is only that learning itself—Prospero's wisdom, art, and magic—which is able to overcome the forces of nature and restore the moral order.

Gonzalo is, as I have said, good. But his goodness untempered by wisdom is so ineffectual in dealing with the real world that in some ways he presents a danger greater than that of Antonio and Sebastian, although his very ineffectuality makes it highly unlikely that this danger will ever become a practical one. The inadequacy of his perception of the world is made clearest in the character of Caliban. Some critics, Langbaum among them, seem not entirely sure what to make of Caliban, and are apparently troubled by their inability to determine from the play whether or not Caliban is human. That seems to me a not very important question; perhaps a stage director might have to face the question of the proper way to have Caliban appear, but in terms of the meaning of the play it is, I think, quite clear what Caliban is. To put it simply, he is the principle of nature itself. At one point Trinculo observes with some wonder "That a monster should be such a natural!" (III, ii, 30–31). Critics are quick to point out that "natural" means idiot, and surely this is the surface meaning. But equally surely Shakespeare's use of the word here is loaded. In his annotations to The Arden Shakespeare edition of the play[5] Frank Kermode glosses the word *natural* as follows: "A monster is by definition unnatural; yet this one is a natural (an idiot)." But isn't the point precisely that the conventional definition held by European civilization is inaccurate? Caliban *is* natural, and he *is* a monster, and he *is* also an idiot. Shakespeare's use of the word *natural* makes it very clear that in the world of the play raw nature is monstrous—remember the storm which introduces us to the world of the play by presenting nature in its most malevolent aspect—and is also to be equated with idiocy in that it is only learning and art—in short, civilization—that can counteract the force of nature.

The first time Prospero speaks to Caliban he addresses him as "Thou earth" (I, ii, 316), thus emphasizing not only his baseness but also his identity with natural forces, the kind of identity implicit in our use of such terms as *mother earth* and *mother nature*. Some critics see Caliban as representing the natural element earth, while Ariel represents the element of air, nature in a more benevolent aspect. To schematize the play in such a way is, I believe, to miss its thematic focus. The matter is a crucial one, and since Langbaum's view is a representative one which raises many significant questions it is worth quoting in full:

> Caliban is natural in that he is earthy and earthbound, low, material. But Ariel is just as natural in that he represents the fluid elements of water and air and also those bodiless energies of nature that strike us as "spiritual." Caliban, whose name may derive from "cannibal," is the natural man seen in one aspect. But Miranda is also natural, and the two are contrasted throughout. Both were brought up in a state of nature; and if Miranda never saw a man other than her father, Caliban never saw a woman other than his mother. Caliban is natural in the sense that nature is rudimentary and mindless; he cannot be educated. Miranda is natural in the sense that we take the Golden Age or the Garden of Eden to be our natural condition. (pp. 189–190)

Langbaum sees Ariel as a two-sided symbol, representing both the fluid elements and the spiritual qualities of nature. No doubt Ariel does represent the "spiritual," but to include spirit as part of nature is to miss the crucial dichotomy of—and antagonism between—nature and spirit, nature and education, nature and art, nature and civilization. Curiously this is a dichotomy that Langbaum himself alludes to just a few lines earlier in saying that the play raises "the question whether nature is not superior to art." Certainly art must be closely identified with spirit, and the very terms of his question suggest, rightly I think, that spirit is not to be identified with nature at all, except to the extent that man's nature allows for the development of spiritual faculties. By insisting that Ariel is natural, Langbaum is able to argue that Miranda too is natural, and that this is her great virtue. He admits shortly afterward that Miranda has indeed been very carefully educated by her father, but this apparently doesn't make her in any significant way unnatural as far as he is concerned. But it is precisely the extent to which she has been educated that she is good, and had she not been subject to Prospero's tutelage she would certainly have been very different. This difference is defined, and the fundamental dichotomy underlying the play made most explicit when Prospero, speaking of Caliban, refers to him as

A devil, a born devil, on whose nature
Nurture can never stick; on whom my pains,
Humanely taken, all, all lost, quite lost.   (IV, i, 188–190)

The word *nurture* as used here includes all those other categories—art, magic, learning, civilization—which the play repeatedly opposes to nature. To see spirit itself—that human faculty out of which all these redemptive qualities grow—as part of nature is surely to overlook the play's thematic pivot.

The main problem with Langbaum's interpretation—the fundamental misconception to which I referred much earlier—is his acceptance of the idea that "the Golden Age or the Garden of Eden [is] our natural condition." To believe that is to make the same mistake made by Gonzalo, to believe in the nobility of the natural man. *The Tempest* makes it quite clear that the Golden Age, and any other similar pastoral ideals, are merely that—ideals, creations of the human imagination. It is important to remember that to whatever extent life on the island is attractive, it is so as a result of the art of Prospero. And since it is learning which can overcome the forces of nature, it is crucially important that Miranda has been educated whereas Caliban has not.

Caliban, then, is the principle of nature itself, the incarnation of the external natural world, or—to put the issue more abstractly—matter. Ariel, on the other hand, represents not the elements of air, as Langbaum suggests, but of the human spirit itself. Caliban and Ariel become symbolic incarnations of the principles that define the play. Significantly Ariel is freed by Prospero's magic, and it is Prospero's magical art that obtains for him the services of Ariel. In terms of the scheme I am defining, it is Prospero's spiritual achievements which enable him to utilize the pure spirit that is Ariel. There is, then, a double meaning when Prospero refers to Ariel as "My brave spirit." On the level of plot he is talking to Ariel, defined by the *dramatis personae* as "a spirit." But on a symbolic—which is to say thematic—level he is addressing the spiritual forces that have made him what he is; in a sense he is addressing his soul.

And yet, in spite of his spiritual accomplishments, Prospero does not release Caliban. It might appear at first that given his magical powers and the services of Ariel Prospero would be able to dispense with Caliban. But one of the very important aspects of Prospero's wisdom is his realization that he cannot do without Caliban, which is another way of saying that he cannot give up his control of the material world. For one thing, to free Caliban would be to lose some things that he cannot do without. When Miranda hesitates to visit Caliban because of his villainous ugliness her father explains his importance to their lives:

But, as 'tis,
We cannot miss him; he does make our fire,
Fetch in our wood, and serves in offices
That profit us.   (I, ii, 312–314)

Man cannot live by spirit alone, as it were. The unique, and implicitly tragic, feature of man is that he is neither pure spirit, like Ariel, nor pure matter, like Caliban, but is caught in an uneasy tension between the two. He strives to be like Ariel but cannot dispense with the services of Caliban.

Prospero, furthermore, cannot free Caliban so long as he is on the island, because to do so would be to unleash the full force of untrammeled nature, a point made strikingly clear by the account of Caliban's original enslavement by Prospero. When Prospero comes to the island he treats Caliban "with human care" (I, ii, 348), until Caliban attempts to rape Miranda. In doing so he is not evil in the way that the conspirators are evil; unlike them, he is not immoral, only amoral, and in attempting to rape Miranda he is merely following the imperatives of his own nature. The results of amoral action may be as detrimental to human society as those of immorality; but Prospero realizes that on a philosophical—as opposed to practical—level they must be viewed differently. This difference Shakespeare makes quite clear in the presentation of Caliban. Although Caliban is surely as potentially dangerous as Antonio and Sebastian, he is not presented as a villain. From the start we are made actively to dislike the conspirators, but the play elicits no such response to Caliban. Which of course is as it should be, for to hate Caliban would be as silly as hating the rain or the wind of a storm. But it would be equally foolish to ignore Caliban and the forces he represents, thereby letting them interfere with the pursuit of human goals. This is what Prospero very quickly realizes, which leads to the subjugation of Caliban. "This island's mine, by Sycorax my mother, / Which thou tak'st from me," Caliban says in one of his complaints to Prospero (I, ii, 333–334), and in one way he is very right. In citing his inherited claim to the island, Caliban suggests the curious fact that Prospero, like his brother, is something of a usurper. But there can be no doubt that in this case, for Prospero, for Shakespeare, and for us, the usurpation is justified. When Prospero arrives on the island it might be the memory of his own exile that makes him attempt to treat Caliban "humanely," which means *kindly* but no doubt also suggests that Prospero tries to treat Caliban as a human. In doing so, however, Prospero makes the same mistake which Gonzalo is to make a dozen years later, that of taking the pastoral dream as fact, of not recognizing the eternal antagonism between the processes of nature and human aspiration. But Caliban's attempted rape of Miranda enables Prospero to recognize the truth very quickly. He learns that nature, while not evil, is indifferent to human values and aspirations, and that the success of the human endeavor requires constant vigilance and the domination of natural force by the arts of human civilization.

And this is the crucial difference between the world of the tragedies and the world of *The Tempest*. In the earlier plays there is, apparently, some moral order external to man, an order which imposes a system of values that man must follow; in such a world moral behavior is probably best understood in terms of a commitment to the proper order of things, a commitment that might well be called religious. But in *The Tempest* there is no such external order to which man must commit himself; there is simply an indifferent and impersonal nature which will follow its own imperative regardless of what man does. In such a world—a world very much like that of modern existentialism—moral behavior is best understood not in terms of religious commitment but in terms of art, that is in terms of all those uniquely human powers which can be used to control the forces of nature and work toward the preservation of human civilization. It is significant that Prospero is not a priest—of whatever kind—but a magician, and that the text continually refers to his special abilities not as supernatural power but as his art.

II

There is one other important difference between the world of the tragedies and that of *The Tempest*. Implicit in the former, as in all theologically oriented views of the universe, is the idea that once the thorns in the side of the moral order are eliminated and the evil extirpated, man is once again at peace with his environment. Men may die, but the fundamental coherence of the universe remains intact. No such assurances are to be found on Prospero's island. His world makes sense only to the extent that man—and man's art—is able to impose some order and meaning upon it. Even more important, in Prospero's world, a world deprived of theological meaning, there can be no final victory against the forces of nature: mortality, which in a theocentric universe is mitigated by the transcendent, is here man's ultimate and insurmountable fate. Nature may be coped with, and some of its disruptive visitations avoided, but in the final analysis nature is implacable, and its final inescapable trump card is death.

All of this necessitates a radically new view of the function of art. Until now I have used the term *art* indiscriminately to refer both to what we would today call art and to what we would now tend to call science. The two are related in that they are both manifestations of man's ability to make sense and order out of his world, but there are important differences between the two. Science, we might say, is man's way of controlling the external world; art, his way of coming to imaginative terms with it. The former deals with material reality, the latter with human attitude. The former consists of ways of dealing with the threats imposed by nature, and at times of avoiding their danger, the latter consists of ways of coming to terms with the final and unavoidable victory of nature over the human organism. To put it in terms of the dramatic structure of the play, the former deals with ways of controlling Caliban, the latter with the best ways of making use of Ariel.

Of these two ways of dealing with the world the former, the scientific, is the more consistent in its purposes. In general one fights a storm much the same way regardless of one's philosophical outlook; although the meaning of a natural disaster may be conceived in different terms, the actual practical process of coping with it will remain largely the same. Thus Prospero's—and Shakespeare's—emphasis on dominating nature, on not assisting the storm, while interesting in its implications, is hardly of decisive importance. But *The Tempest* is about more than the need to use all available human resources to fight the vagaries of nature in order to shore up walls against the inroads of chaos, a need which forms the informing principle of many of the works of Joseph Conrad. The centrality of that need for Conrad leads him to depict a universe in which a dogged perseverance is the highest good, and in which, finally, bitter resignation is the only legitimate way of relating to the inevitable victory of chaos. Shakespeare is able to move far beyond this kind of existential despair, even in a world deprived of theological meaning, by asserting that art is not only a way of fighting against nature—a fight that man always must lose in the last analysis—but is also a way of coming to imaginative terms with the world. Prospero's art, that is to say, involves not only what we would call science, but also what *we* would call art. Even while he is insisting on the need not to give an inch to Caliban, Prospero is demonstrating how man may best use the prerogatives of Ariel, the prerogatives of his own spirit. And Prospero's greatest wisdom is his realization of the limits of the power of the spirit, his recognition that while art can work miracles there is a point at which it must stop, at which its powers cease.

I have been working toward a definition of Prospero's wisdom, which is also the theme and "message" of the play. Let me stop, at this point, and present what I take to be the most important elements of that theme, after which I will return to the text to support my hypothesis. Prospero, it seems to me, realizes that man is finite although his spirit recognizes the infinite and therefore has infinite aspirations; that man's unique curse—and blessing—is that he is neither all spirit like Ariel nor all matter like Caliban: he is matter and subject to the laws of nature, and yet he has awareness of spirit which makes him dissatisfied with the limitations of his corporeal being; that man must leaven his animal nature with his spiritual powers, just as in the outside world he must impose his artifice on the natural material world; that the pastoral myth is not literally true, but that man nonetheless must have such a myth to live by; that the pastoral myth, like all other visions of human perfection, is a wish that grows out of the limitations of the human condition—that the imagination is a way of coping with the unbridgeable gap between the human condition and human aspiration—but that without the double nature of human consciousness even the notion of perfection would not exist; that the glory of the human condition lies precisely in the achievements of the human imagination, and that, as a result, any fundamental change in the human condition is not only impossible but inconceivable in that it would eliminate the very circumstances which led to it; that any attempt to resolve the fundamental ambivalence of the human condition—the split between matter and spirit—must either deny the spirit thus making man no better than Caliban or must deny the body thus alienating man from the physical world in which he lives and without which he would have no existence; that, finally and fundamentally, man's greatness is in his spirit, but that spirit can exist only in man's corporeal being, and that to deny the body in favor of the spirit would be to eliminate the spirit as well.

The passage in which most of these themes are first made manifest occurs in the first scene of Act IV and will repay close attention. While Caliban, Stephano, and Trinculo plot their revenge upon him, Prospero decides that he must bestow upon the betrothed Miranda and Ferdinand "some vanity of mine Art" (l. 41). The word *art* is striking. It suggests, as do any number of other references in the play, that Prospero's magic may be identified with art. But here the nature of that identity is made extremely clear: what Prospero's art creates is a play. The means at his disposal may exceed those of most directors, but the end result is largely the same, a fiction, a projection of the human imagination.

The masque itself relates to the themes of *The Tempest* in two important ways. First, Venus and Cupid are explicitly excluded from the celebration lest they exercise "some wanton charm upon this man and maid" (l. 95). This exclusion reminds both the young lovers, who are the masque's primary audience, and viewers or readers of *The Tempest,* who are the masque's audience once removed, of the importance of Prospero's oft-repeated prohibition against submitting to sexual passion. It is not merely chastity itself that so concerns Prospero. But giving in to sexual desire becomes, as a result of Caliban's attempted rape, a symbol of the forces of natural impulse that must be restrained. This feature of the masque and Prospero's seemingly obsessive insistence on Ferdinand's continence are then directly related to, and expressive of, the view of nature which the play presents.

The second thematically focal feature of the masque is Ceres' final speech (ll. 110–117). In it she repeats in modified form what Gonzalo had said upon first seeing the island; it too is a vision of the pastoral ideal. Now while this ideal may have no place in the attempts of real people to deal with the real world, it surely does have a place in art, as is suggested by Prospero's choice to include it, for Prospero stands in relationship to the masque much as Shakespeare does to *The Tempest*: he is the artist, the magician who simulates reality. As part of a pastoral masque Ceres' speech is hardly worth comment. But Ferdinand's reaction to it is.

> FER.: This is a most majestic vision, and
> Harmonious charmingly. May I be bold
> To think these spirits?
> PROS.:   Spirits, which by mine Art
> I have from their confines call'd to enact
> My present fancies.
> FER.:   Let me live here ever;
> So rare a wonder'd father and a wife
> Makes this place Paradise.   (IV, i, 118–124)

The conversation takes place on two different levels. Ferdinand sees the spirits as having an independent existence. In answering Ferdinand's question Prospero explains that they are merely the spirit of his art, projections or enactments of his imagination. But he answers in such a way as to leave Ferdinand's naiveté intact, and as a result Ferdinand, himself taken in by a vision of pastoral utopia, wishes to remain on the island permanently. Like Gonzalo, he mistakes the world of the imagination for the world of reality. Prospero, not yet ready to undermine Ferdinand's illusions or his innocence, recalls his attention to the masque.

But barely a moment later Prospero himself interrupts the masque when he remembers that Caliban is plotting against his life. In fact what he is doing—at least on a symbolic or thematic level—is waking from the dream of perfection that his imaginative art has created, recalled to the world of material reality by the immediacy of the danger that faces him from Caliban, that is from nature. Gonzalo would live in the dream—and Caliban would kill him; Prospero knows that to live in the dream is to invite death. One might well say that Prospero recognizes the necessity of what Freud called the reality principle.

In dismissing the spirits who have presented the masque, Prospero is not symbolically dispensing with the services of spirit entirely. Here the distinction between art and science becomes important: Prospero must interrupt an imaginative endeavor in order to undertake a very practical one. But before doing so he makes what is surely the most famous and most important speech in the play, in which the relationships between the real world and the world of imaginative perception are explored:

> Our revels now are ended. These our actors,
> As I foretold you, were all spirits, and
> Are melted into air, into thin air:
> And, like the baseless fabric of this vision,
> The cloud-capp'd towers, the gorgeous palaces,
> The solemn temples, the great globe itself,
> Yea, all which it inherit, shall dissolve,
> And, like this insubstantial pageant faded,
> Leave not a rack behind. We are such stuff
> As dreams are made on; and our little life
> Is rounded with a sleep. Sir, I am vex'd;
> Bear with my weakness; my old brain is troubled:
> Be not disturb'd with my infirmity:
> If you be pleas'd, retire into my cell,
> And there repose: a turn or two I'll walk,
> To still my beating mind.   (IV, i, 148–163)

Perhaps the first thing to be noted is that the tone of the speech is certainly not accounted for by Prospero's awareness of the plot against him, a plot that he can deal with without any difficulty. But although he may have no trouble with this particular Caliban at this particular time, he recognizes that the principle of Caliban, earth, will eventually overwhelm the principle of the play, spirit. The recollection of the specific fact of Caliban's plot startles him into an awareness of the more general fact underlying that plot, the fact of mortality. For surely mortality is the theme of the speech that follows.[6] Prospero notes that the vision—that is, the masque—is baseless, which, in this context, means unfounded. But it also suggests that the vision is unfounded because it disregards Caliban, who is best described by the word *base*. Similarly when a few lines later he calls it an insubstantial pageant, he indicates that it lacks substance, matter, material reality—it is entirely an expression of spirit. But as an expression of pure spirit it is untrue to the human experience.

The multiple levels of the speech are clear enough. Prospero uses the evanescence of the masque as a paradigm for the evanescence of the society he has established on the island, of the theater in which the play *The Tempest* is being presented, and of life in general. The word *globe* refers to the masque, the island, the theater of the same name, and finally to the world itself, the globe that is the earth. The stoical acceptance of mutability as essential to the human condition that informs Prospero's speech hardly requires further comment. But the inclusion of a self-conscious reference to the Globe Theatre, to the play as play, does. It is not enough, I think, to say that since the Globe Theatre is part of the real world, it too will fade. That is obvious. Moreover it ignores the idea of art and illusion which the theater represents, which is so important a theme in *The Tempest*, and which in some ways makes the theater—that is the experience of art—significantly different from the real world outside it. To put it more simply, the speech comments not only on the inescapable limitations of the human situation but also on the role of art and imagination in coping with that situation, and finally on the limits of art.

Long before the Globe Theatre as a physical entity ceases to exist, Shakespeare—through Prospero—seems to be saying, the world that currently occupies the Globe, the world of the play called *The Tempest*, will come to an end. The audience, which has interrupted its "real" concerns for an afternoon in order to share the common dream of art, will return to the real world. The speech—like the extraordinary time scheme adopted by Shakespeare for this play in which dramatic time is almost identical with real time, Shakespeare's plays generally being presented between three and six while the action of the play takes place between two and six—points to the parallel between Prospero's art and Shakespeare's. The masque is interrupted twice, first when Ferdinand mistakes art for reality, second when Prospero's recollection of a real danger forces an impatience with his dreams of perfection. *The Tempest*, however, requires no interruption because, unlike the masque, it is perfectly candid about its own limitations. It is, in a sense, about its own limitations, and about the limits of art in general.

But Shakespeare's creation and manipulation of the world of *The Tempest*, if superficially similar to Prospero's presentation of the masque, is, on a more profound level, analogous to Prospero's manipulation of life on his island. Prospero's impatience with the masque when he is reminded of Caliban's plot—that is of mortality—may be seen as a dissatisfaction with the workings of the imagination when they lead one away from a coming to terms with the real world and the moral responsibilities it imposes on man. The masque, the representation of an idealized pastoral utopia, leads to irresponsibility; it brings Ferdinand to the point of repeating Gonzalo's mistake. The island itself, on the other hand, though as much the product of Prospero's art as the masque, does not misrepresent the truth about human life. At first Gonzalo is fooled, but the progress of later developments will open his eyes. Shakespeare is then akin to Prospero. Both men present a pastoral world for our satisfaction. But both—Prospero by manipulating nature and finally by admitting that the island is his work of art, and Shakespeare by presenting us with Prospero and making his play about the limits of art—give us the truth and make it quite clear that the pastoral situation is not a natural one but one that exists only by virtue of man's efforts to impose his imagination on the indifference of the natural world. By this reading Prospero is a model of the artist, and his manipulation of nature on his island a model for the role of the artist in human society: to impose his imaginative ideals on recalcitrant nature to whatever extent possible, but to recognize the limitations of the human spirit in overcoming nature; to live as much as possible with Ariel while remembering that man is partly Caliban.

It is only if we understand the play in this way that Prospero's final abjuration of his magic and his decision to leave his pastoral paradise make sense. When Prospero is ready to leave his island he announces that he will "retire me to my Milan, where / Every third thought shall be my grave" (V, i, 310–311). There is apparently some dispute over the precise meaning of "every third thought," but whatever we take the other two thoughts to be the third one is clearly mortality, and Prospero's return to Milan is, in a sense, a coming to terms with his inevitable end as a human being. Just as the play *The Tempest* is over, and the audience must return to their real world, so Prospero's island paradise is over, and he too must return to the real world.[7] Shakespeare sees the pastoral ideal as a manifestation of the paradox of the imagination: the desire for perfection which can exist only in imperfect beings, the desire to be free of our material limitations which would not exist if we were not matter. Prospero's rejection of the island is therefore a rejection of the world of pastoral fancy, a world which disregards "every third thought" and which, as a result, leads to an inability to come to moral terms with the real world. When Miranda first sees the royal party she is led to marvel at the "goodly creatures" and is convinced that they must come from a "brave new world" (V, i, 182, 183). Because of the limitations on her education resulting from her isolation on the island she mistakes a group of scoundrels, usurpers, drunks, fools, and would be assassins for the cream of mankind. Despite Prospero's efforts, her education by art is incomplete, and a fuller appreciation of what is involved in the human situation will depend on her living in society. This certainly must be one of the reasons why Prospero decides to remove to Milan.

And yet, on a somewhat different level, Miranda is absolutely right in her naive expression of wonder. For the world of human society is in many respects a brave new world when compared with the isolation of the island; it may not be perfect, but perfection is not the human condition, and it may well be that faced with the choice between the perfection of art and the limitations of life Miranda chooses the latter. Significantly, though, when Ferdinand first sees Miranda he is as struck with awe as Miranda herself will be later on. For Ferdinand, who has known only the real world, the spirituality that Miranda embodies is as marvelous as the reality of human society is for Miranda. This is not merely a fanciful way of saying that the grass is always greener on the other side. It is Shakespeare's way of pointing out the perpetual dilemma of the human condition; half matter and half spirit, man strives for a wholeness, attempts to rise above the paradox of his consciousness, but cannot do without the element he attempts to rise above. Caliban is perfect—which is why he is not evil—and Ariel is perfect, but man is not capable of either kind of perfection. And any attempt to reach such perfection involves a misconception of the nature of human life and an abdication of moral responsibility. Prospero, who understands both Miranda and Ferdinand and the limitations of their views, thus chooses to renounce his magic and return to the world of social reality. But his magic, like the magic of any artist, has worked to sharpen his auditors' awareness of the place of man in the world and the nature of human responsibility. Langbaum puts this very well indeed:

> Art is just such an experience of enchantment. The speech in which Prospero breaks his magic wand . . . is his comment on the relation between art and life. For in breaking his wand and taking himself and the others back to Italy, Prospero seems to be saying that the enchanted island is no abiding place, but rather a place through which we pass in order to renew and strengthen our sense of reality. (p. 199)

III

There remains the matter of the tone of the play. I have, in my title, referred to the play as a comedy, and the mood of forgiveness and conciliation which dominates its denouement reinforces one's sense that it is, as does the marriage of Ferdinand and Miranda, of course. Yet it seems odd that a comedy should end with the protagonist clearly looking forward to his own death. And the single most important speech in the work—the one Prospero makes after interrupting the masque—comes awfully close to despair.

It should be noted, though, that Prospero's speech does not end on a desperate note. He seems to come to his senses, as it were, and immediately apologizes to Ferdinand for carrying on as he has; indeed, he refers to his previous statements as the products of infirmity, of a "beating mind." In part, of course, Prospero is merely being tactful. Ferdinand is yet young, on the verge of being married, and Prospero hardly wants to burden him with a kind of existential angst. But Prospero's very tact is an act of kindness which epitomizes the nature of the play's comic resolution, as does Prospero's even greater kindness in forgiving the conspirators.

No doubt every human being is caught in an inescapable existential trap; no doubt "we are such stuff as dreams are made on." But what *The Tempest* seems to imply is that once we have realized this fact we can act accordingly; more specifically, since nature is indifferent to man it is a matter of some importance that men are not indifferent to each other. It is for this reason that Prospero refuses to burden the innocent Ferdinand with his problem. And if Ferdinand's innocence makes him less than fully ready to deal with the real world, the resolution of the play and life in Milan under Prospero's guidance will take care of that in due time. The important thing is that a realization of the truth about life and nature lead not to cynicism, as it has for Antonio and Sebastian, but to an increased benevolence, as it does for Prospero. And that is precisely the comic affirmation of the play: though the universe may be devoid of theological principle, and though nature may be indifferent, cynicism is a mean and an immoral response, for it can only make matters worse; benevolence and human cooperation are the only sensible and moral alternatives. This idea, like so many others in the play, is reinforced in the epilogue when the speaker explains that the only thing standing between him and despair is the indulgence of the audience. The spirit of charity, which alone keeps Prospero from despair, similarly is the only thing that can preserve the actor playing his role from an analogous fate. The play is a comedy because it affirms positive human values, and it affirms them not in spite of but because of the inherent flaws of human existence and the imperfection that is man.

There is, finally, one more reason for the affirmation with which the play concludes. One of the things *The Tempest* deals with is the importance of art. Now whatever else one may want to say about art, it should be clear that it is what Freud calls a substitute gratification; it satisfies needs that cannot be satisfied more directly in the world of immediate experience. In other words art could not exist in a world of perfect creatures leading perfect lives: neither Swift's Houyhnhnms nor the inhabitants of Huxley's Brave New World have any art at all.[8] Art is something people create because their lives are imperfect, and one of the functions of art is to make life as perfect as possible, and to imaginatively explore what perfection would really be like. But obviously art must be all process, and never, in any final sense, product. For the achievement of perfection would eliminate the art which made it possible. Thus Shakespeare, in celebrating man's art, is by implication also celebrating the imperfection of man, his mortality and the double nature of his consciousness, without all of which art would not exist. What Prospero has understood, and what his art—and Shakespeare's—attempts to make clear, is that man's imperfection is inseparable from his glory.

NOTES

[1] Robert Langbaum, "*The Tempest* and Tragicomic Vision," *The Modern Spirit* (New York: Oxford University Press Paperback, 1970), p. 187.

[2] Jan Kott, "Prospero's Staff," *Shakespeare Our Contemporary* (London: Methuen, 1964), p. 180.

[3] Leo Marx, "Shakespeare's American Fable," *The Machine in the Garden: Technology and the Pastoral Ideal in America* (New York: Oxford University Press Paperback, 1967), pp. 34–72. See especially pp. 46–57.

[4] Throughout my essay I will have recourse to such expressions as "the purpose of the play," "the vision of the play," "intention," "meaning," and so on. I hope it is superfluous of me to add that in none of these cases do I mean to indicate that Shakespeare consciously held the views I attribute to the play, or that he consciously intended the play to mean what I claim it means. I am, rather, talking more about that element in the work which can be defined as the intention of the play—as opposed to that of the author—or, alternatively, the meanings intended by the author's second self. It seems to me that one of the most important achievements of recent literary criticism—if not the most important—has been the redemption of the "meaning" of a text from the rigidities of historical intentionality on the one hand, and, on the other, from the aleatory Empsonisms of granting equal status to any and all "meanings" which may be inferred from the text by an ingenious critical methodology. I trust that my reading of *The Tempest* occupies that safe ground cleared by these critical theories and is neither mechanical nor anarchic. In calling the play "existential" I certainly don't mean that Shakespeare was an existentialist, consciously or unconsciously. Merely that the perception of and attitudes to the world expressed in the play are largely those of modern existentialism; and that these perceptions and attitudes—although perhaps very far from Shakespeare's actual purpose in writing the play—are demonstrably there in the work and not merely the creation of critical sophistry.

[5] All my line references are to the 6th edition (1958) of the Arden text.

[6] Kermode suggests that Prospero's perturbation is the result of his sense of ingratitude: "Caliban's

ingratitude recalls that of Antonio—to the one he gave the use of reason, to the other ducal power. The conspiracy afoot reminds him of the trials of the past twelve years, which are now being rapidly re-enacted." I find this reading very unacceptable for two reasons. First it assumes that Prospero really believes that Caliban should have become civilized, when it is quite clear that he knows that his attempts to give reason to Caliban were not only futile but meaningless and silly as well. More important, it hardly accounts for the philosophical force of Prospero's speech. A man faced with ingratitude may get angry, but he normally does not find that ingratitude sufficient reason for stoical speculation on the human condition.

[7] Shakespeare elaborates upon this idea and reinforces the analogy between magician and playwright in the wonderful epilogue to the play. When the actor who has played Prospero says, "Now my charms are all o'erthrown," he is clearly referring both to his charms as Prospero the magician—that is, his charms *within* the fiction—and to his charms as an actor—that is, his charms as the presenter *of* the fiction. Both magic and drama are artifice; and just as Prospero has given up his wand, so the actor has given up his persona. In each case the character is left to face the real world without the benefit of his art. The parallels between artificer and artist in the rest of the epilogue are clear enough.

[8] I hasten to add that neither the land of the Houyhnhnms nor the Brave New World seem to me perfect. But they are perfect in terms of their internal structures and the needs of their inhabitants, who are so satisfied with their lives that they need no substitute gratification at all. Indeed, in Swift's work the very idea of art, which is always to some extent a fabrication and thus a "lie," is unthinkable. The point of all of which is, of course, that for creatures such as we are perfection is not only impossible, it is inconceivable, a point that Samuel Johnson recognized some two centuries ago when, in *Rasselas*, he devoted a chapter to a consideration of "The Wants of Him Who Wants Nothing."

James Smith

CALIBAN

IV. Caliban

Characters in *The Tempest* are subject to perplexities. Certainly commentators on *The Tempest* have shown themselves to be so: among them Mr Morton Luce, although he takes high rank precisely because he pays the perplexities a proper attention. But as a result of his doing so he does not so much offer an explanation of the play as confess that it is inexplicable: *The Tempest,* he concludes, is 'ideal'—itself a perplexing adjective. By it Mr Luce would seem to mean a number of things, between all of which it is not necessary for the moment to distinguish: but two things at least which he does mean are 'praiseworthy' and 'vague'. It is difficult to conceive of a play being both together, or at least to conceive of its being the one because of the other. But in any case, it has already been suggested in this essay that *The Tempest* is not ideal but real; and now I proceed to the suggestion that, whatever else it may be, it is the opposite of vague. Such perplexities as it produces have their origin rather in an abundance than a paucity of details. Whereas a single account of an object or event might have sufficed, two are given. These accounts are contradictory, and so the object appears now to exist, now not to exist: in other words, it is dream-like. Or a single account may be so full of details that these sway hither and thither like a swarm: the mind has difficulty in deciding whether it is faced by one thing or by many, and if by one thing then what is its head, tail or centre. Now the mind is attracted by what seems to be one of these parts, now by another; or what seems to be the same part now attracts and now repels the mind. The object in short appears to exist and not to exist at the same time; it provokes reactions so complex and so incompatible as to put on the appearance of a nightmare.

The first of these cases is that of Alonso's ship. Mr Luce finds a difficulty in some witnesses describing it as split, others as foundered. A landsman sees no

From *Shakespearian and Other Essays* (Cambridge: Cambridge University Press, 1974), pp. 188–211, 243–55. This essay written c. 1954.

objection to its being both: it may, for example, split against a perpendicular rock, and the resulting fragments be immediately swallowed up. What moves even a landsman to objection, is the ship's splitting or foundering and at the same time remaining intact and afloat. Yet that is what is reported. According to the cries of those who are on board, both passengers and crew, the ship is about to split; according to Miranda who is on shore, but near enough to hear the cries, it does split; according to Ariel, who also is near because he is everywhere, it arrives safely in harbour. And later, the same crew who 'gave it out as split' are compelled to agree with Ariel, for the ship is exhibited to them as

> tight and yare and bravely rigged as when
> We first put out to sea. (V. i. 226)

Presumably the passengers agree also, for they find the ship 'tight and yare' enough to embark on it for Naples. Here are flat contradictions between what is seen by the same people at different times, and by different people at the same time.

Nor are such contradictions in any way concealed from the reader. Rather they are paraded before him. For example, they furnish the main matter and, as it would seem, the main motive for some hundred lines of dialogue at the beginning of Act II. When Gonzalo and Adrian maintain that the island provides 'everything advantageous to life', that the grass is lush and lusty and green, and that the air breathes sweetly upon them, Antonio and Sebastian immediately deny all these statements. According to the latter speakers, means of living on the island are 'none or little', the grass is neither lush nor lusty because there is only 'an eye of green in't', the ground is tawny, and the air stinks like that from a fen. This dispute Mr Luce seeks to dismiss as a quibble; but of all possible ways of dealing with it this would seem the least admissible. For it is of the essence of a quibble that, of the two parties to it (if there are no more than two) one at least should be recognized as in the right; while if each of the parties can be recognized as having right on his side, in however different a sense or way, then so much better the quibble. But as between Gonzalo's party and Antonio's, the reader is possessed of no means whatever of deciding, for he knows nothing of the subject of the dispute except what these parties tell him. And if he would seem to know something of the appearance of the company's garments—since in the preceding scene he has heard Ariel assure Prospero that, in spite of their immersion in sea-water, these garments are 'fresher than before'—nevertheless the reader hesitates to come to a decision when this in turn becomes a subject of dispute. For, amongst other things, he notices an uncertainty in Gonzalo, who from a boast that his doublet is 'rather new-dyed than stained', descends to an admission that it is fresher only 'in a sort'. It seems all the more remarkable that he should insist on any sort of freshness. If so weak a disputant is pertinacious in disputing, the reader concludes that dispute between the characters is inevitable.

In any case, the reader is soon, and often, forced into a dispute with himself. After the opening storm he gathers, I think, the impression that the weather on the island is set fair. Yet at the beginning of the second scene of Act II he is startled with the sound of thunder; during the course of the scene, he is informed by Trinculo, the sky is covered by clouds as black as bombards and as ready to shed their liquor. Immediately the scene is over fair weather sets in again; although no interval of time divides it from its neighbours—rather it would seem to be contemporaneous with at least part of them.

Caliban the reader hears complaining of being confined to a 'hard rock', and Prospero he hears confirming this complaint; yet Caliban also boasts of having access to 'every fertile inch' of the island, and Ariel mocks him for forcing access to inches fertile enough at least to bear

Tooth'd briars, sharp furzes, pricking goss and thorns   (IV. i. 180)

Then there is the contradiction between Miranda's remembering 'rather like a dream' that once she had four or five women to attend upon her, and her denial that she remembers any woman's face but her own. She is similarly inconsistent about her acquaintance with the other sex: until Ferdinand's arrival, she says on one occasion, she has seen no man but her father; on another she admits having seen two men, her father, namely, and Caliban.

This last inconsistency may however depend upon another which, according to Mr Luce, is the most striking in the play. 'If all the suggestions as to Caliban's form and features and endowments . . . are collected', he says, 'it will be found that one half render the other half impossible.' If that were true, then Caliban would be, in Mr Luce's terms, a 'vague' or an 'ideal' figure; in language which we have striven to make more exact, he would be dream-like. But as a matter of fact he is not: rather he is one of the most obviously nightmarish figures in the play.

The point is important, not only because of the prominence of the part played by Caliban, but also because it is a part with nothing corresponding to it in the play's congeners—not, at least, in the two we have so far considered. To us therefore it constitutes a characterizing difference of *The Tempest,* and we may hope to gain some light from it. It is necessary for us to study Caliban carefully.

Having addressed ourselves to the task, we find ourselves I think obliged to regret that, in his anxiety to establish a vagueness or ideality, Mr Luce should have overstated, if not mis-stated, the evidence before him. At least he has overstated such of it as concerns Caliban's 'form and features'. For as a matter of fact, very few suggestions about these are thrown out. Stephano it is true addresses Caliban as a cat, and Prospero as a tortoise, while Trinculo upbraids him as 'puppy-headed'. Very possibly however none of these is more than a figurative term. In spite of Caliban's long nails, Stephano may mean no more than that, once wine is poured down his throat, he will begin to 'speak after the wisest'; Prospero probably means no more than that Caliban is lazy, Trinculo than that he is foolish.

Leaving aside all descriptions either obviously or possibly figurative, we are left with two only: Caliban has the form of a fish, say Antonio and Trinculo; many other characters imply, though they may not say—yet some of them do say—that he has the form of a man. And of these two descriptions one, I think, upon examination very soon ceases to appear as such.

'A plain fish and no doubt marketable' (V. i. 268), is Antonio's exclamation when he first sets eyes on Caliban. It might seem easy enough to interpret; Antonio however is speaking not so much to inform as to distract himself and others. Those whom he is addressing have no need of information, for Caliban is before them. And whatever kind of fish the latter may be, he is certainly not a plain one; nor is he any more plainly a fish than he is anything—otherwise it could not have entered even Mr Luce's head to call him 'ideal'. Perhaps therefore it is safer to take the term 'fish', on Antonio's lips at any rate, as another rhetorical figure. As such it is not infrequent in common speech, in which something may be called a 'fish', not because it has gills, but because it is strange.

Therefore Trinculo would seem to be a more useful witness. As he is alone at his first encounter with Caliban, he speaks to distract no one, unless possibly the audience. 'What have we here?' he ruminates, 'a man or a fish?' (II. ii. 25) and following his nose, he decides for the second. 'An ancient and fish-like smell' is however no impossible mark of a human being; as Trinculo himself discovers when at last he ventures to peep beneath Caliban's gaberdine. For then he becomes aware of legs like those of a man, and of fins which are not fins but arms. He needs do no more than touch the body—'warm, o' my troth'—for him to abandon the notion of its fish-like nature. Nor does he ever return to it. If he seems to do so when he calls Caliban 'thou debosh'd fish', (III. ii. 26) it should be remembered that with this phrase he is seeking to requite what he considers to be abuse. Either the adjective or the noun must be figurative and, in view of the fact that the three companions have long been drinking, the odds are heavily in favour of the noun.[1]

With the same phrase, Trinculo seeks to assert superiority by the exercise of his wit. In so far as Caliban is partly a fish he is not wholly a monster, to that extent therefore disqualified for the publishing of lies so monstrous as that Trinculo is 'not valiant'.

But in so far as Caliban is only partly yet not wholly a fish, he is not the less but the more monstrous; and Trinculo is allowing his wit to run away with him. The very insecurity of the joke however serves to make clear the fact that, by the time of its making, the term 'monster' has established itself as a proper appellation for Caliban. As a matter of fact, his most constant companions, who are this same Stephano and Trinculo, only exceptionally call him anything else.

The term can be applied to any kind of creature, whether legged, winged, finned or merely rooted, so long as this creature is not so much unfamiliar as unexpected or improbable in appearance. Men with heads beneath their shoulders, fishes with eyes in their tails, mandrakes bearing rose-blossoms are all in the same sense monsters. This wide variety does not however imply any vagueness in the name which they bear in common, but rather the opposite: since only a precise meaning could first gather and then keep them together. A monster is one of nature's failures or mistakes. It is a creature which, in consequence of some mistake, has failed to reach one of the perfections intended by nature for her creatures. Either the material submitted to her for elaboration was insufficiently responsive, or she herself was insufficiently inattentive during the process of elaboration, or the time for that process was cut short. Or, more briefly, a monster is an abortion, something which should not have been born either as or when it was. This sense may not be so readily accessible to a modern reader as to an Elizabethan; that Elizabethans so unlearned as Trinculo and Stephano were perfectly familiar with it is shown by their occasionally varying their name for Caliban from 'monster' to 'moon-calf'. A moon-calf is a calf, or any kind of offspring, that was born before sufficiently ripe. The weakling moon seems therefore to have operated on it and not, as should have been the case, the potent sun: *Homo hominem generat et sol.*

Since we have dismissed the supposed fishiness of Caliban, and since the only alternative description proposed for him was that of a man, we may I think without more ado assume that he is a human monster. In other words, the perfection for which he was intended and of which he fails is that of humanity. And this is where his nightmarishness enters. To a degree all monsters are suitable for figuring in a nightmare, since at the same time they rouse an expectation and they baulk it. But the contradictory feelings roused by a human monster are exceptionally strong and exceptionally complex. Since the expectation which he baulks is of a perfection similar to our own, at best he seems to mock us; at worst, he may direct a reproach against us, or even an accusation. For no man is absolutely perfect; nor is the division between perfection and imperfection marked by a line, but rather by an area of indeterminate extent, at any end and at every point in which perfection and imperfection blend imperceptibly the one into the other. Or if they are divided by a line, then this is no more stable than the crest of a wave or the boundary of a colour on the pigeon's neck. On this line in one of its positions each of us has his place: but Caliban has his place on the line also, and therefore we are akin to him not only by his humanity but by his monstrosity. No wonder he alarms, as would the most nightmarish figure. Or if we make a laudable attempt to repress this alarm, in the end we succeed in nothing but in replacing it with bafflement. The more details we note about Caliban that make for his monstrosity, the more we find that call to be noted as making for the opposite. We begin to doubt whether we have one thing or many before us, whether we have anything at all. We find ourselves in short in the position of the men on board the *Sea Adventure,* when their mind had lost its judgment and empire.

Let us nevertheless preserve that empire as long as we can, meanwhile noting as many details as possible about Caliban. The first among these would seem to be his physical ugliness, since that is the first to be impressed upon the reader. And the impression is intended to be deep, for Ariel is dressed as a water-nymph and called back upon the stage for no other purpose than, by the contrast he offers to Caliban, to make it so. Yet the ugliness would seem to be of a softer kind, rather ludicrous than horrific: of all the other characters only Miranda and Prospero hinting anything to the contrary, either by action or by word. And of these, Miranda has a special reason for so doing, since in her memory the appearance of Caliban is associated with an attempted rape. As for Prospero, he would not seem to make any clear distinction between disgust at the physical and the moral Caliban. In any case, his solitary reaction cannot be considered to have a significance equal to that of so many others who, rather than turning their eyes away, allow them to dwell on Caliban: either to their scornful or to their tolerant amusement.

A ludicrous ugliness is a heavy cross for a man to bear; not however large enough, if he is a man, to hide the fact. Accordingly, we find the fact recognized not only in the conduct but in the words of the other characters. It must however be admitted that they show no great eagerness to do so: their attitude, rather than one of a decided acceptance or a decided repudiation of Caliban's human appearance resembling that of the reader's hitherto—that is to say, it is an attitude of bafflement. Thus only once does Stephano, the most kindly disposed of all towards Caliban, gratify the latter with the name of 'man-monster'; only once does he go ever so far as to call him 'Monsieur Monster'; for the most part of the time he is content with the name 'servant monster', the anthropomorphic suggestions of which are no more than slight, if indeed they exist. And if Prospero on one occasion allows himself to group Caliban along with Stephano and Trinculo as 'men', and again, a few lines later, as 'fellows', he would seem on that occasion to be attending chiefly to other thoughts; normally at any rate his language is of quite a different kind. On the other hand, Miranda allows herself to compare Caliban with Ferdinand, the paragon of men, and to do so with respect to physical form. And yet, as we have seen, she is also capable of omitting Caliban from the list of men.

Perhaps I had better warn against any attempt to solve the problem of Caliban by putting him down as an ape. However easy, in these days of evolutionism, the solution may appear, it is forbidden not only by chronology but also, I believe, by evolutionary orthodoxy. Of evolution the Elizabethans suspected nothing; in any case it does not proceed, if it does proceed, by way of abortions. Further, there are no creatures of whose difference from himself Caliban is more convinced than he is of that of apes. These he not only fears because they are employed to torment him, he also despises them for the way they 'mow and chatter' (II. ii. 10); 'thou jesting monkey' (III. ii. 45) is the most satisfying insult he can find when Trinculo has given him the lie on the matter nearest his heart; the punishment he most dreads, along with that of being immobilized into a barnacle, is that of degradation into an ape 'with forehead villainous low' (IV. i. 249). Caliban's forehead, it may be presumed, was a perceptibly high one.

A reminder of the fact is not inappropriate as preparation for a study of what Mr Luce calls Caliban's endowments. For of course it is only mental and moral endowments which are in question. Of the physical, Caliban quite obviously possesses at least his proper share. He can eat—he makes his first entrance eating; he can sleep—Prospero reproaches him with sleeping too much; he can move himself and other things—this capacity for locomotion is exploited to the full by Prospero; he is philoprogenitive—according to Prospero, excessively, even unscrupulously so.

Among mental endowments, he possesses to a notable degree that of cunning. Given an end, he is never at a loss to devise the means for obtaining it. The end which he takes as given, and architectonic to all others, is that of vengeance upon Prospero. Accordingly he notes the time at which access to Prospero is least dangerous, and how to circumvent such danger as remains. First Prospero must be deprived of the books which are his weapons of defence; then, and then only, are offensive weapons to be used—a log, a stake or a knife. These Caliban knows himself too cowardly to wield: he is too cowardly to attack even Trinculo, until someone else's blows have lamed the latter. But Stephano, Caliban thinks, is brave; and not altogether foolishly, since the valour of a man when drunk is not necessarily a drunkard's valour. And so Caliban proceeds, by bribery, to devise yet another means to his revenge. Stephano shall have Caliban as a servant, Miranda as a consort, and the island as a kingdom, only if he will consent to act as executioner. He does consent, only, as the reader knows, to fail in the office.

The manner of his failing is such as, by contrast, to suggest that Caliban is endowed not only with cunning but with prudence, and indeed with quite a high measure of it. For having devised means to an end, he remains constantly aware of the temporal priority of the former, and exercises self-control in refraining from any attempt upon the latter until the means have been secured. Stephano on the other hand would seize upon the ends without delay. No sooner has he heard Ariel's music than he is off in pursuit.

This will prove a brave kingdom to me,

he says,

Where I shall have my music for nothing.   (III. ii. 142)

'When Prospero's destroyed', rings Caliban's warning cry; but Stephano will have none of it, preferring to heed Trinculo's 'Let's follow' the music, 'and after do our work.' He commands Caliban to lead the pursuit but Caliban refuses, lagging disconsolately behind. Such at least is a possible interpretation of the speech-headings and, it seems to me, the most plausible one.

Nevertheless he does not abandon Stephano, on whom all his hopes are fixed; he knows of course of no one else upon the island on whom he might fix them. When we next see him, he is exercising a self-control that is nothing less than extraordinary: for he is patient under reproaches that he has done nothing to deserve. It is he, say both Stephano and Trinculo, who is cause of their shins having been pricked with thorns and their noses having been offended with a filthy pool. And yet, as we have seen, Caliban did not lead the chase which brought them to these misfortunes; nor did he tell them that Ariel's music was harmless to follow, only that it was harmless to listen to. The immediately subsequent behaviour of his companions calls for, and meets with, a self-control which is even greater. For they rush upon the glittering garments which Prospero has hung out 'for stale'. Caliban gives expression to anger no more violent than is necessary to restrain them, were they capable of restraint. The garments he condemns as 'trash' or 'luggage'; Trinculo he calls a fool for laying a hand upon them; he himself will have 'none on't'. And he proclaims the punishments to which they are exposing themselves. All is useless, and Caliban must face the punishments along with the other two. He does so in a silence which, like all negatives, can bear no weight of interpretation; it cannot however be interpreted as undignified.

Caliban's self-control and prudence should be borne in mind when his moral endowments come up for consideration. Meanwhile, it may be noted that they are in no way incompatible with ignorance of astronomy. Trinculo may affect to think so; but then Trinculo is a parasite upon learning as upon many other things, and in order to increase his own importance is led to overprize it. Caliban may very well believe both that there is a man in the moon and that Stephano is such a man, without ceasing to be as cunning and as prudent as a number of men, indeed leaders of men, known to history. On the other hand, what might seem repugnant to his possession of any mental or moral qualities whatever is the aphasia with which, according to Prospero (or Miranda), he was once afflicted.

> I pitied thee,
> Took pains to make thee speak, taught thee each hour
> One thing or other: when thou didst not, savage,
> Know thine own meaning, but wouldst gabble like
> A thing most brutish, I endow'd thy purposes
> With words that made them known.[2]   (I. ii. 354)

In interpreting this passage however the philological uncharitableness should be borne in mind which, though at times ascribed as a monopoly to the Greeks, has manifested itself in most places and continues to do so down to modern times. Any unfamiliar speech is readily dismissed as a 'gabble'; so that Prospero's evidence need not be taken to imply that Caliban was ever speechless. In any case, by the time the play opens he has long ceased to be so; and in recognizing that, with a new form of speech, new powers have been conferred upon him he would seem to give invincible proof of the possession of an intellectual nature. In recognizing that he has abused these powers he would seem to prove that he possesses a moral nature also:

> You taught me language, and my profit on't
> Is, I know how to curse.   (ibid. 364)

Like Prospero's speech with which this essay began, this utterance of Caliban's has echoed throughout the world; it can hardly have come from a brute.

Yet a brute is what, according to Prospero, Caliban undoubtedly is; or if not a brute then he is a devil, which is something worse. Either that is he is beneath morality, as incapable of it; or he is averse from it, as incurably malicious. It is scarcely necessary to quote Prospero's fulminations to this effect. 'Abhorred slave', he says,

> Which any print of goodness will not take,
> Being capable of all ill!   (ibid. 353)

or again,

> A devil, a born devil, on whose nature
> Nurture will never stick; on whom my pains,
> Humanely taken, all, all lost, quite lost!   (IV. i. 188)

It is however rarely possible to accept fulminations at their face value; and of itself, the wording of Prospero's makes it clear that they cannot. If Caliban is a 'born devil', then he is no devil except figuratively, for devils are not born. And once attention is fixed upon this figure of Prospero's, he reveals himself I think as failing to justify it. For the charges which he alleges in its support are two: of lust, and of ingratitude.

> I have us'd thee
> ... with humane care, and lodg'd thee
> In mine own cell, till thou didst seek to violate
> The honour of my child.   (I. ii. 346)

If both charges are grave, neither lies beyond the reach of merely human wickedness. And of this truth no one, it would seem, is more aware than Prospero himself. For, to take the less serious charge, he does not think it superfluous to warn Ferdinand against the sin of lust: Ferdinand, whom no one has suspected of falling outside humanity, who on the contrary has enjoyed the highest rank within it, who has received the most careful moral training that men can devise, whom Prospero himself has submitted to a moral probation and whom, in consequence, he has thought worthy of his daughter's hand. Yet even so, he delivers the warning not only once but twice, and then weaves a third repetition of it into a masque provided for Ferdinand's entertainment. Admittedly, the gulf between liability to lust and lustful sin is such as, in the eyes of justice, it cannot be bridged: those under the liability may however bridge it in a single moment, and with a single act. Recognition of them as such would therefore seem to entitle them to charity, at least in speech; however firmly Prospero may be convinced that, with respect to Caliban, he functions as an officer of justice. But it is precisely in speech that Prospero is most notably lacking in charity. As for the second and more serious charge of ingratitude, a similar comment on it is provided by one of the phrases contained in Prospero's warning to Ferdinand. 'The strongest oaths', he admonishes the latter, 'are straws to th'fire i'th' blood' (IV. i. 52). If the strongest oaths, then the closest obligations also; and other passions besides lust may cause these obligations to burn away like straw. If all are to be considered as brutes or as devils who, under the persuasion of passion, have shown themselves ungrateful, then a great part of what is usually considered human history should be called by another name. Indeed, Prospero's vehemence towards Caliban shows itself upon scrutiny as so far beyond justification as to raise the doubt whether the passion which Caliban does entertain towards him, the passion of hate, is not all too easily explicable.

Explicable and no more, for justified it cannot be. It is a completely ruthless hate. The lines in which he not only issues but savours his instructions for the murder of Prospero are by far the most brutal in the play:

> there thou may'st brain him,
> Having first seized his books; or with a log
> Batter his skull, or paunch him with a stake,
> Or cut his wezand with thy knife.   (III. ii. 87)

However, they are not the most diabolic lines; the credit or the shame for uttering which must be allowed to a gentleman of Ferdinand's rank and training: the usurping Duke of Milan who, when reminded that, as a human being, he is supposed to have a conscience, replies:

> I feel not
> This deity in my bosom. Twenty consciences,
> That stand 'twixt me and Milan, candied be they
> And melt ere they molest!   (II. i. 274)

The treachery involved in his plot to murder Alonso has already, in the opening section, been the subject of remark. Therefore perhaps it is sufficient here to add that this treachery is beyond all possibility of explanation. Neither Alonso nor Sebastian has suffered any uncharitableness at Prospero's hands, nor claims to have done so. The sole motive to their crime is, they confess, ambition.

Caliban is then less diabolic than either Antonio or Sebastian. As no one doubts that these are men, it follows that Caliban is not a devil at all. Prospero's alternative suggestion remains to be considered, that he is a brute. And about this the first remark to be made would seem to be that no one brings evidence in its favour, save Prospero himself. Nor would that evidence, from the language in which it is couched, seem to be above suspicion. On the contrary, the whole of Prospero's demeanour towards Caliban rouses suspicion of the strongest kind. If he really believed Caliban to be a brute, for example, he would not rail at him as he does: for it is not intelligent to rail at a brute for the evil he may do, any more than it is to rail at a river for the way in which it flows. If the flow displeases, dykes and dams are constructed to control it. Similarly a brute, if he displeases, is confined and beaten, without apologies to him, to oneself or to anybody. And much of Prospero's railing has the air of being an apology addressed to the universe. These, it may be objected, are merely negative considerations. Positive ones in the same sense are however not lacking. Caliban, we have seen, possesses the power of intelligent choice, which brutes do not: and when this choice is between means and ends, he is capable of standing by a choice of the means, however strongly the ends may attract him. His chief end, the murder of Prospero, must be admitted to be evil. If however he has not, like Antonio and Sebastian, stifled his conscience in order to be free to pursue it, that need not imply he is brutish because of an absence of conscience. He may very well have a conscience and this, as often happens in men, be blinded or blunted by passion to the evil on which he is engaged. Further, there would seem to be occasions when he is not so blinded or blunted. As has been noted, he regrets his cursing: which if he does not clearly repent of, at least he recognizes that repentance would be proper. And if, from the play's opening, he shows himself as, in his conduct towards Prospero, entirely governed by hate, there was a time, he claims, when this was not so: a time when Prospero invited love and gratitude—

> and then I lov'd thee,
> And show'd thee all the qualities o'th'isle,
> The fresh springs, brine-pits, barren place and fertile.   (I. ii. 337)

Prospero does not venture to deny the claim. And that the fount of love and gratitude, though no longer flowing in Prospero's direction, is by no means dry in Caliban's heart is shown by his conduct towards Stephano. The latter hardly needs do more than make a few amiable gestures, utter a few not obviously harsh words to Caliban, for the latter to embarrass him with professions of love:

> I'll show thee every fertile inch o' th' island ...
> I'll show thee the best springs; I'll pluck thee berries,
> I'll fish for thee, I'll get thee wood enough....
> I prithee, let me bring thee where crabs grow;
> And I with my long nails will dig thee pig-nuts;
> Show thee a jay's nest, and instruct thee how
> To snare the nimble marmoset; I'll bring thee
> To clustering filberts, and sometimes I'll get thee
> Young scamels from the rock. Wilt thou go with me?   (II. ii. 153ff.)

The litany is pathetic, both in its own eloquence and in the indifference of him before whom it is poured out.

Caliban is pathetic too in his offer to worship Stephano, for which he has often been condemned. Yet the offer does not hold for long: Caliban is intelligent enough to learn from experience, and when he has done so rapidly degrades Stephano from god to king or lord. Nor while it lasts would the offer seem to be to Caliban's discredit, but rather the opposite. A god is the strongest possible source of authority, and a recognition of authority, together with a willingness to submit to it, is a necessary preliminary to the moral life. For conscience is nothing if not authoritative. Even the mild authority of Alonso is unbearable to Antonio and Sebastian, who stifle conscience.

The moral life is a conflict. Accordingly, those who engage upon it are in need of encouragement, and this they find in the prospect of a time when the causes of conflict shall have been removed. Caliban too enjoys such a prospect. The music of Ariel not only gratifies his senses, it conjures up a vision of paradise:

> Sometimes a thousand twangling instruments
> Will hum about mine ears; and sometimes voices,
>   ... and then, in dreaming,
> The clouds methought would open, and show riches
> Ready to drop upon me.   (III. ii. 135)

Nevertheless he does not follow the music, for he knows that, in this world, paradise is to be enjoyed in prospect only. Thereby as we have seen he shows himself superior in prudence to Stephano and Trinculo. Now I think we may add he shows himself superior to Ferdinand also: at least at the moment when Ferdinand, not content with a passing snatch of the spirits' music, would have them gratify all of his senses for ever. For that is to demand a paradise on earth.

But it is time to halt in our investigation. Having started from a consideration of Caliban's monstrosity, we seem to be on the verge of concluding that no other character in the play is human in a like degree. If so far we have avoided bafflement, it may be we have done so only at the cost of taking a corposant for a planet. Shakespeare is proving his power over us; it was not however part of his intention that his readers should fall victims to a nightmare. And that they should not do so, he provided objects other than Caliban for them to consider. It will therefore be wise for us to change the object before us.

V. The Spirits

In spite of the recommendation with which the last section closed, I find it necessary to return to Caliban. But only for a moment, since my sole object is to get rid of the notion that he is a supernatural being. Mr Luce put it about that he was, or at least one aspect of him: but then Mr Luce held that Caliban was vague, and we have seen that he is rather the opposite; Mr Luce also assumed that the word 'vague' has as synonym, not only the word 'ideal', but the word 'supernatural'. And few would agree with him in this.

Supernatural beings are, not ideal, but at least as real as any other; nor are they vaguely, but at least as precisely known. They can be so, because in no part and in no respect are they compounded of matter. Hence they may be called spiritual substances but, in order to distinguish them as clearly as possible from the spirits which play a prominent part in *The Tempest*, it is perhaps desirable for us to call them 'intellectual substances'. As such, they can exercise control over the world and its inhabitants, in so far as these are not intellectual but material. The purely intellectual substances include God, the good and the evil angels, and the devil as the chief of the latter.

Prospero calls Caliban 'a devil, a born devil' but, as was pointed out in the last section, this cannot be more than a figure of speech. Nor may his description of Caliban as a 'demi-devil', a 'bastard devil' or 'got by the devil himself' be any more than such. Caliban's mother, we are told, was a witch; and witches, we know, were in the habit of accepting devils as their lovers. But it was not inevitable that they should do so, and Sycorax may have been more fastidious or more recalcitrant than the majority of her kind. If indeed Sycorax was a witch—a question which may occupy us later. But whatever answer we may be compelled to return to it makes no difference to the answer required of us now. For the offspring of a union so unnatural as that between a devil and a witch is nothing above nature, but something within nature if not in accordance with it, something preternatural to use the technical term or, to fall back on the term with which we are already familiar, a monster. The characters in the play are fully aware of the important difference between monsters on the one hand, and devils on the other. Stephano, for example, is quite happy to divert himself at the expense of a creature with four legs and two voices so long as, however abnormally shaped, it appears to him normally animate. When however one of the voices addresses him by name, he recoils in fear. For, as he is ignorant that any of his fellows has been washed up on the island, it seems to him that knowledge of his name can have been acquired only by an intelligence surpassing the natural. 'Mercy, mercy', he therefore cries, 'This is a devil and no monster. I will leave him, I have no long spoon' (II. ii. 100).

Stephano's reaction is to be noted, for it is the reaction of all and any characters in the play when they find themselves or believe that they find themselves in the presence of the supernatural. They acknowledge its powers: inclining themselves in reverence and humility if these appear powers for good, recoiling in fear and horror if they appear powers for evil. In the latter case the evil characters, who have set themselves up as rivals to the devil, do not recoil as far as they should; still, they do not deny the existence of the intellectual substance whom they rival. Antonio and Sebastian, when they hear a recital of the crimes they committed long ago and far away from the island, like Stephano conclude that the devil is at work. Unlike Stephano, they do not withdraw but express a wish to fight the devil. Such a wish is absurd, and the condition they seek to impose, that the fight shall be a fair one, only makes the absurdity clearer. As Gonzalo notes, Antonio and Sebastian are 'desperate'—mad, that is, with the same sort if not the same degree of madness as was Ferdinand, when he threw himself out of the ship. He was led to do so by the sight of disturbances in physical nature which seemed to him beyond the power of anything natural to produce. So too the proximate causes of madness is the appearance of Ariel as a harpy and of the 'strange shapes' which, having brought in a table with 'gentle actions and salutations', remove it 'with mocks and mows'. Like the disturbances of the storm, these shapes vanish, and the madness with them. Yet the belief remains, in virtue of which they were able to cause it. When Prospero, somewhat later in the play, hints that, if he wished, he might recite crimes not yet committed but only plotted by Antonio and Sebastian, the latter whispers to the former: 'The devil speaks in him' (V. i. 129). Thereby Prospero is for the moment disconcerted for, as we shall see later, nothing is further from his intentions than to appear as an agent of the devil.

It is as condensations of a firmly held belief in the supernatural that figures of speech such as Prospero's 'born devil', 'bastard devil' are to be explained. No notion can be admitted of explaining the belief itself as a construction upon the figures; for that would be to explain it away, and in consequence the figures would lose much, if not indeed the whole of their force. If Prospero did not believe in the devil's existence, a form of words such as 'born devil', which would then be an empty form, would provide no relief for feelings as vehement as those which he nourishes towards Caliban. Even trivial expressions such as Trinculo's 'The devil take your finger', or Stephano's 'Where the devil should he learn our language?' (II. ii. 68) should not be assumed to coincide with apparently similar expressions on the lips of an unbeliever. For they are different in form, if not in the words out of which they are put together: they are animated by a belief, however sluggishly, at the moment, such a belief may be functioning.

That there can be such moments is proof, paradoxical perhaps but palmary, that the belief is capable of functioning with force. Those who are aware of the supernatural as existing about them everywhere and at all times are under what seems to them the necessity of referring frequently to it. Should time or energy be lacking to do so with a proper formality, they make the reference in a summary way. In consequence they may appear to others, or even to themselves, to treat the supernatural with an undue familiarity: in their eyes, familiarity is not such an offence as neglect would be. For neglect may lead to a weakening of belief, and perhaps to its disappearance. The principle does not need to be argued, perhaps indeed it hardly needs to be stated: for its workings are observable in everyday life. From the conversation of those whose belief in God and the devil is but faint, these names are banished as indecencies; in the conversation of those with a lively faith, on the other hand, God and the whole heavenly hierarchy are liable to be invoked on what might seem indecent occasions.

The principle should be borne in mind when considering the meaning to be attached to such exclamations as Miranda's 'O heavens!' or 'Heaven thank you for it!' It may seem of little importance that these should be dismissed as tricks of speech or empty verbal forms: the critic who allows himself to do so may however find himself similarly dismissing Gonzalo's 'Good angels preserve the king!' (II. i. 304) or the king's own 'Give us kind keepers, Heavens!'—and that is not quite so obviously of little importance. On the other hand, the importance would seem quite sufficiently obvious of allowing a measure of force to Prospero's asseverations that he and Miranda were guided to the island 'by Providence divine', or that, during the voyage thither, she was

> Infused with a fortitude from Heaven,   (I. ii. 153)

the sight of which roused in him

> An undergoing stomach, to bear up
> Against what should ensue.

Most obviously, it would seem most important of all to acknowledge that when Prospero, observing the promise of marriage passed between Ferdinand and Miranda but himself unobserved, uses the words:

> Heavens rain grace
> On that which breeds between them!   (III. i. 75)

—that then he is uttering, not a mere wish or a hope, but a prayer; that when, bestowing Miranda upon Ferdinand, he calls out

> afore Heaven
> I ratify this my rich gift!   (IV. i. 7)

he is not merely protesting the sincerity of his intentions, but taking an oath to that effect; and that when he insists Ferdinand shall not untie Miranda's virgin-knot before

> All sanctimonious ceremonies may
> With full and holy rite be ministered,

he is moved by an anxiety, not merely that human convention shall not be slighted, but that supernatural ordinance shall be obeyed. For if it is not obeyed, supernatural sanction will follow. As Prospero himself says: should Ferdinand defy the warning which is being delivered to him, then

> No sweet aspersion shall the Heavens let fall
> To make this contract grow.

I imagine that no critics would dismiss the appeal to Heaven in this last line as a form of words which is wholly empty; but no critic, I also imagine, can appreciate the force which fills it unless he allows that all the lines quoted in this paragraph are equally full. Yet if he does not, neither does he appreciate the play, one of the central themes of which is Prospero's manner of securing his daughter's happiness. Since that happiness is earthly, it can never be rendered absolutely secure; Prospero however must be understood as rendering it as secure as he thinks he can. According to his ideas, things earthly are secure when set in the supernatural which, in so far as they are good, will protect them; in so far as they are evil will, by its sanctions, procure either their correction or their destruction.

And once it is recognized that the characters in the play conceive of themselves as surrounded at all times and in all places by a supernatural which they must either gratefully respect or desperately fear: then and then only, it seems to me, does another important truth about the play become apparent. This is the truth that Prospero's spirits have nothing to do with the supernatural at all. They are no more supernatural than is Caliban: or rather, they are less so. For if and in so far as he is a human creature, he can enter into relations with the supernatural; whereas the spirits cannot even do that. The proof is that no one in the play regards the spirits as in themselves objects of either respect or fear. At least, no one does so in so far as he does not mistake the spirits for angels or devils, for the supernatural or intellectual substances, that is, which they are not. The newcomers to the island are of course particularly liable to such a mistake, and as we shall see, Prospero encourages them in the making of it; the old established residents of the island on the other hand hardly allow themselves to be aware of the spirits. For these are too insignificant to be worth notice. Caliban for example treats them with the indifference, if also with the tolerance, with which he would treat a band of his own brothers. Of himself, he says,

> they'll nor pinch,
> Fright me with urchin-shows, pitch me i'th'mire,
> Nor lead me, like a firebrand, in the dark
> Out of my way.
>
> (II. ii. 4)

Unfortunately, Prospero employs the spirits as his tormentors, and so by association they become objects of fear to Caliban. That is the reason why, having mistaken Trinculo for a spirit, he throws himself flat upon the ground, and before being touched, perhaps even before being observed, he moans out: 'Do not torment me, O!' His fear is abject, like that of a nervous patient at the dentist's. But it is a fear that the spirits inspire only accidentally and not by their nature; so that, however abject, it can occasionally be laid by. To music that the spirits play, Caliban can listen more than contentedly. When towards the end of *The Tempest* he has his first sight of the courtiers of Naples and Milan, he mistakes them, as he did Trinculo, for spirits: nevertheless, he can spare a moment for their fine clothes. 'O Setebos, these be brave spirits indeed' (V. i. 262), he exclaims. But fine clothes do not soothe him as music can, and so the fear of punishment returns.

The only reference to spirits made by a second old-established resident, Miranda, would seem indifferent to the point of contempt. When Ferdinand is for the first time exhibited before her, 'Believe me, sir', she acknowledges to her father, 'it carries a brave form. But 'tis a spirit', she adds, with the implication that it can be of no possible concern. (I. ii. 415).

Of all the islanders, it is of course Prospero who has most dealings with the spirits. And certainly, he is not to be described as indifferent to them. His dealings are however not only so numerous but so varied that they must be left for a later discussion. At the moment, we may content ourselves with noting that he exploits the airy quickness of Ariel with as little compunction as he does the earthy slowness of Caliban; and that if from time to time he allows himself to express satisfaction with Ariel's services, or amusement at his tricks—'that's my dainty Ariel'— nevertheless he does not hesitate, when occasion seems to him to call for it, to abuse Ariel as 'malignant'.

Two speeches of length, and of an importance equal to their length, are I am aware often quoted as proving either that the spirits are supernatural, or that in some way or other they are related to the latter. These are the speech of denunciation delivered by Ariel as a harpy, and that of farewell addressed by Prospero to the elves. Neither however is easy to interpret, nor are we as yet fully prepared to do so. Therefore I must pass them by, confirming my attention to whatever other evidence seems to point to the same conclusion. It is neither plentiful nor impressive.

First perhaps should be taken Caliban's claim that his master's art is of such power.

> It would control my dam's god Setebos. (I. ii. 374)

As this art finds its chief or perhaps sole ministers in the spirits, here it might be thought we have an instance of the spirits entering not only into relations but into relations of superiority with the supernatural. The divine status of Setebos is however by no means clear. It may be worth noticing that, according to Pigafetta (from whom, through Eden's translation, Shakespeare took the name) he is provided with two horns to his head, hair down to his feet, and the power to cast our fire both before and behind. It is moreover his habit to shake until they burst the bodies of those who make the sign of the cross in his presence. Shakespeare gives no hint that, though encountered in Patagonia, he is possessed of such familiar attributes. It may therefore be Shakespeare's intention that, unlike other pagan gods, Setebos should not be considered as entering into the Christian pandemonium. Perhaps rather he is the sort of god which Caliban, for a passing moment, offers to make of Stephano: a living god, a human idol. In that case, any power which the spirits might exercise over him presents a problem no different from that presented by the power which they actually exercise over Stephano. Or again, Setebos may be of the same nature as the spirits themselves. In any case, he is too obscure to shed light on that nature, or on anything.

Further pieces of evidence might seem to be supplied by Ferdinand. After listening to Ariel's first ditty, he concludes:

> This is no mortal business, nor no sound
> That the earth owes.   (I. ii. 411)

And if earth does not own it then, it would appear, either Heaven or Hell must do so. Ferdinand however is repeating the mistake which we have already observed Trinculo to make on one occasion, and on another Antonio and Sebastian. 'The ditty does remember my drown'd father': unaware of the presence on the island of anyone with a perfectly natural knowledge of that father, Ferdinand falsely attributes a supernatural intelligence to the singer.

Of the salutation with which he greets Miranda:

> Most sure, the goddess
> On whom these airs attend—   (ibid. 427)

it is I fear at last possible, and perhaps it is necessary to complain of as a trick of speech, and an empty verbal form. Among the other advantages of his rank, Ferdinand has enjoyed a classical education, and this encourages the habit, as it confers the power, of elaborately saying little or nothing. *O dea certe* the address of Aeneas to Venus was the more irresponsibly copied, as no responsibility was felt towards the godhead of Venus. Nor does Alonso feel any such responsibility when, as in courtesy bound, he repeats his son's salutation towards the end of the play. Ferdinand has no need to assure him that Miranda is mortal; nor would it occur to Ferdinand to do so, were it not for the antithesis with 'immortal' which he intends in the following line.

The last scraps of possible evidence which occur to me are one or two utterances of Miranda's. But almost before examination they reveal themselves as no evidence at all. When for example she says of Ferdinand:

> There's nothing ill can dwell in such a temple.
> If the ill spirits have so fair a house
> Good things will strive to dwell with it,   (I. ii. 462)

she is using the term spirit, not in what might be called the technical sense peculiar to this play, but in a sense more widely familiar. Christian teaching is in her mind and in particular, I imagine, the parable of the room swept and garnished. Nor when she calls Ferdinand 'a thing divine' is she contrasting him with spirits such as Prospero's, for not even the relation of contrast is possible between these and divinity. As has been pointed out, if Ferdinand were a spirit, he could not be a subject for her concern. He has become very much a subject of that kind; and therefore she contrasts him—her own words make it clear—with all other natural things that are known to her.

Provisionally then I conclude that the spirits have nothing to do with the supernatural. The question rises, with what have they to do? and what are they?

It is a question of extreme difficulty. Usually two answers seem open to the critic, when called upon to specify the dwelling-place or exercising-ground of beings who appear properly to belong neither to earth, Heaven or Hell. He can lodge them in, so to speak, the interstices of the earth; the gaps which, however narrowly, none the less effectively separate one natural kind from another. There Caliban dwells, in so far as he is a monster and not human; there too I suppose dwell the witches of *Macbeth,* in so far as not merely human instruments of the devil. But however important the part assigned to the witches, it is a strictly limited one: confined to the emission of alluring if alarming howls, and to an emission so occasional that no one is much troubled to know exactly whence it proceeds. As for Caliban, he is sufficiently inert to be content with an interstice. But it is impossible for the spirits to be so: they themselves, and not merely their voices, rise and shoot through earth, air and sea, and they do so at all times. ⟨. . .⟩

VIII. Prospero and Caliban

Unlike Ferdinand, Caliban has no need to complain of Prospero's behaviour as 'crabb'd and . . . compos'd of harshness'. The reader observes the fact for himself. No other character but Prospero thinks fit to heap upon Caliban, however villainous or ludicrous in appearance, the burthen of a diabolical ancestry. Even the brutish Stephano occasionally lets fall words of kindness; not so Prospero—or not, at any rate, until the very last scene. And even then, the kindness seems grudgingly measured. To would-be traitors and parricides Prospero grants an immediate remission of guilt; the would-be murderer Caliban must be content, not only with a remission of punishment, but with such a remission in prospect.

Yet by contrast with previous severity, the slightest act of mercy on Prospero's part is such as to startle. Reasons are felt to be required for it; and it is perhaps hardly cynical to suggest that one lies closely to hand. This is the vanishing of an object of dispute between Prospero and Caliban. A few minutes before the latter's entry upon the stage, Prospero has been restored to the sovereignty of Milan. Henceforward the sovereignty of the island is of no interest to him.

In one of his first utterances, Caliban claims that sovereignty for himself, and accuses Prospero of usurpation:

This island's mine, by Sycorax my mother,
Which thou tak'st from me.   (I. ii. 332)

More than once he repeats the claim and the accusation to Stephano:

As I told thee before I am subject to a tyrant,
A sorcerer, that by his cunning hath
Cheated me of the island.   (III. ii. 42)

and again,

> I say by sorcery he got this isle,
> From me he got it.   (ibid. 52)

So strongly convinced is Caliban of the justice of his claim, so deeply wounded therefore at its being ignored, that he develops a litigious fever or madness: in order that the claim may be vindicated, he is willing to forgo all advantages that might result from it. He will make the island over to Stephano, constituting him lord by cession, if only Stephano will undertake that Prospero, who detains the lordship by force, shall be duly punished.

On his side, Prospero gives no sign—at any rate, no immediately legible sign—of being conscious that he deserves punishment. To Ferdinand he presents himself as, without qualification, the lord of the island; to Alonso, he asserts that he was landed there to be the lord—and he regards the landing, it should be remembered, as a directly providential act.

In the pamphlets about Virginia, to which reference has already been made, the sovereignty of newly discovered lands was a topic frequently and laboriously treated of. The critics of colonial enterprise suggested that the English were acting unjustly in intruding themselves into Virginia: for the title to the country, they held, vested not in the English but in the Spaniards; or if not in the Spaniards, then in the native inhabitants.

In so far as the Spanish title reposed, not upon effective settlement, but upon the Bull of 1493, the apologists for the enterprise made, or thought they made, short work of it. Christ's kingdom is not of this world, and therefore the Vicar of Christ—supposing for the moment the Pope to be such—has no authority to give this world's kingdoms away. Nor is the Pope, on the ground that the native inhabitants are idolaters, able to dispossess them in favour of the Spaniards or of anybody. For in the Old Testament we do not see Israel or Judah attacking neighbouring tribes merely on such a ground; nor do Israelitish or Jewish kings, when they themselves fall into idolatry, thereby forfeit their dominion. Gleefully the English Protestants quoted Catholic theologians, such as Vitoria and Cajetan, who had advanced similar views.

However, the main purpose of these Protestants was to justify, not so much the expulsion of the Spanish from the Indies, as the entrance thither of the English. And the more energetically they proclaimed native rights as demanding the former, the more peremptorily did these same rights forbid the latter. In the face of this unsurmountable obstacle, different controversialists adopted different tactics.

William Strachey, for example—of whose *True Reportory* we have already made extensive use—seems to have cultivated a religious rapture such as might, in his own eyes at any rate, raise him above the obstacle and float him over it. In the *History of Travel into Virginia*, which he began about 1612—and which cannot therefore have had any influence on *The Tempest*; but which I quote as an illustration, and possibly an unusually clear illustration, of a temper of the times—he proclaims as 'the . . . only end intended by His Majesty, by the honourable Council for the business, by the Lord General, Lieutenant General, Marshal, and such-like eminent officers . . . together with the general adventurers', not 'common trade and the hope of profit', but 'with all carefulness principally to endeavour the conversion of the natives to the knowledge and worship of the true God and world's Redeemer Christ Jesus'. And if, alongside this 'only end', common trade and the hope of profit happen to be pursued, that he explains is but a consequence of the adventurers' philanthropy. For trade into all parts of the world is the natural right of man, so that, by seeking to prevent it, the natives reveal their ignorance of the 'graces . . . and particularities of humanity'. Their need of enlightenment on political and social matters is, in short, as great as their need of religious enlightenment. The adventurers regard it as their inescapable duty to confer both: 'to exalt privation', says Strachey, adopting a metaphor from alchemy, 'to the highest point of perfection', to transform the crude earth of the natives into the purest gold. And therefore the cause of the Virginia expedition is not only a 'holy cause', but one of 'the most sacred' to which a man can put his hands. Nor has any man done so, except moved by 'pity and religious compassion'; 'our charity suffereth' for the natives, says Strachey, 'until we have derived unto them the true knowledge indeed'. And on this topic he rises to a pitch of eloquence so high as to halt the reader, who is at a loss to know whether to admire his skill, to pity his folly or to reprobate his blasphemy. Our enterprise in Virginia, Strachey claims, is 'the raising and building up of a Sanctum Sanctorum, a holy house and a sanctuary to His Blessed Name amongst infidels; placing them therein on whom it hath now pleased Him both to be sufficiently revenged for their forefathers' ingratitude and treasons, and to descend in mercy to lighten them that sit in darkness, and to direct their feet in the way of peace'.

The author of the *True Declaration*, as the official apologist of the Virginia Council, addresses himself to a wider and a partly sceptical audience. On that account he thinks it prudent to strike a quieter note. The preaching of the Gospel, he explains, might be accomplished in any one of three ways. But of these, the apostolical is no longer to be thought of, since with the ceasing of the gift of tongues and of that of miracles, the divine commission of the apostles has been withdrawn. The second way is imperial, as 'when a prince conquers bodies, that the preachers may feed their souls'. According to the author, this 'may be a matter sacred in the preachers, but I know not how justifiable in the rulers, who for their more ambition do set upon it the gloss of religion. Let the divines of Salamanca discuss the question', he concludes, levelling a usual English reproach against the Spaniards, but doing so with rather more than the usual skill. There remains the third way of 'merchandizing and trade', whereby the natives are brought into a 'daily conversation' with Christians. This is the way reserved for the English. Trade in general is lawful—how otherwise should it have been permitted to Solomon?—English trade to Virginia particularly so, and for a number of reasons. Chief amongst these is the fact that one of the Virginian kings 'sold unto us for copper, land to inherit and inhabit'. By argumentation of this kind, the author of the *True Declaration* seeks to convince the cooler-headed amongst his readers. The warmer-hearted he condescends to rouse by stressing the miraculous rescue of the company on board the *Sea Adventure*. As 'God commanded Elias to flee to the brook Cedron, and there fed him by ravens: so God provided for our disconsolate people on the island in the midst of the sea by fowls—but with an admirable difference. Unto Elias the ravens brought meat, unto our men the fowls brought themselves for meat: for when they whistled . . . the fowls would come and sit on their shoulders, they would suffer themselves to be taken and weighed by our men, who would make choice of the fattest and fairest.' After so affecting a mark of divine favour, who can doubt of the future of Virginia? The *True Declaration* ends with an eloquence drawing its warmth from the same source as Strachey's, but which the author, in view of the diversity of his audience, sees fit to temper with a classic frigidity. Thus he achieves a language at once enthusiastic and decent: 'O all ye worthies, follow the ever-sounding trumpet of a blessed honour—let religion be the first aim of your hopes, *et caetera adjicientur*. . . . The same God that hath joined three kingdoms under one Caesar, will not be wanting to add a fourth . . . Doubt yet not but that God hath determined and demonstrated (by the wondrous preservation of those principal persons which fell upon the Bermudas) that he will raise our state, and build his church in that excellent climate, if the action be seconded with resolution and religion. *Nil desperandum Christo Duce et auspice Christo.*'

All this rhetoric is very fine, and that of the *True Declaration* at least very clever: its main purpose however is but to hide the fact that, at the end, the English find themselves in a similar position to those Spaniards from whom, at the beginning, it was their boasted intention to differ. Like the Spaniards, they allow native rights to be overwhelmed by supposedly conflicting rights of the Gospel. If indeed the Spaniards do so: for in one respect these have an advantage over the English. They are commissioned by two masters or, in so far as they are traders, by three: as preachers by the Pope, as conquerors by the King, and each of them as a trader by his private interest. Any conflict between their preaching, conquering and trading may be referred to an easily conceivable conflict between these authorities, existing independently of themselves. But the Englishman claims to be commissioned by his conscience, and so faces the difficult if not repulsive task of identifying his preaching with his trade. And if conquering prove unavoidable, what then? As Strachey foresees that it might, for he considers the possibility of the Virginian natives failing to appreciate the 'graces . . . and particularities of humanity' which he says trade implies; as the author of the *True Declaration* foresees that it will, for he has no hope of the land bought 'for copper' sufficing for the needs of the colonists. Thereby he abandons the one controversial advantage possibly possessed by the English, and these, he allows, must set about that 'conquering of bodies' which he defied the divines of Salamanca to justify. True, he says that the Virginians will have been the first to engage upon hostilities. But the Spaniards said that also; and when touching upon this topic, the *True Declaration* sounds such a note as might have been sounded by the Spanish conqueror at his reputed worst. The natives, he says, are 'human beasts', in whose fidelity there can be no trust 'except a man will make a league with lions, bears and crocodiles'. The same note had already been sounded by Strachey in the *True Reportory*, towards the end of which he found himself compelled to regret that 'fair and noble intreaty' proved of no beneficial effect upon the Virginians. Rather, it encouraged them in 'the practices of villainy', and so had to be replaced by a 'violent proceeding'. To the stay-at-home Purchas it appeared that this violent proceeding should have been taken from the first; for in printing the *True Reportory* in 1625, he added to the phrase 'fair and noble intreaty' a marginal observation. '*Ad Graecas Calendas!*' he exclaimed, 'can a leopard change his spots?' And so native rights become so entirely overwhelmed as to be forgotten; from the rank of men the natives sank down to that of beasts, incapable of any rights whatever.

It is I think impossible to read the pieces in this debate without being reminded of this phrase which we found in the *True Reportory* on our first dealings with it: 'hoodwinked men'. Only, the participants in the debate are hoodwinked, not as Strachey described the company on board the *Sea Adventure*, but as I suggested the characters in *The Tempest* would prove to be. They are hoodwinked without knowing it, so that it is impossible they should have patience under the disability. Rather than waiting until they shall see, they must immediately make use of their blindness as a seeing. The use they make of it is of an appropriately fantastic kind. Ignorant of their own motives, they miscall both these motives, the actions which result therefrom, and the objects upon which the motives are directed. They reprove the conduct of the Spaniards in the Indies, and at the same time imitate that conduct. Filled with a Christian charity towards the natives, at a slight provocation they overflow with a diabolic hate. Aspiring to exalt the crude earth of the natives to the purest gold, they are ready to stamp it beneath their feet and to scatter it to the winds. Like hoodwinked men they keep on no steady course, but lurch from one side to the other of the path in which it never occurs to them to halt, because they have no notion of being unable to walk down it.

In his dealings with Caliban, at any rate, Prospero appears as a hoodwinked man of this kind. To his making there has gone a part, indeed I think quite a considerable part, both of the Virginia controversialists and of the adventurers into Virginia: some of the former Shakespeare read, with some of the latter he conversed, for they were his friends.

Prospero is fully convinced of his charity towards Caliban. He has 'humanly taken' pains on Caliban's behalf:

> I have us'd thee
> ... with humane care, and lodg'd thee
> In mine own cell.   (I. ii. 346)

Or again:

> I pitied thee,
> Took pains to make thee speak, taught thee each hour
> One thing or other.[3]   (ibid. 354)

If this charity has not produced the effect which, according to supernatural authority, it cannot fail to produce, the fault is not Prospero's, but Caliban's entirely. For
neither of them is life made the sweeter because, says Prospero, Caliban's 'vile race
... had that in't which good natures could not abide to be with'. That a liability to
lust cannot be considered so intolerable a companion has already been suggested,
on the ground that Prospero shows himself tolerant of the same liability in Ferdinand. But now perhaps it is apparent that the suggestion is more deeply and widely
based: neither Caliban's nature nor anyone's can contain anything capable of giving
supernatural authority the lie. What Caliban's nature does contain is something
capable of hiding Prospero's own nature from himself. He believes his charity to be
perfect, when in fact it is otherwise. This something is, in all likelihood, a title to
sovereignty. In its turn, Prospero's imperfect charity blinds him to the existence of
the title: for it allows him to describe Caliban as not a man but a beast, or if not a
beast, then something worse, 'a devil, a born devil'—something at any rate in which
no title can vest. And so Prospero makes a lurch to the opposite side of the path
which he is treading: for as a devil or a beast, Caliban is no more a fitting object of
charity than he is a fitting sovereign, nor would Prospero ever dream of lodging him
in the same cell with Miranda. The hoodwinking continues yet a stage further, as
Prospero convinces himself that he is not only charitable but just. Caliban, he
maintains, is 'deservedly' confined to the rock and kept from the rest of the island,
although if a devil or a beast, it is impossible for him to have deserts. Since human
justice recognizes no rights in such beings, neither does it subject them to penalties:
and Prospero has once more lurched across his own path.

    Whether or not the inconsistencies of his conduct are to be explained only by
a hoodwinking of this kind, they are in fact explicable if it has taken or is taking place.
And perhaps in one passage of the play we can see it doing so. The complexity of
the passage caused the New Cambridge editors to suspect it of being 'patchwork';
rather perhaps that very quality goes to prove its integrity. The passage occurs in
the first dialogue between Prospero and Ariel, and runs as follows:

> PROSPERO: ... then was this island—
> Save for the son that she did litter here,
> A freckled whelp hag-born—not honour'd with
> A human shape.
> ARIEL: Yes, Caliban, her son.
> PROSPERO: Dull thing, I say so.   (I. ii. 281)

'Ariel', say the editors, 'who cleaves to Prospero's very thoughts (IV. i. 165) is
extraordinarily obtuse here.' Or he may, I would suggest, be cleaving more closely
to these thoughts than Prospero finds comfortable. Scrupulous to do nothing less,
if nothing more than justice, Prospero has constructed such a sentence that, if its
parts are taken in the proper order, it concedes humanity to Caliban. 'Then there
were no humans save Caliban on the island.' But Prospero has filled the sentence
with words suggesting that, if a man, Caliban is at the same time a beast. He is not
only a son, but a whelp; if he was born, he was hag-born; in any case, he was not

only born, but littered. Nor is it easy to grasp the proper order of the parts. A long parenthesis separates subject from verb and, dwarfing the former, seems to cry for independent consideration. In that case it implies: 'Nothing that I say can of course have reference to Caliban'. Or if independent consideration is refused, the first word of the parenthesis can only with difficulty be made to depend, as it should, on the last word of the succeeding phrase ('no human shape save Caliban's'), the first word of the phrase temptingly offers itself as dependent on the last of the parenthesis ('hag-born, not honoured with human shape'). And so suggestion pours in from many points upon the reader—from yet more, perhaps, upon the hearer—that Caliban is not a man at all; that those very qualities about him which might make him seem so, emphasize only the more heavily the fact that he is not; that is, with one part of his mind, Prospero is anxious to preserve an appearance of justice, with a larger and a stronger part he is convinced that the appearance is contradictory of the substance. And so he comes near to refusing justice openly. Seeing his master on the verge of an indiscretion, Ariel ventures to correct him. Nothing is more irritating than that thoughts we have been at pains to hide should be exposed, not so much to the sight of others, as to our own. Prospero relieves the irritation with the adjective 'dull': in itself, as the New Cambridge editors are right in noting, a surprising adjective to be applied to Ariel; in the context however perhaps not so surprising, and in any case hardly more so than the adjective 'malignant', which Prospero has similarly applied a few lines earlier.

The reader may have noticed, and if so he will have been amused—indeed, he may have amused himself in this way a number of times before—that, while berating Prospero for presuming to spy into the conscience of other people, I do not appear to have the slightest hesitation in spying into his own. In so far as this difficulty is raised by the whole of my essay, it will be proper to consider it when that whole comes up for review, that is, in the concluding section. With regard to the particular instance of the difficulty now before us, I would plead that I have been arguing from a premiss adopted by the Virginia pamphleteers against the Spaniards and, in so far as Prospero has elements in common with the pamphleteers, shared in by himself. The premiss is that the natives have rights. If the pamphleteers and Prospero, setting out from a premiss of kind, succeed in persuading themselves of an opposite conclusion—if the end of their reflection, like Gonzalo's commonwealth, forgets it beginning—then they invite speculation about their interior. Indeed they demand it, if they are to continue being treated as rational beings and not mere gabblers of the kind to which Prospero, in one of his outbursts against Caliban, would assign the latter. If on the other hand, the premiss may be denied, not shamefacedly and perhaps unconsciously at the end of an argument, but deliberately and boldly at its beginning, speculation such as I have indulged in would be superfluous and therefore impertinent. The consequences of such a denial are both alarming and far-reaching; nevertheless the pamphleteers did not always refrain from it, nor are signs lacking that Shakespeare intended Prospero to be understood as not doing so.

My quotation from Purchas, a few paragraphs ago, was incomplete. In full, the marginal observation which he attached to *True Reportory* runs as follows: '*Ad Calendas Graecas!*' he cries, 'Can a leopard change his spots? Can a savage remaining a savage be civil? Were we not ourselves made and not born civil in our progenitors' days? and were not Caesar's Britons as brutish as the Virginians? The Roman swords were the best teachers of civility to this and other countries near us.' A similar historical reminiscence is made by Strachey himself in his *History of Travel*, when concerned to deny that such violence towards the Virginians as colonization may involve is properly to be considered as an injury to them. 'Had not this violence and this injury been offered unto us by the Romans', he writes, '. . . we might yet have lived overgrown satyrs, rude and untutored, wandering in the woods, dwelling in caves, and hunting for our dinners as the wild beasts in the forests for their prey, prostituting our daughters to strangers, sacrificing our children to idols.' The far-reaching consequences of the denial are perhaps apparent: not only the human individual, but whole groups of humans, such as tribes and nations, are it would seem to be considered as passing through a period of nonage. And during that period they are, like the minor under Roman law, to be exposed to whatever suffering an adult, or at any rate an authorized adult, thinks fit, for their own good or upon any other pretext, to inflict upon them. That the consequences are alarming is equally clear. The human individual defines himself, but who is to define a tribe or a nation? and until that is done, how is its nonage to be limited? To Purchas it might seem obvious that, compared with the Virginians, the English were adult; to a Spaniard, comparing the spacious decency of the Escorial with the crowded squalor of Whitehall, the massive unity of Salamancan theology with the fractious fragments produced at Oxford and Cambridge, the English might seem no less obviously minors. And had the Spaniards succeeded in obtaining a hold on England, they would have lost no time in exposing Oxford and Cambridge theologians to such sufferings as the Inquisition thought they not so much deserved as needed. Yet again, the readiness of the Spaniards to have recourse to an Inquisition might cause them to appear in other nations' eyes less adult than they seemed in their own. By the initial denial of native rights, in short, the chances of a man's being hoodwinked are very greatly increased, increased perhaps even to infinity: for the sole cause of hoodwinking is no longer a blurring of man's sights, on particular occasions or when face to face with a particular object or group of objects; it is also the blurring of what on all occasions is the principal object of his sight, humanity itself. At any time and place, humanity may not as yet have attained to the perfection of existence, may still remain involved in the imperfection of becoming. And though this imperfection may be a falling short of, rather than a deviation from, the proper end of humanity, as imperfect that latter resembles Caliban. It both is and is not, it drags him who observes it in two different directions, it puts on, like Caliban, nightmarish qualities.

And yet, as I said, there are indications that Shakespeare intended Prospero to be understood as making the denial. For not only does the portrait he draws of Caliban closely resemble Strachey's nightmare portrait of our British ancestors—if allowed no daughters to prostitute, no children to sacrifice, Caliban is very much an 'overgrown satyr'; he seeks his dinner in the woods, at least in so far as it consists of pig-nuts, filberts and 'scamels'; he is endowed with a full measure of crocodile cunning and bear-like savagery—not only does Shakespeare draw this portrait, he allows short shrift to those who assert the impossibility of denying rights to any tribe or nation. Or rather, he allows them no shrift at all, but goes out of his way to consign them mercilessly to the hell which gapes for fools.

In Shakespeare's day, the most notorious example of such an assertion was to be found in Montaigne's essay 'On the Cannibals'. The mere title of this essay guarantees its relevance to *The Tempest,* since 'cannibal' and 'Caliban' are in all probability phonetic variants of the same name. Another such variant is 'Caribal' or 'Carib', under which form the name has been assigned by history to that American tribe or nation which offered most effective resistance to European colonizers. Other tribes might flee before the Spaniards or, if they resisted, might be defeated after a struggle lasting days, weeks, months or possibly years; but defeated they would be, and henceforward serve the conquerors. Not so the Caribs, who preferred death to defeat; and who, should they be captured alive, employed every device of savagery and cunning either to make their escape or to render their service valueless. They refused to be Europeanized, and so came to symbolize the colonizing problem, in so far at least as this problem depended, not on geographical but on human factors. But, according to Montaigne's essay, no such problem existed. If the Caribs or cannibals ate human flesh, he maintained, they ate only a very little of it; nor did they so much eat it themselves, as send round the choicer morsels as presents among their friends. And if they executed with a fearsome cruelty their captive enemies, this was no more than they themselves were willing to undergo, should they have the misfortune to be captured. While waiting for the torment, they uplifted both themselves and all who were near them by the songs which they sang. Such songs could not fail of an uplifting effect, since the Carib language employs grammatical terminations similar to those of the Greek. No wife among the Caribs is jealous, no war-lord is ambitious, no member of the nation indeed, of whatever quality, is avid of anything but honour. Yet not even honour leads to strife: 'the very words that import lying, falsehood, treason, dissimulations, covetousness, envy, detraction and pardon, were never heard of amongst them'. In view of all these excellencies, the trouble which the Spaniards were giving themselves to civilize the Caribs could proceed only from a singularly narrow notion of civilization. Undoubtedly, the Spaniards allowed themselves to be unduly impressed by the fact that the Caribs wore no breeches.

Of this rhapsody, Shakespeare shows his opinion by copying out its essential part with hardly more alterations than are required by the metre. Then, not content with entrusting its defence to the fatuous Gonzalo, he permits the worthless Antonio and Sebastian to refute it. That their worthlessness cannot infect and so discredit their refutation, but must rather throw its soundness into relief, is proved by its destiny in the minds and on the lips of generations of Shakespeare readers. They have made it as universally current as is the speech of Prospero's with a consideration of which the present essay began. 'The latter end of his commonwealth forgets the beginning', says Antonio of Gonzalo: and so it must, since the Caribs as Montaigne imagines them dwell in an earthly paradise, and earth in its present state is what paradise has rejected. On such an earth, men's only way of fitting themselves for paradise is to work; which if they neglect, then as Antonio once more observes, they are 'whores and knaves'. Of the soundness of this second part—or corollary—of his refutation, Montaigne's essays themselves would seem to supply a sufficient proof. For written in a library that their [? author] had sought to make as much of an earthly paradise as possible, in large part they record the whoring and the knavery of a mind. But there is no need to go outside *The Tempest* itself for proof. Stephano and Trinculo go whoring after Ariel's music and come to grief. Ferdinand allows his fancy to go whoring after an endless succession of masques to entertain him, and has his entertainment immediately cut short.

Perhaps then Prospero may not be hookwinked about Caliban, the inconsistencies of his conduct towards whom may be evidence rather of an open-eyedness.

NOTES

[1] From here onwards I have followed a single unemended and almost uncorrected typescript. (Edward M. Wilson.)

[2] This speech is attributed to Miranda in the Folio and in New Cambridge Shakespeare. (E. M. W.)

[3] This is taken from the speech attributed to Miranda in the Folio and in the New Cambridge Shakespeare. (E. M. W.)

Jacqueline E. M. Latham

THE TEMPEST AND KING JAMES'S *DAEMONOLOGIE*

The Tempest offers a twentieth-century audience more problems for a full understanding than most of Shakespeare's plays, and these problems are the more insidious because action, language and characters seem transparently clear. Yet the play is highly intellectual and despite the work of scholars who have explored many of the ideas raised by the varied but scant sources there remain elements that still seem to fit uneasily, and one character, Caliban, who eludes even the simplest definition. This essay seeks to develop two aspects of contemporary thought by means of which Caliban can be seen not more clearly but in even greater complexity, and it proposes King James's *Daemonologie* as a possible source for these ideas. Contemporary beliefs about devils could, of course, be found elsewhere, but James's relationship to Shakespeare as patron of the King's Men, the clarity and dialectical skill of his *Daemonologie* as well as its content make the King's famous work a likely source for some of the ideas of Shakespeare's strange play.

The problem of Caliban's birth, while receiving little attention on its own account, crops up from time to time in more general discussions of *The Tempest*. Unfortunately, though many critics agree that Caliban is the touchstone by which the civilised world is judged, his actual status—human, sub-human or demi-devil—is rarely subjected to close examination, and critics tend to take the view which suits their particular interpretation of the play. To cite an obvious example, Professor Kermode, in his brilliant Arden Introduction, places the 'salvage and deformed slave' within the tradition of the European savage man, and in a note added when this edition was in proof, draws attention to *Wild Men in the Middle Ages* by R. Bernheimer, whose views, incidentally, are far more complex than Kermode's brief summary allows.[1] In the same way, Caliban can be seen in the context of the exploration of the New World, corrupted by a supposed civilisation or corrupting the civilised. These are two important dimensions within which Caliban can fruitfully be viewed, but there are others, like the problem of his birth.

For Kermode, 'Caliban's birth, as Prospero insists, was inhuman; he was "a

From *Shakespeare Survey* 28 (1975): 117–23.

born devil", "got by the devil himself upon thy wicked dam". He was the product of sexual union between a witch and an incubus, and this would account for his deformity, whether the devil-lover was Setebos (all pagan gods were classified as devils) or, as W. C. Curry infers, some aquatic demon'.[2] Yet, even in this simple account of Caliban's origin there lurk ambiguities, as I intend to show.

In what would appear to be a key study, 'The Magic of Prospero', C. J. Sisson merely remarks in passing that 'the powers of Sycorax derived from evil communion with the devil, the father of her son Caliban',[3] thus distinguishing the source of her powers from those of Prospero. More recently, Robert Egan in his interesting article 'This Rough Magic: Perspectives of Art and Morality in *The Tempest*' comments, 'Caliban is not a devil—thoroughly evil and unredeemable—but a type of humanity' and in a footnote on the same page adds that Caliban, who makes frequent references to his mother and her god, never mentions an infernal father,[4] apparently missing the point that Setebos is probably his father, in the tradition that false gods are to be identified with devils. Yet Egan is surely correct in his insistence that Caliban's 'qualities as a character are clearly not satanic but human'. There is, then, an apparent contradiction: the text proclaims (and critics sometimes accept) the demonic origin of Caliban: 'A devil, a born devil', cries Prospero (IV, i, 188); yet if we wish to see Caliban as the touchstone of the civilised (or semi-civilised) world, we need to see him in relation to the world of nature or in some definable sense outside it—not, of course, in the world of art but, perhaps, as a symbolic figure, as Bernheimer's book would suggest, representing social, psychological and sexual aspects of man. Alternatively he can be seen as an intermediate link in the chain of being, below man but higher than the animals.

An examination of sixteenth-century views about the incubus may enable certain aspects of *The Tempest* to be seen more clearly. Although it is important to bear in mind R. H. West's wise warning in the first chapter of his study, *The Invisible World*, that 'the literature of pneumatology was rarely so cool and judicial as the ideal required', we can, I think, agree with him that there can be little doubt 'that, within degrees proper to works of art, and each in its own way, these plays [*Doctor Faustus*, *Macbeth* and *The Tempest*] and others accommodate it.'[5]

Traditions of witchcraft in England and on the Continent were very different. This is stressed by Barbara Rosen in her perceptive introduction to the collection of English texts entitled *Witchcraft* and by Keith Thomas in his widely acclaimed *Religion and the Decline of Magic*. In England trials were chiefly concerned with *maleficium*, harm to others, either their person or possessions; the familiar in the form of a domestic creature like cat, toad or fly was also a typically English manifestation. On the other hand, continental witchcraft was frequently concerned with the diabolic nature of the witches' compact and the sexual orgy of the witches' sabbath. As Barbara Rosen says, 'The English witch was frequently unchaste, but in the usual prosaic fashion'.[6] The incubus is, therefore, late in appearing in native accounts of witch trials and Keith Thomas claims that 'the more blatantly sexual aspects of witchcraft were a very uncommon feature of the trials, save perhaps in the Hopkins period', the mid-seventeenth century.[7] We have, then, an odd situation when we look at *The Tempest*. Shakespeare's island world, for all its concern with magic, is far from the witch hunts and trials of his own country. And yet, untypical as Sycorax and Caliban are of the English tradition of witchcraft, there were notorious continental studies of witchcraft (some translated into English) and other ways in which the idea of diabolic intercourse could have become familiar to an educated Elizabethan.

If we accept the likelihood that Shakespeare kept one eye on his royal master while writing *Macbeth* and *The Tempest*, then King James's *Daemonologie*, first published in Edinburgh in 1597 but reprinted in London on James's accession to the English throne, provides a helpful gloss on this aspect of *The Tempest;* it has, moreover, further aspects which suggest that Shakespeare may well have read it closely.[8]

King James was writing in a particular and personal context. *Newes from Scotland Declaring the Damnable Life and Death of Doctor Fian, a Notable Sorcerer* had been published anonymously in Scotland and London in 1591. The story of the tempest, supposedly raised by witchcraft, which sank one boat-load of jewels and provided a contrary wind for King James, though not for his accompanying vessels, is well known. But more significant is that the account of the trial of Dr Fian and the witches included torture, the devil's mark, a witches' sabbath, an obscene kiss,[9] a christened cat bound to the 'cheefest partes' (p. 16) of a dead man, and intercourse with the devil. James followed the trial closely, and when he came to write his *Daemonologie* he explicitly directed it against two sceptics: John Weyer, the German physician, whose *De Praestigiis Daemonum* (1563) remains untranslated, and Reginald Scot, the Kentish author of *The Discoverie of Witchcraft* (1584) which it is thought Shakespeare read. Scot's immensely long and overtly sceptical work serves as an advertisement of the continental views that he is refuting. His sources include Jean Bodin's untranslated *De la démonomanie des sorciers* (1580), Cornelius Agrippa and the notorious *Malleus Maleficarum* (1486?), and though his refutation of the continental writers is based on common sense and a skilful use of *reductio ad absurdum,* he betrays an almost prurient enjoyment of some of the more scabrous tales, including a detailed account, which takes up most of Book IV, of the problems of sexual relations with an incubus, whetting his readers' appetite at the end of Book III by urging those whose 'chaste eares cannot well endure to heare of such abhominable lecheries' to skip the next pages with their 'bawdie stuffe'. His major discussion in Book IV leans heavily upon J. Sprenger and H. Institor's *Malleus Maleficarum.*[10] It seems then likely that the Elizabethan and Jacobean public could derive a fairly full account of continental witchcraft practices from *Newes from Scotland* and from *The Discoverie of Witchcraft,* but even, for example, Samuel Harsnett's *A Declaration of Egregious Popish Impostures,* which Shakespeare knew well, ascribes to Bodin the belief that devils may 'transforme themselves into any shape of beasts, or similitude of men, and may [. . .] have the act of generation with women, as they please'.[11]

King James's *Daemonologie* has a remarkably balanced tone. This derives in part from its dialogue form, in which the good tunes are distributed fairly equally between the credulous Epistemon and the more sceptical Philomathes. The argument is close, clear and free from the tedious capping of scriptural quotations which makes Henry Holland's *A Treatise against Witchcraft* (Cambridge, 1590) such unrewarding reading for us. In chapter 3 of the Third Book Epistemon explains that the devil has two means of effecting the union between himself and a woman—the male authors of works on demonology are strangely reluctant to discuss the mechanics of the succubus. He can steal sperm from a man, dead or alive, and inseminate the witch, or by inhabiting a dead body he can have visible intercourse with her. In both cases the sperm is cold; hence the fact that witches so often report the coldness of union with the devil. Spirits, having no sex, can have no seed of their own; in this James is following the traditional Christian view. A child born of the union of witch and incubus is therefore human. But even the credulous Epistemon is doubtful whether this union can actually take place; this kind of devil, he says, 'was called of old' (p. 67) an incubus or succubus, and his account of the intercourse is hedged with the proviso 'might possibly be performed' (p. 67). So when the inquirer Philomathes asks 'How is it then that they say sundrie monsters have bene gotten by that way' (p. 68), Epistemon can dismiss the notion with 'These tales are nothing but *Aniles fabulae*' and go on to explain that if it were possible '(which were all utterly against all the rules of nature) it would bread no monster but onely such a naturall of-spring, as would have cummed betuixt that man or woman and that other abused person'. The devil's part is merely carrying 'And so it coulde not participate with no qualitie of the same' (p. 68).

James is surprisingly cavalier in dismissing monstrous births as old wives' tales; Shakespeare was obviously more interested in them. There had, after all, been a very long tradition of extraordinary offspring of unusual parentage: Romulus and Remus and Augustus Caesar were, presumably, a tribute to their unusual fathers. In *Mandeville's Travels* the 'fendes of Helle camen many tymes and leyen with the wommen of his generacoun and engendred on hem dyverse folk, as monstres and folk disfigured, summe withouten hedes, summe with grete eres, summe with on eye . . . '.[12] Here we are nearer to the 'mooncalf' of *The Tempest*. But Britain, too, had its monstrous births. Geoffrey of Monmouth's *Historia Regum Britanniae*, incorporating Merlin's prophecies, was popular Tudor propaganda, and gives an account of Merlin's mother being visited in a convent by an incubus in the form of a handsome young man. Nearer home for James is Hector Boece's *Scotorum Historiae* translated by John Bellenden in 1531. In Book VIII chapter 14 he follows an account of Merlin's birth with recent examples of intercourse with the devil, in the last of which the woman is delivered of 'ane monstir of mair terribill visage' than had ever been seen before. From this digression Boece returns quietly to his 'dedis of nobill men'.[13] Shakespeare possibly read Holinshed's close paraphrase of Boece's narrative, which inserted, as Boece had done, the fifteenth-century events immediately after reference to Merlin: 'It is foolishlie supposed that this Merline was got by a spirit of that kind which are called *Incubi*.'[14] Holinshed's scepticism contrasts with Boece's credulity.

Shakespeare emphasises not merely Caliban's demonic paternity but his monstrous birth; he is described as a 'deformed slave' in the list of characters, and in II, ii Stephano calls him a mooncalf and is followed by Trinculo with 'monster', repeated thirteen times in that scene and becoming the name by which Stephano and Trinculo usually address Caliban. Shakespeare is prepared to accept—or exploit—the tradition of having before him many of the same examples as James, as well as *The Mirror for Magistrates,* the 1578 edition of which added the tragedies of Eleanor, Duchess of Gloucester, and her ill-fated husband Humphrey Plantagenet, whose story Shakespeare had told in *2 Henry VI.* In *The Mirror* the Duke says that King Henry II reported:

> that his Auncient Grandame
> Though seeminge in Shape, a Woman naturall,
> Was a Feende of the Kinde that (*Succubae*) some call.[15]

Caliban is not, however, Shakespeare's only 'salvage and deformed slave'. As early as *3 Henry VI* the birth of Richard, Duke of Gloucester, is described in unmistakable terms. After the owl had shrieked, his mother brought forth:

> To wit an indigested and deformed lump,
> Not like the fruit of such a goodly tree.   (V, vi, 51–2)

The most interesting of the references to Richard as monster, however, comes in *Richard III* when Queen Margaret cries:

> Thou elvish-mark'd, abortive, rooting hog!
> Thou that was seal'd in thy nativity
> The slave of nature and the son of hell!   (I, iii, 228–30)

Here Richard, like Caliban, is a monster whose outer form indicates a moral depravity which itself has explicit demonic overtones. As Barbara Rosen points out, 'Imperfection was one of the traditional marks of anything created by the Devil in imitation of God'.[16] (Hence the search for the devil's mark in Continental and Scottish witch-hunts.)

Moreover, the Broadside ballads of the sixteenth century reflect a grossly morbid interest in deformed births where the crudity of description is made more offensive by the moralising tone.[17] Such births were accounted for not by intercourse with Satan but by the more homely sins of vanity, pride or fornication. The Reverend Stephen Batman, too, in *The Doome Warning All Men to Judgement* (1581) gives a hideous collection of monsters illustrated by woodcuts as a warning to blasphemers and adulterous women. Although continental writers are concerned with demonic intercourse, they give similar horrific descriptions of monstrous births, while some take a more naturalistic—though still moralistic—view. N. Remy in Book I chapter 6 of *Daemonolatreiae Libri Tres* (1595) describes the birth of a shapeless mass like a palpitating sponge, arguing that it is the impression of the demon on the mother's imagination that has produced the monstrosity; physically the child is wholly human. Bodin has an account of a hideous monster without head or feet, with a liver-coloured mouth in the left shoulder, and Boguet in *Discours des sorciers* (1590) believes, like the English writers, that monstrous births may be God's punishment for men's sins. A much more scientific view is given in *Des monstres et prodiges* (1573) by the surgeon Ambroise Paré, though his illustrations are quite as extreme as those of Stephen Batman. Anyone who has seen Peter Hall's 1974 production of *The Tempest* for the National Theatre has only to recall the 'living drollery' (III, iii, 21) of 'monstrous shape' (III, iii, 31) bringing in the banquet to have an unforgettable image of these sixteenth-century monsters. Even Stephano's discovery of Caliban and Trinculo under the gaberdine with four legs, two at either end, can be paralleled from contemporary illustrations of headless monsters. Therefore, if King James's reference to monsters is tersely dismissive, it appears to assume both mythical and, more important, popular information; on the other hand, Shakespeare makes his interest manifest, and his monster's relevance to the concerns and images of the age is very close indeed.

King James was clearly more aware of the continental tradition of witchcraft than were most Englishmen, and the chief value for our understanding of *The Tempest* in James's discussion of the incubus is that biologically even Epistemon, the credulous expositor of demonology, would consider Caliban human, as indeed would Reginald Scot and most continental writers. If, then, Shakespeare and his audience like their King were sceptical of the possibility of demonic paternity, then Caliban's essential humanity must be emphasised and his character qualified only by those human factors of nature and nurture so persuasively discussed by Professor Kermode in his Introduction.

At this point the evidence seems decisive, the interpretation of Caliban simply as natural man acceptable and we can return with confidence to accounts of natives in the New World or wild men in the old, forgetting demonology—as most critics have—but perhaps with the image of the monster more clearly fixed in our minds. Yet *The Tempest* is more elusive and interpretation more difficult than is allowed by the argument so far put forward. If Shakespeare had read King James's *Daemonologie,* why did he make Prospero so insistent upon Caliban's demonic nature? After all, though the incubus was not a protagonist in English witch trials, the audience would be likely to accept Prospero's repeated statements with the same kind of willing suspension of disbelief with which in a romance it accepted Ariel and the spirits presenting the Masque.

It seems probably that, as so often, Shakespeare seized upon ambiguities in order to exploit them; Caliban perhaps has more facets than have previously been recognised: as a native of the New World, wild man, demi-devil and monster. As a new-found primitive man he serves as touchstone of the civilisation which has, in one sense, usurped his island as Prospero's throne has been usurped; he seems in this context superior to Trinculo and Stephano though inferior to Ferdinand. As a wild man, he may symbolise the untamed within us, but like Spenser's Sir Satyrane offer hope of ultimate self-discipline. As a man—whether primitive or wild—despite the attempted rape of Miranda and his glorying in the physical details of the proposed murder of Prospero, he may be capable of redemption. However, if we see him as a 'demi-devil' his state is lost; his last intention, to 'seek for grace' (V, i,

295) is, then, a tactical move born of cunning. Moreover, the associations of 'monster' in neo-Platonic, demonic and popular thought emphasise the distortion of human nature by evil; for the twentieth century 'monster' has become trivialised, so that we need to recall its power in the sixteenth century. The reiteration of the word in *King Lear* indicates that Shakespeare felt its force adequate for the most terrible of the tragedies; and the word surely retains some of its strength even in the new context of *The Tempest*. Caliban is literally a malformed creature, a mooncalf; he may, too, take on something of the world's further sense as a creature part brute part human ('a man or a fish?' II, ii, 25); finally, there is the new sixteenth-century sense, exploited in *Lear*, of moral depravity. The connotations, therefore, of 'monster' serve to emphasise Caliban's evil. Moreover, the moralising interpretation of monsters in contemporary popular writing may also give some support to the view of Caliban as externalising Prospero's own propensity to evil, since for Prospero, as for the audience, Caliban's monstrous form must, as I have shown, have had a religious and moral message lost to us. Prospero's concession, 'this thing of darkness I/Acknowledge mine' (V, i, 275–6), now takes on a new resonance.

King James's *Daemonologie*, however, has further relevance to *The Tempest*. His Preface includes a reference to the power of magicians who can 'suddenly cause be brought unto them, all kindes of daintie disshes, by their familiar spirit'. This point is developed more fully in Book I chapter 6. Here Epistemon repeats the traditional view (only to reject it) that at the fall of Lucifer some spirits fell into the elements of air, fire, water and land, the spirits of air and fire being 'truer' (p. 20) than those of water and land. However, he grants a spirit the ability to carry news 'from anie parte of the worlde' (p. 21) and refers to the 'faire banquets and daintie dishes, carryed in short space fra the farthest part of the worlde' (p. 22). In this the devil deceives through his agility, as he does when he produces 'impressiones in the aire' of 'castles and fortes' (p. 22). The similarity of this to *The Tempest* is obvious; even the 'insubstantial pageant' (IV, i, 155) of Prospero's great speech is prefigured.

There remains some slight additional evidence that Shakespeare had read the *Daemonologie*.[18] James, as one would expect, refers to magicians making circles, as Prospero does to charm the court party in Act V. More interesting, however, in chapter 2 of Book I James gives the three ways the devil 'allures' (p. 7) persons by the 'three passiones that are within our selves' (p. 8). These are curiosity, thirst of revenge and 'greedie appetite of geare' (p. 8). Although James goes on to relate the allurement of curiosity to magicians or necromancers, and the last two to sorcerers and witches, they remain oddly relevant to three important temptations in *The Tempest* as a whole. First, it is the curiosity of Prospero that has led to his secret studies and to his downfall as Duke of Milan. Second, though Antonio was dry for sway Prospero overcomes his thirst for revenge saying 'the rarer action is/In virtue than in vengeance' (V, i, 27–8). Finally the greedy appetites of the three men of sin could be tempted by the illusory banquet, and Trinculo and Stephano, too, are far from controlling their unrestrained passions when confronted by the 'geare' that Prospero displays to distract them.

NOTES

[1] *The Tempest*, ed. F. Kermode (1958), Introduction, pp. xxxix, lxii–lxiii. All quotations from *The Tempest* are from this, the sixth, edition. References to passages in other Shakespeare plays are from the single-volume Oxford edition of W. J. Craig.

[2] *The Tempest*, Introduction, p. xl.

[3] *Shakespeare Survey, 11* (Cambridge, 1958), 75.

[4] *Shakespeare Quarterly*, 23 (1972), 179.

[5] *The Invisible World* (Athens, Georgia, 1939), p. 4.

[6] *Witchcraft* (1969), p. 338 footnote.

[7] *Religion and the Decline of Magic* (1971), p. 568.

[8] I have used the Bodley Head Quarto of the *Daemonologie* edited by G. B. Harrison (1924). All quotations from the work are followed by parenthetical page references which are identical with the 1597 edition. *Newes from Scotland* is usefully included in the same volume, but since the original is unpaginated the page reference refers only to the reprint.

[9] English innocence is demonstrated by Peele's *The Old Wives' Tale* where Madge telling the burlesque romance to her sleepy listeners threatens them, 'Hear my tale, or kiss my tail.'

[10] This remained unavailable in English until Montague Summers edited and translated it in 1928.

[11] *A Declaration of Egregious Popish Impostures* (1603), p. 133. It should be noted that Shakespeare echoes Harsnett in *The Tempest*. See II, ii, 10–11 and Kermode's note.

[12] *Mandeville's Travels*, ed. M. C. Seymour (Oxford, 1967), p. 160. I owe this example to R. R. Cawley's pioneering study, 'Shakspere's use of the Voyagers', *PMLA*, XLI (1926), 722.

[13] *The Chronicles of Scotland*, trans. J. Bellenden, ed. R. W. Chambers and E. C. Batho, The Scottish Text Society, 3rd ser. (Edinburgh and London, 1938), I, 348.

[14] *Holinshed's Chronicles of England, Scotland and Ireland, Scotland* (London, 1808), V, 146. In the same volume Holinshed refers to Alphonse, King of Naples, and his son, Ferdinand, p. 454.

[15] *The Mirror for Magistrates*, ed. L. B. Campbell (New York, 1960), p. 447.

[16] *Witchcraft*, p. 18.

[17] See J. H. Pafford's Arden edition of *The Winter's Tale* (1963) for his footnote list of references on p. 105.

[18] H. N. Paul, *The Royal Play of Macbeth* (1950), pp. 255ff. and K. Muir, *Shakespeare's Sources*, I (1957), p. 178, provide some of the evidence.

Lucy S. McDiarmid and John McDiarmid

ARTIFICE AND SELF-CONSCIOUSNESS IN AUDEN'S *THE SEA AND THE MIRROR*

Auden's "guess," in 1966, was that *The Orators* sprang from an "unconscious motive . . . to exorcise certain tendencies in myself by allowing them to run riot." [1] In similar language Auden has written of Goethe:

> The work of a young writer—*Werther* is the classic example—is sometimes a therapeutic act. He finds himself obsessed by certain ways of thinking and feeling of which his instinct tells him he must be rid before he can discover his authentic interests and sympathies, and the only way he can be rid of them forever is by surrendering to them. . . . Having gotten the poison out of his system, the writer turns to his true interests. . . . [2]

In Auden's own career expulsion of the poison does not occur only in *The Orators;* for him, repudiation of "certain ways of thinking and feeling" is almost a ritual. His long poems, especially, are often exorcisms of the imagination. In *The Age of Anxiety,* a night of intoxicated excursions to idyllic landscapes and remote islands ends with the return to a drab New York in the middle of World War II. Abandoning fantasy, the characters are "reclaimed by the actual world where time is real and in which, therefore, poetry can take no interest." In so recent a poem as "City without Walls" the same pattern recurs. A neurotic voice drones on in insistent alliterative lines for twenty-one stanzas, rehearsing the horrors of "Megalopolis," before daybreak ushers in the ordinary, a new voice whose "Go to sleep now for God's sake" silences the self-indulgent imagination. After its vision of the nativity *For the Time Being* also lets us down with a thump in reality, "where . . . Newton's mechanics would account for our experience,/And the kitchen table exists because I scrub it."

The Sea and the Mirror is unusual among Auden's poems because it begins with disenchantment. [3] Some "therapeutic act" has preceded the poem. The characters of *The Tempest* appear as they would after Shakespeare's play, and are introduced by a stage manager: we are behind the scenes of the illusion from the

From *Contemporary Literature* 16, No. 3 (Summer 1975): 353–77.

start. Of all people, the stage manager is most likely to know that the world of art is only a temporary, artificial suspension of ordinary life:

> The aged catch their breath,
> For the nonchalant couple go
> Waltzing across the tightrope
> As if there were no death. . . .   (p. 351)

And Prospero, when he appears, has already decided to dismiss Ariel. Each successive character, in fact, is relieved that he is no longer deluded. As Sebastian says: "I smile because I tremble, glad today/To be ashamed, not anxious, not a dream" (p. 371). Although there is no single questing figure, *The Sea and the Mirror* could be seen as a search for solid ground to end on. Each speaker seems to be saying, "At last! Reality!" The poem consists of a series of endings, or to use Auden's metaphor, attempts to leave a theater. But whereas in *The Orators* and *The Age of Anxiety* the illusion is clearly broken from, the theater left behind once and for all, in *The Sea and the Mirror* substantiality is elusive, and recedes before the speakers as they seem to move closer to it. Deliverance comes only with the acknowledgment that we are always on stage.

The Sea and the Mirror shares its pursuit of the real with its source. Auden's work is subtitled "A Commentary on Shakespeare's *The Tempest*," and perhaps it is best to see its status as derived from that of *The Tempest*'s own self-commentary—Prospero's speeches after the masque ("Our revels now are ended") and after the dramatic action of *The Tempest* ("Now my charms are all o'erthrown"). Both instances of *The Tempest*'s self-reference end on a note of concession, as one world gives way to another. The masque gives way to the greater substantiality of the world of conspiracies and murders, as that world will itself some day "Dissolve/And . . . leave not a wrack behind." The distancing of the masque caused by the intrusion of Caliban's plot provides the occasion for the distancing of life. In the epilogue the real world's dependent position mirrors art's, and the audience's Prospero's: "As you from crimes would pardoned be,/Let your indulgence set me free." Each speech places the play and, by analogy, life, in a series of worlds all alike conceding their insubstantiality and dependence on the next.

The Tempest is distanced by *The Sea and the Mirror* as the masque was by Prospero's speech, but of course *The Sea and the Mirror* is no less poetry itself than "Our revels now are ended." That is, the distancing *The Sea and the Mirror* provides does not make it "life" to *The Tempest*'s "art." Rather, the relation suggests, like Prospero's speeches, a greater consciousness of artificiality: the movement toward truth is actually the movement toward greater awareness of artifice. If we assume the whole poem to be a commentary on a previous performance of *The Tempest*, then each of the three main sections—"Prospero to Ariel," "The Supporting Cast," and "Caliban to the Audience"—is simultaneously more real and yet more artificial than that which preceded it. The only thing that is real, according to *The Sea and the Mirror*, is our own artificiality—"our incorrigible staginess," Caliban calls it.

Each section acts as a *Verfremdungseffekt* for the previous ones, distancing successively *The Tempest*, Prospero, Antonio, and the beginning of Caliban's speech.[4] The estranging of one section by the next is subtlest in the shifts of setting that occur, yet the changing context of *The Sea and the Mirror* is one of its most important features. Monroe Spears writes, "There is the implicit setting of a theater, after a performance of *The Tempest*," and John Blair, "The poem takes place in no space." [5] Although before the main body of *The Sea and the Mirror* there is a brief preface spoken by "The Stage Manager to the Critics," he does not locate himself in space, and he does not literally "introduce" Prospero. A Roman numeral I comes between the "Preface" and "Prospero to Ariel" to separate the two speakers and their worlds. There is no single answer to the question, where are these people, because each one sees himself, and therefore *The Tempest*, in different ways.

Prospero, the first speaker, seems to be beginning where Shakespeare left off. He is addressing Ariel, and begins, "Stay with me, Ariel, while I pack" (p. 352), so one assumes he is in his cell on the island. One of his last lines—"Here comes Gonzalo/With a solemn face to fetch me" (p. 359)—implies that the whole world of the last pages of Shakespeare's play is still around him. Prospero asserts a number of times that over the years on the island he has acquired self-knowledge, and speaks in sadder-but-wiser tones:

> Now, Ariel, I am that I am, your late and lonely master
>   Who knows what magic is:—the power to enchant
> That comes from disillusion.   (pp. 353-54)

His previous life is a "dream" from which he is now waking. But in spite of his new understanding, Prospero's "space" is not significantly different from that of *The Tempest*. Auden's Prospero differentiates himself chronologically, but not ontologically, from Shakespeare's. *The Tempest* for Prospero is merely the past. The segment of his life recorded in *The Tempest* covers what Prospero might call his "escapist" period, but it is nonetheless on a continuum with the present. He does not see the life he is entering as different in status from the life he is leaving.

In the first speech of "The Supporting Cast, Sotto Voce," Antonio refers to sails, passengers, and crew, and sees the other characters "Dotted about the deck" (p. 360), so he is apparently on the ship going back to Italy. His world is not part of Shakespeare's play but exists through an imaginative extension of that world. Prospero had said, "I'll promise you calm seas, auspicious gales," and Antonio begins, "As ... the sky is auspicious and the sea/Calm as a clock, we can all go home again" (p. 360). From Antonio's greater physical distance, *The Tempest* looks somewhat insubstantial. Antonio's first tercet, with its reference to Circe ("As all the pigs have turned back into men," p. 360) casts doubt on the nature of events at the end of *The Tempest*. There is something witchy about Prospero, and although the magical high jinks are supposed to be over, the last scene was suspiciously artificial. In fact, Antonio's language imputes to *The Tempest* the status of a work of art. What is really art has, he thinks, been disguising itself as life:

... it undoubtedly looks as if we
Could take life as easily now as tales
Write ever-after. . . .   (p. 360)

Miranda and Ferdinand seem to Antonio about as life-like as lovers on a postcard: "Two heads silhouetted against the sails—And kissing, of course" (p. 360). He goes through the cast by type—"The lean Fool . . . the dear old butler"—and analyzes *The Tempest* with the aesthetic detachment of a critic:

... the royal passengers [are] quite as good
As rustics, perhaps better, for they mean

What they say, without, as a rustic would,
Casting reflections on the courtly crew.   (p. 360)

Prospero is merely the arranger of a *nature morte* ("Your grouping could not be more effective," p. 360) and the finale of *The Tempest* is the fragile, temporary effect of a spell: "given a few/Incomplete objects and a nice warm day,/What a lot a little music can do" (p. 360).

As *The Tempest* begins to seem like a painting, a *tableau vivant*, or even a Shakespearean play, it recedes from the world of *The Sea and the Mirror*. Like Prospero in his farewell to Ariel, Antonio is saying, "That wasn't real, this is." Although Auden's Prospero professes to feel as if he were awake after a dream, and sober after drink, the world he imagines around him is still that of the play; he has not even left the island, but is still packing his bags and chatting with Ariel. Antonio never gives a name or status to *The Tempest*'s world but the names implied by his images—*tableau vivant*, magical spell, fairy tale—all emphasize its artificiality. Whatever it is, it is not life.

Caliban gives this artificial status a name—*The Tempest* is a play. More than suspiciously fictive or masquerading as life, *The Tempest* was a work of art from start to finish. His speech is entitled, "Caliban to the Audience," so the status of *The Tempest*, as well as his "space," is implicit to the title. Now, at any rate, we are in a theater after a performance of *The Tempest*. The audience, "having dismissed [their] hired impersonators" (p. 373), are faced with someone who does not impersonate but appears as his real self. Caliban presents himself as life after art. Caliban's understanding of his context, or "space," is the third stage in what we can now see as a progression defined by increasing awareness of the fictive status of *The Tempest*. In the final paragraphs of his speech Caliban will come to see his own status, too, as artificial.

There is a progressive self-consciousness in the styles of the three main sections that works in tandem with the growing sense of artificiality.[6] Prospero's style is as little conscious of itself as a style as he is aware of any touch of artifice in *The Tempest*. Style and setting both glide unnoticeably into the "real." Casual and colloquial, the speech is full of such ordinary phrases as, "Stay with me," "Thanks to your service," "I don't know," and "To you that doesn't matter." The meter, syllabic verse of thirteen and eleven syllables alternately, is as unobtrusive as the language. In a sentence like, "So at last I can really believe I shall die" (p. 352), the diction and cadences of the spoken language fit easily into the meter. Although a reader is of course aware that this is not an exact transcript of spontaneous speech, the conversational tone and frequent reminders of Ariel's listening presence ("You, I suppose . . .") do give the impression that we are overhearing whatever Prospero has to say to Ariel.

Antonio, by contrast, makes himself conspicuous through his style. His voice dominates the second part of *The Sea and the Mirror*. "The Supporting Cast, Sotto Voce" consists of ten speeches by the rest of the cast as they evaluate their particular disenchantments. With the exception of Antonio, all are grateful for the awakening Prospero has sponsored. Antonio darts out from hiding and inserts himself in the lulls between their eloquent and sincere speeches to sing a mocking refrain. His stanzas—symmetrical in their form and in their variations—are like flourishes, waves of a plumed cap, that call attention to the speaker. Each stanza echoes the lyric it follows only to pervert its imagery and mock its sincerity. After Ferdinand's love sonnet, for instance, comes the response:

> One bed is empty, Prospero,
>   My person is my own;
> Hot Ferdinand will never know
> The flame with which Antonio
>   Burns in the dark alone.   (p. 362)

Alonso's discussion of kingship and government is countered by the lines:

> One crown is lacking, Prospero,
>   My empire is my own;
> Dying Alonso does not know
> The diadem Antonio
>   Wears in his world alone.   (p. 369)

And so for ten stanzas Antonio tells us,"My will is all my own," "My person is my own," "My nature/language/audience/empire/compass/conscience/humor/magic is my own." Antonio is the source of a pattern so obtrusive we begin to see the "supporting cast" as more subject to Antonio's spell than Prospero's.

Just as Antonio was sufficiently aware of artifice in *The Tempest* to see the play as a tale or a picture, so he speaks in a style conscious of itself as a style: each stanza is perfect for its place, specially contrived to follow a certain lyric, and all repeat the identical five-line form.[7] The style of the stanzas, with their insistent, identical rhymes and their circumambulating pattern, is distinctly artificial. Prospero's lines might seem to suggest overheard speech, but Antonio's stanzas are consciously crafted poetry. Although they are addressed to Prospero, his presence is not suggested in this part as Ariel's was in the first section; *we* are Antonio's real audience. In the pattern of repetitions with variations set up by the refrain there is a nascent awareness of an audience to appreciate the craftsmanship. This awareness, however, does not break through the surface until the third part of *The Sea and the Mirror.*

Antonio may be a dashing villain with wavy mustachios, lurking in corners and popping out, conscious of his kinship with Richard and Edmund, but Caliban out-does him in "staginess." With Caliban, the style of *The Sea and the Mirror* recedes even further from some conversational norm. He is, of course, *on* a stage, like a performer, while Antonio is only on the boat going home. Caliban is histrionic, florid, and extreme. He enters like a soft-shoe dancer waving his boater and twirling his cane. His smile—and he is grinning hard—has two layers, one for the audience and one for himself. As a performer he must smile to entertain, but as a stylist he is conscious of his own artifice and enjoys it. His sentences are full of superfluous phrases which add no nuances of meaning but serve only to display the performer's agility. He comes onstage acutely conscious of his audience. Here is part of his first sentence:

> If now, having dismissed your hired impersonators with verdicts ranging from the laudatory orchid to the disgusted and disgusting egg, you ask, and, of course, notwithstanding the conscious fact of his irrevocable absence, you instinctively *do* ask for our so good, so great, so dead author to stand before the finally lowered curtain and take his shyly responsible bow for this, his latest, ripest, production, it is I—my reluctance is, I can assure you, co-equal with your dismay—who will always loom thus wretchedly into your confused picture, for. . . .   (pp. 373–74)

Caliban may not be a hired impersonator, but he is certainly a voluntary one. After distinguishing himself from actors, he proceeds to take on a series of roles (the audience, Shakespeare, himself), announcing after the first that he is returning for the moment to his "officially natural role" (p. 384). The phrase is an oxymoron—does Caliban mean that "officially" his role is to be "natural"? Is he still Shakespeare's Caliban, who allegorically represents "nature" to Ariel's "art"? Or does he mean that he has officially—i.e., for the sake of his audience—a "natural" role, a basic, unar-tificial self, to which he will return between impersonations? Either way, the word "natural" still refers to something artificial. If the self to which he returns is merely a role, there is no "natural" self, but only a series of artificial ones. Caliban is conscious that even his "official" self is a "stagy" one, that while he may be removing one hat with the right hand and slowly putting on the next with his left, he is never bare-headed.

This "stagy" presentation, a sequence of "acts" rather than a single speech, is suggestive of a progression in the poem's ideas. If all modes of personation are equally artificial, there is no such thing as an objectively real self. With each suc-cessive section of *The Sea and the Mirror*, more of life comes to be seen as subjective. A gradual shift of focus away from objective reality is implicit in the change of setting from island to stage, and the change of style from colloquial to artificial. The increasing complexity of structure in the various sections—from Prospero's casual musings with their brief lyric interruptions to Caliban's "baroque profusion of distinctions and elaborations" [8] is evidence of the will's growing readiness to choose, to determine, and to create its world. As the poem develops, the characters' beliefs about the relative strengths of objective and subjective reality shift from Prospero's deterministic view of the world to Caliban's existentialism. Viewing Prospero and Antonio at first as characters in a play, Caliban clings to a belief in his own reality. Only at the very end, in a moment of vision and humility, does Caliban come to consider himself just as artificial as the others, and acknowledges with confessional relief his "incorrigible staginess."

The division of life into mutually incompatible escapist and naturalistic realms is implicit in Prospero's chief linguistic habit, the pairing of opposites. The balance of clauses in his second sentence—"share my resigning thoughts/As you have served my revelling wishes" (p. 352)—is an emblem of the way Prospero thinks. A few lines later his syntax and cadences make the same contrast between a world where revelling is the predominant mood and wishing the customary form of mental activity, and one where all thought is sober: "Ages to you of song and daring, and to me/Briefly Milan, then earth" (p. 352). The prevalence of pairs—shadow/substance, dream/wake, drunk/sober, moonshine/daylight, smooth song/rough world—suggests that Prospero's world, like his language, is polarized. The lyrics Prospero bursts into at intervals during his speech—"Could he but once see Nature," "Sing first that green remote Cockaigne," and "Sing, Ariel, sing"—are another instance of the separation of "song" from "thought," as if the two modes were the "songs of Apollo" and the harsh "words of Mercury."

In Prospero's scheme of things Milan is objective reality, immutable fact—a world in which no human choice or act of will can be effectual. Trapped in this prison, the child Prospero felt like a "sobbing dwarf/Whom giants served only as they pleased" (p. 353). The grotesque extremes of this vision of the relation between parent and child imply a world defined by its power to oppress. Only in magic, which the child practiced "To ride away from a father's imperfect justice" (p. 353), were choices possible. Prospero's exile on the island was a brief sojourn in a fantasy land of freedom. All the subjective, world-creating activities associated with the island—magic, art, language—seem incompatible with a return to Milan: "But now all these heavy books are no use to me any more, for/Where I go words carry no weight" (p. 353). When Prospero thinks of schooling himself for the real world's suffering, he sees speech as his biggest temptation:

> When the servants settle me into a chair
> In some well-sheltered corner of the garden,
> And arrange my muffler and rugs, shall I ever be able
> To stop myself from telling them what I am doing,—
> Sailing alone, out over seventy thousand fathoms—?
> Yet if I speak, I shall sink without a sound
> Into unmeaning abysses. Can I learn to suffer
> Without saying something ironic or funny
> On suffering? I never suspected the way of truth

> Was a way of silence where affectionate chat
> Is but a robber's ambush and even good music
> In shocking taste. . . .   (p. 358)

Music, "affectionate chat," and "saying something ironic or funny/On suffering" are
all detours from the silent, stoic "way of truth." His speech itself is a last indulgence,
a "something ironic or funny/On suffering" before the passive suffering begins.

Although Prospero claims to have recognized that art offers us an "echo" and
a "mirror," his speech ends in "song" rather than "thought," and the lyric itself belies
the recognition. Prospero is still thinking in the same polarities as he imagines Ariel

> Entrancing, rebuking
> The raging heart
> With a smoother song
> Than this rough world. . . .   (p. 359)

Art is still a kind of lullaby for Prospero, and life unpleasant. His last words are a plea
for Ariel to sing to him as "Trembling he takes/The silent passage/Into discomfort"
(p. 359).

In Part II, as I mentioned above, the grateful comments of the "Supporting
Cast" are countered by Antonio's denials: "I am I, Antonio,/By choice myself alone."
More self-conscious than Prospero, Antonio is also conscious, as Prospero is not,
of the power of choice in the world, his ability to affect if not to control reality:

> . . . as long as I choose
>
> To wear my fashion, whatever you wear
> Is a magic robe; while I stand outside
> Your circle, the will to charm is still there.
>
> As I exist so you shall be denied. . . .   (p. 361)

The antiphonal pattern of speeches and stanzas demonstrates formally the intrac-
tability of will which Antonio's opening speech states explicitly. There are two
structures in tension in "The Supporting Cast," one the circular dance of Prospero's
plan, the other the dance broken by Antonio's refusal to join. The cast all acknowledge themselves to have been the swaggering "extravagant children" Prospero
called them, and in appropriate poetic forms describe their joy at having "received
a second life." Miranda says, "we/Are linked as children in a circle dancing" (p. 373),
and without Antonio's speech or refrains the characters form such a pattern, linked
through the marriage of the first and last, Ferdinand and Miranda. The speeches
pair off symmetrically, making partners of the two lovers, the two drunkards, the
false and true courtiers, and the two sets of friends. The hinge of the symmetrical
pairs is the king Alonso, whose speech is about the "tightrope" or middle way
between the sea and the desert, the "temperate city" precariously balanced between opposite extremes:

2	Ferdinand		Miranda	10
3	Stephano		Trinculo	9
4	Gonzalo		Sebastian	8
5	Adrian and Francisco		Master and Boatswain	7

6 Alonso

(Numbers indicate the order of the speeches: Antonio's is first.)

Without Antonio, Part II would look like the dance Miranda describes, the circle of perfection, with the "children" linked together by Prospero's benevolent manipulations. Antonio's speech, coming first, ruins the geometric pattern; as he says, "I stand outside/Your circle" (p. 361). The stanzas which follow each of the nine speeches virtually unlink them, forming a counterspell to undo Prospero's magic. Every success of Prospero's—for instance, Sebastian's "I smile because I tremble, glad today/To be ashamed, not anxious, not a dream" (p. 371)—is countered by Antonio's equal and opposite verbal force. Auden does not have Antonio assert his will through silence, as Shakespeare did. In *The Sea and the Mirror,* the "way of silence" is Prospero's submissive way of truth; the way of choice is a way of speech.

If the power of speech is related to the power of will, then Caliban is living in a world of great freedom, since his address to the audience is half again as long as the rest of the work. From the vantage of his speech, patterns in the whole work can be seen which could only be dimly apprehended before. This most self-conscious section of the poem uses terms—audience, role, performance—which serve to clarify and explain the form of the whole poem. For instance, the awareness of an audience which was suggested by Antonio's language, with its flourishes and arabesques, is much stronger in the third section, since Caliban is on a stage.

In a similar way, the self-reflectiveness is very apparent in the third section, since that section reflects the whole poem in miniature. The structure of Caliban's speech, with its three "roles" parallel to the poem's three main sections in their growing subjectivity and self-consciousness, reveals the latent self-reflection in "The Supporting Cast." The shadowy presence of Prospero's choreography is obscured by Antonio's stanzas, but it is there *in potentia.* In its third section *The Sea and the Mirror* is so self-conscious that it refers almost exclusively to itself, but that self-reference is part of the poem's development. The opinions dramatized in the "roles" are seen as inadequate, even as Antonio deprecates Prospero's achievement. In presenting even his own opinions as a role parallel to the other two Caliban reaches the ultimate degree of self-consciousness. *The Sea and the Mirror* follows to its logical conclusion the structure suggested by its conception: it is a work of art reflecting another work of art, and as it progresses it turns inward and reflects itself more and more. The "baroque profusion" of its final section is not random imaginative excess but an intricately executed pattern of accumulating subjectivity.

The audience whose "echo" Caliban speaks in his first role is like the one Brecht so disparagingly describes: "They stare at the stage as if spellbound,"[9] The magical term is apt, because the audience's life, like Prospero's, is polarized into golden and drab worlds. Its own daily life the audience describes as "the wearily historic, the dingily geographic, the dully drearily sensible" (p. 376), in wearily alliterated phrases. Art, like Prospero's island, is a realm of beauty and "freedom without anxiety," utterly separate from the "shambling slovenly makeshift" world. The "native Muse" is beautiful precisely because she is "other":

> We most emphatically do *not* ask that she should speak to us, or try to understand us; on the contrary our one desire has always been that she should preserve forever her old high strangeness, for what delights us about her world is just that it neither is nor possibly could become one in which we could breathe or behave. . . .   (p. 378)

Hungry for its few glimpses of beauty, the audience is naturally indignant with Shakespeare for including "the absolutely natural . . . utterly negative" in *The Tempest*. It complains to him histrionically that the Muse's soirées have been spoiled:

> How *could* you, you who are one of the oldest habitués at these delightful functions . . . be guilty of the incredible unpardonable treachery of bringing along the one creature . . . she is not at any hour of the day or night at home to. . . .   (p. 376)

The audience's extended social metaphor and fussy style—replete with Gallicisms and italicized phrases—expose its "role" as caricature, ridiculing the notion of a "real" life. Like Prospero, the audience devotes its final thoughts to Ariel, but in quite a different vein. We do not laugh when Prospero asks Ariel, the "unanxious one," to sing to him as he enters the world of discomfort; but when the audience reacts in horror at the thought that Ariel has not been confined at the end of the play we see through their indignant "bourgeois" reaction to Caliban's glee:

> We want no Ariel here, breaking down our picket fences in the name of fraternity, seducing our wives in the name of romance, and robbing us of our sacred pecuniary deposits in the name of justice. (p. 384)

Through Caliban's sophistication the view which Prospero expressed in nostalgic sincerity is distorted into parody.

In his second "role" Caliban delivers "a special message" from Shakespeare to budding magicians. Like "The Supporting Cast," the message is constructed as a confrontation between choice and limitation. As a counter-manipulator, Antonio is limited by Prospero just as Prospero is limited by him. Antonio can "choose to wear [my] fashion," but not much more. The idea of choice is just being born in that section, and it is not yet powerful. Antonio's limitation is suggested by his reiteration—he can only say the same thing over and over again. The artist in Shakespeare's message can choose a lot more, and Caliban emphasizes choice in his first sentence: "So . . . you have decided on the conjurer's profession" (p. 384). The message is a fable in which an Everyartist has "heard imprisoned Ariel call for help," liberated him, and launched a promising career. He reaches a pitch of success but finally, tired of giving orders to Ariel, peremptorily frees him. Before his very eyes, refusing to go away, Ariel turns into Caliban, and the artist is forced to confront "a gibbering fist-clenched creature with which you are all too unfamiliar . . . the only subject that you have, who is not a damn amenable to magic but the all too solid flesh you must acknowledge as your own" (p. 387). Shakespeare's message ends on a note of admonition: Caliban and the artist must accept one another's necessary presence, keeping their "hopes for the future, within moderate, very moderate, limits" (p. 390).

The artist has complete freedom—up to a point. One aspect of life remains "not . . . amenable to magic," i.e. choice: the flesh. Flesh remains an uncontrolled alien outside of the domain of the spirit. Shakespeare, in Auden's opinion, still believed in some degree of determinism. In the next role, Caliban addresses the audience "on behalf of Ariel and myself," and the combination suggests a break with the notion that the fleshly Caliban is of a different ontological order than the spiritual Ariel. The two characters, though opposites, are now two aspects of the same realm.

Caliban presents his and Ariel's opinions in conscious parallel with the two previous roles. The third part of his speech is simultaneously itself and a reflection of itself; that is, it is both part of the third section of *The Sea and the Mirror*, and a reflection of that third section, as the other two roles reflect Parts I and II. The self-conscious presentation of the self is appropriate to this role's conception of living as role-playing. The waking to consciousness which is occurring as the poem develops is seen here as a "fall" from a fluid state into a condition of distinctions between fantasy self and real self, role and identity. The speech at this point is virtually explaining its own method: commentary has become self-commentary. Resistance to the utter subjectivity now implied takes the form of nostalgia, and this stage is characterized as a *loss of unawareness:*

> All your clamour signifies is this: that your first big crisis, the breaking of the childish spell in which, so long as it enclosed you, there was, for you, no mirror, no magic, for everything that happened was a miracle—it was just as extraor-dinary for a chair to be a chair as for it to turn into a horse; it was no more absurd that the girding on of coal-scuttle and poker should transform you into noble Hector than that you should have a father and mother who called you Tommy—and it was therefore only necessary for you to presuppose one genius, one unrivalled I to wish these wonders in all their endless plenitude and novelty to be, is, in relation to your present, behind, that your singular trans-parent globes of enchantment have shattered one by one, and you have now all come together in the larger colder emptier room on this side of the mirror which *does* force your eyes to . . . reckon with the two of us. . . . (pp. 390–91)

The clause dependent on the pronoun "which" is suspended in time, like childhood, for almost as long as the syntax can bear, though its own dependence as well as the grammatical necessity of a verb to follow "crisis" doom it to death from the start. The most fragile and vulnerable illusions of childhood—when, for

Wordsworth, "the earth and every common sight/To me did seem apparalled in celestial light,/The glory and the freshness of a dream"—are carefully protected between dashes ("it was just as extraordinary . . .") within a dependent clause from the brutal realities of the indicative voice. After the suspension the words of the clause strain at the syntax before "is" breaks in with the unalterable facts of existence.

In a way, Caliban's central expository sentence recapitulates the same disenchantment that Auden is turning over in his mind in the whole poem—the breaking of the magic spell, the end of the play, the fall into self-conscious awareness. Plays end in infinite regress in *The Sea and the Mirror:* the whole poem follows some hypothetical performance of *The Tempest;* Caliban faces the audience after his performance in it; here, in simile, an audience faces Caliban and Ariel; and in the last pages of Caliban's speech, he and Ariel face themselves. The "larger colder emptier room" is literally where Caliban's audience is as it hears him speak, but the description is only a metaphorical explanation of their fallen state.

In the previous role Caliban and Ariel were servants to a master artist, and his decisions determined the nature of his life as well as his career. Here also they receive "fatal foolish commands," but what is determined is not merely the self but the world; we are artists not merely of our lives but of the whole context which surrounds us. This responsibility is seen as the beginning of a journey manifestly unlike the one Prospero mentioned. The "Journey of Life" requires no silent stoic submissiveness but a recognition of "three or four decisive instants"; the "way of truth" is a way of choices.

"Stagestruck" at all the possibilities before them, the members of the audience may become dissatisfied with their "minor roles" and attempt to avoid the complexities of a world whose nature is entirely subjective. They may, on the one hand, decide to try to put Caliban "in charge" and beg for release into the state Auden has called a "Hell of the Pure Deed." [10] Longing for the simplicities of childhood, they will find themselves only in a "secular stagnation." Alternately those who want to live in a world beyond choice rather than before it will, according to Caliban, put Ariel in charge. Longing to be delivered from "this hell of inert and ailing matter," they create an equal and opposite hell of "the Pure Word," where "Everything suggests Mind." Those who insist on refusing the responsibility of their subjectivity get a world in which they are imprisoned rather than free.

After a final admonition to the audience, Caliban's efforts collapse in disgust and contempt, and he wishes he had had "the futile honour of addressing the blind and the deaf" (p. 399). The tone really reflects Caliban's frustrations with himself; the third role represented his own opinions, and he has nowhere to go. In a kind of hell himself, Caliban is not aware of the full implication of his own phrase, "officially natural role." His hell is the same as Prospero's and Antonio's, belief in one's own reality. Although he danced jauntily onto the stage with a sophisticated consciousness of his own style, he saw himself nevertheless as replacing "impersonators." They were art, he was life.

Then, in a quantum leap in consciousness of artificiality, Caliban distances himself from his own speech, comparing his function to a dramatist's and, implicitly, his remarks to a play. Although this is only an intensification of the movement we have seen all along, it is a turning point, because it is the first step toward acknowledging what Auden calls the "unnecessary" status of our lives. In seeing the remarks he had earlier contrasted with the speech of "impersonators" as themselves a play, Caliban recognizes that nothing is absolute; that in an infinite series of distancings all life could be seen as art. In a method appropriate to the idea of infinite regress Caliban creates similes within similes, never returning to the place of the original tenor but entering deeper into the hypothetical worlds of the vehicles. As the status of Caliban's remarks appears to be getting more artificial, it is, paradoxically, getting closer to the truth. Moving through similes within similes, in the most tenuous touch with the world of the work, to the life on the other side of them, Caliban in a state of visionary receptiveness reaches the absolute.

The first simile, in which Caliban compares himself to a dramatist, begins as if it were an epic simile but turns into a narrative, and the world of the vehicle soon acquires independent importance. The original point of tangency is the frustration felt by both Caliban and the dramatist in relation to their audience. Any artist's "aim and justification" is

> to make you unforgettably conscious of the ungarnished offended gap between what you so questionably are and what you are commanded without any questions to become. . . .　　　　　　　　　　　　　　(p. 400)

We are "commanded," in the Sermon on the Mount, to become perfect: "Be ye perfect, even as your Father in Heaven is perfect." The artist must indicate our condition of estrangement from the truth and dramatize how "Wholly Other" the truth is. Somehow he must show us that although we are commanded to become perfect, perfection is outside our state of existence altogether. The audience's tendency to "interpret any sight and sound to their advantage" dooms this attempt to failure:

> for the more truthfully [the artist] paints the condition, the less clearly can he indicate the truth from which it is estranged, the brighter his revelation of the truth in its order, its justice, its joy, the fainter shows his picture of your actual condition in all its drabness and sham, and . . . the more sharply he defines the estrangement itself . . . the more he must strengthen your delusion that an awareness of the gap is in itself a bridge. . . .　　　　　　(pp. 399–400)

The audience will resist acknowledging their "unnecessary" status and the distance of the Necessary from their own lives. The only solution for the artist is to

> give all his passion . . . to the task of "doing" life . . . as if it lay in *his* power to solve this dilemma—yet of having at the same time to hope that some unforeseen mishap will intervene to ruin his effect, without, however, obliter-

ating your disappointment, the expectation aroused by him that there was an
effect to ruin. . . .   (p. 400)

If the audience is going to take the play to their own advantage, they will have
to be shown how artificial the play is. If the "effect" is "ruined," they will be
conscious of it *as* an "effect," a display, a scene—something collapsible. The interruption is not important in itself but in its power to distance what it interrupts. The
play's artificiality will be exposed, and the audience will be made conscious of
dramatic illusion as an illusion.

Caliban never returns to the tenor of his simile; he never returns, that is, to
his own problems with his audience. As he enters deeper into the world of his
simile Caliban speculates about the genesis of the "dramatist's" play, wondering
what originally inspired his "imitative passion." The language in which Caliban poses
his question implies a foreknowledge of the answer, since he is seeking

> some large loose image to define the *original drama* which aroused his imi-
> tative passion, the first *performance* in which the players were their own
> audience, the worldly *stage* on which their behaving flesh was really sore and
> sorry—for the floods of tears were not caused by onions, the deformities and
> wounds did not come off after a good wash. . . .   (p. 401, emphasis mine)

Caliban cannot even use the word "life" because it sounds too absolute. In this
context it might suggest a radical difference in status between whatever aroused
the imitative passion and the imitation itself, and by this time Caliban is beginning to
realize the utter artificiality of all we consider real.

The answer to Caliban's question must be a simile, since he was looking for an
"image," and the world of the final simile becomes the context for the rest of his
speech. Like its mother simile, it becomes a narrative, and the original point of
comparison is forgotten as the world of the vehicle becomes the world of the
speech. The vehicle, or answer—"the greatest grandest opera rendered by a very
provincial touring company indeed"—is a performance full of mishaps, an "effect"
ruined in every detail:

> Sweating and shivering in our moth-eaten ill-fitting stock costumes which with
> only a change of hat and rearrangement of safety-pins, had to do for the
> *landsknecht* and the Parisian art-student, bumping into, now a rippling palace,
> now a primeval forest full of holes, at cross purposes with the scraping bleating
> orchestra we could scarcely hear for half the instruments were missing and the
> cottage piano which was filling-out must have stood for too many years in
> some damp parlour, we floundered on from fiasco to fiasco. . . .
>
> (p. 401)

In his description of the "original drama" Caliban appeared to be distinguishing
between art and life. He wanted an image for the performance in which tears were
not caused by onions, deformities and wounds did not come off with washing,
suicides could not take curtain calls, and so forth. It is paradoxical that his image for

what he so carefully defines as *not* artificial is a play whose artificiality is obtrusively present. The opera is a succession of unforeseen mishaps and illusion-breaking incidents. What is really indisputably real, Caliban is saying, is our artificiality. To see life as a play is the logical next step after seeing one's own speech as a play, and the final stage in the progressive growth of awareness of subjectivity.

Caliban acknowledges his own personal artificiality and, in "contrition and surrender," dives into his own simile. The direction of his movement is reversed from that of his first appearance, when he stood in front of the "finally lowered curtain" and distinguished himself from "hired impersonators": "Our performance— for Ariel and I are, you know this now, just as deeply involved as any of you— ... has been so indescribably inexcusably awful ... " (p. 401). Performing, in the simile, is tantamount to behaving or living, an activity in which Caliban acknowledges his imperfection. If life is also a bungled performance, it is one that constantly reveals its contingent, unnecessary state, that its landscapes are scenery, its clothes costumes, its music cacophony. All its attempts to pass itself off as absolute only show more obviously its insubstantiality.

The actors in the simile accept their failure: they stand "down stage with red faces and no applause," knowing that "no effect ... came off." They give up when they "see [them]selves as [they] are," performers in a play, people whose lives are unnecessary. They give up assumptions about what performing can do, acknowledging that perfection, or reality, lies outside the zone of their endeavors. Caliban's pace slows, and his sentences become shorter and simpler as the buoyant self-confidence which had propelled his verbosity fails him: "There is nothing to say. There never has been,—and our wills chuck in their hands—There is no way out. There never was ..." (p. 402). Acceptance of their imprisonment in contingency opens the way to the truth. Resigning themselves to imperfection, they have a vision of Perfection:

> it is at this moment that for the first time in our lives we hear, not the sounds which, as born actors, we have hitherto condescended to use as an excellent vehicle for displaying our personalities and looks, but the real Word which is our only *raison d'être.*   (p. 402)

When Caliban's style picks up speed again, it has not changed; his "incorrigible staginess" is still there. But now he understands that in spite of estrangement from the truth

> we are blessed by that Wholly Other Life from which we are separated by an essential emphatic gulf of which our contrived fissures of mirror and proscenium arch—we understand them at last—are feebly figurative signs....
>   (p. 402)

In this new understanding of the metaphor of the stage, in which "all our meanings are reversed," Caliban is on stage and the more real world on the other side of the "essential emphatic gulf" is that of the Absolute, the Life which is defined in terms of its "otherness" from our own. As Caliban amplifies his vision in a succession of images, the rhythm of his prose builds up in a crescendo of progressively shorter sentences to the final restored relation. The "perfected Work," at first seen as if hazily from a distance, comes into closer focus:

> it is just here, among the ruins and the bones, that we may rejoice in the perfected Work which is not ours. Its great coherences stand out through our secular blur in all their overwhelmingly righteous obligation; its voice speaks through our muffling banks of artificial flowers and unflinchingly delivers its authentic molar pardon; its spaces greet us with all their grand old prospect of wonder and width; the working charm is the full bloom of the unbothered state; the sounded note is the restored relation.   (pp. 402–03)

This is the perfect version of the "greatest grandest opera," whose coherences show off our structures as a "secular blur," and whose blooms expose our flowers as stage properties. At first the coherences "stand out" as if at the end of a broad avenue. Then the voice speaks, audible but still "through" the flowers to us. After the pardon is delivered, forgiving our pride for ever hoping to identify words with the Word, the distance is diminished: the spaces seem to reach out and greet us. The combination of the present participle ("working") and noun signifying a finished product ("bloom") suggests the reconciliation of process and product, performing and perfected Work. The musical note signifies the harmony of the restored relation between fact and value, artificial and real, man and God.

The short poems that stand outside the three main sections of *The Sea and the Mirror*—the Stage Manager's Preface, and Ariel's Postscript—are usually seen as "frames" for the "triptych" between them.[11] One does feel a certain symmetry in their positions, but the lyrics are just as much phases in the poem's development as the three parts themselves. The Preface, the main part of the poem, and the Postscript form a progression crucial to the poem's meaning; they reveal how *The Sea and the Mirror* becomes what it describes.

Like the three inner sections as a whole, each lyric follows the pattern of a movement from art to life to some absolute which makes art and life both look insubstantial. The scene of Prospero's masque in *The Tempest* (IV.i) is perhaps the source of this pattern, as it develops from Ferdinand's association of the masque with paradise, through the disappearance of the masque, and finally the disappearance of life and art both in "Our revels now are ended." Prospero's speech lacks Auden's third term, however: Our "little life is rounded with a sleep," but it is not clear what, if anything, surrounds the sleep or whose dream we are. Auden's versions of this concession end facing heavenward, towards a life real because it is "Wholly Other."

The Stage Manager, for example, begins with Ferdinand's misconception. The circus he describes is a magical world, as suspended in time as the tightrope-walkers in space:

> The aged catch their breath,
> For the nonchalant couple go
> Waltzing across the tightrope
> As if there were no death.... (p. 351)

By contrast the audience's world seems more real; after the performance they drop with a jolt into time:

> We are wet with sympathy now;
> Thanks for the evening; but how
> Shall we satisfy when we meet,
> Between Shall-I and I-Will,
> The lion's mouth whose hunger
> No metaphors can fill? (p. 351)

In the last stanza circus and audience, art and life, disappear together, inverted in that leap of understanding which suddenly sees the world as a stage before an audience of angels. Auden does to Shakespeare's lines what the Stage Manager does to the analogy of stage and world—he juggles them around and juxtaposes words and images in an artful rearrangement which shifts our sense of value:

> ... this world of fact we love
> Is insubstantial stuff:
> All the rest is silence
> On the other side of the wall;
> And the silence ripeness,
> And the ripeness all. (p. 352)

The Stage Manager's final lines constitute a grammatical version of the changing conception of the real. The identity between subject and predicate signified by the verb "to be" fosters a gradual transformation, and the nouns progress successively from "this world" to "insubstantial stuff" to "silence" to "ripeness" to "all." Through a verbal recapitulation of concession, fact disintegrates before the silence which gradually emerges as the source of all value.

This inversion is the same one that Caliban expresses at the end of his speech: "all our meanings are reversed," and the "contrived fissures of mirror and proscenium arch" are understood as "feebly figurative signs" for the gulf between man and God. Caliban's imagery repeats the Stage Manager's, since he finds, on the other side of the proscenium arch, "the full bloom of the unbothered state." In fact, Caliban makes the discovery which the Stage Manager's speech describes. Prospero's and Antonio's sections, in their expanding awareness, are stages in the approach to this discovery.

Ariel's song is the third and final recognition of insubstantiality. The most concrete of the three, it fully embodies the idea of concession, of acquiescence in one's insubstantiality. "Fleet persistent shadow," Ariel himself embodies the insubstantiality of *The Tempest*'s metaphors of clouds, mists, vanishing, fading and melting. Ariel's self-definition as a "shadow" suggests that the life which he reflects is substantial and real. From an expression of the dependence of art on life—"Helplessly in love with you,/Elegance, art, fascination,/Fascinated by/Drab mortality" (p. 403)—Ariel moves to an evocation of the ultimate powerlessness of both. Caliban and Ariel

> Can, alas, foretell,
> When our falsehoods are divided,
>   What we shall become,
> One evaporating sigh,

                    . . . I   (p. 404)

Ariel's song literally evaporates, its last syllable a weak echo of its penultimate word. Like the work it ends, Ariel's poem is a concession. With it the whole *Sea and the Mirror* concedes itself out of existence.

If *The Sea and the Mirror* is a distorted mirror of *The Tempest,* its distortions tell us something about Auden's habits of mind. Auden once wrote that *The Tempest* ends "sourly," and in a way *The Sea and the Mirror* explores the sourness.[12] Shakespeare's Prospero twice "forgives" Antonio in language distinctly unforgiving, qualifying his forgiveness the first time with the phrase, "unnatural though thou art," and the second time prefacing it with the parenthetic "whom to call brother/Would even infect my mouth." Caliban's hostilities to the master whose skull he wants to better ("or paunch him with a stake,/Or cut his wezard") seem too suddenly converted to contrition and obedience:

> PROSPERO: As you look
> To have my pardon, trim it handsomely.
> CALIBAN: Ay, that I will; and I'll be wise hereafter,
> And seek for grace.

The Sea and the Mirror allows the two who rebelled against Prospero's authority in Shakespeare's play to have their say, and to have the last words.

More than anything else, Auden's "revisions" of Shakespeare reveal a new view of the relation between Prospero and Caliban. *The Sea and the Mirror* distorts *The Tempest* according to the stipulation that "the last shall be first, and the first last." The reversal corroborates Auden's complaints about *The Tempest* in his essay "Balaam and His Ass":

> *The Tempest* seems to me a manichean work, not because it shows the relation of Nature to Spirit as one of conflict and hostility, which in fallen man it is, but because it puts the blame for this upon Nature and makes the Spirit innocent.[13]

The structure of *The Sea and the Mirror* is a kind of Christian judgment, placing the proud Prospero in the lowliest position. As the speaker of the first of the three sections, he is the most naive and the least self-conscious. The beast Caliban, the final speaker, is the most sophisticated, and his self-consciousness ultimately leads him to the vision of grace which Shakespeare left him seeking. One could say that Auden has "put down the mighty from their seat,/And hath exalted the humble and meek."

The rereading of *The Tempest* is as Freudian as it is Christian. The fool is granted the vision of God, but this fool is "natural" in another sense. Shakespeare's Caliban may have trotted off stage obediently, but Auden's refuses to leave it. He is, after all, "the dark thing you could never abide to be with." From both Christian and Freudian points of view, Auden's interpretation of Caliban is reminiscent of his reading of another anarchic figure, Falstaff. The Hal of *Henry IV, Part II* does not come to terms with Falstaff and what he represents; he merely suppresses him with superior legal force.[14] In "The Prince's Dog" Auden goes so far as to suggest that Falstaff is morally superior to Hal, "the supernatural order of Charity as contrasted with the temporal order of Justice symbolized by Henry of Monmouth."[15]

Auden's dislike of Hal is his dislike of temporal justice, of moral compromise, of "a practical reckoning with time and place." Auden's feelings about Prospero are more closely related to his ideas about the artist. The structure of *The Sea and the Mirror* could also be interpreted as a deliberate incapacitating of the artist, who emerged successful at the end of *The Tempest.* Auden concluded *The Enchafèd Flood* with a similar abrogation, in words more normative than descriptive:

> We live in a new age in which the artist neither can have such a unique heroic importance nor believes in the Art-God enough to desire it ... in which the heroic image is not the nomad wanderer through the desert or over the ocean, but the less exciting figure of the builder, who renews the ruined walls of the city.[16]

In his "commentary" on *The Tempest,* Auden is grappling not with Shakespeare but with the idea of the artist's "unique importance." Although this is an idea which Auden associates with Romanticism, and with writers such as Tennyson and Rimbaud, it is really his own bogeyman, the escapism and solipsism he is exorcising in *The Orators, The Age of Anxiety,* and "City without Walls." *The Sea and the Mirror* is subtler than those works because each character asserts his own disenchantment. The Prospero of *The Sea and the Mirror* seems to be the perfect hero for Auden: in wry, conversational tones and Kierkegaardian language he rejects magic for "the way of truth." But the characters in *The Sea and the Mirror* are often less wise than they appear. Only when Prospero is seen as the first character in a progression defined by increasing awareness is he properly understood. As the poem moves from Prospero's confident declarations to Caliban's visionary receptiveness, it reveals two simultaneous motions, a movement inward toward full acceptance of subjectivity, and a movement outward toward freedom. Auden is following the dictum Yeats's death inspired him to express:

> In the prison of his days
> Teach the free man how to praise.

NOTES

[1] W. H. Auden, *The Orators* (London: Faber and Faber, 1966), p. 8.

[2] W. H. Auden, "Writing," *The Dyer's Hand* (New York: Vintage Books, 1968), p. 18.

[3] W. H. Auden, *The Sea and the Mirror*, in *The Collected Poetry of W. H. Auden* (New York: Random House, 1945). Parenthetical page references in the text will be to this edition.

[4] Like Auden, Brecht thought art should "disenchant," and in his discussions of the typical audience's relation to the play on stage he uses similar imagery: "they stare at the stage as if *spellbound,* which is an expression from the Middle Ages, an age of witches and obscurantists." Bertolt Brecht, "Kleines Organon für das Theater" (1948), *Versuche* 12, para. 26, p. 119. As quoted in Martin Esslin, *Brecht: The Man and His Work* (Garden City: Doubleday, 1961), p. 124.

[5] Monroe K. Spears, *The Poetry of W. H. Auden* (New York: Oxford Univ. Press, 1968), p. 218. John Blair, *The Poetic Art of W. H. Auden* (Princeton: Princeton Univ. Press, 1965), p. 108.

[6] The relatively greater "reality" of Caliban's world was expressed more crudely in an early draft of Auden's "Ladies and gentlemen, please keep your seats./An unidentified plane is reported/Approaching the city. Probably only a false alarm/But naturally we cannot afford/To take any chances. So all our lights are out/And we must sit in the dark. I can guess/What you are thinking: How odd this feels: to be sitting/In a theatre when the final curtain has fallen/On a dream that ended agreeably with wedding bells/Substantial rewards for the good, and for the bad/Nothing worse than a ducking...." The unidentified plane distances the play and calls attention to it as a play—as an insubstantial group of scenes which can disappear in a moment. The artificiality of the play stands out in clear relief against the world it has suddenly given way to. In the final version Auden's revisions of the third section made the style congruent with the awareness of artifice. As quoted in Spears, p. 249.

[7] The final stanza has one extra line, as if Antonio were penning an extra swirl under his signature.

[8] Spears, p. 219.

[9] Esslin, p. 124.

[10] The terms "Hell of the Pure Word" and "Hell of the Pure Deed" are found in Auden's "Swarthmore Chart." The original copy of this chart is in the Special Collections of McCabe Library, Swarthmore College. For a discussion of it see Kenneth Lewars, "Auden's Swarthmore Chart," *Connecticut Review,* 1, No. 2 (1968), 44–56.

[11] For the idea of a "triptych," see Edward Callan's unpublished dissertation "A Study of the Relationship of Structure to Meaning in W. H Auden's Major Poems, 1940–1955," Univ. of South Africa, Pretoria, 1958, pp. 95ff. As cited in Blair, p. 107.

[12] Auden, "Music in Shakespeare," *The Dyer's Hand,* p. 526.

[13] Auden, "Balaam and His Ass," *The Dyer's Hand,* p. 130.

[14] As Jonas Barish writes in "The Turning Away of Prince Hal," *Twentieth Century Interpretations of Henry IV, Part One,* ed. R. J. Dorius (Englewood Cliffs: Prentice-Hall, 1970), p. 85, "Where his counterparts in the comedies incorporate the holiday or the dream into their fuller waking lives, the new king dismisses it....Instead of a synthesis, in which an enlarged sense of human possibility emerges from the dialectic between duty and holiday ... we have a forcible sundering of the two kinds of experience, and a walling of them off into the noncommunicating realms of Good and Bad."

[15] Auden, "The Prince's Dog," *The Dyer's Hand,* p. 198.

[16] Auden, *The Enchafèd Flood* (New York: Random House, 1950), p. 153.

G. Wilson Knight
CALIBAN AS A RED MAN

As a contribution to a book on Shakespeare's style, my essay may at first seem inappropriate, though as it develops its placing should appear more assured. I am to point to certain analogies between Caliban and the Red Men of America.[1] We cannot say what Shakespeare knew about them, but he probably heard accounts. Some aspects of Caliban, especially what others say of him, I do not stress, being concerned rather with Caliban's own outlook. In pursuance of this argument, I rely primarily on a stylistic judgement.

At his first entry he addresses Prospero and Miranda:

CALIBAN: As wicked dew as e'er my mother brushed
With raven's feather from unwholesome fen
Drop on you both! A south-west blow on ye
And blister you all o'er!
PROSPERO: For this, be sure, to-night thou shalt have cramps,
Side-stitches that shall pen thy breath up; urchins
Shall, for that vast of night that they may work,
All exercise on thee; thou shalt be pinched
As thick as honeycomb, each pinch more stinging
Than bees that made 'em.
CALIBAN: I must eat my dinner.
This island's mine, by Sycorax my mother,
Which thou tak'st from me. When thou cam'st first,
Thou strok'st me and made much of me, would give me
Water with berries in't, and teach me how
To name the bigger light, and how the less,
That burn by day and night; and then I loved thee,
And showed thee all the qualities o' th'isle,
The fresh springs, brine-pits, barren place and fertile.

From *Shakespeare's Styles: Essays in Honour of Kenneth Muir*, edited by Philip Edwards, Inga-Stina Ewbank, and G.K. Hunter (Cambridge: Cambridge University Press, 1980), pp. 205–20.

Cursèd be I that did so! All the charms
Of Sycorax, toads, beetles, bats, light on you!
For I am all the subjects that you have,
Which first was mine own king: and here you sty me
In this hard rock, whiles you do keep from me
The rest o' th' island.   (*The Tempest*, I,ii,321–44)

That is our introduction.

Nature is Caliban's mental stock-in-trade. It may be impregnated by the evil charm of his mother Sycorax, who is conceived as a witch of great power, as one

That could control the moon, make flows and ebbs,
And deal in her command without her power.   (V,i,270–1)

That means, presumably, could use the Moon's power without herself possessing it. Prospero calls her practices 'earthy' and her sorceries 'terrible', though 'for one thing she did/They'—the people of Argier or Algiers—'would not take her life' (I,ii,263–73); what that was, we are not told. Such is Caliban's descent. Prospero addresses him as 'thou earth', 'tortoise', 'poisonous slave', 'hag-seed' (I,ii,314, 316, 319, 365). He threatens Caliban with more torments.

At first all had gone smoothly, till Caliban tried to violate Miranda. He had been taught language and introduced to the higher heavenly powers. Caliban in his turn showed earth-nature to Prospero, 'all the qualities o' th' isle'. He is uniquely at home with earth-nature. His curses are weighted with it, and even in his slavery he is imprisoned by Prospero 'in this hard rock' (I,ii,343).

Caliban bears certain traces of savages as they were viewed by colonial adventurers. Their talk would often have been considered meaningless. In his *Shakespeare* Mark van Doren says that Caliban's language comes with difficulty, as though speech is hard for him.[2] Prospero refers to the time

when thou didst not, savage,
Know thine own meaning, but wouldst gabble like
A thing most brutish.   (I,ii,355–7)

However brutish he may have been, this closeness to nature demands respect. He is one with the heavier elements of earth and, to some extent, water, and his contacts cover nature's springs and fertility. Most important of all for our immediate comparison is his claim that the island is *his;* as the Red Men of America, to this hour, are persistent in their claim that they have been robbed of their land. Their land, to the Red Men, was as a living entity of which they were part.

We next meet Caliban with a burden of wood, collected for Prospero, whom he still curses:

All the infections that the sun sucks up
From bogs, fens, flats, on Prosper fall, and make him
By inch-meal a disease!   (II,ii,I–3)

There is thunder which Caliban, as indeed did the Red Men, regarded as coming from the spirits:

> His spirits hear me,
> And yet I needs must curse. But they'll nor pinch,
> Fright me with urchin-shows, pitch me i' th' mire,
> Nor lead me, like a firebrand, in the dark
> Out of my way, unless he bid 'em; but
> For every trifle are they set upon me;
> Sometime like apes that mow and chatter at me,
> And after bite me; then like hedgehogs which
> Lie tumbling in my barefoot way, and mount
> Their pricks at my footfall; sometime am I
> All wound with adders, who with cloven tongues
> Do hiss me into madness.   (II,ii,3–14)

We have a new variation on animal life. As in Caliban's curses, the animals are still spiritually impregnated, but this time by spirits controlled by Prospero. Here Caliban is aware of spirits within animal forms, as the Red Men felt through animal life to spirits. This spiritual apprehension somehow, as through his curses earlier, does not prevent the animals being real to us as animals. We feel the clustering and thickly inhabited jungle, with the noise of apes and its dangerous serpents. Caliban is vividly aware of spirits in animal or human form. At Trinculo's entry he thinks him, too, a spirit; as savage tribes sometimes do when confronted by strangers. The term is used by Caliban when he first sees the whole community of strangers from the ship: 'These be brave spirits indeed' (V,i,261).

Our 'Indian' comparisons have verbal support, though whether Indians of east or west is intended is not clear. When Stephano enters he finds Caliban and Trinculo hiding together under Caliban's 'gaberdine', and, seeing limbs only, thinks it some trick of 'savages and men of Ind' (II,ii,55). Trinculo had earlier associated Caliban with a 'dead Indian': he had a 'fish-like smell' but was 'legged like a man, and his fins like arms' (II,ii,35).

We shall next inspect passages which will show Caliban as a nature force. Whether as spirit-powers or as their ordinary selves, he is one with earth's creatures; 'all the qualities o' th' isle' (I,ii,337) come to us unmediated by any particular 'style' of expression; or we might say we have the perfection of style in its apparent absence. In Caliban's words we shall find a 'close-up' of nature, and this apparent closeness seems to be unique in Shakespeare's nature poetry. He has always a vast resource at his disposal. There are nature-spirits in *A Midsummer Night's Dream* and there is Perdita's flower-dialogue in *The Winter's Tale*. His tragedies have elemental tempests, and references to fierce animals, lion, bear, wolf and boar. There is pretty nearly every sort of nature, located or atmospheric, in reference or setting; but all are, in the comparison I am now making, used, as it were, for a literary or dramatic purpose, and so in a way distanced. Even the stallion in *Venus and Adonis*, the boar and hunted hare, yes, and the wonderful snail (ll. 1033–6), might be called descriptive triumphs and are to that extent lacking in spontaneity. I am thinking on the lines of Tolstoy's final tenets, wherein he repudiated all artistic sophistication.[3] Caliban's nature has an actuality beyond the literary; he speaks as one embedded in it, as sophisticated man cannot be. This embeddedness somehow gets across to us in his words; it may be called a matter of 'style' but if so it is a style that does not submit to analysis; even the term 'transparent' is inapposite. The literary surface is absent and reality presented as though beside us, as in a close-up, again the best phrase I can think of to give the quality of Caliban's talk.

Comparison with the Red Men is obvious. With them, animal and elemental life is throughout emphatic. They bear animal and elemental names: Black Elk, Sitting Bull, Crazy Horse, Red Cloud, Shooting Star. In their ritual dances they wear animal disguises.[4] In trance they converse with talking animals.[5] Animals and spirits are felt in unison, or identification. The earth and higher elements are remembered; in their names, in prayers and invocations, in their belief in the supernal powers of lightning and thunder. To Earth's stones and rock they attribute vitality. Like Robinson Jeffers, they felt reality rising from 'earth's stony core'; when they made a treaty, they used to call on Earth, pounding it with a staff: 'What has the earth got to say?'[6] One's feet should be able to 'hear the very heart of Holy Earth'.[7] Caliban's earthiness is, by the Red Men's standards, wholly honourable.

We have a trio: Stephano and Trinculo, a drinking servant and a jester, who both speak in prose; and Caliban, who speaks almost wholly in poetry, the difference in style reflecting their status. Caliban is trembling with fear of what he regards as spirits sent by Prospero to torment him, and given drink by Stephano to calm him. The drink works rapidly upon him:

> These be fine things, an if they be not sprites.
> That's a brave god, and bears celestial liquor.   (II,ii,108–9)

So

> I'll swear upon that bottle to be thy true subject, for the liquor
> is not earthly.   (II,ii,116–17)

He thinks Stephano has dropped from heaven (II,ii,127). Here he corresponds exactly to the Red Men, who were easily dominated, often to their ruin, by European drink, despite the knowledge of drugs, such as mescalin, held by certain tribes; and they smoked freely.[8] Caliban's phrase 'celestial liquor' corresponds to the Red Men's name for whisky, which they called 'Holy Water'.[9]

The drink at first seems to loosen Caliban's speech to a new freedom, so that his innate feeling for nature is unleashed. He will show Stephano 'every fertile inch o' th' island' (II,ii,138). Again:

> I'll show thee the best springs; I'll pluck thee berries;
> I'll fish for thee, and get thee wood enough.
> A plague upon the tyrant that I serve!
> I'll bear him no more sticks, but follow thee,
> Thou wondrous man.   (II,ii,150–4)

Trinculo's comment is: 'A most ridiculous monster, to make a wonder of a poor drunkard'. True: Caliban has no intellectual judgement; his gifts are of another order. Next, with growing pride in his expertise:

> I prithee let me bring thee where crabs grow;
> And I with my long nails will dig thee pig-nuts;
> Show thee a jay's nest, and instruct thee how
> To snare the nimble marmoset. I'll bring thee
> To clust'ring filberts, and sometimes I'll get thee
> Young scamels from the rock. (II,ii,157–62)

What scamels are is not known: I imagine them as limpets. Here his nature poetry is at its best. W. H. Clemen observes the amount of 'sensuous and concrete detail' contained in these lines.[10] Caliban has pleasure and just pride in revelation of nature's secrecies, her ways and habits.

Caliban's kinship with animals does not preclude hunting them. The Red Men were characterised by their simultaneous love of nature in trees and in animals together with control and use of natural resource. In that classic document of Red Indian life and culture, Longfellow's *Hiawatha* (VII), trees are cut down and shaped for a canoe. Sympathy is accorded their complaint, but they finally agree. When a woman, to make a basket, cuts the roots of a tree, she prays to it not to be angry.[11] These are compact miniatures of the Red Men's nature-philosophy. In hunting, they used every part of the buffalo, each for a special purpose, observing full respect for the creature they had killed. There was normally no hunting for pleasure and no wanton destruction of arboreal life. In human affairs they could both inflict and endure suffering; they seem to have been unique among races in acceptance, without sentimentality, of the conditions of incarnate life, both its wonders and its agonies. Caliban's words breathe natural kinship, love, and understanding, but also mastery, through man's place in the created scheme.

In *The Oregon Trail,* Francis Parkman notes

> a curious characteristic of the Indians, who ascribe intelligence and a power of understanding speech to the inferior animals; to whom indeed, according to many of their traditions, they are linked in close affinity; and they even claim the honour of a lineal descent from bears, wolves, deer or tortoises. (p. 210)

The drink intoxicates Caliban. Wildly he chants his new freedom. He has in Stephano a new master, and will desert Prospero. There will be no more unwilling labour but instead

> 'Ban 'Ban Ca-Caliban
> Has a new master—Get a new man! (II,ii,173–4)

He is quite drunk. The fall of the Red Men is often regarded as due to their having given way to the 'fire-water' brought by Europeans.[12] In 1849 Francis Parkman wrote:

With the stream of emigration to Oregon and California, the buffalo will dwindle away, and the large wandering communities who depend on them for support must be broken and scattered. The Indians will soon be abased by whisky and overawed by military posts; so that within a few years the traveller may pass in tolerable security through their country. Its danger and its charm will have disappeared together.[13]

That is at least honest. Parkman also refers often to the treachery of the Indians. He might be thinking of Caliban who now plans, perhaps because he is under the influence of the drink, to get Stephano to murder Prospero:

> I am subject to a tyrant, a sorcerer, that by his cunning hath cheated me of the island.   (III,ii,40–1)

Prospero's 'sorcery' corresponds—in our admittedly quite arbitrary comparison—to gunpowder and European technology in general, which the primitive mind certainly regarded as a kind of magic.

Again the reiterated—and just—complaint:

> I say, by sorcery he got this isle;
> From me he got it.   (III,ii,49–50)

The general case of the Red Men as against white robbery is well stated in the many Indian complaints compiled by T. C. McLuhan in *Touch the Earth*.[14] Caliban continues:

> I'll yield him thee asleep,
> Where thou mayst knock a nail into his head.   (III,ii,57–8)

His murderous thoughts are crude and ugly:

> Why, as I told thee, 'tis a custom with him
> I' th' afternoon to sleep; there thou mayst brain him,
> Having first seized his books; or with a log
> Batter his skull, or paunch him with a stake,
> Or cut his wezand with thy knife. Remember
> First to possess his books; for without them
> He's but a sot, as I am, nor hath not
> One spirit to command: they all do hate him
> As rootedly as I.   (III,ii,83–91)

Caliban knows that Prospero relies on his 'books'; without them he is powerless. His magic is to this extent a magic of learning, not so far away from European science; which may indeed be supposed to be covered by his early use of the term 'liberal arts' (I,ii,73), in which what we should call 'science' was embryonic. He commands spirits tyrannically and that they resent it may be true: Ariel cries for freedom. We may suppose that Prospero's command of nature-spirits and nature in general is of the same order as western callousness in using nature for our immediate ends, regardless of consequences. Today the Red Men assert regularly that they have never been guilty of ravaging, despoiling, and pollution. Respect for the rights of the environment was intrinsic to the Indian way of life. In comparison our own record is appalling. Prospero is to Caliban a callous slave-master: 'They all do hate him as rootedly as I.' That is how nature may feel under the tyranny of technology. Indians assert that the white man's greed 'has blinded him to the pain he has caused Mother Earth by his quest for what he calls natural resources'.[15]

Caliban and his companions go ahead, bent on murder. Prospero, knowing their purpose, has set out a rich array of 'glistering apparel' to distract them. Stephano and Trinculo are ravished by it. We have an indirect correspondence to the Europeans' greed for gold, which the Red Men saw as a kind of worship, driving them 'crazy';[16] and they suffered grimly because of it, being driven from land where gold could be found. When Trinculo first sees the 'glistering' show, Caliban's scorn registers his superiority: 'Let it alone thou fool;/it is but trash.' His accent exactly corresponds to the Red Men's inability to understand the Europeans' gold-lust. He warns them a second time: 'What do you mean/To dote thus on such luggage?' (IV,i,229–30)

They are now trapped: *A noise of hunters heard. Enter divers* Spirits, *in shape of dogs and hounds, hunting them about'*. Prospero uses animals, or spirits as animals, for harsh purposes; there is no evidence in him of a kindly approach to animal life. We heard earlier of his punishing Caliban with the sting of bees (I,ii,329–30), and Caliban describes at length other instances, as we have seen. The hounds are sympathetically viewed, but then they are half humanised and used for a cruel purpose; the joy of a hunt is innately cruel. We are given their names:

PROSPERO: Hey, Mountain, hey!
ARIEL: Silver! there it goes, Silver!
PROSPERO: Fury, Fury! There, Tyrant, there! Hark, Hark!   (IV,i,254–6)

Two of Prospero's names are harshly toned, but Ariel's corresponds with his own quicksilver quality. The pleasure and excitement of a hunt is before us. They are hunting human beings; we may remember that hounds were used to track runaway slaves. Prospero has more torments in store:

Go charge my goblins that they grind their joints
With dry convulsions, shorten up their sinews
With agèd cramps, and more pinch-spotted make them
Than pard or cat o'mountain.   (IV,i,257–60)

Another callous reference to animals, very different from the ingrained sympathy of Caliban's 'nimble marmoset' (II,ii,160), or his later exquisite:

Pray you, tread softly, that the blind mole may not
Hear a foot fall.   (IV,i,194–5)

This is perhaps Caliban's best natural 'close-up'. Prospero speaks from a superiority, Caliban from an identity, with the animal creation.

The Tempest is full of spirits, in one shape or another; but if we concentrate on Caliban, my sole present purpose, we can say that he is sometimes aware of spirits in animals and sometimes speaks of nature direct. In both modes, the animals, as animals, are vividly present, and probably more so than when others speak of them, in *The Tempest* or elsewhere in Shakespeare. The style has an authenticity beyond that of Shakespeare's style of reference elsewhere, which may be called at the lowest 'fanciful' and at the best 'literary'.

Now what I am leading up to is this: *exactly the same applies to Caliban's style in respect of extra-sensory perceptions.* In *The Tempest* spirits may activate animals, or may, as by Caliban and once by Miranda (I,ii,409–11), be confused with human beings; or each may function alone. The general conception, widely understood, may, despite what is due to artifice and plot-fabrication, be allowed to give us a sense of spiritual reality behind or within phenomena; a reality, or essence, that makes phenomena live. So it is not strange to find that what is true of Caliban's nature poetry is true also of his spiritual poetry. His words have the same immediacy of style.

Before I approach Caliban's lines on music, it is as well to make an apology. I am working now, as not before, at what is called 'literary criticism'. As a critic rather than an interpreter, I have what may seem some strange, though tentative, judgements. I myself have always a hankering for facts. I tend to respect Byron's statement, thinking of *Marino Faliero,* in his letter to John Murray of 2 April 1817, that 'pure invention is but the talent of a liar'. I have for long been critical of *Macbeth* for subjecting its protagonist to an unfair treatment of the sources, and have often suggested that the stage record of ill luck attending performances may accordingly be due to the activity of inimical spirit-powers. My own personal books have been strongly factual, as were *Atlantic Crossing, The Dynasty of Stowe,* my poems *Gold-Dust,* and still more the biography of Jackson Knight, my brother.[17] True, imagination has given them a colouring, and factual report in the biography included, necessarily, spiritualistic experience. Faithfulness to the factual, if honest, will include much that is strange. I certainly never regard the 'factual' as excluding the 'supernatural' or things beyond ordinary sense-perception.

This emphasis on the factual, or on 'reality', accounts for my high rating of Shakespeare's accomplishment in Shylock. The poetic conception and treatment is used to present to us a Jew as a well-known figure with an aura of racial attributes; yet, as misfortune closes in on him, he has the thrust and realism of great tragedy. The coalescence of actuality and imagination is perfect. Beside him it is easy to see Macbeth and Lear as extravagances. Othello covers a racial problem, like Shylock, with a personality well realised, the all-important and dramatically dominating handkerchief being so dissolved into his personal aura that its semi-superstitious nature is discounted; but the plotting is arbitrary, as Shylock's story is not. Shylock is so well done that he is, like Falstaff, in danger of ruining the drama in which he occurs.

These are personal studies, and it may be because Macbeth and Lear are more dissolved into their separate poetic universes that they are less acceptable as persons; and that may be part of a yet greater task. I do not know. All I emphasise is that, as rounded *persons,* Shylock, Falstaff and possibly Othello stand out. For a whole play, *Timon of Athens,* discussed fully in my recent (1977) *Shakespeare's Dramatic Challenge,* has, as a whole, something of the impact I am trying to describe, exerting the pressure of reality: Hazlitt well says that of all his plays Shakespeare was here most 'in earnest'. It has no extrinsic supernatural machinery though a kind of supernature is in the action: Timon as Promethean semi-superman, his 'god'-given Gold and his Nirvana ending. Timon's nature-contacts and critique of society correspond, point by point, to the Red Men's culture. The play has, of course, faults, presumably being in an unrevised state; and Timon, as a person, is not without looseness of delineation. In both *The Merchant of Venice* and *Timon of Athens* riches, the central concern of the European world, are a primary concern.

If all, or some, of this be allowed, then Caliban with his rich earth-contacts, which correspond so closely with those of aboriginal natives, and especially the Red Men of North America, undoubtedly qualifies as an outstanding Shakespearian delineation in the realistic mode. His nature-contacts enclose a whole range of animals. They may be blended with spirits, in his curses and his thought of Prospero's use of them to torment him, or he may feel them directly. But what I would point to is the way they affect us, whatever the reference: the 'raven's feather' of his curses, the 'tumbling hedgehogs' of his torment, the 'nimble marmoset' and 'blind mole' of direct apprehension, all are equally living and vivid presences verbally conveyed. I hazard again the suggestion that they hold a reality beyond any others in Shakespeare; the rest are more 'literary', at the best more 'imaginative'. With Caliban, as Lear says of Edgar, we have 'the thing itself' (*King Lear,* III,iv,106).

Now as the Red Indians, whom John Cowper Powys calls 'this most original and formidable race among all the children of men',[18] had wonderful spiritual apprehensions, so also does Caliban. The Red Men lived in a richly peopled universe beyond normal sensory perception. They believed in spirits within animals and men; they had superlative visionary experiences; they heard atmospheric voices, songs and music, and, above all, they dreamed; honoured dreams were a large part of their life. The record is clear in *Black Elk Speaks* (see n. 1) and elsewhere.

When Caliban and his companions hear Ariel's song, the Europeans are afraid of this invisible, ghostly music. Not so Caliban. It is to him part of his normal, clairvoyant, apprehension, and he speaks lines on the intimations around us which do not relate merely to Ariel's song, but have a purely general implication:

> Be not afeard. The isle is full of noises,
> Sounds, and sweet airs, that give delight, and hurt not.
> Sometimes a thousand twangling instruments
> Will hum about mine ears; and sometime voices
> That, if I then had waked after long sleep,
> Will make me sleep again; and then, in dreaming,
> The clouds methought would open and show riches
> Ready to drop upon me, that, when I waked,
> I cried to dream again.   (III,ii,130–8)

The riches of Caliban's vision contrast with the 'trash' of the glistening robes set to entrap them as the two aspects of riches contrast in *The Merchant of Venice* and *Timon of Athens.*

These were the lines at which my brother murmured with subdued intensity, during a performance of *The Tempest* by Charles Doran's Company which we attended together at Oxford in 1922, 'What does it mean?'—thereby prompting, perhaps inaugurating, my life's work in Shakespearian interpretation. With all the critical confidence I can muster, I assert that these few marvellous lines, like Caliban's nature poetry, and for the same deep reason, transfix us with a direct, convincing and unique report of the powers surrounding us. Our perceptions are normally constricted to an arbitrary selection of phenomena. Were they not, we might, as Alexander Pope has it, 'die of a rose in aromatic pain'.[19] The absurdity of our normal supposition that the nature of the surrounding universe is limited to our normal sense-perception has been admirably discussed in Arthur Ford, *The Life Beyond Death*, recounted by Jerome Ellison.[20] Abnormal children who have difficulties of communication may none the less have experience of voices and music unknown to normality. As with a radio, we may not know how to turn on the switch; but the music in the atmosphere and the voices are there for when the switch is on, none the less. For Caliban the switch is always on; he makes no distinction between man and spirit, the natural and the supernatural, and sees and hears what to us is wonderful; his every accent is there to prove it. We forget the occasion. We are, for the moment, outside *The Tempest,* but inside the universe; a spiritualistic universe. The universe of the Red Men.

In *Black Elk Speaks* we have a true and mainly autobiographical account of how Black Elk as a youth was caught up into a heavenly vision which fertilised his life, laying on him commands to serve his people. He had extra-sensory experience, travelling back to America in spirit when he was in Europe with a circus. He practised spiritual healing. The story is interthreaded with animals. At his central visionary experience we are told:

> All the universe was silent, listening; and then the great black stallion raised his voice and sang . . . His voice was not loud, but it went all over the universe and filled it. There was nothing that did not hear, and it was more beautiful than anything can be. It was so beautiful that nothing anywhere could keep from dancing. (Ch. III, p. 39)

We are reminded of Caliban's 'thousand twangling instruments'; it is a similar, vast, music, travelling the universe. 'Voices', like Caliban's, of all kinds are on page after page of Black Elk's story.

> In a sacred manner they have sent voices.
> Half the universe has sent voices.
> In a sacred manner they have sent voices to you.   (Ch. XVI, p.137)

Voices are everywhere. There are dreams too, as in Caliban's speech. Dreams are universally respected by primitive cultures, but were probably rated more highly, and were more habitually experienced and used, by the Red Men than by any other culture on record. Indian medicines or charms, we are told in *The Oregon Trail*, 'are usually communicated in dreams' (Ch. XV, p. 212). Of a healer in *Black Elk Speaks* we hear that he performed 'after he had sung a certain sacred song that he had heard in a dream' (Ch. II, p. 21). Dreams are the opening to the higher, visionary, consciousness. There was 'a dreamer religion', to whose devotees dreams were 'the sole source of supernatural power'.[21]

Finally, when Black Elk tries to recapture his early transcendent experience while his people are wilting under European oppression and injustice, recalling his lost vision and the failure of his life's work, at the book's heart-rending end, he cries to the great spirits:

> Again, and maybe the last time on this earth, I recall the great vision you sent me. It may be that some little root of the sacred tree still lives. Nourish it then, that it may leaf and bloom and fill with singing birds. Hear me, not for myself, but for my people; I am old. Hear me that they may once more go back into the sacred hoop,[22] and find the good red road, the shielding tree!

With tears running down his cheeks, the old man raised his voice to a thin high wail, and chanted:

> In sorrow I am sending a feeble voice, O Six Powers of the World. Here me in my sorrow, for I may never call again. O make my people live!

For some minutes the old man stood silent, with face uplifted, weeping in the drizzling rain.[23]

So too Caliban weeps for the riches he had glimpsed: 'I cried to dream again.'

For Caliban nature and spirits are one; and what is true of his nature poetry is true equally of his spiritual apprehensions. Here too, I see them as out-spacing all Shakespeare's other spiritual adventures, great as they may be. Of these, the most dramatically exciting are composed of the traditional, and to that extent factual, elements: the black magic of *Macbeth,* traditional folklore; the Ghost in *Hamlet,* a blend of folklore and theology; the vision of Jupiter in *Cymbeline,* Roman mythology; the angels in *Henry VIII,* Christian. Though great as drama, and often the greater for their use of tradition, they remain artefacts. For equivalents to Caliban's lines, where the extra-sensory is so cogently, yet simply, experienced, bearing every impress of actuality, we can point to Joan's defence in *I Henry VI* (V,iv,36–53); to Glendower's spirit-music in *I Henry IV* (III,i,226–8, 233–5); to the healing scene in *All's Well That Ends Well;*[24] and to the resurrection of Hermione in *The Winter's Tale,* which comes from the will to place esoteric possibilities within a normal plot. These do not, however, so wonderfully compact the whole truth as Caliban's lines; which indeed, in their statement of mysteries beyond ordinary perception, may be allowed to make good sense of Shakespeare's symbolic powers elsewhere. They might even be seen as an introduction to the Shakespearian universe; and perhaps this has something to do with *The Tempest's* being placed first in the Folio. Caliban's lines are comprehensive and unique. This may be, as with his nature poetry, a question of style, though its style is, necessarily, slightly different. It does not, as psychic descriptions so often do, lack vigour, but is fully, and imagistically, alive, to be experienced by the reader, or listener, as an immediacy.

If, as Dr Johnson said,[25] there is always in criticism room for an appeal beyond literature to life itself, then the quality of Caliban's poetry, in both its natural and supernatural contacts, becomes apparent. In it Shakespeare forecasts what may be the future of world-literature, concerned less with the fictional than the factual, but with a factuality that encompasses the supernatural.

In the story, Caliban realises his foolishness in thinking Stephano a god, and seeks for 'grace' (V,i,295). That is a reasonable ending, which we might set beside the conclusion to *Hiawatha*, where the Red Men are to be converted to Christianity; which again, given the period of composition, we may regard as a normal conclusion. What is important, however, is not the end, but the events that form the main substance.

Something, but far from all, of Caliban's natural kinship and its higher extensions is given by Robert Browning's 'Caliban upon Setebos', so admirably studied in Thomas Blackburn's *Robert Browning.*[26] There is more in Beerbohm Tree's approach, in costume, make-up, and general sympathy, as recorded in his illustrated souvenir edition of *The Tempest.*[27] Tree's sensitivity to Shakespeare's poetry is evident from his bird-song interlude in his production of *Much Ado About Nothing*, long before Caroline Spurgeon's researchers into Shakespeare's imagery, and his Weird Women actually seen floating in 'fog and filthy air' in *Macbeth* (I,i,12); as well as in his own vocal recordings from *Richard II, Julius Caesar* and *Hamlet*. But never was his status in poetic understanding more evident than in his electing to act Caliban himself, and his building up of the part even at the cost of some overbalance. I am thinking of his conclusion, as pictorially illustrated in the souvenir, showing Caliban alone on the island rocks, and looking out sadly, according to the stage-direction, on the departing ship. A copy is shown in my *Shakespearian Production.*[28]

Here our analogy collapses. The Red Men would have been glad enough to see the last of the Europeans.

Postscript, October 1977

Since composing my essay, my attention has been drawn by Professor Gāmini Salgādo to Leslie A. Fiedler's *The Stranger in Shakespeare,*[29] which contains a careful study of *The Tempest* in relation to its forecast of colonisation, paying exact regard to Caliban. Some of my own points are made: see especially the reference to European 'technology' (Ch. IV,p. 238). Mr Fiedler observes throughout 'a kind of music' and 'natural rhythm' in Caliban's talk (p. 235). I should point also to the brilliant analyses in D. G. James's *The Dream of Prospero.*[30]

I have concluded recent performances of my dramatic recital[31] with a short delineation of Caliban in Red Indian guise.

NOTES

[1] For my Red Indian material I rely on the following books: John G. Neihardt, *Black Elk Speaks* (London, 1974; first published 1961); Frank Waters, *Masked Gods* (New York, 1973; first published 1950); Ralph

T. Coe, Catalogue of the 'Sacred Circles' Exhibition, Hayward Gallery, London, October 1976–January 1977 (Arts Council of Great Britain, 1977); Carlos Castaneda, *The Teachings of Don Juan* (Harmondsworth, 1976; first published 1968); Francis Parkman, *The Oregon Trail* (Harmondsworth, 1949; first published 1849); T. C. McLuhan, *Touch the Earth* (London, 1973; first published 1972).

[2] Mark van Doren, *Shakespeare* (New York, 1939), pp. 325–6. In his notes on *The Tempest*, Dr Johnson quotes Warburton as follows: 'It was a tradition, it seems, that Lord Falkland, Lord C. J. Vaughan, and Mr Seldon concurred in observing, that Shakespeare had not only found out a new character in his Caliban, but had also devised and adapted a *new manner of language* for that character' (*Johnson on Shakespeare*, ed. Walter Raleigh (London, 1908, repr. 1909), p. 66).

[3] Relevant thoughts on Tolstoy are developed in my *Christian Renaissance* (London, 1962), Ch. III, pp. 38–40.

[4] Waters, *Masked Gods*, Part Two.

[5] Neihardt, *Black Elk Speaks*, Ch. III, pp. 28–9, 42.

[6] Murray Hickey Ley, Papers lodged at Notre Dame University (South Bend, Indiana, USA), *Introductions* [booklet], pp. 24, 27.

[7] McLuhan, *Touch the Earth*, p. 90.

[8] For drugs, see Castaneda, *The Teachings of Don Juan*.

[9] Neihardt, *Black Elk Speaks*, Ch. X, p. 100.

[10] *The Development of Shakespeare's Imagery* (London, 1951), Ch. XIX, p. 187.

[11] McLuhan, *Touch the Earth*, p. 40.

[12] McLuhan, *Touch the Earth*, pp. 83, 102, 104, 141, 161.

[13] *The Oregon Trail*, Ch. XIV, p. 176.

[14] See pp. 85, 87, 91–2, 96–7, 107, 131, 156, 169.

[15] Letter by a group of Indians to President Nixon, quoted in McLuhan, *Touch the Earth*, p. 170.

[16] Neihardt, *Black Elk Speaks*, Ch. II, p. 18.

[17] *Jackson Knight: A Biography* (Osney Mead, Oxford, 1975).

[18] In his *Autobiography* (London, 1934), Ch. XI, p. 548.

[19] *An Essay on Man*, I, 200.

[20] London, 1974 (first published 1972), Ch. I, pp. 38–41, also Ch. V, p. 114.

[21] McLuhan, *Touch the Earth*, pp. 56, 178n.

[22] For the importance of 'hoops' or circles in Red Indian culture, see the Catalogue for 'Sacred Circles', noted above (n. 1), pp. 18–19. Also see McLuhan, *Touch the Earth*, p. 178.

[23] Postscript to Neihardt, *Black Elk Speaks*, pp. 190–1.

[24] Discussed in my *The Sovereign Flower* (London, 1958), Ch. II, pp. 148–54.

[25] 'Preface to Shakespeare', in *Johnson on Shakespeare* (see n. 2, above), p. 16.

[26] London, 1967, Ch. IV, pp. 155–61.

[27] London, 1904.

[28] London, 1964.

[29] London, 1973.

[30] Oxford, 1967, pp. 81, 106, 111–14.

[31] Described in *Shakespeare's Dramatic Challenge* (London and New York, 1977).

Virginia Mason Vaughan

CALIBAN'S THEATRICAL
METAMORPHOSES

Since Caliban's first appearance in 1611, Shakespeare's monster has undergone remarkable transformations.[1] From drunken beast in the eighteenth century, to noble savage and missing link in the nineteenth, to Third World victim of oppression in the mid-twentieth, Caliban's stage images reflect changing Anglo-American attitudes toward primitive man. Shakespeare's monster once represented bestial vices that must be eradicated; now he personifies noble rebels who symbolize the exploitation of European imperialism.

Caliban's malleability derives, perhaps, from his scant 180 lines and his ambiguous image in Shakespeare's text. In the 1623 Folio (where *The Tempest* was first printed), Caliban appears in the cast of characters as a "salvage and deformed slave." Of his slavery the text leaves no doubt: throughout the play he is called a slave, and he ruefully admits it himself. The text is also persistent, though imprecise, about Caliban's deformity. Before the monster appears on stage, Prospero says that except for Caliban, the island had not been "honored with a human shape" when he arrived (I.ii.282–83); later Prospero calls Caliban a "mis-shapen knave" (V.i.268). But the play's only details about Caliban's appearance are several references to fish-like features. Trinculo initially calls him a "fish" who is "Legg'd like a man; and his fins like arms" (II.ii.25–35). On closer view, however, Trinculo decides that "this is no fish, but an islander" (II.ii.36–37). Later Trinculo describes Caliban as a "debosh'd fish" (III.ii.25) and "half a fish and half a monster" (II.ii.28). Near the end of the play Antonio refers to him as "a plain fish" (V.i.266). Prospero once calls him "thou tortoise" (I.ii.317), though the epithet probably refers to Caliban's dilatoriness rather than to his appearance. Not surprisingly, Caliban has often been portrayed on the stage or in illustrations with scales, fins, and other aquatic attributes.

"Monster" is Caliban's most frequent sobriquet. The term appears in the text 40 times, usually with a pejorative adjective: "shallow," "weak," "credulous," "most perfidious and drunken," "puppyheaded," "scurvy," "abominable," "ridiculous," "howling," "drunken," "ignorant," and "lost." Only "brave" might be considered a

---

From *Shakespeare Quarterly* 36, No. 4 (Winter 1985): 390–405.

favorable modifier, but it is almost certainly meant sarcastically. More neutral are "servant-monster," "man-monster," and "poor monster." To the extent that monster implies physical deformity, these abundant reminders strengthen the notion of Caliban as grotesque. They do nothing, however, to clarify our picture of him.

Neither do other references to Caliban. He is often called "mooncalf," suggesting stupidity and an amorphous shape. According to Pliny's *Natural History* translated into English in 1601, a mooncalf is "a lumpe of flesh without shape, without life."[2] Once Caliban is called "this thing of darkness," possibly to imply a dusky skin though more likely to indicate a faulty character. And once Prospero calls him "thou earth." On other occasions he is termed "a freckled whelp hagborn," and once he is "Hag-seed." Several times Caliban's parentage—his mother was an Algerian witch, his father was the devil—is invoked, as in "demi-devil" and "a born devil." From this confusion of epithets no clear image emerges. Shakespeare seems to have invited his actors and directors to see Caliban however they wished. They have not been reluctant to accept his invitation.

I

Edmond Malone reported in his 1821 Variorum edition that Caliban had always appeared dressed in animal skins:

> The dress worn by this character, which doubtless was originally prescribed by the poet himself, and has been continued, I believe, since his time, is a large bearskin, or the skin of some other animal; and he is usually represented with long shaggy hair.[3]

How Malone knew what Shakespeare prescribed we cannot say. The closing of all public theatres during the Interregnum destroyed all but the most scattered clues about how Shakespeare's plays were originally performed. When the playhouses opened again in 1660, Shakespeare's fellow actors were dead; the theatre as Shakespeare had known it was transformed to suit Restoration audiences.[4]

In 1660 William Davenant, who claimed a close relationship with Shakespeare, formed an acting company under the Duke of York's patronage. An agreement of 12 December 1660 gave Davenant's actors exclusive rights to nine of Shakespeare's plays, including *The Tempest*. But Shakespeare's text struck Davenant as unsuitable for Restoration tastes. Collaborating with John Dryden, in 1667 he produced an adaptation: *The Tempest; or, The Enchanted Isle*. Dryden and Davenant simplified Shakespeare's characters, added an extra boy and girl (Hippolito and Dorinda) and a she-monster named Sycorax, inserted moralistic songs and sayings, and rearranged scenes and changed episodes—all in accord with contemporary notions of decorum. Dryden and Davenant also padded the Stephano-Trinculo plot with two new sailors, Ventoso and Mustacho, who join in comic machinations to take control of the island and to win the affections of Sycorax. This version, later combined with songs and scenes from Shadwell's operatic treatment (1674), became extremely popular.[5] Other operatic productions were staged in the 1690s (Purcell), 1756 (Garrick), and 1776–79 (Covent Garden). Even non-operatic versions had more music, song, and dance than Shakespeare's text indicates. From the Restoration to the mid-eighteenth century, then, *The Tempest* was a musical extravaganza.

Caliban in the Dryden-Davenant *Tempest* is a lecherous drunk. As a burlesque slave to Stephano and Trinculo, he makes love to his sister, Sycorax. Later he tries to couple Sycorax with Trinculo, a scheme motivated by his own ambition. Caliban's lines from the original *Tempest* are so cut and altered that he becomes the epitome of monstrousness, a non-human symbol of human iniquity.

Shakespeare's text portrays Caliban as a primitive man who poses basic questions about the values and benefits of Jacobean "civilization." In the Dryden-Davenant *Tempest,* this function belongs to Hippolito, a beautiful young man who is kept in a cave by Prospero, separated from Miranda (and her sister Dorinda), because of the magician's fear that the youth will be destroyed by a woman. Hippolito is of noble birth but is brought up without the benefits of culture and education. He was designed by Davenant, says Dryden in his Preface to the 1670 edition, as a counterpart for Miranda. Hippolito is "a Man who has never seen a Woman; that by this means those two Characters of Innocence and Love might the more illustrate and commend each other."[6] Drawing upon long-established European traditions, Dryden and Davenant may have meant Hippolito to represent a benign version of the wild man.[7] He lives in a state of nature. He uses reason to understand his world, but he is unsophisticated in the courtly arts of love and dueling. He does not understand the difference between love and lust, nor can he comprehend that he is to pledge himself to one woman only. Dorinda, Miranda, Ferdinand, and Prospero undertake his education, and as the play concludes it is Hippolito who exclaims "O brave new world that hath such people in't!"

Where does that leave Caliban? He is no longer natural man but a savage monster who reflects European fears of the non-European world. Two of Dryden's mariners reveal their conception of "salvages":

> MUSTACHO: Our ship is sunk and we can never get home agen: we must e'en turn Salvages, and the next that catches his fellow may eat him.
>
> VENTOSO: No, no, let us have a government; for if we live well and orderly, Heav'n will drive the Shipwracks ashore to make us all rich, therefore let us carry good Consciences, and not eat one another.[8]

Dryden's Caliban is just such a "salvage." As the play closes, he resolves to be more wise, but he is incapable of suing for grace as did Shakespeare's Caliban.[9]

When Samuel Pepys saw *The Enchanted Isle,* he described it as "the most innocent play that ever I saw." He admired the Dryden-Davenant echo song between Ferdinand and Ariel, but he did not mention Caliban.[10] In ensuing years, this version—with songs and scenes from Shadwell's opera added—played continually to crowded audiences. This *Tempest* was produced at the Theatre Royal, Drury Lane, almost every year from 1701 to 1756, its popularity unabated.

In March 1756, however, David Garrick, actor-manager for the Drury Lane, experimented with a new operatic *Tempest.* Garrick pruned Shakespeare's lines, incorporated Dryden-Davenant material, and added 32 songs by John Christopher Smith. Larded with arias for the major characters, the opera had even less space for Caliban. In any early scene, Trinculo refers to Caliban as an amphibious monster, but no sooner is the "dear tortoise" introduced than he is forgotten. The opera contains no resolution to the Stephano-Trinculo subplot except a drinking song in Act III.[11] This opera, not surprisingly, failed. After a short run and some bad reviews, Garrick admitted defeat and closed it.

The following year (20 October 1757) Garrick offered a new version, billed as "written by Shakespeare." It returned to the First Folio, minus 432 lines and with 14 added. Part of Garrick's growing effort to restore Shakespeare's original text, the production was a success.[12] It ran nearly every year until 1787, when John Philip Kemble substituted his own acting text. Kemble reintroduced Dorinda and Hippolito, but he eliminated Sycorax, Ventoso, and Mustacho. His Caliban had Shakespeare's original lines.[13] This hodgepodge persisted until 1838 when William Charles Macready returned to Shakespeare's text.

Despite the paucity of details about the actors who played Caliban during the Restoration and the early eighteenth century, it is clear that Caliban was a minor role. Actors were selected for a voice and figure that could portray the monster's grotesque qualities. Edward Machan, a lame actor who failed as Richard III, acted Caliban at Phillips' Booth in Bartholomew Fair during 1749.[14] Edward Berry (1700–1760), Caliban in Garrick's restoration of the original text, was notable for his huge body and booming voice and was accused of howling on all occasions.[15] James Dance, also known as James Love (1721–74), acted Caliban at Drury Lane from 1765 to 1769. As one commentator notes, "Roles like Jaques, Sir Toby Belch, Caliban, Jobson, and Falstaff were suited to his manner, his unwieldly figure, and a voice described ... 'as somewhat asthmatical, and abounding with many inharmonious tones.'"[16]

Caliban was also played by comedians who had some musical talent. Charles Bannister, Drury Lane's Caliban for nearly thirty years (1777 into the 1800s), was praised for a voice "which he used ... both as a tool of the mimic's trade and with near-operatic skill in dramatic singing." He also boasted a "Herculean figure."[17] Another comedian, Charles Blakes, portrayed Caliban from 1759 to 1763: Blakes sang sea songs during most intervals. In *Tempest* productions, this must have seemed an appropriate pastime for the fishy monster.[18]

Caliban's relative insignificance to eighteenth-century productions is understandable. Caliban did not suit the age's notions of comedy. As early as Shadwell, argues Stuart M. Tave in his study of eighteenth-century comic theory, theatre critics had "ruled out natural imperfections as fit objects for satire." Caliban's grotesque deformities were not the proper vehicle for good-natured wit. Moreover, his natural folly was inappropriate to an art form that should deal with artificial follies. Only with the Romantic movement's appreciation of humor mixed with pathos could theatregoers respond to Caliban's poetic imaginings and longing for freedom.[19]

Caliban did not suit the eighteenth-century definition of a Noble Savage. If anyone in the Dryden-Davenant version had that role, it had to be Hippolito. In an age of reason that believed "the proper study of mankind is man,"[20] Caliban was too irrational, too inhuman, to warrant serious consideration. To generalize broadly, the eighteenth century was concerned with mankind as a social unit, civilized by generally accepted norms of behavior and commonly held beliefs. The poet's province was human nature—the collective wisdom of human experience. Thus, when Samuel Johnson praised Shakespeare in his *Preface,* he admired the poet's "just representations of general nature."[21] Sub-human, idiosyncratic, passionate (as opposed to rational), and uncivilized, Caliban was not likely to become the age's favorite dramatic character.

Unlike the Noble Savage, Caliban did not point to the possibility of progress by civilized man if left untrammeled by social institutions.[22] Instead Caliban suggested the absolute need for such institutions. Like Gulliver's Yahoos, Caliban's monstrousness revealed the lower aspects of human appetite. Since he represented bestial desires without the control of right reason, he could never be considered sympathetically as a human being.

Caliban's image would shift with the times. With the rise of Romanticism, the Noble Savage no longer had to be a man of reason. He could be instead a creature of emotion and sensibility. He could be seen as one who depended on intuition for a direct apprehension of nature. Like Wordsworth's poet, Caliban could express his natural affinities in the "spontaneous overflow of powerful feelings."[23] As a result, Caliban's image was to change drastically during the nineteenth century.

II

In the early nineteenth century, Caliban's role became more desirable. When John Emery (1777–1822) played Caliban to John Philip Kemble's 1806 Prospero, he captured more than the audience's laughter, according to an anonymous witness:

> ... this roughness as well as awe, Emery most inevitably displayed, particularly in the vehement manner and high voice with which he cursed Prospero, and the thoughtful lowness of tone, softened from his usual coarse brutality, with which he worshipped his new deity.... [He] approached to terrific tragedy, when he described the various tortures inflicted on him by the magician, and the surrounding snakes that "stare and hiss him into madness...." The monster hugged and shrunk into himself as he proceeded, and when he pictured the torment that almost turned his brain, glared with his eyes, and gnashed his teeth with an impatient impotence of revenge.[24]

Emery's dramatic interpretations invoked elements of Caliban that had been neglected in earlier productions. Now there was scope for Caliban's poetic sensibilities and tragic suffering as well for his grotesquerie.

Contemporary critical assessments of Caliban also revealed a shift from dismissal based on his lack of enlightened reason to a romantic appreciation of his poetic suggestiveness. In his lecture on *The Tempest* (1811–12), Samuel Taylor

Coleridge described Caliban not as a sotted monster, but as a "noble being; a man in the sense of the imagination, all the images he utters are drawn from nature, and are highly poetical."[25] William Hazlitt agreed. He saw Caliban as Shakespeare's portrait of "the human animal rude and without choice in its pleasures, but not without the sense of pleasure or some germ of the affections."[26]

In the privacy of their studies, Coleridge and Hazlitt were free to respond to Shakespeare's original text. Yet on stage, both at Drury Lane and at Covent Garden, the Kemble-Dryden-Davenant version persisted. William Charles Macready played Prospero in 1821, 1824, and again in 1833, but he did so unhappily. Later he described the acting version he was forced to use as a "*mélange* that was called Shakespeare's *Tempest,* with songs interpolated by Reynolds among the mutilations and barbarous ingraftings of Dryden and Davenant." Macready found the performances tedious and lamented that his role was a "stupid old proser of commonplace which the acted piece calls Prospero."[27] It is not surprising then that when in 1838 Macready revived the *Tempest* as Shakespeare had originally conceived it, the new production confirmed the romantic critics' more sympathetic conceptions of Caliban.

Caliban was by then a more important character, played by George Bennett, an actor who excelled in tragic as well as comic roles. Besides Caliban, he was remembered for performances of Sir Toby Belch, Pistol, Enobarbus, Bosola, and Apemantus. Bennett's performance inspired at least one member of the audience to see Caliban in a fresh light. Bennett, argued Patrick MacDonnell, delineated "the rude and uncultivated savage, in a style, which arouses our sympathies." To MacDonnell Caliban was no longer merely a comic butt; he had become "a creature, in his nature possessing all the rude elements of the savage, yet maintaining in his mind, a strong resistance to that tyranny which held him in the thraldom of slavery."[28] Bennett began the stage tradition of lunging at Prospero during the opening confrontation, then recoiling from a wave of the magic wand, and finally writhing in impotent fury.[29] Here the modern Caliban, victim of oppression, was born.

Macready's *Tempest* ran for 55 performances, netting an average income of 230 pounds a night. In his journal Macready confessed his pleasure: "I look back on its production with satisfaction, for it has given to the public a play of Shakespeare's which had never been seen before, and it has proved the charm and simplicity and poetry." Macready's journal entries indicate that even when he felt he had been "cold" or "indifferent" in the part, he was well received and generally called back by the audience."[30]

Macready's innovative production was soon followed by rival versions. Two surviving promptbooks provide valuable insights into Caliban's new role. The first was Samuel Phelps's (1804–78) at Sadler's Wells Theatre in 1847. Phelps had performed with Macready at Covent Garden and portrayed Antonio in the 1838 *Tempest.* When Parliament withdrew the exclusive privileges of Drury Lane and Covent Garden in 1844, Phelps formed a company that specialized in higher drama. In his 1847 *Tempest* Phelps acted Prospero; George Bennett again portrayed Caliban.

According to the promptbook, the 1847 Caliban was still fairly bestial. Nevertheless, he was a man-beast, not simply a monster. His first entrance is carefully described: "Enter Caliban. Opening L of Flat/Crawling out on all fours as a Beast, rises & threatening Prospero, who raises his wand & checks him. Caliban recoils as if spell struck" (p. 24)."[31] As he describes the fresh springs and brine pits, Caliban is to be "stamping and gabbling with fury" (p. 25). (Much of this stage business was to become standard, repeated in promptbooks throughout the century.) Prospero's reminders of his magical power make Caliban afraid, and he exits "tremblingly." He rebels in II.ii, indignantly discarding his burden of wood. He drinks thirstily throughout the scene, while crawling and kneeling at Stephano's feet. In III.ii Caliban, like Stephano and Trinculo, is literally falling-down drunk. Says the promptbook: "Caliban speaks his other speeches either kneeling or sitting on all fours like a   beast" (p. 62). When Ariel mischievously causes Stephano to strike Trinculo, "Caliban shows a strong and savage expression of joy" (p. 64). This Caliban is surely comical, but both in his anger and his poetry he displays human dignity.

By the mid-nineteenth century Shakespearean drama was being acted regularly in America as well as in England.[32] On 11 April 1854, the comedian William Burton portrayed Caliban at his own theatre in New York. Visitors from the Northeast thronged to his theatre to see Burton impersonate Dickensian characters. They expected broad and coarse humor. His Caliban, however, was more than comic. His friend and biographer W. L. Keese recalled that

> His *Caliban* we have tried to forget rather than remember, it terrified us and made us dream bad dreams, but for all of that, we know that it was a surprising impersonation.[33]

An anonymous author, writing in the *New York Times* on 20 June 1874, recalled Burton's Caliban:

> A wild creature on all fours sprang upon the stage, with claws on his hands, and some weird animal arrangement about the head partly like a snail. It was an immense conception. Not the great God Pan himself was more the link between man and beast than this thing. It was a creature of the woods, one of nature's spawns; it breathed of nuts and herbs, and rubbed itself against the back of trees.

The stage directions from Burton's promptbook bear out this portrayal. Throughout his speech to Prospero (I.ii), Caliban "roars or yells with rage." His gaberdine is a large skin, not a cloak. Later he clings to Stephano's keg, growls when he loses it, and paws Stephano's leg to get it back again. Burton's Caliban was meant to be animal-like; and his ferocity was awesome.[34]

Prompt copy for Charles Kean's extravagant 1857 production at the Princess's Theatre is equally revealing. In accord with standard stage business, John Ryder's Caliban flies at Prospero after his opening speech and then shrinks back when Prospero extends his magic wand. The gaberdine scene is milked for all its humor with the following interplay:

Trinculo nudges Stephano not to give all the wine to Caliban and then goes round at back to RH. Cal takes a long pull at the bottle. Trin. looks at him in surprise. Cal turns and looks savagely at Trinc.[35]

Ryder's costume was later described in Thomas Barry's acting edition:

Brown fleshings, covered with hair, green nails, toes and fingers, fins on shoulders and arms, calf of legs, webbed fingers and toes, goggles on eyes, wolf skin skirt, wild wavy wig, beard, and moustache.[36]

In the Kean costume book at the Folger Shakespeare Library, Caliban has long toenails and fingernails and is covered with bushy brown fur.[37] The era of the apish Caliban had begun.

III

During the mid-nineteenth century, costumes such as John Ryder's emphasized Caliban's animal characteristics. Occasionally, however, the costumer went to extremes. Dutton Cook insisted in a 1871 review that George Rignold's "Caliban is perhaps needlessly repulsive of aspect, and the tusks and pasteboard jaws worn by the actor have the disadvantage of hindering his articulation."[38] Despite such difficulties, from Emery's performance on, actors conveyed not only Caliban's savagery but his tragic sense of Prospero's injustice. The result was performances human in their emotional power, animal in appearance and behavior.

The conception of Caliban as an amphibian, somewhere between brute animal and human being, was made more explicit and timely in Daniel Wilson's book, *Caliban: The Missing Link* (1873). Wilson associated Caliban with Darwin's missing link; to him, Shakespeare's monster personified the evolutionist's theoretical "intermediate being, lower than man." Wilson noted Caliban's fish-like appearance and related it to Darwin's view that humanity evolved from some species of aquatic animal. At the same time he contended that "though by some scaly or fin-like appendages, the idea of a fish or sea-monster, is suggested to all, the form of Caliban is, nevertheless, essentially human." Wilson concluded that "We feel for the poor monster, so helplessly in the power of the stern Prospero, as for some caged wild beast pining in cruel captivity, and rejoice to think of him at last free to range in harmless mastery over his island solitude."[39]

Gradually Caliban the ape man evolved on stage. Lady Benson recalled in her memoirs that in preparation for productions of *The Tempest* during the 1890s, F. R. Benson "spent many hours watching monkeys and baboons in the zoo, in order to get the movements and postures in keeping with his 'makeup.'" She described his costume as "half monkey, half coco-nut," and noted that he "delighted in swarming up a tree on the stage and hanging from the branches head downwards while he gibbered at 'Trinculo.'" Benson also initiated the stage business (continued by Beerbohm Tree) of appearing with a real fish in his mouth.[40]

Tyrone Power's costume for the 1897 Augustin Daly production was similarly apish. The color sketch in Daly's souvenir album shows a human form covered with brown fur. He wears a green tunic (shades of Tarzan) and sports metallic scales around his calves. His long nails and hairy face bespeak his animal qualities; his erect posture and expression suggest the human.[41]

Power's costume, according to a *New York Times* critic (7 April 1897) is conventional, but his 'mask' and wig are "most unhappy, while his delivery of the poetry lacks melody." To William Winter, reviewer for the *New York Daily Tribune* (also 7 April 1897), Caliban represented a "brutish creature, the hideous, malignant clod of evil, in whom nevertheless, the germs of intelligence, feeling and fanciful perception are beginning to stir." Winter praised Power's "half-bestial, half-human aspect, the rude grisly strength, the intense, sustained savage fury and the startling gleams of thought." However one judges Power's performance, it is clear that he—and Daly—saw Caliban as a pre-civilized missing link. Caliban the ape man has crossed the Atlantic.

Beerbohm Tree also stressed Caliban's humanity in his production of 1904. In the preface to his acting edition, Tree argued that Caliban had a human shape and that "in his love of music and his affinity with the unseen world, we discern in the soul which inhabits this elemental man the germs of a sense of beauty, the dawn of art."[42] Tree's costume consisted of fur and seaweed; significantly, he also wore a necklace of shells and coral. When this Caliban hears the island's music, he dances and tries to sing. At the beginning of Act III, scene ii, he listens to the isle's sweet music while weaving a wreath of flowers for Stephano: "Placing the wreath on his head, he looks at himself in the pool." The most famous scene of this production was a final tableau that shows the Neapolitans sailing home:

> Caliban creeps from his cave and watches. . . . Caliban listens for the last time to the sweet air [Ariel's song], then turns sadly in the direction of the departing ship. The play is ended. As the curtain rises again, the ship is seen on the horizon, Caliban stretching out his arms toward it in mute despair. The night falls, and Caliban is left on the lonely rock. He is king once more.
>
> (p. 63)

Tree noted that at this moment "we feel that from the conception of sorrow in solitude may spring the birth of a higher civilization."[43] Despite his primitive origins, Tree's Caliban expressed deep human sensibilities and aspirations. Perhaps this "deformed savage"—image of humanity's earliest ancestors—could become civilized.

Belief in human progress also animated Caliban's portrayal in Percy MacKaye's mammoth community masque, performed at Lewisohn Stadium in New York (1916). MacKaye wanted his Caliban to symbolize "that passionate child-curious part of us all [whether as individuals or as races], groveling close to his aboriginal origins, yet groping up and staggering—with almost rhythmic falls and back-slidings—toward that serener plane of pity and love, reason and disciplined will, where Miranda and Prospero commune with Ariel and his spirits."[44] Caliban is aspiring humanity; his education consists of pageants depicting human civilization from ancient Egypt to the present. He is also entertained by scenes from Shakespeare's plays, manufactured through Prospero's art. Although a monster at first, MacKaye's Caliban learns by trial and error to reject Lust, Death, and War. Finally, he learns how to love. Caliban illustrates MacKaye's conviction that humanity had progressed from bestiality to civilization.

The Darwinian Caliban persisted well into the twentieth century. Gordon Crosse praised Robert Atkins' Caliban at the Old Vic (1920–25) because "He showed with superlative art the malevolent brute nature with the dim, half-formed, human intellect just breaking through." [45] G. Wilson Knight records that he played Caliban at Toronto (1938) wearing heavy gray furs over a complete covering of green grease paint which blended "the slimy reptilian and savagely human." [46] In 1938 Robert Atkins again depicted Caliban, this time as an aspiring and frustrated Neanderthal. English productions of 1940 and 1951 presented Caliban as a pre-historic figure, newly crawling out of the slime. [47]

The Darwinian Caliban demonstrated humanity's capacity for continued growth and improvement. He sensed the island's beauty and slowly learned to sue for grace. During World War II, however, Western civilization plunged back into the savagery from which it had supposedly emerged. *The Tempest* no longer seemed an airy comedy; as the play darkened, Prospero became a cruel taskmaster, Caliban his unwilling victim.

IV

After 1945 a growing number of literary critics began to view *The Tempest* as Shakespeare's study of the colonists' adventures in the New World. If Prospero's enchanted island was an image of America, then surely Caliban, the island's indigenous inhabitant, must be Shakespeare's portrait of an American Indian. [48] In addition to Shakespeare's monster and Third World native peoples—of whatever continent or country—who had been colonized by Europeans and were now throwing off their foreign governors and asserting independence. Like Caliban (so the argument goes), most colonized peoples are disinherited, subjugated, and exploited. Like him, they learned a conqueror's language and values. Like him, they endured enslavement and contempt by European usurpers. Eventually, like Caliban, they rebelled.

Though it began as a source of discussion during the 1950s—with precursors in the 1930s and '40s—Caliban's politicized image did not penetrate the theatre until the late 1960s. By then Caliban had become a role often reserved for black actors. In the all-white theatrical world of the 1940s and '50s, few parts were open to members of minority groups. Caliban, an alien creature, could be played by a black man; the strangeness, seemingly part of the costume, need not startle the predominantly white audience. But once the tradition was established, the role became politicized.

Canada Lee first broke the color barrier. In 1945 he portrayed Caliban in Margaret Webster's New York *Tempest.* Lee wore a scaly costume and grotesque mask, moved with an animal-like crouch, and emphasized Caliban's monstrousness. *The Saturday Review* noted that "Canada Lee's Caliban is a monster, fearsome, badgered, and pathetic. His only trouble is that he keeps all of Caliban's poetry earth sprung, too." [49] Lee's performance won modest praise; the role of Caliban was now open, but the transformation was slow.

Earle Hyman assayed the part in 1960 at the American Shakespeare Festival in Connecticut. Hyman too played up Caliban's monstrosity, wearing inflated belly and legs and a grotesque headpiece. Judging from the photograph in *Shakespeare Quarterly,* he looked anything but human.[50] In 1962 James Earl Jones used similar tactics, though his interpretation was more reptilian. Alice Griffin described Jones's Caliban as "a savage, green-faced lizard darting his red tongue in and out, lunging clumsily at what he wanted, and yelping when he was denied it." [51]

Jones's and Hyman's Calibans looked to the past. For the rest of the 1960s and beyond, Caliban changed from monster to vehicle for contemporary ideas. The following survey is admittedly cursory, but it does reflect the breadth of Caliban's politicization during the 1960s and '70s.

Influenced by Jan Kott's harsh interpretation of the play as a study in violence, Peter Brook directed a production in 1963 at Stratford-upon-Avon in which Roy Dotrice played Caliban as a Java man "who represented emergent humanity." [52] His phallic gestures conveyed primitive man's raw sexuality. Brook continued this motif in 1968 with an experimental rendition of *The Tempest* at the Round House in London. Brook used Caliban and his hypothetical mother Sycorax in order to

> represent those evil and violent forces that rise from man himself regardless of his environment. The monster-mother is portrayed by an enormous woman able to expand her face and body to still larger proportions.... Suddenly, she gives a horrendous yell, and Caliban, with black sweater over his head, emerges from between her legs: Evil is born.

As the action proceeded in Brook's version, Caliban raped Miranda, escaped from Prospero, and took over the island. The experiment continued in a mime of homosexual rape, Caliban on Prospero. And the play ended with broken voices intoning Prospero's epilogue.[53]

Brook's experiment clearly differed from Shakespeare's original, but it charted the way to new interpretations of Caliban. Now the role represented power more than subjugation. Henry Baker, for example, embodied Caliban's violence in the 1970 Washington Summer Shakespeare production. Jeanne Addison Roberts described Baker as "darkly beautiful in his glistening fish scales" and "powerful and intractable from beginning to end." Baker never obeyed Stephano's command to kiss his foot, never cowered, never uttered the final resolve to be wise and sue for grace. To Roberts, "Baker's black skin, his somewhat flawed enunciation, a minstrel-show mouth painted grotesquely in a greenish face, and the use of the word 'slave' evoked instantly for the Washington audience the American Negro." [54] Caliban was now a black militant, angry and recalcitrant.

Jonathan Miller employed similar dynamics in his 1970 production at the Mermaid Theatre. Miller's Caliban, Rudolph Walker, was an uneducated field Negro "in contrast to Ariel, a competent, educated 'houseboy.'" Set in the world of Cortez and Pizarro, Miller's version reflected the complex interrelations of colonial masters and their subjugated natives.[55]

Variations on the colonial theme persisted through the 1970s. The New York Shakespeare Festival presented Jaime Sanchez as a Puerto Rican Caliban in 1974,[56] and in the same year Denis Quilley's Caliban at London's National Theatre was likened by reviewers to James Fenimore Cooper's Chingachgook. Quilley's Caliban was the noble savage, "with one side of him as a man, and the other side half emerging from animality." [57] David Suchet's Caliban (Stratford-upon-Avon, 1978) was a composite version of the Third World native, a generalized conception of primitive man. John Velz reported that Suchet's Caliban combined both West Indian and African.[58] Another reviewer described Suchet's Caliban as a "naked, dark-skinned primitive, with a bold head and bloodshot eyes; ... his exploitation was strongly emphasized." [59]

The climax of Caliban's politicization came, perhaps, during 1980–81, when productions around the world emphasized what had become the standard interpretation. In the popular imagination Caliban now represented any group that felt itself oppressed. In New York, he appeared as a punk rocker, complete with cropped hair, sunglasses, and a Cockney accent.[60] In Augsburg, Germany, Caliban continued as a black slave who performed African dances and rituals during the Stephano-Trinculo scenes.[61] In Connecticut, Gerald Freedman viewed Caliban as an aspect of Prospero's character—the libido that cannot be controlled. At the same time, he cast Joe Morton, a black actor, in the part and had him sing his freedom catch to jazz tunes. Libido or no, this Caliban still symbolized a repressed minority.[62] The Globe Playhouse of Los Angeles, using a cast of mixed nationalities, assigned Caliban to Mark Del-Castillo Morante, who portrayed him as an American Indian. The *Shakespeare Quarterly* review suggests that Del Castillo-Morante's interpretation reflected Montaigne's essay and the historical background of the American Indian circa 1610.[63]

While 1981 marks the apogee of Caliban's colonial image, it may also indicate the shape of things to come. Joe Morton, the black actor who played Caliban for Gerald Freedman in Connecticut, performed the role a second time at The Mount, a summer theatre in Lenox, Massachusetts. This time, however, the actor's blackness was insignificant. Peter Erickson describes the effect:

Caliban's costume consisted of a narrow, flared leather cape as a tail; a daggerless scabbard dangling from his waist; leather gloves, which blended in with his blackened skin, gave the illusion of enormous hands; a mask of light brown body paint which ... left large circles around the eyes. ... This Caliban was typically on or near the ground—he walked bent over at the waist, torso swaying up and down or shaking vigorously in an animal-like posture.... An assortment of convincing groans and growls served as background, imbuing his language with striking visceral impact.[64]

No longer a political symbol, Caliban had returned to his monstrous origins.

V

Ralph Berry wrote in 1983 that "Nowadays, directors have gone off Caliban: I suspect that they are bored with symbols of colonial oppression, and have wrung all the changes they can on Red Indians and Rastafarians."[65] Future productions will test this observation, but it seemed apt enough during the Trinity Repertory Company's 1982 production in Providence. To convey Caliban's monstrousness, Adrian Hall strapped Richard Cavanaugh's feet to three foot stools. As Caliban clomped across the stage, he was grotesque indeed. Some in the audience worried more about how Caliban would fall to his hands and knees than about his lines or characterization, but at least the portrayal was original. This production suggests, however, that even with Caliban, there are limits to innovations.

But rather than a forecast of things to come, the Trinity Theatre Caliban will probably remain an aberration. For, as this survey suggests, when Caliban speaks Shakespeare's original lines, he usually stirs an audience's imagination. Shakespeare's monster continues to provoke horror at his appearance, awe at his language, and laughter at his antics. He is in many respects society's image of the "other"; but he is also, as Auden mused, that thing of darkness we must acknowledge as our own. As we ourselves change, our perceptions of Caliban—our own darkness—change. In the evolving image of Caliban we see a reflection of Anglo-American intellectual history. But we also see our ever-changing selves.

NOTES

[1] Citations from The Tempest are taken from the Arden edition, ed. Frank Kermode (London: Methuen, 1954). I am grateful to both Charles H. Shattuck and Alden T. Vaughan for editorial and substantive advice on early versions of this article.

[2] C. Plinius Secundus, The Historie of the World, trans. Philemon Holland (London, 1601).

[3] Edmond Malone, ed., The Plays and Poems of William Shakespeare (London: F.C. and J. Rivington, et al., 1821), XV, 13. Malone suggests that Caliban was Shakespeare's version of a Patagonian. See pp. 11–14.

[4] See George Odell, Shakespeare from Betterton to Irving (1920; rpt. New York: Dover Publications, 1966), I, 1–42 for a full account of changes in the Restoration theatre. Also see Montague Summers, Shakespeare Adaptations (London: Jonathan Cape, 1922), pp. xvii–cvii.

[5] Christopher Spencer, ed., Five Adaptations of Shakespeare (Urbana: Univ. of Illinois Press. 1965), p. 5.

[6] John Dryden, The Tempest: or, The Enchanted Isle (London, 1670), sig. A2ᵛ. A facsimile edition is George Robert Guffey, ed., After the Tempest (Los Angeles: William Andrews Clark Memorial Library, 1969).

[7] See Richard Bernheimer, Wild Men in the Middle Ages (Cambridge, Mass.: Harvard Univ. Press, 1950).

[8] Dryden, p. 19.

[9] Ibid.

[10] Samuel Pepys, *The Diary of Samuel Pepys*, ed. Robert Latham and William Matthews (Berkeley: Univ. of California Press, 1974), VIII, 522.

[11] See David Garrick, *The Tempest: An Opera* (London, 1756). Reproduced in Guffey.

[12] Charles Beecher Hogan, *Shakespeare in the Theatre: 1701–1800* (Oxford: Clarendon Press, 1952), II, 636–38.

[13] See *John Philip Kemble Promptbooks*, ed. Charles H. Shattuck (Charlottesville: Univ. Press of Virginia, 1974), VIII.

[14] Philip Highfill, Jr., Kalman A. Burnim, and Edward A. Langhans, *A Biographical Dictionary of Actors, Actresses, Musicians, Dancers, Managers, and Other Stage Personnel in London, 1660–1800*, IX (Carbondale: Southern Illinois Univ. Press, 1982), 402.

[15] Ibid., II, 64.

[16] Ibid., IX, 360.

[17] Ibid., I, 262.

[18] Ibid., II, 150.

[19] Stuart M. Tave, *The Amiable Humorist* (Chicago: Univ. of Chicago Press, 1960), p. 94.

[20] See Alexander Pope, "An Essay on Man," *The Poems of Alexander Pope* (New Haven: Yale Univ. Press, 1963).

[21] Samuel Johnson, "Preface to Shakespeare," *Johnson: Prose and Poetry*, ed. Mona Wilson (Cambridge, Mass.: Harvard Univ. Press, 1967).

[22] For a discussion of the Noble Savage, see Robert F. Berkhofer, *The White Man's Indian* (New York: Alfred A. Knopf, 1978), pp. 72–79.

[23] See the Preface to the second edition of *Lyrical Ballads* (1800), reprinted in William Wordsworth, *Selected Poems and Prefaces*, ed. Jack Stillinger (Boston: Houghton Mifflin, 1965), pp. 445–64.

[24] From a transcription in the flyleaf of Folger *Tempest* Promptbook No. 4. Source unknown.

[25] Samuel Taylor Coleridge, *Coleridge on Shakespeare: The Text of the Lectures of 1811–1812*. ed. R. A. Foakes (Charlottesville: Univ. Press of Virginia, 1971), pp. 112–13.

[26] William Hazlitt, *Characters of Shakespeare's Plays* (London, 1817), pp. 118–20.

[27] *The Journal of William Charles Macready, 1832–1851*, abr. and ed. by J. C. Trewin (London: Longmans, Green, 1967), pp. 15–16. A description of Caliban's costume at Drury Lane (1824) and Covent Garden (1827) in the Folger *Tempest* Promptbook No. 7 reads, "Entire dress of goat skin; long claws on the fingers; very dark flesh legs; the hair long, wild, and ragged."

[28] Patrick MacDonnell, *An Essay on the Play of* The Tempest (London: John Fellowes, 1840), pp. 16–19.

[29] See Arthur Colby Sprague, *Shakespeare and the Actors: The Stage Business in His Plays; 1600–1905* (Cambridge, Mass.: Harvard Univ. Press, 1944), p. 41.

[30] *The Diaries of William Charles Macready, 1833–1952*, ed. William Toynbee, 2 vols. (London: Chapman and Hall, Ltd., 1912), I, 474–504; II, 5–9.

[31] Citations of stage directions for the Samuel Phelps 1847 production are taken from Folger *Tempest* Promptbook No. 13. Page numbers are indicated in parentheses.

[32] See Charles H. Shattuck, *Shakespeare on the American Stage: From the Hallams to Edwin Booth* (Washington: Folger Shakespeare Library, 1976); and Lawrence W. Levine, "William Shakespeare and the American People: A Study in Cultural Transformation," *American Historical Review*, 89 (1984), 34–66.

[33] William L. Keese, *William E. Burton: Actor, Author, and Manager* (New York: G. P. Putnam's Sons, 1885), p. 175.

[34] See Folger *Tempest* Promptbook No. 12.

[35] See Charles Kean's promptbook, Folger *Tempest* Promptbook No. 10, p. 37.

[36] Cited from Folger *Tempest* Promptbook No. 4.

[37] Charles Kean's costume book, Folger Art Volume d 49, dated 1853.

[38] From a clipping inserted in Folger *Tempest* Promptbook No. 4. Source unknown.

[39] Daniel Wilson, *Caliban: The Missing Link* (London: Macmillan and Co., 1873), p. 9.

[40] Lady Benson, *Mainly Players: Bensonian Memoirs* (London: Thornton Butterworth, 1926), p.179.

[41] Augustin Daly's Souvenir Album, Folger Art Volume b 31, includes color drawings for each character in addition to photographs, playbills, and clippings from *The Tempest*'s stage history.

[42] *Shakespeare's Comedy The Tempest as Arranged for the Stage by Herbert Beerbohm Tree* (London: J. Miles & Co., 1904), p. xi. The ensuing stage directions are cited from this edition.

[43] Ibid., p. xi.

[44] Percy MacKaye, *Caliban by the Yellow Sands* (Garden City: Doubleday, Page, and Co., 1916), p. xv.

[45] Gordon Crosse, *Shakespeare Playgoing, 1890–1952* (London: A. R. Mowbray and Co., 1953), p. 58.

[46] G. Wilson Knight, *Shakespearian Production* (London: Routledge & Kegan Paul, 1968), p. 164.

[47] See William Babula, *Shakespeare in Production, 1935–1978: A Selective Catalogue* (New York: Garland, 1981), pp. 307–21.

[48] See Charles Frey, "*The Tempest* and the New World," *Shakespeare Quarterly*, 30 (1979), 29–41.

[49] *Saturday Review*, 10 February 1945, p. 29.

[50] Claire McGlinchee, "Stratford, Connecticut, Shakespeare Festival, 1960," *Shakespeare Quarterly*, 11 (1960), 469–72.

[51] Alice Griffin, "The New York Season 1961–1962," *Shakespeare Quarterly*, 13 (1962), 555.

[52] Robert Speaight, "Shakespeare in Britain," *Shakespeare Quarterly*, 14 (1963), 419–31.

[53] Margaret Croyden, "Peter Brook's *Tempest*," *The Drama Review*, 3 (1968–69), 125–28.

[54] Jeanne Addison Roberts, "The Washington Shakespeare Summer Festival, 1970," *Shakespeare Quarterly*, 21 (1970), 481–82.

[55] Robert Speaight, "Shakespeare in Britain," *Shakespeare Quarterly*, 21 (1970), 439–40.

[56] M. E. Comtois, "New York Shakespeare Festival, Lincoln Center, 1973–74," *Shakespeare Quarterly*, 25 (1974), 405–6.

[57] Robert Speaight, "Shakespeare in Britain, 1974," *Shakespeare Quarterly*, 25 (1974), 389–94.

[58] John Velz, "*The Tempest*," *Cahiers Elisabethains*, 14 (1978), 104–6.

[59] Roger Warren, "A Year of Comedies: Stratford 1978," *Shakespeare Survey*, 21 (1979), 203.

[60] Maurice Charney and Arthur Ganz, "Shakespeare in New York City," *Shakespeare Quarterly*, 33 (1982), 218–22.

[61] Werner Habicht, "Shakespeare in 'Provincial' West Germany," *Shakespeare Quarterly*, 31 (1980), 413–15.

[62] For a description of Morton's performance, see Errol G. Hill, "Caliban and Ariel: A Study in Black and White in American Productions of *The Tempest* from 1945–1981," *Theatre History Studies*, 4 (1984), 1–10.

[63] Joseph H. Stodder and Lillian Wilds, "Shakespeare in Southern California and Visalia," *Shakespeare Quarterly*, 31 (1980), 254–74.

[64] Peter Erickson, "A *Tempest* at the Mount," *Shakespeare Quarterly*, 32, (1981), 188–90.

[65] Ralph Berry, "Stratford Festival Canada, 1982," *Shakespeare Quarterly*, 34 (1983), 95.

Kenneth Maclean

CALIBAN IN SHAKESPEARE AND BROWNING

We can only harm Robert Browning by bringing him into comparison with Shakespeare: so goes a common critical judgment.[1] But while historical and aesthetic change makes such a comparison difficult, in assuming prohibitive differences we may well miss valuable grounds of relation. However special his use of the dramatic speaker, Browning obviously learned from Shakespeare and identified himself in a number of particular instances with Shakespeare's art. Shakespeare ought to provide a frame of reference, even if by contrast, for the enlightenment of any poem in which his thematics and characterization are directly involved. Browning's "Caliban upon Setebos" is such a poem; and, while it is a poem of frequent study, it does not seem to have been carefully enough considered in this way.[2] Especially, certain crucial categories of theme and imagery have been neglected. These categories are substantially dependent on seeing Shakespeare's Caliban, of *The Tempest,* as a symbolic figure drawn from the archetypal thematology of the Wild Man as Jungian "Shadow," the same kind of projection seen in Browning's ironically structured, if satirically directed, work.[3]

Some consideration of the Wild Man typology associated with both artists is initially necessary, although that typology itself is formidably complex. For application to Shakespeare and Browning, it involves two thematically related, yet categorically different appearances. First, there is the literary and artistic appearance of the Wild Man figure, most highly developed in his (or her or its) reification as the expression of represented human universals—life, death, human survival, and the threat to that survival. These universals are expressed through the Wild Man's linkage to the human unconscious, what one Jungian interpreter calls, in a chapter title, "Shadow: The Archetypal Enemy."[4] Secondly, behind and within this reification is the persistent, human, historical struggle to understand the ambiguities of human nature itself, represented in art, myth, and folklore by the mixing of animal and human characteristics.

Historically, the Wild Man (or woman or hermaphrodite) differentiates him-

From *Victorian Poetry* 25, No. 1 (Spring 1987): 1–16.

self in a bewildering abundance of ways. Depending on the definition of the source one applies, he may appear as demon or devil, faun, satyr, werewolf, giant, wild herdsman, malevolent cannibal, or "Noble Savage." These appearances are generally basic to the association of the figure with moral universals of both positive and negative kinds: death or the preservation of life, rapacious lust or protectiveness.[5] The general historical evolution of the figure toward the "Noble Savage" is not consistent. One of the earliest known Wild Man figures, Enkidu of the Sumerian epic *Gilgamesh,* is one of the most natural and positive. The Wild Man figures of Judaism and Christianity, as of Greco-Roman culture, are generally of the monstrous types, although the redemptive attitudes of Christianity modified the monstrosity in many specific ways (Bernheimer, p. 8, passim).

That Shakespeare's Caliban is a member of the typological succession of the Wild Man, especially as that succession enters the centuries of colonialization, has been a general assumption of recent scholarship and criticism.[6] The primary stimulation to this scholarship was, perhaps, Frank Kermode's edition of *The Tempest,* in which he briefly considered the Wild Man in the context of Elizabethan life and drama and linked Shakespeare's "Salvage and Deformed Slave" to "the wild or salvage man of Europe, formerly the most familiar image of mankind without the ordination of civility."[7]

Symbolically, Kermode finds Caliban representative of the natural common denominator of what he terms "The Vigour of Vice" in *The Tempest,* opposed to "The Magic of Nobility" in Prospero (pp. li, liv). The two central characters thus come to represent allegories on human moral status as it was understood in the Elizabethan world, an interpretation correct as far as it goes but limited as considered against a more psychological reading. The establishment of grounds for such a psychological reading in the historical context of Shakespeare's civilization may be aided by a quotation from another Wild Man interpreter, historian Hayden White. Commenting on the situation just before the opening of the Renaissance, White develops a tradition of interpretation for the Wild Man figure:

> By the end of the Middle Ages, the Wild Man has become endowed with two distinct personalities, each consonant with one of the possible attitudes men might assume with respect to society and nature. If one looked upon nature as a horrible world of struggle, as *animal* nature; and society as a condition . . . preferable to the natural state, then he would continue to view the Wild Man as the antitype of the *desirable humanity,* as a warning of what men would fall into if they definitively rejected society and its norms. If, on the other hand, one took his vision of nature from . . . what might be called *herbal* nature, and saw society, with all its struggle, as a fall away from natural perfection, then he might be inclined to populate that nature with wild men whose function was to serve as antitypes of *social* existence. The former attitude prevails in a tradition of thought which extends from Machiavelli . . . and Vico down to Freud and Jean-Paul Sartre. The latter attitude is represented by Locke and Spenser, Montesquieu and Rousseau, and has recent champions in Albert Camus and Claude Lévi-Strauss. (In *Wild Man,* p. 28)

These are, respectively, the ways White sees the essentially Biblical and the essentially naturalistic attitudes toward the Wild Man. And while he does not develop any directly psychological application, the suggestion of Freud among those adopting an "animal struggle" reaction to nature implies the countering, and elaboration, of such a position in Freud's colleague and opponent, Carl Jung. Where Jung would stand in terms of these alternatives is problematical, since Jung would find the threat to well-being personified neither in terms of physical struggle only, nor in society, but in human nature itself affecting or conditioning these applications.

A recent writer on Jung's psychology of self-realization, of "Individuation," describes Jung's development of a psychological theory of balance in the understanding of Jungian "Self" against interference of "Shadow," that "aspect of the Self which remains unconscious because it is repressed by the *superego* or unactivated by the environment" (Stevens, p. 300). Jung's substitution of "Shadow" for "Id," or seen another way, his combining of "id" and "ego" in developing a self-balancing superego, suggests an unconscious amenable to self-analysis and reduces sharply that suggested attachment to the "animal struggle" alternative which White seems to suggest produced the monstrous Wild Man as an archetype influencing Freud. Similarly, Jung's sense of confrontation between the individuating self and the superego suggests in a limited way, at least, that conflict with social forces which originates, in White's sense, the "Noble Savage" type of Wild Man figure.

Certainly Shakespeare's Caliban, as he appears in *The Tempest,* can be read in the direction of either of White's late medieval (suggesting modern) alternatives. Some evidence of Shakespeare's participation in the Wild Man typology is clear in the play. Caliban's descriptively mixed species, his suggested original speechlessness, aphasia (including his stammer), his lust, his carrying of logs and his suggested use of a log for the killing of Prospero (III.ii.87) are all examples of the Wild Man characteristics suggested by Bernheimer and White (Bernheimer, pp. 2–13, 17, 34; White, pp. 18–19, passim).

But the Wild Man as the artist must treat him is not simply a figure of man drawn from the natural or social struggle, but a figure of man in a human, individuating, self-realizing struggle which involves, in *The Tempest,* both Prospero and Caliban, and in Browning's poem the representative "Shadow" which the search for a balanced Self struggles to transcend. Browning's severe narrowing of the dramatic context of Shakespeare's play, his substantial avoidance of the Prospero character, is more than an inevitable characteristic of the monologue; it is a condition of his narrowed and interiorized ironic perspective as a man and as a modern artist.[8] The isolation of his speaker transcends soliloquy as we would understand it in the dramatist; it is perhaps the chief contrast with Shakespeare, whose Wild Man is, after all, a more limited thinker than Browning's philosophically developed, if primitive, personification of the warfare between man and creation. It is this sense of strangeness that Shakespeare's Wild Man comes on stage to represent in its effects on the ordinary human perception of what it means to be a man. And Browning may also be satirizing the ordinary human perception of what it means to be a believer in his tyrannically materialistic age.[9]

Again, Shakespeare's "bemused sense of strangeness" (the word "strange" itself runs like a latent thematic strain through Shakespeare's play) seems to be a probing toward a definition of human nature itself, for if the Wild Man in Shakespeare's play is, as Kermode put it, "the lowest common denominator" of humanity in the play, he is also the most general symbolic expression of the ambiguous potentials of humanity, and of the human reaction to them; he is monster and charmed dreamer, vengeful savage and childlike learner, fearful slave and seeker after freedom, all these sui generis and in the universal, so that Prospero, too, shares in them. Prospero's vices as they become active in the play stem mainly from his failed and reactive relation to Caliban, if also from his relation to the world: he is mage and failed prince, partisan of justice and slavemaster, figure of noble mercy and vengeful, unyielding moralist. His reaction to Caliban is so strong as to create a puzzle and a problem in the play, especially in the final scenes where every evil *except* Caliban's it seems, stands forgiven. Yet surely one cannot doubt Shakespeare's human sympathy and identification with suffering in Caliban's lines describing the island as paradise of dreams: "The clouds methought would open, and show riches/Ready to drop upon me; that, when I wak'd,/I cried to dream again" (III.ii.139–141). The "riches" of course can be ambiguous in Caliban's understanding, but the imagery is implicitly of rain, the most common natural image of the healing or regenerative "grace" that Caliban vows to "seek for" in the closing lines of the drama. It is, of course, too, his imaginative sense of another "graceful" self emergent in dreams, overcoming physical limitations of time and reality. But it is these limitations which dominate Prospero's responses to Caliban's imaginatively germinating potentials; Caliban is to the life-injured slave-master of Act I, Scene ii, "thou earth," and "filth," and to the otherwise forgiving philosopher of Act V, a "thing of darkness": nightmare figure to him, perhaps, rather than any figure of healing dreams. Prospero seems to see in Caliban more than any mere figure of animal nature. He seems to see in him the "beast" in the Wild Man figure. And the implication is substantial that the manifestation of "Shadow" in Caliban takes on the character of a universal threat transcending the Wild Man as typology, takes the shape of the ultimate psychological threat of death itself. Shakespeare's parallel description of the servant of rapine, Time, in his early *The Rape of Lucrece,* indicates, presumably, the direction of his imaged thought about death. Lucrece describes Time as "Misshapen Time, copesmate of ugly Night," and as "false slave to false delight,/Base watch of woes, sin's pack-horse, virtue's snare" (ll. 925-928). Time is bound up with sin in his Christian thought; with that heraldic sense of the Wild Man depicted by Albrecht Dürer nearly nine decades before the beginning of Shakespeare's career, with the Wild Man as Death.[10]

In this context it is natural, even conventional, that Prospero's conflict with Caliban should be based in the sexual assault on Miranda. Sex and death are related universals of man's experience which evade and threaten his "control." Prospero's exaggeration of the principle of virginity (not innocence) between Ferdinand and Miranda (IV.i.13–23), almost to the point of self-parodoy as the Puritan papa, is, of course, a reaction to Caliban, but it also confirms the larger anxiety he seems to feel. The multitude of death references in the play (countered, to be sure by references of "sea-change," spiritual transcendence) forms the thematic background for the Prospero-Caliban relationship, for the conflicts and the potentials of the dethroned leader and the ambiguously described animal-human being.

If much of *The Tempest* is dominated by figurative death associated with sleep, dreams, and spells, literal death persists behind the illusions and verbal tropes. Often, figurative death seems to offer a moral test of the characters, extending toward death in the spiritual, Christian sense (sin), or toward spiritual vitality (virtue or innocence). The brave struggler against the sea, the Boatswain, returns with his men from the "dead of sleep," under Prospero's spell (V.I.230). The dreams of literally deadly and evil men are suggested in the "sleepy language" of Antonio and Sebastian, plotting murder and usurpation while Gonzalo and Alonso take their natural rest (II.i.203–291). Plotting the killing of Prospero, Caliban, however, does not deal in figurative terms: his are the honest, if brutal, terms of the Wild Man: "with a log/Batter his skull, or paunch him with a stake" (III.ii.87–88).

Prospero furthers the death imagery and its moral implications as the play enters its final acts. Rather than hearing the consolation in the unearthly music of Ariel's song as it is heard by Ferdinand (I.ii.407–410), Prospero seems increasingly to brood on the illusory qualities of life (IV.i.152–158) and his own psychological state nearing the end of it. His "old brain is troubled," he says, and, after the marriage of his daughter, he tells Alonso that he will return to Milan, but not to the triumph of his princely restoration, rather to that scene where, "Every third thought shall be my grave" (V.i.311).[11] This death, which will preoccupy what he has earlier called his "beating mind" (V.i.163), seems not transformed to any "sea change," but expressed as a continuously recurrent thought, like the bell which Ariel sings of in its clocklike tolling.

It is this obsessive thought then, with which the audience leaves Prospero, just after his penultimate indirect reference to Caliban: "this thing of darkness I/Acknowledge mine" (V.i.275–276). It seems reasonable, following this thematic direction, to read Caliban as Prospero's demon of death, that is, as Shakespeare's brilliantly intuitive understanding of the force of death (and its Christian association in sin) on human attitudes and behavior. Granted this representation, the distance between the artistic consciousness of Shakespeare and of Robert Browning may not be so great as has been supposed, although social and anthropological history, especially the history of ideas, plays a strong role in the apparent differences between the two artists in relation to the Caliban theme.

The interiorization of the Wild Man, his coming-to-be as a psychological figure distinguished from his appearances in social myth and religious commentary, involves, fundamentally, the individualization process inherent in Western democratization, a process so complex in its particular effects as to be impossible to describe briefly, although some outlines do exist. Karl Mannheim describes his sociological understanding of the interiorization process in Western culture as being demonstrated, for example, in such characteristic phenomena as the shifting of words such as "villain" and "noble" from external designations of social rank to internal qualities of character. He refers, further, to the shift from external to internal standards for the evaluation of the literary hero producing, eventually, such a sharp interiorization as the Romantic weltanschauung.[12] Our modern sense of irony as a literary method, with its sharply defensive, individualistic reaction to social demands placed on the artist's values by the larger audience, "the public," is most likely psychologically parallel to what has been considered Browning's reactively Romantic literary form, the dramatic monologue.[13]

But of more immediate pertinence to this writing is the interiorization of the Wild Man figure in particular, bearing its own marks of the Romantic transformation, its own commentary on what the figure was or is to become. Peter L. Thorslev, Jr., calls into recognition the terms of this direction in a swift summary:

> Rousseau was the first to "internalize" the Wild Man, to suggest that he lives on in all of us, that when we strip ourselves of the evils as well as of the refinements of civilization, we find naked savages. So long as this naked savage is also noble, the prospect is not unpleasant. . . . In the nineteenth century, however, when the civilized man looked within to discover his primitive unconscious, ever more frequently it was not the brave and open face of the Noble Savage which greeted him, but the dark face of Dionysus. (In *Wild Man*, p. 298)

The Wild Man reappears as the "dark face" of the living and dying god Dionysus or in his representations, as Bernheimer suggests, as a connection with the classical gods of death and the underworld, Hades or Orcus (pp. 42–44). Shakespeare would simply have said "devil," a characterization which has been convincingly applied to Browning's Caliban.[14] Still, the difference in the relationship of the two artists lies in the individualization of Browning's "devil" away from its original archetype, in the increased complexity and "civilization" of his character, in the severe narrowing of Browning's "dramatization."

Suffice it to say that Browning's Caliban is a post-Romantic (modern) Wild Man, not an Elizabethan or a medieval one. And although the Wild Man was apparently able to appear as his medieval self as late as 1886 (Bernheimer, p. 120), neither Shakespeare's nor Browning's figure can be understood except by extension beyond the image of primitive or natural man. In Browning's poem he has become a sophisticated savage; a modern, island-dwelling self, understood best in a symbolic context similar to that of Shakespeare's character—as a demon of the material circumstances of man, but seemingly without the relieving potentials of the original. If the premier Caliban stands symbolically for the potentials of change (death being such change, depending on the understanding of it), Browning's character would seem to stand for just the opposite, for the rigidity of absolute intellectual changelessness, for what Browning saw, probably, as the savage worship of a universal tyranny of the self projected as almighty and destructive power. That power, as his Wild Man projects it theologically, is rigidly causal and at the same time perversely uncreative, so that as God, Setebos' power is above all fear instilling, death dealing. The creature of this concept of divine power, Caliban, is neither a purely natural wild man, nor purely a creature in process toward humanity and civilization, although there are implicit elements of both in his characterization. He is most intentionally to Browning a parody (the form without the content, the mind without the values) of man as a religious believer when belief is reduced to death dealing, to a defensive solipsism which sees its God as death and its own ability to deal in destruction as an assertion of dignity, its "creative" imitation of the source. This characterization is of course more than a parody of primitive man; it entails a profound criticism of anthromorphically believing humanity as Browning and as we have known it.

In physical terms Browning's Caliban seems to live what Bernheimer describes as a Wild Man life of "bestial self-fulfillment directed by instinct rather than volition, and devoid of all those acquired tastes and patterns of behavior which are part of our adjustment to civilization" (p. 4). In mental and symbolic terms, he is obviously quite something else. But the marked limitation of the potentials of dramatic change in the specific character, seemingly built into the imagery of the poem, makes it hazardous to assume any evolutionary direction of development in either the physical or the mental character. This is true even though the seed ground, the human potential for such development is clearly present in the character. This limitation of potentiality can be seen centrally in the "death's head" imagery. This imagery gathers itself most specifically in the lines in which Caliban describes building the runic burial mound which he is pleased simply to knock down again (ll. 192–199). But elements of this imagery are contained in the opening and closing passages of description; first, just before Caliban addresses the problem of Setebos, and again after he is driven back into terrorized silence by what he perceives as his God's avenging arrival. The opening passage first:

> Will sprawl, now that the heat of day is best,
> Flat on his belly in the pit's much mire,
> With elbows wide, fists clenched to prop his chin.
> And, while he kicks both feet in the cool slush,
> And feels about his spine small eft-things course,
> Run in and out each arm, and make him laugh:
> And while above his head a pompion-plant
> Coating the cave-top as a brow its eye,
> Creeps down to touch and tickle hair and beard,
> And now a flower drops with a bee inside,
> And now a fruit to snap at, catch and crunch.

About half of the opening passage, these lines are enough to suggest the first mood of childlike relaxation and physical enjoyment in a context almost exotic enough to suggest paradise. And yet, at the center of it is an image that seems to recur throughout the poem; the cave suggests an eye, an organ of vision over which the mockingly common pumpkin (with a play on "pomp" in the use of the French word) spreads its growth like a "brow." The suggested frame of vision is a "cave," and the common image of the seat of intellect, the "brow," is formed by the frond of a common garden vegetable. Behind the opening mood of childlike, sensuous enjoyment appears a more sinister burden of meaning. The whole passage suggests the "head" of Caliban: chin, brow, eye, the beard—Caliban's vision extending out of a hollow darkness. The lines themselves might be unremarkable enough if the eye and the various contexts of Caliban's way of seeing did not constantly recur throughout the poem, and if the imagery of the "head" were not picked up so centrally in the burial mound passage previously mentioned, as well as most dramatically in the final terrified lines: "Ha! The wind / Shoulders the pillared dust, death's house o' the move" (ll. 287–288).

This entire complex structuring—childlike enjoyment played off against more sinister thematology developing throughout the poem—suggests the Jungian concept of the gathering aspects of the Shadow: the counterpart of the conscious ego, "growing and crystallizing apace with it," and having aspects of the childlike and primitive which may serve to "vitalize and embellish" life even as its potentials for conflict also assume shape (Jacobi, p. 113). It would seem that Browning's artistic instinct has reached into a psychological parallel to the whole cultural process of life itself, "evolutionary" if one wishes to see it that way, but also profoundly and naturally human.[15]

Browning apparently believed in the straining forward of nature toward God at God's own direction.[16] In this there is always an implicit possibility of a materialistically "bound" humanity, limited by an inadequate "evolution" of consciousness to a self-projecting savagery of thought on any cultural level of existence. Browning's Caliban is truly the interiorized Wild Man in social terms as well as, implicitly, in the psychological terms mentioned here.

Certainly Browning's image of Setebos in the shouldered wind of "death's house o' the move" conditions our understanding of his Caliban as a death-worshipper, unable to transcend in any imaginative way the terms and conditions of what he can observe. The subtitle, then, of Browning's poem concerning "Natural Theology on the Island" is clarified if we see the poem as many have, as a satire on inductive theology. But it is not simply a mistaken theology that Browning has in mind, it would seem, but a practice of theology, a religion, that is for him profoundly disturbing.

Worshipping death, or God as the "head" (brain, mind) of death, is inevitably suicidal. That Browning saw this suicidal, or at least self-brutalizing, self-destructive impulse in the "eye" of his parodic believer, his psychological Wild Man, can be seen in returning to the imagery of the poem. That it is an imagery of religious fear and that the center of that fear makes death its only solace (l. 250) can hardly be missed in the plainer statements of the poem. But the ritual development of that fear is more subtle, perhaps, than has been recognized, and more conscious of its inheritance from Shakespeare. Caliban blinds the "sea-beast, lumpish" with which he identifies himself in relation to Prospero (ll. 163–169) and later proposes to sacrifice his sea-beast Caliban to the "orc" while he performs a ritual act of self-mutilation as a propitiation to Setebos. The heavy irony of self-hatred and projected self-mutilation (including the earlier symbolic "self"-blinding) suggests far more than savage confusion. It is a loss of vision far more humanly devastating than the drunken worship of folly by Shakespeare's character, and it makes ironic the contrast with Shakespeare's imagery of potentiality in "sea-change," the potentials of discovered "grace" in his Wild Man. This is the mind of an inductive "natural theology" as Browning understands it, the belief in, and imitation of, God as a destructive force.

The proposition that Browning profoundly disapproved of such a theology and was entirely engaged in satirizing it has been, as noted, a basis of dispute among his critics. Yet if the natural theology of his Caliban is not the only aspect of the character that focuses the poet's attention, it is certainly his substantial target; and if the imagery of the poem is read carefully, it is hard to see how one can miss Browning's deep disturbance at the profound moral emptiness and human danger of such a theology. Caliban's "vision" of his deity is suicidal, or at least consciously self-destructive, and bold as his language and intelligence may sometimes become (carefully put off from himself in the third person), his worshipful response can only be fear and hatred of his God; his sense of projected self can only be self-destructive, even as he realizes, almost with longing, that "with the life, the pain shall stop" (l. 250).

As suggested previously, the images and associations of eye, head, brain, and mind elaborate this self-destructive visionary worship, for it is the ironically developing "death's head" which, suggesting itself in the opening image of Caliban, continues in Browning's emphasis on the visionary organ—the eye—in rhetorical as well as imagistic terms. His intention seems to have been to define Caliban's "spiritual" world as simply a projection of Caliban's experience in a universe of ethically dead objects or "things" to be seen and experimented with and pleased or injured by, bearing no meaning or significance to him outside of that experience itself.

Beginning with the "eye" of Caliban's cave, Browning uses the noun or adjective form of the word "eye"—"eyed," "eyesore," and so on—ten times in forming contexts suggesting aspects of literal or figurative vision, exclusive of the related verbs "sees," "spied," "looks," and so forth. The first "'eye" of the cave is used to observe a spiderweb created by the sunlight (l. 13), an image of the natural trap as Caliban understands it (and as ordinary worshipers might have heard it used in sermons). This is the web which "some great fish breaks at times" in a beautiful exchange of the images of light and animal grace which Caliban cannot really express (Browning may intend the "great fish" of Jonah's Biblical experience, in that case a divine instrument). Caliban, further, "spied" the frigid stream fish, a reduced analogy, perhaps, to the "great fish," which he can understand only in terms of an imprisonment like his own, in a reduced mirror of the aching cold of Setebos, longing for and hating the outer "warmth" (ll. 31–43). Discussing Setebos' creation further, Caliban comes to a passage which extends the materialization of his description of natural creation to a myopic factitiousness.[17] The "plain word" of the magpie, for example, is never clear as a direct image, but makes clear only Caliban's rush to establish the "prize," the excitement of its capture. The rest of the imagery of the passage is similarly reductive:

Yon otter, sleek-wet, black, lithe as a leech;
Yon auk, one fire-eye in a ball of foam,
That floats and feeds; a certain badger brown
He hath watched hunt with that slant white-wedge eye
By moonlight; and the pie with the long tongue
That pricks deep into oakwarts for a worm,
And says a plain word when she finds her prize,
But will not eat the ants; the ants themselves
That build a wall of seeds and settled stalks
About their hole—He made all these and more,
Made all we see, and us, in spite: how else?   (ll. 46–56)

The implication here is that Caliban is not really capable of seeing for more than a fleeting moment, not capable of comprehending the variety and beauty which he himself describes. The comparison of the otter to a "leech" (like the reduction of the greater to the lesser fish?) and the shift of the brilliant description of the auk downward "one fire-eye in a ball of foam" to a mere creature "That floats and feeds" is the typical processing of Caliban's mind away from the potential of insight into the flat material triviality of superficial sense data. And one should not miss the fact that the eye again is prominent in all of this reduction. Indeed the ambiguous syntax of lines 48–49 suggests the unity of Setebos' vision ("He") with that of the "slant white-wedge eye" of the badger, not in the beauty of the image which Caliban sees only casually, but in the deadly instinct of Caliban's sense of natural purpose—hunter and hunted: "Made all we see, and us, in spite: how else?" What is sensed must be what is real and what is real must be limited absolutely to the terms of what is sensed. Any pain—or ugliness or evil—then, if God is to be "real," must somehow be a part of His malice as it is mentally treated by Caliban, since, being powerful and logical, He would not have created an "eyesore" for any other reason. The reductively developed metaphor of vision is pursued further in Caliban's drunken imaginings of himself as a bird and as the creator of a bird which he might then torture, this the reduction of a potential poetic symbol to a mere opportunity for cruelty. This purpose, he inductively reasons, must have been his creator's designs for him, and what is religion if not the imitation of one's deity? Thus Caliban imagines the envious smashing of the one seeming "art" object he can conceive, the pipe that makes "the cry my maker cannot make" (l. 124), the pipe's suggestion of transcendence stamped into dust.

So the limitation that must be placed on Setebos is the power of the "Quiet"—the "something quiet o'er his head,/Out of His reach, that feels nor joy nor grief" (ll. 132–133). And the concept of the Quiet brings forth the first explicit statement of how Caliban literally "sees" his God, in the form of a "many-handed . . . cuttle-fish," a reduced "sea-beast" again, and one representative of the bottom-dwelling, devouring self-identity which Caliban apparently worships. Again, in a single image, Caliban reduces the spiritual potentiality of his idea of deity to an extreme of the material, to a creature of deep, perhaps "buried," primitivism. One is reminded of the psychological despair of Eliot's Prufrock, longing for the destruction of his own consciousness: "I should have been a pair of ragged claws/Scuttling across the floors of silent seas."

As has been previously suggested, hatred anthropomorphized into deity can only imply self-hatred in the anthropomorphizing mind. And this translates easily enough into the hatred of existence itself. In this line of thought, disregard for Browning's Biblical subscript to the poem (Psalms 50.21: "thou thoughtest that I was altogether such an one as thyself") is engaged in only at great peril to his clear intention. This writer concludes that Browning saw the poem as a demonstration of the anthropomorphizing reductiveness of common religion carried to the full extreme of primitivism allowed by the Caliban, or Wild Man, mythology.[18] If so, this is certainly the reductive process of one method of irony, if not specifically the mode of satire. The target would be materialistic worship in any age, but specifically the age of Bishop Blougram, who acts for, talks for, lives "for this world now" (l. 769); of the age of the companion piece to "Caliban upon Setebos" in *Dramatis Personae,* "Mr Sludge, 'The Medium'." It is, in short, the demonstration of narcissistic religious materialism in an age from which the sense of God as Browning wished to hold it was disappearing. Caliban's demonstration of the poet's vision of the material, institutional church in such an age is made in the previously developed "burial mound" passage. In it, "making," the activity in which Shakespeare's world saw man and God joined, is made ironic:

> 'Falls to make something: 'piled yon pile of turfs,
> And squared and stuck there squares of soft white chalk,
> And, with a fish-tooth, scratched a moon on each,
> And set up endwise certain spikes of tree,
> And crowned the whole with a sloth's skull a-top
> Found dead i' the woods, too hard for one to kill.
> No use at all i' the work, for work's sole sake;
> 'Shall some day knock it down again: so He.   (ll. 192–199)

Perhaps this building is, as F. E. L. Priestley suggests, in "all the ironic force of bitter parody," a temple.[19] If so, the parody is bitter indeed, for it seems to suggest ironically the figurative temple in Matthew—the symbolic prophecy of Jesus concerning his own death and resurrection in the destruction and rebuilding of the "temple," a prophecy taken literally, and so entirely misunderstood by his audience. Caliban's seeming self-parody in constructing the useless pile of turfs surmounted by the cruelly (obsessively?) suggestive "spikes of tree" (the cross?) and domed by the remnant skull of a sloth, all to be "knocked down again," suggests a primitive, ritual worship of death and triviality behind the child's-play gestures, a self-projection into a cruel and idle creator. Further, it most likely suggests Browning's understanding of the diseased materialization of the "temple," the church, that which has turned it into a burial mound rather than a dome of creation and spirit. The temple is again, even literally under the animal skull, a "death's head."

If the concept of God which Browning wished to hold was that of a truly creative principle of Becoming implicit in life, surely his Wild Man poem demonstrates the antithesis of that principle—the spiritual death-in-life which Browning's kind of artist faces in the agony of historical religious failure. This is symbolically the domination of the social world of faith (and of creativity, of art) by a characterized intelligence which, granting its force, is not really that of an imaginative questioner who may enlighten the intellect by his bold challenge to its conventions; this Caliban is rather a primitively environed logician whose limited system of reasoning runs on its rigid rails of envy and hatred through a world of manifold potentials to which he is ironically self-blinded. While it is possible to make too much out of Browning's sense of his Wild Man's importance, it is also possible to make too little out of that sense. As the extension out of the artist's psychological construct into our own understanding, his Caliban becomes the Shadow, too, of our own interiorized fears as we struggle to master our own deaths-in-life—aesthetic, religious, ethical, or whatever they may be. He (with his ancestor in Shakespeare) must stand for our own primitive, disruptive, substantially unrealized and thereby "uncreated" selves.

Browning himself seemed to have some sense of what we call the archetype in his use of the Wild Man. In his letter to F. J. Furnivall concerning the poem, he concludes: "Then, as to the divergence from Shakespeare's Caliban—is it so decided? . . . True, 'he was a very different thing at the end of the play from what he was at the beginning,'—but my Caliban indulges his fancies long before even that beginning." [20] The emphasis lies in two directions: the recognition of the rigidly unchanging quality of his own as opposed to Shakespeare's figure and the final emphasis on the timelessness of the Wild Man. Crucial to the meaning of both emphases is the lack of a transcending principle in Browning's representation of the archetype as contrasted with Shakespeare's. This "lack" suggests, again, Browning's search not for a character so much as for an interiorized principle of human problem in characterized form—the most penetrating quality of all, perhaps, in his mastery of the dramatic monologue. The emphasized "lack" is, finally, a profoundly tragic issue: the historic human inability to live with and by, rather than under, natural change—the blindness, to repeat once more, to Becoming.

In their use of the archetype of the Wild Man, Browning—a pioneer modern poet—and Shakespeare—the greatest of his predecessors—have much in common. Both artists use the Wild Man to develop the theme of death; Shakespeare's Wild Man taking on the threatening representation in the mind of Prospero, Browning's Wild Man becoming an embodiment of the poet's sense of the failure of the soul of man in the spiritual world which he understood to be forming itself as the world around him. Both can be said to have seen Caliban as both a human presence, a social figure of alienation and struggle, and as a feared, death-associated symbol. If Shakespeare's Caliban is the purer mythic figure, Browning's represents (and topically parodies) what the Victorian artist saw in the religious civilization of his own age. In his inheritance of figure and theme and his extension of these into the socially alienated feeling of the modern artist, Browning brings Caliban into clearer connection with the Wild Man archetype as it has developed in the twentieth century. [21]

NOTES

[1] Lionel Trilling and Harold E. Bloom, eds., *Victorian Prose and Poetry* (New York, 1973), p. 494.

[2] A notable exception is Arnold Shapiro, "Browning's Psalm of Hate: 'Caliban upon Setebos,' Psalm 50, and *The Tempest*," *Papers on Language and Literature*, 8 (1972), 53–62. I do not agree entirely with Shapiro's ultimate interpretation of Caliban in Shakespeare (and Browning) as, simply, a Biblical demi-devil, but this characterization is related to the Wild Man history which I discuss. His judgment that the thought processes which the poem studies "are, unfortunately, all too modern," parallels, as well, my own understanding. Ruby Cohn, *Modern Shakespeare Offshoots* (Princeton, 1976), pp. 267–307, studies the major appearances of Caliban into this century.

[3] Jolande Jacobi sees Caliban as a "Shadow" figure: *The Psychology of C. G. Jung* (New Haven, 1973), p. 110.

[4] Dr. Anthony Stevens, *Archetypes* (New York, 1982), p. 210.

[5] The definitive study is Richard Bernheimer, *Wild Man in the Middle Ages* (Cambridge, Massachusetts, 1952). Bernheimer's ch. 2 is the major discussion of types. Timothy Husband, *The Wild Man: Medieval Myth and Symbolism* (New York, 1982), pp. 1–17, summarizes Bernheimer and adds valuable extension into artistic representations. See, for example, his Figs. 129, 130, pp. 194–196, for Dürer's association of the Wild Man with death and rapine. *The Wild Man Within,* ed. Robert Dudley and Maximillian E. Novak (Pittsburgh, 1972), draws together social science as well as literary opinion on the figure; this collection will be subsequently referred to as *Wild Man.*

[6] See, for example, Philip Brockbank, "*The Tempest:* Conventions of Art and Empire," in *Later Shakespeare,* ed. John Russell Brown and Bernard Harris, Stratford-upon-Avon Studies, 8 (New York, 1967), pp. 183–201.

[7] Sixth Arden edition (Cambridge, Massachusetts, 1958), pp. xxxviii–xxxix. This is my source for *The Tempest;* further reference is in the text.

[8] I judge Browning's poem to be both satiric in its literary design and ironic in its method. The fusion is considered by Claudette Kemper, "Irony Anew, with Occasional Reference to Byron and Browning," *Studies in English Literature 1500–1900,* 7 (1967), 705–719, esp. 707. See also E. Warwick Slinn, *Browning and the Fictions of Identity* (London, 1982), esp. pp. 1–19. Terrell Tebbetts, "The Question of Satire in 'Caliban upon Setebos'," *Victorian Poetry,* 22 (1984), 365–381, finds Browning's satiric strategy to be an intuitional one on Caliban's thought rather than on the content of the poem. This position parallels my argument at several points.

[9] Although satire has traditionally been seen to be the intention of the poem, a number of influential critics have demurred, unable to find "Natural Theology" a substantial enough ground for satire. Along with Tebbetts I find the ground for satire not only in the belief but in the satirized believer. Michael Timko's "Browning upon Butler; or, Natural Theology in the English Isle," *Criticism,* 7, (1965), 141–150, is a thorough analysis of Browning's contemporary theological targets. The anti-satire critics have drawn valuable attention to the means of the poem, its persona. Summaries of the controversy may be found in William C. DeVane, *A Browning Handbook,* 2nd ed. (New York, 1955), pp. 299–302, and, more recently, in Shapiro (pp. 55–59).

[10] As I have said, the figure of the Wild Man is ambiguous in the context of life and death. Bernheimer points out the Wild Man's "very strong" association "with Orcus, the Italic god of death and the underworld" (p. 42). The association is interesting in relation to Browning's Caliban as he assumes that Setebos might have clad him in "an orc's armour." (l. 177; all citations from the poem are taken from *Robert Browning: The Poems,* ed. John Pettigrew and Thomas J. Collins, 2 vols. [New Haven, 1981]). Jung did not directly associate his "Shadow" principle with the manifestation of, or the fear of, death, but had much to say of the destructive effects of the Western concept of death as psychological end of things. See Barbara Hannah, "The Beyond (Death and Renewal in East and West)," in *In the Wake of Jung,* ed. Molly Tuby (London, 1983), pp. 112–127. The death threat to spiritual personality, personified in Caliban, seems evident (if differently conveyed) in both artists I am considering.

[11] This line of discussion was suggested by Theodore Weiss, whose poem "Every Second Thought" follows the retired and death-expectant Prospero home to Milan, in *A Slow Fuse* (New York, 1984), pp. 68–82.

[12] *Essays on Sociology and Social Psychology* (New York, 1953), pp. 296–298.

[13] Irony and alienation in the Romantic weltanschauung are deftly considered by Charles I. Glicksberg, *The Ironic Vision in Modern Literature* (The Hague, 1969), pp. 5ff. Slinn (pp. 8, 17–18, passim) considers the dramatic monologue in these terms. E. D. H. Johnson, *The Alien Vision of Victorian Poetry,* Princeton Studies in English, 34 (Princeton, 1952), is the definitive study.

[14] Park Honan, "Belial upon Setebos," *Texas Studies in English*, 9 (1964), 89–98.

[15] W. David Shaw, *The Dialectical Temper* (Ithaca, 1968), pp. 201–203.

[16] E. LeRoy Lawson, *Very Sure of God* (Nashville, 1974), pp. 143–145.

[17] Robert Langbaum, *The Poetry of Experience* (New York, 1957), p. 138.

[18] John Howard, in "Caliban's Mind," *Victorian Poetry*, I (1963), 249–257, develops the "subhuman" primitivism, but rejects the centrality of any satire. Caliban seems to me human enough, and I see primitivism and satire to be complementary in the poem.

[19] "Some Aspects of Browning's Irony," in *Browning's Mind and Art*, ed. Clarence Tracy (London, 1968), p. 135.

[20] *The Letters of Robert Browning*, ed. Thurman L. Hood (New Haven, 1933), p. 228.

[21] Chief among these is W. H. Auden's *The Sea and the Mirror, The Collected Poetry of W. H. Auden* (New York, 1945), pp. 373–403. Auden's Caliban, like Aimé Césaire's in *Une Tempete*, represents the "Shadow" as implicitly or directly a racial outcast. A valuable recent study by Virginia Mason Vaughan traces the physical appearance of the Caliban figure from the seventeenth century to the most recent dramatic interpretations. See "'Something Rich and Strange': Caliban's Theatrical Metamorphoses," *Shakespeare Quarterly*, 36 (1985), 390–405.

Meredith Anne Skura

THE CASE OF COLONIALISM
IN *THE TEMPEST*

For many years idealist readings of *The Tempest* presented Prospero as an exemplar of timeless human values. They emphasized the way in which his hard-earned "magical" powers enable him to re-educate the shipwrecked Italians, to heal their civil war—and, even more important, to triumph over his own vengefulness by forgiving his enemies; they emphasized the way he achieves, if not a wholly "brave," at least a harmoniously reconciled new world. Within the last few years, however, numbers of critics have offered remarkably similar critiques of this reading. There is an essay on *The Tempest* in each of three recent anthologies of alternative, political, and reproduced Shakespeare criticism, and another in the volume on estranging Renaissance criticism; *The Tempest* was a focus for the 1988 SAA session on "Shakespeare and Colonialism" and was one of the masthead plays in the Folger Institute's 1988 seminar on new directions in Shakespeare studies.[1] Together, the revisionists call for a move to counteract some "deeply ahistorical readings" of *The Tempest*,[2] a play that is now seen to be not simply an allegory about "timeless"[3] or universal experience but rather a cultural phenomenon that has its origin in and effect on "historical" events, specifically in English colonialism. "New historicist" criticism in general, of which much recent work on *The Tempest* is a part, has itself begun to come under scrutiny, but the numerous historical reinterpretations of *The Tempest* deserve closer attention in their own right,[4] and they will be the subject of the rest of this essay.

In assessing the "new" historicist version of the play, it is important to realize that here, even more than in other new historical criticism, an historical emphasis in itself is not new. Since the early nineteenth century *The Tempest* has been seen in the historical context of the New World, and Frank Kermode, citing the early scholars, argued in the fifties that reports of a particular episode in British efforts to colonize North America had precipitated the play's major themes.[5] In 1609 nine ships had left England to settle the colony in Jamestown, Virginia, and the *Sea Venture*, carrying all of the colonial officers, had disappeared. But its passengers

From *Shakespeare Quarterly 40*, No. 1 (Spring 1989): 42–69.

reappeared in Virginia one year later, miraculously saved; they had wrecked off the Bermudas, until then believed demonically dangerous but now found to be providentially mild and fruitful. These events, much in the news in the year just preceding *The Tempest*, have long been seen as a relevant context for the play by all but a very few critics.[6] These earlier historical interpretations generally placed the play and its immediate source in the context of voyaging discourse in general, which stressed the romance and exoticism of discoveries in the Old as well as the New world. Even the "factual" reports in this discourse, as Charles Frey notes, were themselves colored by the romance of the situation, for better and for worse; and the traditional view was that *The Tempest*'s stylized allegory abstracts the romance core of all voyagers' experience.[7]

Nor had traditional criticism entirely ignored either Prospero's flaws[8] or their relation to the dark side of Europe's confrontation with the Other. Kermode had identified Caliban as the "core" or "ground" of the play, insofar as confrontation with this strange representative of "uncivilized" man prompts the play's reexamination of "civilized" human nature. Harry Levin, Leslie Fiedler, Leo Marx, and others had suggested that in trying to understand the New World representatives of "uncivilized" human nature, Prospero, like other Europeans, had imposed Old (and New) World stereotypes of innocence and monstrosity on the Native Americans, distorting perception with hope and fear.[9] Fiedler's landmark book had indeed placed *The Tempest* suggestively in the context of a series of plays about the Other (or, as he called it in 1972, the "Stranger") in Shakespeare, showing Caliban's resemblance to the demonized women, Moors, and Jews in the canon. O. Mannoni had added that, in this process, Prospero displayed the psychology of colonials who projected their disowned traits onto New World natives.[10]

Why, then, so many recent articles? In part they are simply shifting the emphasis. Revisionists claim that the New World material is not just present but is right at the center of the play, and that it demands far more attention than critics have been willing to grant it. They argue that the civil war in Milan that had ousted Prospero should be recognized as merely an episode in a minor dispute between Italian dynasties, of little import compared to the transatlantic action;[11] they show how the love story can be seen as a political maneuver by Prospero to ensure his return to power in Milan,[12] and how even Caliban's attempted rape of Miranda can be seen as an expression not merely of sexual but also of territorial lust, understandable in its context.[13]

These recent critics are not simply repeating the older ones, however; they are making important distinctions. First and most explicitly, they are not calling attention to history in general but rather to one aspect of history: to power relations and to the ideology in which power relations are encoded.[14] The revisionists look not at the New World material in the play but to the play's effect on power relations in the New World. What matters is not just the particular Bermuda pamphlets actually echoed in the play but rather the whole "ensemble of fictional and lived practices" known as "English colonialism," which, it is now being claimed, provides the "dominant discursive con-texts"[15] for the play. (Though the term "colonialism" may allude to the entire spectrum of New World activity, in these articles it most often refers specifically to the use of power, to the Europeans' exploitative and self-justifying treatment of the New World and its inhabitants— and I shall use it in that sense.) If Caliban is the center of the play, it is not because of his role in the play's self-contained structure, and not even because of what he reveals about man's timeless tendency to demonize "strangers," but because Europeans were at that time exploiting the real Calibans of the world, and *The Tempest* was part of the process. It is no longer enough to suggest that Europeans were trying to make sense of the Indian; rather, the emphasis is now on the way Europeans subdued the Indian to "make sense/order/money—not of him, so much as out of him."[16] Revisionists argue that when the English talked about these New World inhabitants, they did not just innocently apply stereotypes or project their own fears: they did so to a particular effect, whether wittingly or unwittingly. The various distortions were discursive strategies that served the political purpose of making the New World fit into a schema justifying colonialism.[17] Revisionists therefore emphasize the discursive strategies that the play shares with all colonial discourse, and the ways in which *The Tempest* itself not only displays prejudice but fosters and even "enacts" colonialism by mystifying or justifying Prospero's power over Caliban.[18] The new point is that *The Tempest* is a political act.

Second, this shift in our attitude toward the object of interpretation entails a less explicit but extremely important move away from the psychological interpretation that had previously seemed appropriate for the play (even to its detractors) largely because of its central figure who, so like Shakespeare, runs the show. Where earlier criticism of Prospero talked about his "prejudice," the more recent revisionists talk about "power" and "euphemisation." Thus, a critic writing in 1980 argued that *The Tempest*'s "allegorical and neoplatonic overlay masks some of the most damaging prejudices of Western civilization";[19] but by 1987 the formulation had changed: "*The Tempest* is . . . fully implicated in the process of 'euphemisation', the effacement of power," in "operations [that] encode struggle and contradiction even as they, or *because* they, strive to insist on the legitimacy of colonialist narrative."[20]

Psychological criticism of the play is seen as distracting at best; one recent critic, for example, opens his argument by claiming that we need to conceive *The Tempest* in an historical context that is not "hamstrung by specious speculations concerning 'Shakespeare's mind'."[21] Even in less polemical examples the "political unconscious" often replaces, rather than supplements, any other unconscious; attention to culture and politics is associated with an implicit questioning of individuality and of subjective experience. Such a stance extends beyond an objection to wholesale projections of twentieth-century assumptions onto sixteenth-century subjects, or to psychological interpretations that totally ignore the cultural context in which psyches exist. As Frederick Jameson argued in a work that lies behind many of these specific studies, it derives from the desire to transcend personal psychology altogether, because Freud's psychology remains "locked into the category of the individual subject."[22] The emphasis now is on psychology as a product of culture, itself a political structure; the very concept of a psyche is seen to be a product of the cultural nexus evolved during the Renaissance, and indeed, psycho-analysis itself, rather than being a way of understanding the Renaissance psyche, is a marginal and belated creation of this same nexus.[23] Thus the revisionists, with Jameson, may look for a "political unconscious" and make use of Freud's insights into the "logic of dreams"[24]—the concepts of displacement, condensation, the manage-ment of desire[25]—but they do not accept Freud's assumptions about the mind—or the subject—creating that logic.[26] The agent who displaces or manages is not the individual but the "collective or associative" mind; at times it seems to be the text itself, seen as a "libidinal apparatus" or "desiring machine"[27] independent of any individual creator.

The revisionist impulse has been one of the most salutary in recent years in correcting New Critical "blindness" to history and ideology. In particular it has revealed the ways in which the play has been "reproduced" and drafted into the service of colonialist politics from the nineteenth century through G. Wilson Knight's twentieth-century celebration of Prospero as representative of England's "coloniz-ing, especially her will to raise savage peoples from superstition and blood-sacrifice, taboos and witchcraft and the attendant fears and slaveries, to a more enlightened existence."[28] But here, as critics have been suggesting about new historicism in general, it is now in danger of fostering blindness of its own. Granted that something was wrong with a commentary that focused on *The Tempest* as a self-contained project of a self-contained individual and that ignored the political situation in 1611. But something seems wrong now also, something more than the rhetorical ex-cesses characteristic of any innovative critical movement. The recent criticism not only flattens the text into the mold of colonialist discourse and eliminates what is characteristically "Shakespearean" in order to foreground what is "colonialist," but it is also—paradoxically—in danger of taking the play further from the particular historical situation in England in 1611 even as it brings it closer to what we mean by "colonialism" today.

It is difficult to extrapolate back from G. Wilson Knight's colonialist discourse to seventeenth-century colonialist discourse without knowing more about the par-ticulars of that earlier discourse. What is missing from the recent articles is the connection between the new insights about cultural phenomena like "power" and "fields of discourse" and the traditional insights about the text, its immediate sources, its individual author—and his individual psychology. There is little sense of how discourse is related to the individual who was creating, even as he was participating in, that discourse. The following discussion will suggest how such a relation might be conceived. Sections I and II briefly elaborate on *The Tempest*'s versions of prob-lems raised by new historicist treatment of the text and its relation to the historical context; sections III and IV go on to suggest that the recognition of the individuality of the play, and of Shakespeare, does not counter but rather enriches the under-standing of that context. Perhaps by testing individual cases, we can avoid the circularity of a definition that assumes that "colonialism" was present in a given group of texts, and so "discovers" it there.

I

How do we know that *The Tempest* "enacts" colonialism rather than merely alluding to the New World? How do we know that Caliban is part of the "discourse of colonialism"? To ask such a question may seem perversely naive, but the play is notoriously slippery. There have been, for example, any number of interpretations of Caliban,[29] including not only contemporary post-colonial versions in which Caliban is a Virginian Indian but also others in which Caliban is played as a black slave or as "missing link" (in a costume "half monkey, half coco-nut"[30]), with the interpretation drawing on the issues that were being debated at the time—on the discursive contexts that were culturally operative—and articulated according to "changing Anglo-American attitudes toward primitive man."[31] Most recently one teacher has suggested that *The Tempest* is a good play to teach in junior colleges because students can identify with Caliban.

Interpretation is made even more problematic here because, despite the claims about the play's intervention in English colonialism,[32] we have no *external* evidence that seventeenth-century audiences thought the play referred to the New World. In an age when real voyages were read allegorically, the status of allegorical voyages like Prospero's can be doubly ambiguous, especially in a play like *The Tempest*, which provides an encyclopedic context for Prospero's experience, presenting it in terms of an extraordinary range of classical, biblical, and romantic exiles, discoveries, and confrontations.[33] Evidence for the play's original reception is of course extraordinarily difficult to find, but in the two nearly contemporary responses to Caliban that we do know about, the evidence for a colonialist response is at best ambiguous. In *Bartholomew Fair* (1614) Jonson refers scornfully to a "servant-monster," and the Folio identifies Caliban as a "salvage and deformed slave"[34] in the cast list. Both "monster" and "salvage" are firmly rooted in the discourse of Old World wild men, though the latter was of course also applied to the New World natives. In other words, these two seventeenth-century responses tend to invoke the universal and not the particular implications of Caliban's condition. A recent study of the play's history suggests that "if Shakespeare, however obliquely, meant Caliban to personify America's natives, his intention apparently miscarried almost completely."[35]

Despite this lack of contemporary testimony, the obvious reason for our feeling that the play "is" colonialist—more so than *The Winter's Tale* or *Henry VIII*, for example, which were written at roughly the same time—is, of course, the literal resemblance between its plot and certain events and attitudes in English colonial history: Europeans arrive in the New World and assume they can appropriate what properly belongs to the New World Other, who is then "erased." The similarities are clear and compelling—more so than in many cases of new historical readings; the problem, however, is that while there are also many literal differences between *The Tempest* and colonialist fictions and practice, the similarities are taken to be so compelling that the differences are ignored. Thus Caliban is taken to "be" a Native American despite the fact that a multitude of details differentiate Caliban from the

Indian as he appeared in the travelers' reports from the New World.[36] Yet it does seem significant that, despite his closeness to nature, his naiveté, his devil worship, his susceptibility to European liquor, and, above all, his "treachery"—characteristics associated in writings of the time with the Indians—he nonetheless lacks almost all of the defining external traits in the many reports from the New World—no superhuman physique, no nakedness or animal skin (indeed, an English "gaberdine" instead), no decorative feathers,[37] no arrows, no pipe, no tobacco, no body paint, and—as Shakespeare takes pains to emphasize—no love of trinkets and trash. No one could mistake him for the stereotyped "Indian with a great tool," mentioned in passing in *Henry VIII*. Caliban in fact is more like the devils Strachey expected to find on the Bermuda island (but didn't) than like the Indians whom adventurers did find in Virginia, though he is not wholly a monster from the explorers' wild tales either.[38]

In other ways, too, it is assumed that the similarities matter but the differences do not: thus Prospero's magic occupies "the space *really inhabited in colonial history* by gunpowder"[39] (emphasis mine); or, when Prospero has Caliban pinched by the spirits, he shows a "similar sadism" to that of the Haitian masters who "roasted slaves or buried them alive";[40] or, when Prospero and Ariel hunt Caliban with spirit dogs, they are equated to the Spaniards who hunted Native Americans with dogs.[41] So long as there is a core of resemblance, the differences are irrelevant. The differences, in fact, are themselves taken to be evidence of the colonialist ideology at work, rationalizing and euphemizing power—or else inadvertent slips. Thus the case for colonialism becomes stronger insofar as Prospero *is* good and insofar as Caliban *is* in some ways bad—he did try to rape Miranda—or is *himself* now caught trying to falsify the past by occluding the rape and presenting himself as an innocent victim of Prospero's tyranny. Prospero's goodness and Caliban's badness are called rationalizations, justifications for Prospero's tyranny. Nor does it matter that the play seems *anti*-colonialist to the degree that it qualifies Prospero's scorn by showing Caliban's virtues, or that Prospero seems to achieve some kind of transcendence over his own colonialism when at the end of the play he says, "This thing of darkness I acknowledge mine."[42] Prospero's acknowledgement of Caliban is considered a mistake, a moment of inadvertent sympathy or truth, too brief to counter Prospero's underlying colonialism: in spite of the deceptively resonant poetry of his acknowledgement, Prospero actually does nothing to live up to the meaning which that poetry suggests;[43] it has even been argued that Prospero, in calling Caliban "mine," is simply claiming possession of him: "It is as though, after a public disturbance, a slaveowner said, 'Those two men are yours; this darkie's mine.' "[44]

Nonetheless, in addition to these differences that have been seen as rationalizations, there are many other differences as well that collectively raise questions about what counts as "colonialist discourse" and about what, if anything, might count as a relevant "difference." Thus, for example, any attempt to cast Prospero and Caliban as actors in the typical colonial narrative (in which a European exploits a previously free—indeed a reigning—native of an unspoiled world) is complicated by two other characters, Sycorax and Ariel. Sycorax, Caliban's mother, through whom he claims possession of the island, was not only a witch and a criminal, but she came from the Old World herself, or at least from eastern-hemisphere Argier.[45] She is a reminder that Caliban is only half-native, that his claim to the island is less like the claim of the Native American than the claim of the second generation Spaniard in the New World.[46] Moreover, Caliban was not alone when Prospero arrived. Ariel either came to the island with Sycorax or was already living on the island—its true reigning lord[47]—when Sycorax arrived and promptly enslaved him, thus herself becoming the first colonialist, the one who established the habits of dominance and erasure before Prospero ever set foot on the island. Nearly all revisionists note some of these differences before disregarding them, though they are not agreed on their significance—on whether they are "symptoms" of ideological conflict in the discourse, for example, or whether Shakespeare's "insights exceeded his sympathies."[48] But however they are explained, the differences *are* discarded. For the critic interested only in counteracting earlier blindness to potentially racist and ideological elements in the play, such ignoring of differences is understandable; for his or her purposes, it *is* enough to point that *The Tempest* has a "political unconscious" and is connected in *some* way to colonialist discourse without specifying further.

But if the object is, rather, to understand colonialism, instead of simply identifying it or condemning it, it is important to specify, to notice how the colonial elements are rationalized or integrated into the play's vision of the world. Otherwise, extracting the play's political unconscious leads to the same problems Freud faced at the beginning of his career when he treated the personal unconscious as an independent entity that should be almost surgically extracted from conscious discourse by hypnotizing away the "defenses." But, as is well known, Freud found that the conscious "defenses" were as essential—and problematic—as the supposedly prior unconscious "wish," and that they served purposes other than containment.[49] Indeed, in most psychoanalytic practice since Freud, the unconscious—or, rather, unconscious mentation—is assumed to exist in texts rather than existing as a reified "id," and interpretation must always return to the text.

As in the case of the personal unconscious, the political unconscious exists only in texts, whose "defenses" or rationalizations must be taken into account. Otherwise interpretation not only destroys the text—here *The Tempest*—as a unique work of art and flattens it into one more example of the master plot—or master ploy—in colonialist discourse; it also destroys the evidence of the play as a unique cultural artifact, a unique voice in that discourse. Colonialist discourse was varied enough to escape any simple formulation, even in a group of texts with apparent thematic links. It ranged from the lived Spanish colonialist practice of hunting New World natives with dogs to Bartholomew Las Casas's "factual" account lamenting and exposing the viciousness of that hunt,[50] to Shakespeare's possible allusion to it in *The Tempest*, when Prospero and Ariel set spirit dogs on Caliban, to a still earlier Shakespearean allusion—or possible allusion—in the otherwise non-colonialist *A Midsummer Night's Dream,* when Puck (who has come from India himself) chases Greek rude mechanicals with illusory animals in a scene evoking an entirely English conflict. The same "colonialist" hunt informs radically different fictions and practices, some of which enact colonialism, some of which subvert it, and some of which require other categories entirely to characterize its effect.

It is not easy to categorize the several links between *The Tempest* and colonialist discourse. Take the deceptively simple example of Caliban's name. Revisionists rightly emphasize the implications of the cannibal stereotype as automatic mark of Other in Western ethnocentric colonialist discourse,[51] and, since Shakespeare's name for "Caliban" is widely accepted as an anagram of "cannibal," many read the play as if he *were* a cannibal, with all that the term implies. But an anagram is not a cannibal, and Shakespeare's use of the stereotype is hardly automatic.[52] Caliban is no cannibal—he barely touches meat, confining himself more delicately to roots, berries, and an occasional fish; indeed, his symbiotic harmony with the island's natural food resources is one of his most attractive traits. His name seems more like a mockery of stereotypes than a mark of monstrosity, and in our haste to confirm the link between "cannibal" and "Indian" outside the text, we lose track of the way in which Caliban severs the link *within* the text.[53] While no one would deny *some* relation between Caliban and the New World natives to whom such terms as "cannibal" were applied, what that relation is remains unclear.

To enumerate differences between *The Tempest* and "colonialist discourse" is not to reduce discussion of the play to a counting contest, pitting similarities against differences. Rather, it is to suggest that inherent in any analysis of the play as colonialist discourse is a particular assumption about the relation between text and discourse—between one man's fiction and a collective fiction—or, perhaps, between one man's fiction and what we take for "reality." This relation matters not only to New Critics trying to isolate texts from contexts but to new Historicists (or just plain historicists) trying to put them back together. The relation is also vital to lived practices like censorship and inquisitions—and there are differences of opinion about what counts in these cases. Such differences need to be acknowledged and examined, and the method for reading them needs to be made more explicit before the implications of *The Tempest* as colonialist discourse can be fully understood.

II

Similar problems beset the definition of the "discourse" itself, the means of identifying the fictional—and the "lived"—practices constituting "English colonialism" in 1611. Given the impact of English colonialism over the last 350 years, it may again seem perversely naive to ask what colonialist discourse was like in 1611, as opposed to colonialism in 1911 or even in 1625, the year when Samuel Purchas asked, alluding to the "treachery" of the Virginian Indians, "Can a leopard change his spots? Can a Savage remayning a Savage be civill?" Purchas added this comment when he published the 1610 document that Shakespeare had used as his source for *The Tempest,* and Purchas has been cited as an example of "colonialist discourse."[54] Purchas does indeed display the particular combination of exploitative motives and self-justifying rhetoric—the "effacement of power"[55]—that revisionists identify as colonialist and which they find in *The Tempest.* But, one might reasonably ask, was the discursive context in 1611, when Shakespeare was writing, the same as it would be fourteen years later, when Purchas added his marginal comment?[56]

There seems, rather, to have been in 1611 a variety of what we might call "New World discourses" with multiple points of view, motives, and effects, among which such comments as Purchas's are not as common as the revisionist emphasis implies. These are "colonialist" only in the most general sense in which all ethnocentric cultures are always "colonialist": narcissistically pursuing their own ends, oblivious to the desires, needs, and even the existence of the Other. That is, if this New World discourse is colonialist, it is so primarily in that it *ignores* Indians, betraying its Eurocentric assumptions about the irrelevance of any people other than white, male, upper-class Europeans, preferably from England. It thus expresses not an historically specific but a *timeless* and universal attitude toward the "stranger," which Fiedler described in so many of Shakespeare's plays. We might see this discourse as a precondition[57] for colonialism proper, which was to follow with the literal rather than the figurative colonizing of New World natives. But to assume that colonialism was already encoded in the anomalous situation in 1611 is to undermine the revisionist effort to understand the historical specificity of the moment when Shakespeare wrote *The Tempest.*

It is not easy to characterize the situation in 1611. On the one hand, Spain had long been engaged in the sort of "colonialist discourse" that revisionists find in *The Tempest;* and even in England at the time there were examples of colonialist discourse (in the rhetoric, if not yet often in the lived practices) produced by those directly involved in the colonialist project and expecting to profit from it. The official advertisements in the first rush of enthusiasm about Virginia, as well as the stream of defenses when the Virginia project began to fail, often have a euphemistic ring and often do suggest a fundamental greed and implicit racism beneath claims to be securing the earthly and spiritual well-being of the Virginia natives.[58] ("[We] doe buy of them the pearles of earth, and sell to them the pearles of heauen."[59]) These documents efface not only power but most practical problems as well, and they were supplemented by sermons romanticizing hardships as divine tribulation.[60] Scattered throughout this discourse are righteous defenses of taking land from the Indians, much in the spirit—and tone—of Rabbi Zeal-of-the-Land Busy defending his need to eat pig. (This was also the tone familiar from the anti-theatrical critics—and, indeed, occasional colonialist sermons included snipes at the "Plaiers," along with the Devil and the papists, as particular enemies of the Virginia venture.[61])

On the other hand, even in these documents not only is the emphasis elsewhere but often there are important contradictory movements. For example, "A True Declaration," the official record of the Bermuda wreck, refers once to the Indians as "humane beasts" and devotes one paragraph of its twenty-four pages to the "greedy Vulture" Powhattan and his ambush. It notes elsewhere, however, that some of the English settlers themselves had "created the *Indians* our implacable enemies by some violence they had offered," and it actually spends far more time attacking the lazy "scum of men" among the settlers, who had undermined the colony from within, than demonizing the less relevant Indians.[62]

And on the whole, the exploitative and self-justifying rhetoric is only one element in a complex New World discourse. For much of the time, in fact, the main conflict in the New World was not between whites and Native Americans but between Spain and England. Voyages like Drake's (1577–80) were motivated by this international conflict, as well as by the romance of discovery and the lure of treasure—but not by colonizing.[63] Even when Raleigh received the first patent to settle and trade with the New World (1584), necessitating more extended contact with Native Americans, the temporary settlements he started in the 1580s were largely tokens in his play for fame and wealth rather than attempts to take over sizable portions of land from the natives.[64]

Only when the war with Spain was over (1604) and ships were free again did colonization really begin; and then "America and Virginia were on everyone's lips."[65] But this New World discourse still reflects little interest in its inhabitants. Other issues are much more widely discussed. For example, what would the New World government be like? Would James try to extend his authoritarianism to America? *Could* he? This was the issue, for example, most energizing Henry Wriothesley, Shakespeare's Southampton, who led the "Patriot" faction on the London Virginia Council, pushing for more American independence.[66] (As for James's own "colonial discourse," it seems to have been devoted to worries about how it would all affect his relations with Spain,[67] and to requests for flying squirrels and other New World "toyes."[68]) Of more immediate interest, perhaps, to the mass of real or armchair adventurers were the reports of New World wealth that at first made Virginia known as a haven for bankrupts and spendthrifts, as well as for wild dreamers—followed by the accounts of starvation, rebellion, and hardship brought back by those who had escaped from the reality of colonial existence. Now the issue became "Is it worth it?" The official propaganda, optimistic about future profits, was soon countered by a backlash from less optimistic scoffers challenging the value of the entire project, one which sent money, men, and ships to frequent destruction and brought back almost no profit.[69]

Even the settlers actually living with the natives in the New World itself were—for entirely non-altruistic reasons—not yet fully engaged in "colonialist" discourse as defined by revisionists. In 1611 they had not managed to establish enough power to euphemize; they had little to be defensive about. They were too busy fighting mutiny, disease, and the stupidities of the London Council to have much energy left over for Indians. It is true that no writer ever treated Native Americans as equals—any more than he treated Moors, Jews, Catholics, peasants, women, Irishmen, or even Frenchmen as equals; travellers complacently recorded kidnapping natives to exhibit in England, as if the natives had no rights at all.[70] And it is true that some of their descriptions are distorted by Old World stereotypes of wild men or cannibals—though these descriptions are often confined to earlier *pre*-colonial explorers' reports.[71] Or, far more insidiously, the descriptions were distorted by stereotypes of unfallen innocent noble savages—stereotypes that inevitably led to disillusionment when the settlers had to realize that the Indians, like the land itself, were not going to fulfill their dreams of a golden world made expressly to nurture Englishmen. The "noble savage" stereotype thus fueled the recurring accusation of Indian treachery, a response to betrayal of settlers' fantasies as well as to any real Indian betrayal,[72] and one to which I will return in discussing *The Tempest*.

But, given the universality of racial prejudice towards New World natives along with all "Others," in this early period the movement was to loosen, not to consolidate, the prejudices brought from the Old World. The descriptions of these extended face-to-face encounters with Native Americans were perhaps even more varied than contemporary responses to Moors and Jews, who were usually encountered on the white man's own territory, where exposure could be limited and controlled. The very terms imported from the Old World to name the natives— "savages" or "naturals"—began to lose their original connotations as the differing descriptions multiplied and even contradicted themselves. The reports range from Harriot's widely republished attempt at scientific, objective reporting (1588) which viewed natives with great respect, to Smith's less reliable adventure stories (1608– 31), disputed even in his own time by Purchas. And although these do not by any means live up to our standards for non-colonialist discourse, their typical attitude is a wary, often patronizing, but live-and-let-live curiosity, rather than the exploitative erasure which would later become the mark of colonialist discourse. So long as the conflicts remained minimal, Native Americans were seen as beings like the writers;[73] further, tribes were distinguished from one another, and recognition was granted to their different forms of government, class structure, dress codes, religion, and language.[74] And when conflict did trigger the recurring accusation of "treachery," the writers never presented the Indians as laughable Calibans, but rather as capable, indeed formidable, enemies whose skill and intelligence challenged that of the settlers.

Horrors had already been perpetrated by the Spanish in the name of colonialism; not learning from these—or perhaps learning all too well—the English would soon begin perpetrating their own. But that lay in the future. When *The Tempest* was written, what the New World seems to have meant for the majority of Englishmen was a sense of possibility and a set of conflicting fantasies about the wonders to be found there; these were perhaps the preconditions for colonialism—as for much else—but not yet the thing itself.

To place colonialist discourse as precisely as possible within a given moment (like stressing the differences between *The Tempest* and colonialist discourse) is not to reduce the discussion to a numbers game. What is at stake here is not a quibble about chronology but an assumption about what we mean by the "relevant discursive context," about how we agree to determine it, and about how we decide to limit it. Here too there are differences of opinion about what counts, and these differences need to be acknowledged, examined, and accounted for.

III

My point in specifying Shakespeare's precise literal and temporal relation to colonialist discourse—in specifying the unique mind through which the discourse is mediated—is not to deny that the play has *any* relation to its context but to suggest that the relation is problematic. In the effort to identify Caliban as one more colonialist representation of the Other, we fail to notice how remarkable it is that such a Caliban should exist. In 1611 there were in England no literary portrayals of New World inhabitants and certainly no fictional examples of colonialist discourse.[75] Insofar as *The Tempest* does in some way allude to an encounter with a New World native (and I will for the remainder of this essay accept this premise), it is the very first work of literature to do so. There may be Indians, more or less demonized, in the nonliterary discourse. Outside of Shakespeare, however, there would be none in literature until two years after *The Tempest*, when they began to appear—feathers and all—in masques.[76] And Shakespeare went out of his way to invent Caliban: Strachey's account of the wreck on the uninhabited Bermuda islands—Shakespeare's main New World source—contains, of course, no island natives.[77] For these Shakespeare had to turn elsewhere in Strachey and in others who described the mainland colony in Virginia. Shakespeare was the first to show one of *us* mistreating a native, the first to represent a native from the inside, the first to allow a native to complain on stage, and the first to make that New World encounter problematic enough to generate the current attention to the play.

To argue for Shakespeare's uniqueness is not to argue that as fiction *The Tempest* is above politics, or that as a writer of fiction Shakespeare transcended ideology. It does imply, however, that if the play is "colonialist," it must be seen as "prophetic" rather than descriptive.[78] As such, the play's status immediately raises important questions. Why was Shakespeare—a man who had no direct stake in colonization—the first writer of fiction to portray New World inhabitants? Why then? Shakespeare had shown no signs of interest in the New World until *The Tempest*, despite the fact that there had been some colonial activity and some colonialist rhetoric for several years among those who did have a stake in it. How did the colonialist phenomenon spread?

To hasten over Shakespeare's reaction to colonialism as if it were not a question but a conclusion is to lose one of the most important bits of data we may ever have about how such things as colonialism—and discourse—work. Problematic as it may be to speculate about an individual mind, it is even more problematic to speculate about the discourse of an entire nation or an entire period. One way to give substance to such large generalizations is to trace, in as much detail as may be available, the particulars on which they are based. Here the particulars include the individuals who produced, as well as reproduced, the larger cultural discourse—especially individuals like Shakespeare, who, more than almost any other, both absorbed and shaped the various conflicting discourses of the period.

To do this, as I have been arguing, it is necessary to consider the entire play, without deciding prematurely what is "only a distortion" or "only an irrelevance." In addition, however, we must also look to a context for *The Tempest* that is as relevant as colonialist discourse and perhaps even more essential to the presence of colonialism in *The Tempest* in the first place—that is, to the context of Shakespeare's own earlier "discourse." Only then can we see how the two fields of discourse intersect. In making use of the New World vocabulary and imagery,

Shakespeare was in part describing something much closer to home—as was Jonson when he called the London brothel district "the Bermudas,"[79] or as would Donne when he found his America, his "new founde land," in the arms of his mistress. Or as was Dudley Carleton in a gossipy letter from London about Lord Salisbury enduring a "tempest" of reproof from a lady; or Sir Ralph Winwood in trying to "begin a new world by setting himself and his wife here at home."[80]

Long before writing *The Tempest*, Shakespeare had written another play about a ruler who preferred his books to government. Navarre's academy in *Love's Labor's Lost* was no island, but, like an island, it was supposed to be isolated from territorial negotiations. And Navarre, oblivious to colonial issues, though certainly not exempt from timeless aristocratic prejudice, brought his own version of Ariel and Caliban by inviting Armado and Costard to join him. Like Prospero, he asked his "Ariel" to make a pageant for him, and he imprisoned his "Caliban" for trying to "do" a wench. His relation to the two is not a matter of colonization but rather of condescension and ironic recognition, as Navarre is forced to see something of himself in the conflict between fiery Armado's over-active imagination and earthy Costard's lust.[81] Only much later did this pattern come to be "colonial."

The Tempest is linked in many other ways not only to *Love's Labor's Lost* but also to the rest of the canon, as continued efforts of critics have shown,[82] and it is revealing to see how, in each case, the non-colonial structures become associated with colonialist discourse. Indeed, the very details of *The Tempest* that revisionists see as marking the "nodal point of the play's imbrication into this discourse of colonialism"[83] are reworkings of similar moments in earlier and seemingly pre-colonial plays. The moment I will focus on for the rest of this paper is the one that many revisionists take as the strongest evidence in the play for the falseness of Prospero's position—the moment when the hidden colonialist project emerges openly,[84] when the "political unconscious" is exposed.[85] It occurs when Caliban's plot interrupts the pageant Prospero is staging for Ferdinand and Miranda, and Prospero is so enraged that Miranda says she has never seen him so angry. The explanation, it has been suggested, is that if psychology matters at all, Prospero's anger here, like his anger earlier when Caliban tried to rape Miranda, derives from the politics of colonialism. It reveals Prospero's political "disquiet at the irruption into consciousness of an unconscious anxiety concerning the grounding of his legitimacy" on the island.[86]

But the dramatic context counters the assumption that politics is primary in this episode. Like Caliban, Prospero differs in significant ways from the stereotyped "real life" characters in colonial political drama. Unlike the single-minded colonial invader, Prospero is both an exile and a father; and the action of the play is initiated when both these roles are newly activated by the arrival of Prospero's old enemies, those who had exiled him as well as his daughter's husband-to-be. At the moment of Prospero's eruption into anger, he has just bestowed Miranda on his enemy's son Ferdinand[87] and is in the midst of presenting his pageant as a wedding gift, wrapped in a three-fold warning about chastity.[88] If Prospero is to pass on his heritage to the next generation, he must at this moment repress his desire for power and for revenge at home, as well as any sexual desire he feels toward Miranda.[89] Both desires are easily projected onto the fishily phallic Caliban, a walking version of Prospero's own "thing" of darkness. Not only has Caliban already tried to rape Miranda; he is now out to kill Prospero so that he can turn Miranda over to Stephano ("she will give thee brave brood"); and Caliban does not even feel guilty. Caliban's function as a walking screen for projection may help explain why Caliban's sin does not consist in cannibalism, to which, one assumes, Prospero was never tempted, but rather in Prospero's own repressed fantasies of omnipotence and lust.[90] Of course Prospero is also angry that Caliban is now threatening both his authority on the island and his justification of that authority; but the extraordinary intensity of Prospero's rage suggests a conjunction of psychological as well as political passion.

This conjunction of the psychological and the political not only appears here in *The Tempest* but also characterizes a surprising number of Prospero-like characters in Shakespeare's earlier plays who provide a suggestive context for *The Tempest*. All through the canon one finds characters who escape from active lives to some kind of pastoral retreat, who step aside form power and aggression—and usually from sexuality as well—and from all the forbidden fantasies in which these are enacted. But while each adopts a disinterested stance, as if having retired behind the scenes, each sees life as a play and manipulates others still on stage in a way that suggests a fascination with what he has rejected and assigned to the "Others." And each of these has his "Caliban" and his moment of sudden, irrational anger when his "Caliban" threatens to overstep the limits defining him as "other" and separating him from "Prospero." At this moment of confrontation, boundaries threaten to disappear and hierarchies are menaced. And in each of the earlier plays, this moment is indicative of inner conflict, as the earlier "Prospero" figure confronts someone who often has neither property nor power to colonize, and whose threat is largely symbolic. In all these plays Shakespeare is dealing not just with power relations but also with the psychology of domination, with the complicated ways in which personal psychology interacts with political power.

As early as the mid-1590s, two figures show some resemblance to Prospero. Antonio, the merchant of Venice, sees the world as "A stage where every man must play a part, / And mine a sad one" (1.1.78–79). Almost eagerly accepting his passive lot, he claims to renounce both profit and love. But, as Marianne Novy suggests, a repressed self-assertion is hinted at in the passive/aggressive claims he makes on Bassanio and comes out clearly when he lashes out at the greedy and self-assertive Shylock with a viciousness like Prospero's toward Caliban, a viciousness he shows nowhere else.[91] He admits calling the Jew a dog and says,

> I am as like to call thee so again,
> To spet on thee again. . . .   (1.3.130–31)[92]

A related and similarly problematic exchange occurs in the *Henry IV* plays, written a year or so later, where role-playing Prince Hal, during his temporary retreat from power, had found a version of pastoral in Falstaff's tavern. After reclaiming his throne, when he finds that Falstaff has also come from the tavern to claim a role in the new kingdom, Hal suddenly repudiates Falstaff with a cruelty as cold as Prospero's anger at Caliban—and equally excessive: "I know thee not, old man." In both these cases, though the resemblance to Prospero is clear, the relation to an historically specific colonialism is hard to establish.

Then in *As You Like It* (1599) and *Measure for Measure* (1604) come the two exiled or self-exiled Dukes who leave home—one to "usurp" the deer in the forest (2.1.21–28), the other to "usurp" the beggary in the Vienna streets (3.2.93)—and who most resemble Prospero. Duke Senior in *As You Like It* is banished to the pastoral Forest of Arden, where he professes himself utterly content to live a life notable for the absence of both power and women (a "woeful pageant," he calls it cheerfully [2.7.138]). He is saved from having to fight for power when his evil brother (unlike the one in Shakespeare's source) conveniently repents and hands back the dukedom; but an ambivalence about sexuality is at least suggested when this mildest of men lashes out at Jaques, precisely when Jaques returns from melancholy withdrawal and claims the fool's license to satirize society's ills—to "cleanse the foul body of the infected world."[93] "Fie on thee!" says the Duke,

> . . . thou thyself has been a libertine,
> As sensual as the brutish sting itself,
> And all th' embossed sores, and headed evils,
> That thou with license of free foot has caught,
> Wouldst thou disgorge into the general world.   (2.7.65–69)

Jaques seems to have touched a nerve. Elsewhere Jaques makes a claim on behalf of the deer in the forest rather like the claim Caliban makes for himself on the island, complaining that Duke Senior has "usurped" these "velvet friends"; he even makes it "most invectively," having, like Caliban, learned how to curse. Just as in the case of Caliban, we cannot laugh away the claim the way the Duke does. But Jaques's complaint seems intended more as an insight into the Duke than a comment on the deer—whom Jaques later kills anyway.

The touchiest of these precursors, Vincentio in *Measure for Measure* (1604), is the one who most closely resembles Prospero. He too prefers study to government, and he turns over his power to Angelo, claiming "[I] do not like to stage me to their eyes" (1.1.68)—but then he steps behind the scenes to manipulate the action. Like Prospero, Vincentio sees his manipulation as an altruistic means of educating his wayward subjects into chastity, repentance, and merciful mildness; but it seems to serve more private needs of self-definition as well. For it first allows him, as "ghostly father," to deny any aggressive or sexual motives of his own, and then allows him to return at the end to claim both power and sexual rewards as he resumes his dukedom and claims Isabel.[94] Vincentio's "Caliban" is the libidinous and loose-tongued Lucio, who not only indulges his own appetites but openly accuses the Duke of indulging his, so that it is unusually clear in this case that the "Caliban" figure is a representation of the Duke's own disowned passions. Lucio's slanders include the claim that the Duke has "usurp[ed] the beggary he was never born to," but, like Jaques speaking for the deer, he is more concerned with revealing the Duke's contradictory desires here than with defending beggars' rights. Goaded by Lucio's insubordination, the Duke lashes out at him as he does at no one else and threatens a punishment much worse than the one he assigned to the would-be rapist and murderer Angelo or to the actual murderer Barnardine.

In the case of all of these "Prosperos," it is hard to see the attack on "Caliban" as part of a specifically colonialist strategy, as a way of exploiting the Other or of rationalizing illegitimate power over him rather than over what he represents in "Prospero" himself. To a logical observer, the Prospero-attack seems at best gratuitous—and the more frightening for being so. It has no political rationale. The "political" attack always takes place outside the play's old world, after the characters' withdrawal to a second world that is not so much a new world as one that projects, exaggerates, turns upside down, or polarizes the conflicts that made the old world uninhabitable. In the case of each earlier "Prospero," the conflicts seem internal as well as external, so that when he moves out to meet his "Caliban," he is always meeting himself. Political exile is also presented as self-estrangement, a crisis of selfhood expressed in social and geographical divisions. And in each case, Shakespeare exposes the fragility of such arrangements, whether they take the form of the pastoralization of the forest of Arden, or of the scapegoating of Shylock in Venice, or of Falstaff's carnival misrule in the tavern, or of the theatricalizing of the prison in Vincentio's Vienna, or of Prospero's "colonizing" of a utopian island.

Whatever varying political role each earlier "Caliban" plays as inhabitant of his second—or second-class—world, each seems to embody a similar psychological quality. In each case he displays the overt self-assertion that the retired or retiring "Prospero" cannot—or wishes not to—muster for himself, and that for Shakespeare seems to be the mark of the Other. Each is an epitome of what Shakespeare (perhaps in his own punning ambivalence about acknowledging it as his own) elsewhere calls "will."[95] This "will" includes a range of forbidden desires and appetites often attributed to the Other and always associated with the "foul body," as Jaques calls it; or with the fat appetitive body, as in Hal's picture of Falstaff; or with the body as mere pounds of flesh and blood; perhaps with what we might call, after Bakhtin, the "grotesque" body. And it is defined in opposition to the ethereal, or ariel, virtues such as "mercy," "honor," and "chastity" characterizing the various "Prosperos."

The "will" of these "Calibans" can carry suggestions of primitive oral greed, as in Shylock's desire to "feed fat" his revenge with a pound of human flesh, in Falstaff's voracious appetite, or in Caliban's name. Or it emerges in a rampant sexual greed, as in Falstaff, in Jaques's past, in Lucio, perhaps even in Shylock's reproductive miracles with sheep, and of course in Caliban himself. But the most alien aspect of self-assertion or "will" in these plays emerges in a primitive vengefulness. This vengefulness is associated with an infantile need to control and dominate and with the scatological imagery of filth—with a disgust at the whole messy, physical world that always threatens to get out of control. Thus Shylock's drive for revenge is linked to his Jonsonian "anal" virtues ("fast bind, fast find"), to his fecal gold, and to his tightly locked orifices ("stop my house's ears, I mean my casements" [2.5.34]). Thus, too, Duke Senior's description of Jaques "disgorging" his "embossed sores" suggests that he is projecting onto Jaques his disgust at the idea of "the foul body of the infected world"—and his fear that Jaques will "disgorge" and overflow his boundaries rather than cleanse; Jaques's very name associates him with this scatological vision. Caliban, very much concerned with revenge, also takes on a taint of anality through the words of Trinculo and Stephano. The latter sees Caliban hiding under his garbardine with Trinculo and takes Caliban for a monster whose first act is to "vent" a Trinculo—a Gargantuan act of defecation; Trinculo elsewhere complains that Caliban led them to a "foul lake" that o'erstunk their feet till they smelled "all horse-piss."[96]

Thus, although Caliban is like the New World natives in his "otherness," he is linked at least as closely to Shakespeare's earlier "Calibans." What is interesting in any attempt to understand *The Tempest*'s uniqueness in other aspects is that in Caliban for the first time Shakespeare shows "will," or narcissistic self-assertion, in its purest and simplest form as the original "grandiosity" or "megalomania" of a child,[97] for the first time he makes the representative of bodily existence a seeming child whose ego is a "body ego," as Freud said, a "subject" whose "self" is defined by the body. There is a childishly amoral—and almost asexual—glee in Caliban's sexuality ("O ho, O ho, would't had been done!" he says of the attempted rape [1.2.349]) and a childish exaggeration in his dreams of revenge ("brain him / . . .or with a log / Batter his skull, or paunch him with a stake, / Or cut his wezand with thy knife" [3.2.88–91]).[98] Like a child he thinks often about his mother,[99] and now that she is gone, he dreams of riches dropping from heaven and cries to dream again; like a child he was taught language and shown the man in the moon.[100] And like an imperious child he is enraged when his pie in the sky does not appear. If he rebukes Prospero for first stroking and then disciplining him, if he objects to being made a subject when he was "mine own king" (1.2.342), this is the rebuke made by every child, who begins life as "His Majesty the Baby," tended by his mother, and who is then subjected to the demands of the community,[101] represented by the father. Childhood is the period in which anyone—even the most powerful Elizabethan aristocrat—can experience the slave's side of the master/slave relation, its indignities, and the dreams of reversal and revenge it can imbue. Appropriate and acceptable in a baby, all these traits (like Caliban himself) "with age [grow] uglier" (4.1.191)—and far more dangerous.

Caliban's childishness has been dismissed as a defense, another rationalization of Prospero's illegitimate power.[102] But if it is a defense, it is one which itself is revealing. Caliban's childishness is a dimension of the Other in which Shakespeare seems extremely interested.[103] It is a major (not peripheral) source both of Caliban's defining characteristics and of what makes his relation to Prospero so highly charged. Caliban's childish innocence seems to have been what first attracted Prospero, and now it is Caliban's childish lawlessness that enrages him. To a man like Prospero, whose life has been spent learning a self-discipline in which he is not yet totally adept, Caliban can seem like a child who must be controlled, and who, like a child, is murderously enraged at being controlled. Prospero treats Caliban as he would treat the willful child in himself.

The importance of childishness in defining Caliban is suggested by the final *Tempest* precedent to be cited here, one that lies behind Prospero's acknowledgement of Caliban as his own thing of darkness—and in which the Caliban figure is literally a child. This figure is found in *Titus Andronicus,* where a bastard child, called "devil" and "slave," is cast out by his mother but rescued by his father, who promises—in language foreshadowing Caliban's imagery in *The Tempest*—to raise him in a cave and feed him on berries and roots.[104] Here the father is black Aaron the Moor, and the childish thing of darkness, whom Aaron is at some pains to acknowledge his, is his own literally black son. What is remarkable about this portrait of a barbarian father and son is that Aaron's is the only uncomplicated parental love in a play-world where civilized white men like Titus kill their own children on principle. It is a world, by the way, which contains the only literal (if unwitting) cannibal in Shakespeare's plays, the child's white mother. Unlike Titus, Aaron can love his child because he can identify with him; as an "uncivilized" black man, he can accept the greedy, sensual, lawless child in himself: "This is my self, the vigor and the picture of my youth," he says (4.2.108). This love, which comes easily to Aaron in acknowledging his own flesh and blood, is transformed in *The Tempest* to Prospero's strained and difficult recognition of a tribal Other whose blackness nonetheless figures his own.

The echoes of Aaron not only suggest the family resemblance between Prospero and Caliban. They also suggest that here Shakespeare is changing his earlier version of authority. In the earlier play it is white Titus who—like Prospero—gives away his power and is betrayed; but it is black Aaron who is stigmatized as the vengeful villain. And Titus maintains this black-and-white distinction even while savagely carrying out his own revenge. But distinctions in *The Tempest* have become less rigid. By merging his fantasy about a "white" (but exiled and neurotically puritanical) duke with his fantasy about a villainous (but loving) "black" father, Shakespeare for the first time shows, in Prospero, a paternal leader who comes back to power by admitting rather than denying the "blackness" in himself. Prospero may not, as several revisionists point out, physically *do* much for Caliban at the end; however, what he *says* matters a great deal indeed, for his original transgression, when he first defined Caliban as the Other, was intellectual as well as physical. When Prospero finally acknowledges Caliban, although he is a long way from recognizing the equality of racial "others," he comes closer than any of Shakespeare's other "Prosperos" to acknowledging the otherness within, which helps generate all racism—and he comes closer than anyone else in colonialist discourse. Prospero acknowledges the child-like Caliban as his own, and although he does not thus undo hierarchy, he moves for the first time towards accepting the child in himself rather than trying to dominate and erase that child (along with random vulnerable human beings outside himself) in order to establish his adult authority.

Thus, although Shakespeare may, as the revisionists claim, to some degree reproduce Prospero's colonialist vision of the island, the play's emphasis lies not so much in justifying as in analyzing that vision, just as Shakespeare had analyzed the origins of dominance in the earlier plays. The play insists that we see Prospero's current relation to Caliban in terms of Prospero's own past; it contains the "colonial" encounter firmly within the framing story of his own family history. And though that history does not extend backward to Prospero's own childhood, it does begin with family ties and Miranda's memory of "the dark backward and abysm of time" (1.2.50), before either she or Prospero had known the Other. Prospero was then, he thought, in total harmony with his world and himself, happy in his regressive retreat to his library-Eden; he was buffered from reality, he thought, by a "lov'd" brother so linked to himself and his own desires that Prospero had in him a trust with no "limit, / A confidence sans bound" (1.2.96–97), like the trust that Miranda must have had in the women who "tended" her then. Only when Antonio's betrayal shattered that trust and Prospero was ousted from Eden—newly aware of both the brother as Other and of himself as a willful self in ópposition—did he "discover" the island and Caliban. In a sense, then, Caliban emerged from the rift between Prospero and Antonio,[105] just as Ariel emerged from Sycorax's riven pine. Once the brother has shown that he is not identical to the self, reflecting back its own narcissistic desire, then he becomes the Other—and simultaneously rouses the vengeful Other in the self. In *The Tempest* the distance that a "colonialist" Prospero imposes between self and Other originated in a recoil from the closest relation of all; it was a recoil that in fact *defined* both the "distant" and the "close," the public and the private—the political and the personal—as separate realms. When Prospero acknowledges Caliban, he thus partly defuses an entire dynamic that began long before he had ever seen the island.

IV

When Shakespeare created a childish "Caliban," he was himself rounding out a dynamic process that had begun as long ago as the writing of *Titus Andronicus.* We will never "know" why Shakespeare gave to this final version of his exile story a local habitation incorporating aspects of colonialist discourse. But the answer lies not only in that discourse but also in him and in what was on his mind. Some of the most "specious" speculations about Shakespeare's mind have been stimulated by his presumed resemblance to Prospero at the end of the play: past his zenith, on the way to retirement, every third thought turned to his grave. Without trying speciously to read minds, however, it seems safe to say that to some degree Shakespeare had been for several years concerned with the aging, loss, mortality, and death that recur in so much of what we know he was writing and reading at the time. To this degree, both the play and its context deal with the end of the individual self, the subject and the body in which it is located. It is the end of everything associated with the discovery of self in childhood, the end of everything Caliban represents—and thus the greatest threat to infantile narcissism since His

Majesty the Baby was first de-throned. John Bender has noted that the occasion of the play's presumed court debut in 1611 was Hallowmas, the feast of winter and the time of seasonal celebrations figuring the more final endings and death associated with winter.[106] As part of the celebrations, Bender suggests, the play might have served to structure a communal response to the recurring "seasonal mentality" brought on by the reminder of mortality. Whether or not this is true, that which "recurs" in seasons and communities comes only once to individuals; and as the final stage in Shakespeare's own "seasonal" movement from *A Midsummer Night's Dream* to *The Winter's Tale,* the play can be seen as staging a final "crisis of selfhood" and of betrayal like those in the earlier exile plays—but this time a far more extreme one.[107] For those who rage against the dying of the light, it is a crisis that awakens the old infantile narcissistic demand for endless fulfillment and the narcissistic rage and vengefulness against a world that denies such satisfactions.[108]

To one on the threshold of retirement from the Old World, the New World is an appropriate stage on which to enact this last resurgence of the infantile self. We take for granted the historical conditions generating utopian visions in the voyagers' reports outside the play. What the example of Caliban's childish presence in the play suggests is that for Shakespeare the desire for such utopias—the golden worlds and fountains of youth—has roots in personal history as well as in "history." The desire has been shaped by the most local as well as by the largest, collective, material constraints: by being born small and weak in a world run by large, strong people with problems of their own; by being born in "a sexed and mortal body"[109] that must somehow become part of a social and linguistic community. Caliban's utopia of sweet voices and clouds dropping riches (3.2.137–43) draws most directly on the infantile substratum that colored Columbus's report when he returned from his third voyage convinced "that the newly discovered hemisphere was shaped like a woman's breast, and that the Earthly Paradise was located at the high point corresponding to the nipple."[110] But the play's other "utopias" draw on it too. Gonzalo's utopia is more socialized ("nature should bring forth, / . . . all abundance, / To feed my innocent people" [2.1.163–65]); Prospero's pageant utopia is more mythic (a world without winter, blessed by nurturing Ceres); but, like Caliban's, their utopias recreate a union with a bounteous Mother Nature. And, like every child's utopia, each is a fragile creation, easily destroyed by the rage and violence that constitute its defining alternative—a dystopia of murderous vengeance; the interruption of Prospero's pageant is only the last in a series of such interruptions.[111] Each is the creation of a childish mind that operates in binary divisions: good mother/bad mother, love/rage, brother/Other.

That Shakespeare was drawn to the utopian aspects of the New World is suggested by the particular fragment of New World discourse that most directly precipitated (Kermode's suggestive term) the play—the Bermuda pamphlets, which record what was "perhaps the most romantic incident associated with America's beginnings."[112] What attracted Shakespeare, that is, was the story in which a "merciful God," a loving and fatherly protector, rescued a whole shipload of people from certain death; it was a story that countered thoughts of winter with reports of magical bounty in the aptly named "Summer Islands."

The concerns that made Shakespeare's approach to colonialist discourse possible may have been operative later in other cases as well. In analyzing the colonialist discourse growing out of political motives, it is important not to lose touch with the utopian discourse growing out of a different set of motives. Without reducing colonialism to "the merely subjective and to the status of psychological projection,"[113] one can still take account of fantasies and motives that, though now regarded as secondary, or as irrelevant to politics, may interact with political motives in ways we have not yet begun to understand—and cannot understand so long as we are diverted by trying to reduce psychology to politics or politics to psychology. The binary dynamics of infantile utopian fantasies can, for example, help explain why frustrated settlers succumbed *so easily* to the twin stereotypes of the Native Americans as innocent primitives who would welcome and nurture the settlers, and as hopelessly treacherous Others. They can serve as a reminder that the desire for friendship and brotherhood can be as destructive as a desire to exploit. Reference to irrational, outdated infantile needs can help explain why the settlers, once they actually did begin colonizing, set out with such gratuitous thoroughness to "reduce" the savage to civility. As James Axtell describes the process, "In European eyes, no native characteristic was too small to reform, no habit too harmless to reduce."[114] Such behavior seems to go beyond any immediate political or material motive and seems rather to serve more general psychological needs stirred up by conflict with the natives. The recent emphasis on the colonists' obvious material greed and rational self-interest—or class-interest—has unnecessarily obscured the role of these less obvious irrational motives and fantasies that are potentially even more insidious.

Shakespeare's assimilation of elements from historical colonialist discourse was neither entirely isolated from other uses or innocent of their effects. Nonetheless, the "colonialism" in his play is linked not only to Shakespeare's indirect participation in an ideology of political exploitation and erasure but also to his direct participation in the psychological aftereffects of having experienced the exploitation and erasure inevitable in being a child in an adult's world. He was not merely reproducing a preexistent discourse; he was also crossing it with other discourses, changing, enlarging, skewing, and questioning it. Our sense of *The Tempest*'s participation in "colonialist discourse" should be flexible enough to take account of such crossings; indeed our notion of that in which such discourse consisted should be flexible enough to include the whole of the text that constitutes the first English examples of fictional colonialist discourse.[115]

NOTES

[1] Two of the earliest of these critiques were actually written, although not published, by 1960: George Lamming, "A Monster, a Child, a Slave" (1960) in *The Pleasures of Exile* (London: Allison and Busby, 1984); James Smith, "*The Tempest*" (1954) in *Shakespearian and Other Essays*, ed. E. M. Wilson (Cambridge: Cambridge Univ. Press, 1974), pp. 159–261. Two more articles, less politicized, followed in the sixties: Philip Brockbank, "*The Tempest*: Conventions of Art and Empire" in *Later Shakespeare*, eds. J. R. Brown and B. Harris (London: Edward Arnold, 1966), pp. 183–201; and D. G. James, "The New World" in *The Dream of Prospero* (Oxford: Clarendon Press, 1967), pp. 72–123.

The recent group, returning to the political perspective of the first two, includes: Stephen Greenblatt,

"Learning to Curse: Aspects of Linguistic Colonialism in the Sixteenth Century" in *First Images of America*, ed. Fredi Chiappelli, 2 vols. (Los Angeles: Univ. of California Press, 1976), Vol. 2, 561–80; Bruce Erlich, "Shakespeare's Colonial Metaphor: On the Social Function of Theatre in *The Tempest*," *Science and Society*, 41 (1977), 43–65; Lorie Leininger, "Cracking the Code of *The Tempest*," *Bucknell Review*, 25 (1980), 121–31; Peter Hulme, "Hurricanes in the Caribbees: The Constitution of the Discourse of English Colonialism" in *1642: Literature and Power in the Seventeenth Century*, Proceedings of the Essex conference on the Sociology of Literature, eds. Francis Barker et al. (Colchester: Univ. of Essex, 1981), pp. 55–83; Paul N. Siegel, "Historical Ironies in *The Tempest*," *Shakespeare Jahrbuch*, 119 (Weimar: 1983), 104–11; Francis Barker and Peter Hulme, "Nymphs and Reapers Heavily Vanish: The Discursive Con-texts of *The Tempest*" in *Alternative Shakespeares*, ed. John Drakakis (London and New York: Methuen, 1985), pp. 191–205; Terence Hawkes, "Swisser-Swatter: Making a Man of English Letters" in *Alternative Shakespeares*, pp. 26–46; Paul Brown, " 'This Thing of Darkness I Acknowledge Mine': *The Tempest* and the Discourse of Colonialism" in *Political Shakespeare: New Essays in Cultural Materialism* (Ithaca, N.Y., and London: Cornell Univ. Press, 1985), pp. 48–71; Peter Hulme, *Colonial Encounters: Europe and the Native Caribbean, 1492–1797* (London and New York: Methuen, 1986), pp. 89–134; Thomas Cartelli, "Prospero in Africa: *The Tempest* as Colonialist Text and Pretext" in *Shakespeare Reproduced: The Text in History and Ideology*, eds. Jean Howard and Marion O'Conner (New York: Methuen, 1987), pp. 99–115; I would include two essays by Stephen Orgel somewhat different in their focus but nonetheless related: "Prospero's Wife" in *Rewriting the Renaissance*, eds. Margaret Ferguson et al. (Chicago: Univ. of Chicago Press, 1986), pp. 50–64, and "Shakespeare and the Cannibals" in *Cannibals, Witches, and Divorce: Estranging the Renaissance*, ed. Marjorie Garber (Baltimore and London: Johns Hopkins Univ. Press, 1987), pp. 40–66.

[2] Hulme, *Colonial Encounters*, p. 94.

[3] See, for example, Paul Brown, "This Thing of Darkness," p. 48.

[4] In fact Edward Pechter, in one of the earliest of such scrutinies, cited several of the recent *Tempest* articles as especially problematic. See "The New Historicism and Its Discontents: Politicizing Renaissance Drama," *PMLA*, 102 (1987), 292–303. See also Howard Felperin, "Making It 'Neo': The New Historicism and Renaissance Literature," *Textual Practice*, 1 (1987), *Renaissance*, 16 (1986), 13–43; and Anthony B. Dawson, "*Measure for Measure*, New Historicism, and Theatrical Power," *Shakespeare Quarterly*, 39 (1988), 328–41.

[5] *The Tempest*, The Arden Shakespeare, ed. Frank Kermode (London: Methuen, 1954), p. xxv. For an account of the work of earlier scholars exploring the connections between the play and these documents, see Kermode, pp. xxv–xxxiv, and Charles Frey, "*The Tempest* and the New World," *Shakespeare Quarterly*, 30 (1979), 29–41.

[6] E. E. Stoll and Northrop Frye are the only exceptions I have seen cited.

[7] Recently there has been a renewed emphasis on the romance elements. See Gary Schmidgall, "*The Tempest* and *Primaleon*: A New Source," *Shakespeare Quarterly*, 37 (1986), 423–39, esp. p. 436; and Robert Wiltenberg, "The *Aeneid* in *The Tempest*," *Shakespeare Survey*, 39 (1987), 159–68.

[8] See, for example, Harry Berger's important essay, "Miraculous Harp: A Reading of Shakespeare's *Tempest*," *Shakespeare Studies*, 5 (1969), 253–83.

[9] Harry Levin, *The Myth of the Golden Age in the Renaissance* (Bloomington: Indiana Univ. Press, 1969); Leslie A. Fiedler, *The Stranger in Shakespeare* (New York: Stein and Day, 1972); Leo Marx, "Shakespeare's American Fable," *The Machine in the Garden* (London and New York: Oxford Univ. Press, 1964), pp. 34–72.

[10] O. Mannoni, *Prospero and Caliban: The Psychology of Colonization*, trans. Pamela Powesland (1950; rpt. New York: Praeger, 1964).

[11] Hulme, *Colonial Encounters*, p. 133.

[12] Hulme, *Colonial Encounters*, p. 115; Barker and Hulme, p. 201; Orgel, "Prospero's Wife," pp. 62–63.

[13] Orgel, "Shakespeare and the Cannibals," p. 55.

[14] As Paul Werstine wrote in the brochure announcing the NEH Humanities Institute on "New Directions in Shakespeare Criticism" (The Folger Shakespeare Library, 1988), "To appreciate *The Tempest* . . . today . . . we must understand discourses of colonialism, power, legitimation."

[15] Barker and Hulme, p. 198.

[16] Hawkes, "Swisser-Swatter," p. 28.

[17] Thus stereotypes, for example, served as part of a "discursive strategy . . . to locate or 'fix' a colonial other in a position of inferiority . . ." (Paul Brown, modifying Edward Said on orientalism, p. 58).

[18] Actually, this point too is a matter of emphasis. R. R. Cawley ("Shakspere's Use of the Voyagers in *The Tempest*," *PMLA*, 41 [1926], 688–726) and Kermode, among others, had noted in passing some

similarities between the play's view of Caliban and the distortions of colonialist self-serving rhetorical purposes; but revisionists take this to be the important point, not to be passed over.

[19] Leininger, "Cracking the Code of *The Tempest,*" p. 122.

[20] Paul Brown, pp. 64, 66. Brown also contends that *The Tempest* "exemplifies ... a moment of *historical* crisis. This crisis is the struggle to produce a coherent discourse adequate to the complex requirements of British colonialism in its initial phase" (p. 48).

[21] Hulme, *Colonial Encounters,* p. 93. Later he does grant a little ground to the psychological critics in allowing that their "totally spurious" identification of Prospero with Shakespeare yet "half grasps the crucial point that Prospero ... is a dramatist and creator of theatrical effects" (p. 115).

[22] "From the point of view of a political hermeneutic, measured against the requirements of a 'political unconscious,' we must conclude that the conception of wish-fulfillment remains locked in a problematic of the individual subject ... which is only indirectly useful to us." The objection to wish-fulfillment is that it is "always outside of time, outside of narrative" and history; "what is more damaging, from the present perspective, is that desire ... remains locked into the category of the individual subject, even if the form taken by the individual in it is no longer the ego or the self, but the individual body.... *the need to transcend individualistic categories and modes of interpretation is in many ways the fundamental issue for any doctrine of the political unconscious*" (*The Political Unconscious: Narrative as a Socially Symbolic Act* [Ithaca, N.Y.: Cornell Univ. Press, 1981], pp. 66, 68, italics added).

[23] Stephen Greenblatt, "Psychoanalysis and Renaissance Culture," *Literary Theory/Renaissance Texts,* eds. Patricia Parker and David Quint (Baltimore: Johns Hopkins Univ. Press, 1986), 210–24.

[24] Jameson, p. 12. So, too, Freud's "hermeneutic manual" can be of use to the political critic (p. 65).

[25] "Norman Holland's suggestive term," Jameson, p. 49.

[26] Jameson, p. 67. Cf. Paul Brown, "My use of Freudian terms does not mean that I endorse its ahistorical, Europocentric and sexist models of psychical development. However, a materialist criticism deprived of such concepts as displacement and condensation would be seriously impoverished ..." (p. 71, n. 35).

[27] James discussing Althusser (p. 30) and Greimas (p. 48).

[28] *The Crown of Life* (1947; rpt. New York: Barnes & Noble, 1966), p. 255.

[29] See Trevor R. Griffiths, " 'This Island's Mine': Caliban and Colonialism," *Yearbook of English Studies,* 13 (1983), 159–80.

[30] Griffiths, p. 166.

[31] Virginia Mason Vaughan, " 'Something Rich and Strange': Caliban's Theatrical Metamorphoses," *Shakespeare Quarterly,* 36 (1985), 390–405, esp. p. 390.

[32] Erlich, "Shakespeare's Colonial Metaphor," p. 49; Paul Brown, p. 48.

[33] Even St. Paul in his travels (echoed in the play) met natives who—like Caliban—thought him a god.

[34] Hulme produces as evidence against Shakespeare these four words from the cast list, which Shakespeare may or may not have written ("Hurricanes in the Caribbees," p. 72).

[35] Alden T. Vaughan, "Shakespeare's Indian: The Americanization of Caliban," *Shakespeare Quarterly,* 39 (1988), 137–53. He argues that the intention miscarried not only at the time but also for the three centuries following. He adds, "Rather, from the Restoration until the late 1890s, Caliban appeared on stage and in critical literature as almost everything but an Indian" (p. 138).

[36] Hulme, while noting Caliban's "anomalous nature," sees the anomaly as yet another colonialist strategy: "In ideological terms [Caliban is] a compromise formation and one achieved, like all such formations, only at the expense of distortion elsewhere" ("Hurricanes in the Caribbees," pp. 71, 72). This begs the question: Caliban can only be a "distortion" if he is intended to represent someone. But that is precisely the question—*is* he meant to represent a Native American? Sidney Lee noted that Caliban's method of building dams for fish reproduces the Indians'; though he is often cited by later writers as an authority on the resemblance, the rest of his evidence is not convincing ("The Call of the West: America and Elizabethan England," *Elizabethan and Other Essays,* ed. Frederick S. Boas [Oxford: Clarendon Press, 1929], pp. 263–301). G. Wilson Knight has an impressionistic essay about the relationship between Caliban and Indians ("Caliban as a Red Man" [1977] in *Shakespeare's Styles,* eds. Philip Edwards, Inga-Stina Ewbank, and G. K. Hunter [London: Cambridge Univ. Press, 1980]). Hulme lists Caliban's resemblances to Caribs ("Hurricanes in the Caribbees"), and Kermode cites details taken from natives visited during both the Old and the New World voyages.

[37] The Indians who would appear in Chapman's 1613 masque would be fully equipped with feathers. See R. R. Cawley, *The Voyagers and Elizabethan Drama* (Boston: D. C. Heath; London: Oxford Univ. Press, 1938), p. 359, and Orgel, "Shakespeare and the Cannibals," pp. 44, 47

[38] Shakespeare had apparently read up on his monsters (R. R. Cawley, "Shakspere's Use of the Voyagers," p. 723, and Frey, passim), but he picked up the stereotypes only to play with them ostentatiously

(in Stephano's and Trinculo's many discredited guesses about Caliban's identity) or to leave them hanging (in Prospero's identification of Caliban as "devil").

[39] Hulme, "Hurricanes in the Caribbees," p. 74.

[40] Lamming (n. 1, above), pp. 98–99.

[41] Lamming, p. 97; Erlich, p. 49.

[42] The play also seems anti-colonialist because it includes the comic sections with Stephano and Trinculo, which show colonialism to be "nakedly avaricious, profiteering, perhaps even pointless"; but this too can be seen as a rationalization: "This low version of colonialism serves to displace possibly damaging charges ...against properly-constituted civil authority on to the already excremental products of civility, the masterless" (Paul Brown, p. 65).

[43] Greenblatt, "Learning to Curse," pp. 570–71; Leininger (n. 1, above), pp. 126–27.

[44] Leininger, p. 127.

[45] As Fiedler's book implies (n. 9, above), she is less like anything American than like the Frenchwoman Joan of Arc, who also tried to save herself from the law by claiming she was pregnant with a bastard; Joan simply wasn't as successful (see pp. 43–81, esp. p. 77).

[46] See Brockbank, p. 193. Even these details can be discounted as rationalizations, of course. Paul Brown, for example, explains Sycorax's presence as a rationalization: by degrading her black magic, he argues, Shakespeare makes Prospero seem better than he is (pp. 60–61). Hulme notes that Sycorax may be Prospero's invention, pointing out that we never see any direct evidence that she was present (*Colonial Encounters*, p. 115). Orgel links Caliban's claims of legitimacy by birth to James I's claims ("Prospero's Wife," pp. 58–59).

[47] See Fiedler, p. 205.

[48] Erlich, "Shakespeare's Colonial Metaphor," p. 63.

[49] The trend, moreover, is to move away from anthropomorphic terms like "repression" or "censorship," themselves inherited from the political terminology on which Freud drew for his own. Like the vocabulary of "scientific" hydraulics on which Freud also drew for his notions of libido flowing and damming up, the older terms are being replaced by contemporary terminologies more appropriate to describing a conflict among meanings or interpretations, rather than between anthropomorphized forces engaged in a simple struggle "for" and "against."

[50] Spaniards, he writes, "taught their Hounds, fierce Dogs, to teare [the Indians] in peeces" (*A Briefe Narration of the Destruction of the Indies by the Spaniards* [1542 (?)]. Samuel Purchas, *Purchas His Pilgrimes*, 20 vols. [Glasgow: Maclehose and Sons, 1905–1907], Vol. XVIII, 91). This was apparently a common topos, found also in Eden's translation of Peter Martyr's *Decades of the Newe Worlde* (1555), included in Eden's *Historie of Trauaile* (1577), which Shakespeare read for *The Tempest*. It was also used by Greene and Deloney (Cawley, *Voyagers and Elizabethan Drama*, pp. 383–84).

[51] Hulme, "Hurricanes in the Caribbees," pp. 163–66; see also Orgel on this "New World topos" in "Shakespeare and the Cannibals," pp. 41–44.

[52] Neither was Montaigne's in the essay that has been taken as a source for the play. Scholars are still debating about Montaigne's attitude toward cannibals, though all agree that his critical attitude toward *Europeans* was clear in the essay.

[53] This blend of Old and New World characteristics, earlier seen as characteristic of New World discourse, is acknowledged in many of the revisionist studies but is seen as one of the rhetorical strategies used to control Indians.

[54] William Strach[e]y, "A True Reportorie ...," *Purchas*, Vol. XIX, p. 62. For the citation of Purchas as colonialist, see Hulme, "Hurricanes in the Caribbees," p. 78, n. 21.

[55] Paul Brown, p. 64.

[56] This is an entirely separate question from another that one might ask: How comparable were Purchas's remarks, taken from the collection of travelers' tales which he edited, censored, and used to support his colonialist ideal, on the one hand, and a play, on the other? In *Purchas*, Richard Marienstras argues, "the multiplicity of interpretations modulates and reinforces a single ideological system. The same can certainly not be said of ... *The Tempest*" (*New Perspectives on the Shakespearean World*, trans. Janet Lloyd [Cambridge: Cambridge Univ. Press, 1985], p. 169). This entire book, which devotes a chapter to *The Tempest*, is an excellent study of "certain aspects of Elizabethan ideology and ... the way these are used in Shakespeare" (p. 1).

[57] See Pechter (n. 4, above). This kind of "condition," he argues, is really a precondition in the sense that it is assumed to be logically (if not chronologically) prior. It is assumed to have the kind of explanatory power that "the Elizabethan world view" was once accorded (p. 297).

[58] See, for example, the following contemporary tracts reprinted in *Tracts and Other Papers Relating*

Principally to the Origin, Settlement, and Progress of ... North America, ed. Peter Force, 4 vols. (1836–47; rpt. New York: Peter Smith, 1947): R. I., *"Nova Brittania:* OFFERING MOST Excellent fruites by Planting IN VIRGINIA. Exciting all such as be well affected to further the same" (1609), Vol. 1, No. 6; "Virginia richly valued" (1609), Vol. 4, No. 1; "A TRVE DECLARATION of the estate of the Colonie in Virginia, With a confutation of such scandalous reports as haue tended to the disgrace of so worthy an enterprise" (1610), Vol. 3, No. 1; Sil. Jourdan. "A PLAINE DESCRIPTION OF THE BARMVDAS, NOW CALLED SOMMER ILANDS" (1613), Vol. 3, No. 3.

In *The Genesis of the United States,* ed. Alexander Brown, 2 vols. (New York: Russell & Russell, 1964), see also; Robert Gray, "A GOOD SPEED to Virginia" (1609), Vol. 1, 293–302; "A True and Sincere declaration of the purpose and ends of the *Plantation* begun in *Virginia* of the degrees which it hath received; and meanes by *which it hath beene advanced:* and *the ... conclusion* of *His Majesties Councel* of that Colony ... untill by the mercies of GOD it shall *retribute to a fruitful harvest to the Kingdome of heaven, and this Common-Wealth"* (1609), Vol. 1, 337–53; "A Publication by the Counsell of Virginea, touching the Plantation There" (1609), Vol. 1, 354–56; R. Rich, "NEWES FROM VIRGINIA. THE LOST FLOCKE TRIUMPHANT ..." (1610), Vol. 1, 420–26.

[59] "A Trve Declaration," p. 6.

[60] Alexander Brown, in *The Genesis of the United States,* reprints extracts from the following pertinent documents: William Symonds, "VIRGINIA: A SERMON PREACHED AT WHITECHAPPEL ..." (1609), Vol. 1, 282–91; Daniel Price, "SAVLES PROHIBITION STAIDE ... And to the Inditement of all that persecute Christ with a reproofe of those that traduce the Honourable Plantation of Virginia" (1609), Vol. 1, 312–16; and, most important, William Crashaw's sermon titled "A New-Yeeres Gift to Virginea," and preached, as the title page announced, before "Lord La Warre Lord Governour and Captaine Generall of Virginia, and others of [the] Counsell ... At the said Lord Generall his ... departure for Virginea ... Wherein both the lawfulnesses of that action is maintained and the necessity thereof is also demonstrated, not so much out of the grounds of Policie, as of Humanity, Equity and Christianity" (1610), Vol. 1, 360–75.

[61] In Alexander Brown, see William Crashaw for two of these references (in "A Newe-Yeeres Gift to Virginea" [1610], and "Epistle Dedicatory" to Alexander Whitaker's *"Good Newes from Virginia"* [1613], Vol. 2, 611–20); and see Ralphe Hamor in *A True Discourse of the Present Estate of Virginea* (1615), Virginia State Library Publications, No. 3 (Richmond: Virginia State Library, 1957).

[62] Pp. 16, 17.

[63] For the general history of the period, see David Beers Quinn, *England and the Discovery of America, 1481–1620* (New York: Alfred A. Knopf, 1974); Alexander Brown's *Genesis* identifies similar shifting motives in the history of colonization. Such voyages were made famous by often-reprinted accounts, especially in collections by Richard Eden and Richard Hakluyt, both of whose anthologies Shakespeare would consult for *The Tempest.* In the introductory material in these collections, as in the voyages themselves, the self-interest is obvious but so mixed with excitement and utopian hopes, and so focused on competition with Spain, that the issue of relation to Indians was dwarfed by comparison.

[64] If he didn't succeed in establishing a settlement, he would lose his patent. His interest in the patent rather than the colony was shown by his apparent negligence in searching for his lost colony (Quinn, n. 63, above, p. 300). He could hold onto his patent only so long as their was hope that the colonists were still alive; clearly the hope was worth more to Raleigh than the colony.

[65] Matthew P. Andrews, *The Soul of a Nation: The Founding of Virginia and the Projection of New England* (New York: Scribner's, 1943), p. 125. An entire popular literature developed, so much so that the Archbishop of York complained that "of Virginia there be so many tractates, divine, human, historical, political, or call them as you please, as no further intelligence I dare desire" (quoted in Andrews, p. 125).

[66] It is this issue rather than the colonialism that stimulated an earlier period of political commentary on the New World material in *The Tempest:* Charles M. Gayley, *Shakespeare and the Founders of Liberty in America* (New York: Macmillan, 1917); A. A. Ward, "Shakespeare and the Makers of Virginia," *Proceedings of the British Academy,* 9 (1919); see also E. P. Kuhl, "Shakespeare and the Founders of America: *The Tempest,*" *Psychological Quarterly,* 41 (1962), 123–46.

[67] Contributing to the welter of contradictory discourses was the Spanish ambassador's flow of letters to Spain insisting, not irrationally, that the whole purpose of maintaining a profitless colony like Jamestown was to establish a base for pirate raids against Spanish colonies.

[68] Letter from Southampton to the Earl of Salisbury, 15 December 1609, in Alexander Brown, Vol. 1, 356–57.

[69] The quantity and quality of the objections, which have not on the whole survived, has been judged by the nature of the many defenses thought necessary to answer them. See notes 58, 60, 61.

[70] A practice that Shakespeare did not admire if Stephano and Trinculo are any indication.

[71] As are the two monsters cited as possible prototypes for Caliban by Geoffrey Bullough (*Narrative and Dramatic Sources of Shakespeare,* 8 vols. [New York: Columbia Univ. Press, 1958], Vol. 8, 240). There were exceptions, of course, as in George Percy's *Observations... Of the Plantation of... Virginia* (1606), in *Purchas,* Vol. XVIII, 403–19.

[72] See Karen Ordahl Kupperman, *Settling with the Indians: The Meeting of English and Indian Cultures in America, 1580–1640* (Totowa, N.J.: Rowman and Littlefield, 1980), pp. 127–29. The origins of this nearly universal belief in Indian treachery are of course multiple, ranging from the readiness of the English to project their fears onto any available victim, whether Indians or mariners (who were also regularly accused of treachery in these narratives), to the prevailing stereotypes of the Other, to specific English acts of provocation, to the general tensions inherent in the situation. Without arguing for any one of these, I merely wish to suggest that the notion of "colonialist discourse" implies a complex situation.

[73] Even as proto-white men, their skin as tanned rather than naturally black, etc. See Kupperman, and Orgel, "Shakespeare and the Cannibals."

[74] Greenblatt, in his study of the ways in which white men "colonialized" Indians, emphasizes the degree to which whites assumed that the Indians had *no* language. Although he notes that there were exceptions, he makes it sound as if these exceptions were rare and were largely confined to the "rough, illiterate sea dog, bartering for gold trinkets on a faraway beach," rather than to the "captains or lieutenants whose accounts we read" ("Learning to Curse," pp. 564–65). On the contrary, even the earliest travelers had often included glossaries of Indian terms in their reports (e.g., the Glossary in the introductory material of Eden's translation of Martyr's *Decades* [1555], as well as in various later English reports reprinted in *Purchas His Pilgrimes* [1625]); and in reading through Purchas's helter-skelter collection, one is struck by the number of writers who grant automatic respect to the Indians' language. A possibly figurative rather than literal force for comments on the Indians' "want of language" is suggested by Gabriel Archer's account of a 1602 voyage. Here it is the English, not the Indians, who are deficient in this respect: they "spake divers Christian words, and seemed to understand much *more then we, for Want of Language, could comprehend*" ("Relation of Captain Gosnold's Voyage," *Purchas,* Vol. XVIII, 304, italics mine).

[75] See R. R. Cawley, *Voyagers and Elizabethan Drama,* passim, and *Unpathed Waters: Studies in the Influence of the Voyagers on Elizabethan Literature* (Princeton, N.J.: Princeton Univ. Press, 1940), pp. 234–41. Neither of R. R. Cawley's two books about the voyagers' influence on contemporary English literature cites any pre-1611 passage of more than a few lines. It is true that in the 1580s Marlowe's plays took off from the general sense of vastness and possibility opened up by voyages to the New as well as to the Old World. In addition Drayton wrote an "Ode to the Virginia Voyage," perhaps expressly for the settlers leaving for Jamestown in 1606; and one line in Samuel Daniel's "Musophilis" has a colonialist ring: he speaks of "vent[ing] the treasure of our tongue ... T' inrich unknowing Nations with our stores." True, too, that in a quite different spirit Jonson, Marston, and Chapman collaborated in *Eastward Ho* (1605) to make fun of gallants flocking to Virginia with expectations as great as those bringing foolish victims to Face and Subtle's alchemical chimeras. But while Marlowe participates in the spirit of romantic adventure associated with voyaging and treasure-hunting, and *Eastward Ho* satires it, neither deals at all with the New World or with the New World natives.

[76] The three brief exceptions are references to Spanish cruelty to Indians, all published before the truce with Spain. The Stationers' Register lists "The crueltie of ye Spaniardes toward th[e] Indians, a ballad" (1586) and "Spanishe crueties" (1601), now lost. Robert Greene notes in passing that the Spaniards hunted Indians with dogs, while by contrast the English treated the natives with "such courtesie, as they thought the English Gods, and the Spaniardes both by rule and conscience halfe Devils" (*The Spanish Masquerado* [1589], *Life and... Works,* ed. Alexander B. Grosart, 15 vols. [London and Aylesbury: privately printed, 1881–86], Vol. V. 282–83). See Cawley, *Voyagers and Elizabethan Drama,* pp. 385–86.

[77] When Strachey finishes with his account of the Bermuda episode and turns to a description of Virginia, he does devote one sentence to the Indians' treachery.

[78] See Frey, p. 31.

[79] In his edition of *The Tempest,* Kermode notes this parallel with *Bartholomew Fair* (2.6.76–77), "Looke into any Angle o' the towne, (the Streights, or the Bermuda's)... " (p. 24, n. 223).

[80] Letter from Carleton to Chamberlain, August 1607, in Alexander Brown, Vol. 1, 111–13.

[81] Many other similarities link *The Tempest* to the earlier play, including some which might have been taken to suggest *The Tempest*'s focus on the New World. Thus, for example, Stephano cries out when

he first sees Caliban, "Do you put tricks upon's with salvages and men of Inde, ha?" (2.2.58–59). But Berowne, though rooted in the Old World, resorts to similarly exotic analogies to describe the passion which Rosaline should inspire in his colleagues. Who sees her, he says,

That, (like a rude and savage man of Inde),
At the first op'ning of the gorgeous east,
Bows not his vassal head . . . ?

(*Love's Labor's Lost*, 4.3.218–20)

See Kermode's note on the line in *The Tempest*.

[82] Specific resemblances between subplots here and the plots of other plays have been noted (between the plot to murder Alonso and *Macbeth*, between Ferdinand's courtship of Miranda and *Romeo and Juliet*, etc.). See Alvin B. Kernan, "The Great Fair of the World and the Ocean Island: *Bartholomew Fair* and *The Tempest*," in *The Revels History of Drama in English*, 8 vols., eds. J. Leeds Barroll, Alexander Leggatt, Richard Hosley, Alvin Kernan (London: Methuen, 1975), Vol. III, 456–74. G. Wilson Knight has described the place of *The Tempest* in Shakespeare's overarching myth of the tempest. Even more suggestive, Leslie Fiedler has traced the less obvious personal mythology that provides a context for the play. Drawing on marginal details, he shows the play's concern with themes that pervade the entire canon, such as the interracial marriage that here, not accidentally, initiates the action of the play. His work is the starting point for mine.

[83] Barker and Hulme, p. 198.

[84] Hulme, *Colonial Encounters*, p. 133.

[85] Paul Brown, p. 69.

[86] Barker and Hulme, p. 202.

[87] The last time Prospero got so angry that Miranda had to apologize was when Ferdinand began to court Miranda.

[88] See A. D. Nuttall's discussion of the blend of colonialist and sexual tensions in *The Tempest*, "Two Unassimilable Men, " in *Shakespearian Comedy*, Stratford-upon-Avon Studies 14 (London: Edward Arnold, 1972), pp. 210–40, esp. p. 216.

[89] The incestuous impulse implicit in the situation is even clearer in Shakespeare's own earlier romances; both Fiedler and Nuttall, among others, have explored these in the context of the vast literature of romance that lies behind the play. See also Mark Taylor, *Shakespeare's Darker Purpose: A Question of Incest* (New York: AMS Press, 1982).

[90] Fielder, p. 234.

[91] Marianne Novy, *Love's Argument: Gender Relations in Shakespeare* (Chapel Hill and London: Univ. of North Carolina Press, 1984), pp. 63–82.

[92] All Shakespeare quotations are from *The Riverside Shakespeare*, ed. G. Blakemore Evans (Boston: Houghton Mifflin, 1974). The earlier group of critics who had pointed out the racist assumptions in Antonio's behavior made many of the same points recently made on Caliban's behalf. The two cases are indeed similar, and although both can be seen as examples of "colonialism"—with the word "colonialism" used very loosely as it is today for any exploitative appropriation—the more historically specific "colonialist discourse" does not seem to be the appropriate context for Shylock.

[93] Nuttall (n. 88, above) notes the strangeness of the Duke's explosion and the fact that Jaques's request for a fool's license "has shaken Duke Senior" (p. 231).

[94] See Richard P. Wheeler's analysis in *Shakespeare's Development and the Problem Comedies: Turn and Counter-Turn* (Berkeley and Los Angeles: Univ. Of California Press, 1981).

[95] Primarily of course in the sonnets, but in the plays as well. See Novy's discussion of self-assertiveness in Shylock.

[96] Caliban later joins the two courtly servants in appropriately scatological double entendres.

[97] Norman N. Holland, "Caliban's Dream," *The Design Within: Psychoanalytic Approaches to Shakespeare*, ed. M. D. Faber (New York: Science House, 1970), pp. 521–33.

[98] Compare Antonio's cold calculations as he plans to kill Alonso.

[99] Albeit in a "My mommy is going to get you" fashion.

[100] Nuttall, p. 225.

[101] So, too, any child might complain that he was taught to speak and now his "profit on 't" is to be trapped in the prison house of language.

[102] See Leininger, p. 125, for the most effective presentation of this view; also Paul Brown, p. 63.

[103] Here, too, Shakespeare seems unusual. Not until our child-centered, post-Freudian age do we find writers so directly representing the aliens on our galactic frontier as children—whether as innocents like Steven Spielberg's E.T. or as proto-savages like his Gremlins. Others has associated the primitive with metaphorical childhood: De Bry's 1590 edition of Harriot's *Briefe and True Report* and, later, Purchas's

version of Strachey associated the primitive Indians with the childhood of the English nation, and writers spoke of the Indians as "younger brethren" (Kupperman, n. 72, above, p. 170). What is unusual in Shakespeare is the emphasis and the detailed portrayal of emotional as well as cognitive childishness. Leah Marcus argues, in another context, that the English in the chaotic and disorienting intellectual context of the seventeenth century were especially susceptible to dreams of the golden age—and to sympathetic portrayals of childhood wholeness (*Childhood and Cultural Despair* [Pittsburgh, Pa.: Univ. of Pittsburgh Press, 1978]). Most of the instances of such portrayals did not appear until later in the century, however.

[104] Edward A. Armstrong, *Shakespeare's Imagination* (Lincoln: Univ. Of Nebraska Press, 1963), p. 52.

[105] Might the brothers' definition by opposition perhaps have influenced Shakespeare's choice of names: *Prospero* and *Antonio?*

[106] John B. Bender, "The Day of *The Tempest,*" *English Literary History,* 47 (1980), 235–58.

[107] It also marks Shakespeare's return to the pattern of withdrawal from active life used in *Love's Labor's Lost*—but this time with a difference. The earlier play had shown young men hoping to conquer death by forswearing the body and what it represents.

[108] Elliot Jacques offers a related account, in Kleinian terms, of the role of infantile demands and emotions in the effort to come to terms with death in "Death and the Mid-life Crisis," *International Journal of Psychoanalysis,* 46 (1965), 502–14.

[109] John Forrester, "Psychoanalysis or Literature?" *French Studies,* 35 (1981), 170–79, esp. p. 172.

[110] Cited in Levin (n. 9, above), p. 183.

[111] See Bender (n. 106, above) on the way dreams are always followed by violence in the play; the violence is not a cause of the problem on the island but rather an effect.

[112] Andrews (n. 65, above), p. 126.

[113] Jameson cites as being "very much in the spirit of [his] present work" the concern of Deleuze and Guattari "to reassert the specificity of the political content of everyday life and of individual fantasy-experience and to reclaim it from ... reduction to the merely subjective and to the status of psychological projection" (*The Political Unconscious,* n. 22, above, p. 22).

[114] *The Invasion Within: The Contest of Cultures in North America* (Oxford: Oxford Univ. Press, 1985), p. 54.

[115] The original version of this essay was presented at a session on "Psychoanalysis and Renaissance History," chaired by Richard Wheeler at the 1987 MLA annual meeting. The current version has greatly benefited from careful readings by Janet Adelman, Anne and Rob Goble, Carol Neely, Marianne Novy, Martin Wiener, and several anonymous readers.

CONTRIBUTORS

HAROLD BLOOM is Sterling Professor of the Humanities at Yale University and Henry W. and Albert A. Berg Professor of English at the New York University Graduate School. He is a 1985 MacArthur Foundation Award recipient, served as the Charles Eliot Norton Professor of Poetry at Harvard University (1987–88), and is the author of nineteen books, the most recent being *The Book of J* (1990). Currently he is editing the Chelsea House series Modern Critical Views and The Critical Cosmos, and other Chelsea House series in literary criticism.

JOHN W. DRAPER was the author of numerous works on Shakespeare and English literature; among them are *The Funeral Elegy and the Rise of English Romanticism* (1929), *The Humors of Shakespeare's Characters* (1945), and *Stratford to Dogberry: Studies in Shakespeare's Earlier Plays* (1961).

BARBARA MELCHIORI is Professor of English at Rome University and is the author of *Il gusto di Henry James* (1974) and *Terrorism in the Late Victorian Novel* (1985).

MIKE FRANK is Professor of English at Bentley College (Waltham, MA) and is a co-editor of *Mark Twain's Letters* (1987).

JAMES SMITH was lecturer of English at the Instituto Pedagógico at Caracas (1940–41), director of the British-Venezuelan Cultural Center (1941–46), and Chairman of English at the Roman Catholic University of Tribourg, Switzerland (1947–63). His articles have been gathered in *Shakespearian and Other Essays* (1974).

JACQUELINE E. M. LATHAM is Principal Lecturer in English at Kingston Polytechnic and is the editor of *Critics on Virginia Woolf* (1970).

LUCY S. MCDIARMID is Professor of English at Villanova University. She is the author of *Saving Civilization: Yeats, Eliot, and Auden between the Wars* (1984) and *Auden's Apologies for Poetry* (1990).

JOHN MCDIARMID teaches at New College (Sarasota, FL) and has written on English Renaissance Humanism, drama, and poetry.

G. WILSON KNIGHT taught drama and English Literature at the University of Leeds. He published many innovative studies of Shakespeare and the English Romantic poets, including *The Wheel of Fire* (1930), *The Imperial Theme* (1951), and *The Starlit Dome* (1959).

KENNETH MACLEAN is Professor of English at Seattle University and has published a book of poetry, *Blue Heron Sky* (1990).

MEREDITH ANNE SKURA is Professor of English at Rice University in Houston and is the author of *The Literary Use of the Psychoanalytic Process* (1981).

BIBLIOGRAPHY

Armstrong, Edward A. "The Painted Jay." In *Shakespeare's Imagination: A Study of the Psychology of Association and Inspiration.* London: Lindsey Drummond, 1946, pp. 66–71.

Barker, Francis, and Peter Hulme. "Nymphs and Reapers Heavily Vanish: The Discursive Con-texts of *The Tempest.*" In *Alternative Shakespeares,* edited by John Drakakis, London: Methuen,1985, pp. 26–46.

Bloom, Harold, ed. *William Shakespeare's* The Tempest. New York: Chelsea House, 1988.

Bradbrook, M. C. "Romance Farewell! *The Tempest.*" *English Literary Renaissance* 1 (1971): 239–49.

Brailow, David G. "Prospero's 'Old Brain': The Old Man as Metaphor in *The Tempest.*" *Shakespeare Survey* 14 (1981): 285–303.

Brandes, George. *William Shakespeare.* London: William Heinemann, 1898.

Bratman, David. "Caliban between the Worlds." *Mythlore* 12, No. 4 (Summer 1986): 46–53.

Breight, Curt. " 'Treason Doth Never Prosper': *The Tempest* and the Discourse of Treason." *Shakespeare Quarterly* 41 (1990): 1–28.

Brockbank, Philip. "*The Tempest:* Conventions of Art and Empire." *Later Shakespeare* (Stratford-upon-Avon Studies 8), edited by John Russell Brown and Bernard Harris. London: Edward Arnold, 1966, pp. 180–201.

Brown, E. K. "The First Person in 'Caliban upon Setebos.' " *Modern Language Notes* 66 (1951): 392–95.

Brown, Paul. " 'This Thing of Darkness I Acknowledge Mine': *The Tempest* and the Discourse of Colonialism." In *Political Shakespeare: New Essays in Cultural Materialism,* edited by Jonathan Dollimore and Alan Sinfield. Ithaca: Cornell University Press, 1985, pp. 48–69.

Bushnell, Nelson Sherwin. "Natural Supernaturalism in *The Tempest.*" *PMLA* 47 (1932): 684–98.

Callan, Edward. "Auden's Ironic Masquerade: Criticism as Morality Play." *University of Toronto Quarterly* 35 (1966): 133–43.

Comito, Terry. "Caliban's Dream: The Topography of Some Shakespeare Gardens." *Shakespeare Studies* 14 (1981): 23–54.

Conniff, Brian. "The Modern Lyric and Prospero's Island." *Twentieth Century Literature* 34 (1988): 84–112.

Corfield, Cosmo. "Why Does Prospero Abjure His 'Rough Magic'?" *Shakespeare Quarterly* 36 (1985): 31–48.

Cutts, John. "Music and the Supernatural in *The Tempest:* A Study in Interpretation." *Music and Letters* 39, No. 4 (October 1958): 346–48.

Daniell, David. The Tempest: *An Introduction to the Variety of Criticism.* Atlantic Highlands, NJ: Humanities Press International, 1989.

Dawson, Anthony B. "Tempest in a Teapot: Critics, Evaluation, Ideology." In *"Bad" Shakespeare: Revaluation of the Shakespeare Canon,* edited by Maurice Charney. Rutherford, NJ: Fairleigh Dickinson University Press, 1988, pp. 61–73.

Dessen, Alan C. "Elizabethan Drama and the Modern Reader." In *Elizabethan Drama and the Viewer's Eye.* Chapel Hill: University of North Carolina Press, 1977, pp. 3–31.

DeVane, William Elijah. " 'Caliban upon Setebos.' " In *A Browning Handbook.* 2nd ed. New York: Appleton-Century Crofts, 1955, pp. 299–302.

Echeruo, M. J. C. "The 'Savage Hero' in English Literature of the Enlightenment." *English Studies in Africa* 15 (1972): 1–13.

Egan, Robert. "This Rough Magic: Perspectives of Art and Morality in *The Tempest.*" *Shakespeare Quarterly* 23 (1972): 171–82.

Erlich, Bruce. "Shakespeare's Colonial Metaphor: On the Social Function of Theatre in *The Tempest.*" *Science and Society* 41 (1980): 121–31.

Felperin, Howard. "Making It 'Neo': The New Historicism and Renaissance Literature." *Textural Practice* 1 (1987): 262–77.

———. "Undream'd Shores: *The Tempest.*" In *Shakespearean Romance.* Princeton: Princeton University Press, 1972, pp. 246–83.

Fiedler, Leslie. "Caliban or Hamlet: An American Paradox." *Encounter* 26, No. 4 (April 1966): 23–27.

Frey, Charles. "*The Tempest* and the New World." *Shakespeare Quarterly* 30 (1979): 29–41.

Frye, Northrop. "Introduction to *The Tempest.*" New York: Pelican Books, 1970, pp. 14–24.

Gervinus, G. G. "*The Tempest.*" *Shakespeare Commentaries.* Translated by F. E. Bunnet. 4th ed. London: Smith, Elder, & Co., 1892, pp. 787–800.

Gilbert, Allan H. "*The Tempest*: Parallelism in Characters." *Journal of English and Germanic Philology* 14 (1915): 63–74.

Goldsmith, Robert Hillis. "The Wild Man on the English Stage." *Modern Language Review* 53 (1958): 481–91.

Gray, Henry David. "The Sources of *The Tempest.*" *Modern Language Notes* 35 (1920): 321–30.

Greenberg, Herbert. "The Failure of Caliban and Ariel." In *Quest for the Necessary: W. H. Auden and the Dilemma of Divided Consciousness.* Cambridge: Harvard University Press, 1968, pp. 117–71.

Griffiths, Trevor R. " 'This Island's Mine': Caliban and Colonialism." *Yearbook of English Studies* 13 (1983): 159–80.

Grudin, Robert. "*The Tempest*: Prospero as Hero of Contrariness." In *Shakespeare and Renaissance Contrariety.* Berkeley: University of California Press, 1979, pp. 185–211.

Hamilton, Donna B. *Virgil and* The Tempest: *The Politics of Imitation.* Columbus: Ohio State University Press, 1990.

Hankins, John E. "Caliban the Bestial Man." *PMLA* 62 (1947): 793–801.

Harris, Wendell V. "Browning's Caliban, Plato's Cosmogony, and Bentham on Natural Religion." *Studies in Browning and His Circle* 3, No. 2 (Fall 1975): 95–103.

Hartwig, Joan. "Cloten, Autolycus, and Caliban: Bearers of Parodic Burdens." *Shakespeare's Romances Reconsidered,* edited by Carol McGinnis Kay and Henry E. Jacobs. Lincoln: University of Nebraska Press, 1978, pp. 91–103.

Hawkes, Terence. "Swisser-Swatter: Making a Man of English Letters." In *Alternative Shakespeares,* edited by John Drakakis. London: Methuen, 1985, pp. 26–46.

Henze, Richard H. "*The Tempest*: The Rejection of a Vanity." *Shakespeare Quarterly* 23 (1972): 420–34.

Holderness, Graham. "*The Tempest*: Spectacles of Disenchantment." In *Shakespeare: Out of Court Dramatizations of Court Society* by Graham Holderness, Nick Potter, and John Turner. New York: St. Martin's Press, 1990, pp. 136–94.

Holland, Norman N. "Caliban's Dream." *Psychoanalytic Quarterly* 37 (1968): 114–24.

Honan, Park. "Belial upon Setebos." *Tennessee Studies in Literature* 9 (1964): 87–98.

Howard, John. "Caliban's Mind." *Victorian Poetry* 1 (1963): 249–57.

James, D. G. "The New World." In *The Dream of Prospero*. Oxford: Clarendon Press, 1967, pp. 72–123.

Knight, Charles. "*The Tempest.*" In *Studies of Shakespeare*. London: Charles Knight, 1849, pp. 377–86.

Knight, G. Wilson. "The Final Plays." In *The Shakespearean Tempest*. New York: Oxford University Press, 1932, pp. 218–66.

Knox, Bernard. "*The Tempest* and the Ancient Comic Tradition." In *English Stage Comedy* (English Institute Essays 1954), edited by W. K. Wimsatt, New York: Columbia University Press, 1955, pp. 52–73.

Leavis, F. R. "The Criticism of Shakespeare's Late Plays." In *The Common Pursuit*. London: Chatto & Windus, 1952, pp. 173–81.

Leininger, Lorie. "Cracking the Code of *The Tempest.*" *Bucknell Review* 25 (1980): 121–31.

Luria, Maxwell S. "Standing Water and Sloth in *The Tempest.*" *English Studies* 49 (1968): 328–31.

McClosky, John C. "Caliban, Savage Clown." *College English* 1 (1940): 354–57.

McDowell, Frederick P. W. " 'The Situation of Our Time': Auden in His American Phase." In *Aspects of American Poetry: Presented to Howard Mumford Jones*, edited by Richard M. Ludwig. Columbus: Ohio State University Press, 1962, pp. 223–55.

McFarland, Thomas. "So Rare a Wondered Father: *The Tempest* and the Vision of Paradise." In *Shakespeare's Pastoral Comedy*. Chapel Hill: University of North Carolina Press, 1977, pp. 146–75.

McPeek, James A. S. "The Genesis of Caliban." *Philological Quarterly* 15 (1946): 378–81.

Marx, Leo. "Shakespeare's American Fable." In *The Machine in the Garden: Technology and the Pastoral Idea in America*. New York: Oxford University Press, 1964, pp. 34–72.

Meyers, Jeffrey. "Savagery and Civilization in *The Tempest, Robinson Crusoe* and *Heart of Darkness.*" *Conradiana* 2 (1970): 171–79.

Moulton, Richard G. "How *The Tempest* Is a Drama of Enchantment." In *Shakespeare as a Dramatic Artist: A Popular Illustration of the Principles of Scientific Criticism*. Oxford: Clarendon Press, 1893, pp. 246–83.

Nelson, Gerald. *Changes of Heart: A Study of the Poetry of W. H. Auden*. (Perspectives in Criticism 21). Berkeley: University of California Press, 1969, pp. 21–55.

Nevo, Ruth. "Subtleties of the Isle: *The Tempest.*" In *Shakespeare's Other Language*. New York: Methuen, 1987, pp. 130–52.

Nuttall, A. D. *Two Concepts of Allegory: A Study of Shakespeare's* The Tempest *and the Logic of Allegorical Expression*. New York: Barnes & Noble, 1967.

———. "Two Unassimilable Men." In *Shakespearian Comedy* (Stratford-upon-Avon Studies 14), edited by Malcolm Bradbury and David Palmer. London: Edward Arnold, 1972, pp. 210–40.

Orgel, Stephen. "Prospero's Wife." In *Rewriting the Renaissance*, edited by Margaret Ferguson et al. Chicago: University of Chicago Press, 1986, pp. 50–64.

———. "Shakespeare and the Cannibals." In *Cannibals, Witches, and Divorce: Estranging the Renaissance*, edited by Marjorie Garber. Baltimore: Johns Hopkins University Press, 1987, pp. 40–66.

Peterson, Douglas L. "*The Tempest:* 'Remember, for That's My Business with You.' " In *Time, Tide, and Tempest: A Study of Shakespeare's Romance*. San Marino, CA: The Huntington Library, 1973, pp. 214–54.

Reed, Henry. "W. H. Auden in America." *New Writing and Daylight* 6 (1945): 131–35.

Replogle, Justin. *Auden's Poetry*. Seattle: University of Washington Press, 1969.

Sawyer, Tom. "The Shadow in the Garden: Auden's Jungian Quest." *Ariel* 15, No. 1 (January 1984): 67–85.

Schmidgall, Gary. "*The Tempest* and *Primaleon:* A New Source." *Shakespeare Quarterly* 37 (1986): 423–39.

Shannon, Sheila. "Topical Commentaries." *Spectator* No. 6098 (1945): 433.

Shapiro, Arnold. "Browning's Psalm of Hate: 'Caliban upon Setebos,' Psalm 50, and *The Tempest.*" *Papers on Language and Literature* 10 (1972): 53–62.

Sharp, Sister Corona. "Caliban: The Primitive Man's Evolution." *Shakespeare Studies* 14 (1981): 267–83.

Shaw, W. David. "Rhetoric at the Religious Stage." In *The Dialectical Temper: The Rhetorical Art of Robert Browning.* Ithaca: Cornell University Press, 1968, pp. 192–203.

Smith, Stan. " 'My Father's Prick': The Long Poems." In *W. H. Auden.* Oxford: Basil Blackwell, 1985, pp. 152–67.

Spears, Monroe K. "*The Sea and the Mirror.*" In *The Poetry of W. H. Auden: The Disenchanted Flood.* New York: Oxford University Press, 1963, pp. 218–30.

Summers, Joseph H. "The Anger of Prospero: *The Tempest.*" In *Dreams of Love and Power: On Shakespeare's Plays.* Oxford: Clarendon Press, 1984, pp. 137–58.

Taylor, George Coffin. "Shakespeare's Use of the Idea of the Beast in Man." *Studies in Philology* 42 (1945): 530–43.

Timko, Michael. "Browning upon Butler; or, Natural Theology in the English Isle." *Criticism* 7 (1965): 141–50.

Tracy, C. R. " 'Caliban upon Setebos.' " *Studies in Philology* 35 (1938): 487–99.

Vaughan, Alden T. "Caliban in the 'Third World': Shakespeare's Savage as Sociopolitical Symbol." *Massachusetts Review* 29 (1988): 219–313.

———. "Shakespeare's Indian: The Americanization of Caliban." *Shakespeare Quarterly* 39 (1988): 137–53.

William, David. "*The Tempest* on the Stage." In *Jacobean Theatre* (Stratford-upon-Avon Studies 1), edited by John Russell Brown and Bernard Harris. New York: St. Martin's Press, 1960, pp. 133–57.

Willis, Deborah. "Shakespeare's *Tempest* and the Discourse of Colonialism." *Studies in English Literature 1500–1900* 29 (1989): 277–89.

Wilson, Daniel. *Caliban: The Missing Link.* London: Macmillan, 1873.

Wiltenberg, Robert. "The *Aeneid* in *The Tempest.*" *Shakespeare Survey* 39 (1987): 759–68.

Witt, Robert W. "Caliban upon Plato." *Victorian Poetry* 13 (1975): 136.

Wolfe, Thomas P. "Browning's Comic Magician: Caliban's Psychology and the Reader's." *Studies in Browning and His Circle* 6, No. 2 (Fall 1978): 7–24.

Young, David. "Rough Magic: *The Tempest.*" In *The Heart's Forest: A Study of Shakespeare's Pastoral Plays.* New Haven: Yale University Press, 1972, pp. 146–91.

Zabus, Chantal. "A Calibanic Tempest in Anglophone and Francophone New World Writing." *Canadian Literature* No. 104 (Spring 1985): 35–50.

Zimbardo, Rose. "Form and Disorder in *The Tempest.*" *Shakespeare Quarterly* 14 (1963): 49–56.

ACKNOWLEDGMENTS

"The Tempest" by Elmer Edgar Stoll from *PMLA* 47, No. 3 (September 1932), © 1932 by the Modern Language Association of America. Reprinted by permission of the Modern Language Association of America.

"The Tempest" by Harold C. Goddard from *The Meaning of Shakespeare* by Harold C. Goddard, © 1951 by The University of Chicago. Reprinted by permission of The University of Chicago Press.

"Introduction" to *The Tempest* (Arden Edition) by Frank Kermode, © 1954 by Methuen. Reprinted by permission of Routledge.

"Balaam and His Ass" by W. H. Auden from *The Dyer's Hand and Other Essays* by W. H. Auden, © 1962 by W. H. Auden. Reprinted by permission of Random House, Inc., and Faber & Faber Ltd.

"Prospero's Staff" by Jan Kott from *Shakespeare Our Contemporary* by Jan Kott, translated by Boleslaw Taborski, © 1964 by Panstwowe Wydawnictwo Naukowe and Double-day, a division of Bantam Doubleday Dell Publishing Group, Inc. Reprinted by permission of Doubleday, a division of Bantam Doubleday Dell Publishing Group, Inc.

"The Tempest and the Renaissance Idea of Man" by James E. Phillips from *Shakespeare Quarterly* 15, No. 2 (Spring 1964), © 1964 by the Shakespeare Association of America, Inc. Reprinted by permission of *Shakespeare Quarterly.*

"Hunt the Symbol" by William Empson from *Essays on Shakespeare* by William Empson, © 1986 by William Empson. Reprinted by permission.

"Miraculous Harp: A Reading of Shakespeare's *Tempest*" by Harry Berger, Jr., from *Shakespeare Studies* 5 (1969), © 1970 by The Center for Shakespeare Studies. Reprinted by permission of *Shakespeare Studies.*

"The New World Savage as Stranger; or, ' 'Tis New to Thee' " by Leslie A. Fiedler from *The Stranger in Shakespeare* by Leslie A. Fiedler, © 1972 by Leslie A. Fiedler. Reprinted by permission of the author.

"The Tempest: Speaking Your Language" by Terence Hawkes from *Shakespeare's Talking Animals: Language and Drama in Society* by Terence Hawkes, © 1973 by Terence Hawkes. Reprinted by permission of Hodder & Stoughton Publishers.

"Learning to Curse: Aspects of Linguistic Colonialism in the Sixteenth Century" by Stephen J. Greenblatt from *First Images of America: The Impact of the New World on the Old,* Volume 2, edited by Fredi Chiappelli et al., © 1976 by the Regents of the University of California. Reprinted by permission of the University of California Press.

"Ruling Taste and the Late Plays" by John D. Cox from *Shakespeare and the Dramaturgy of Power* by John D. Cox, © 1989 by Princeton University Press. Reprinted by permission of Princeton University Press.

"Monster Caliban" by J. W. Draper from *Revue de Littérature Comparée* 40, No. 4 (October–December 1966), © 1966 by *Revue de Littérature Comparée*. Reprinted by permission of *Revue de Littérature Comparée*.

"Upon 'Caliban upon Setebos'" by Barbara Melchiori from *Browning's Poetry of Reticence* by Barbara Melchiori, © 1968 by Barbara Melchiori. Reprinted by permission.

"Shakespeare's Existential Comedy" by Mike Frank from *Shakespeare's Late Plays: Essays in Honor of Charles Crow*, edited by Richard C. Tobias and Paul G. Zolbrod, © 1974 by Richard C. Tobias and Paul G. Zolbrod. Reprinted by permission of the editors.

"Caliban" by James Smith from *Shakespearian and Other Essays* by James Smith, © 1974 by Cambridge University Press. Reprinted by permission of Cambridge University Press.

"*The Tempest* and King James's *Daemonologie*" by Jacqueline E. M. Latham from *Shakespeare Survey* 28 (1975), © 1975 by Cambridge University Press. Reprinted by permission of Cambridge University Press.

"Artifice and Self-Consciousness in Auden's *The Sea and the Mirror*" by Lucy S. McDiarmid and John M. McDiarmid from *Contemporary Literature* 16, No. 3 (Summer 1975), © 1975 by the Board of Regents of the University of Wisconsin System. Reprinted by permission of The University of Wisconsin Press.

"Caliban as a Red Man" by G. Wilson Knight from *Shakespeare's Styles: Essays in Honour of Kenneth Muir*, edited by Philip Edwards, Inga-Stina Ewbank, and G. K. Hunter, © 1980 by Cambridge University Press. Reprinted by permission of Cambridge University Press.

"Caliban's Theatrical Metamorphoses" (originally titled "'Something Rich and Strange': Caliban's Theatrical Metamorphoses") by Virginia Mason Vaughan from *Shakespeare Quarterly* 36, No. 4 (Winter 1985), © 1985 by The Folger Shakespeare Library. Reprinted by permission of *Shakespeare Quarterly*.

"Caliban in Shakespeare and Browning" (originally titled "Wild Man and Savage Believer: Caliban in Shakespeare and Browning") by Kenneth Maclean from *Victorian Poetry* 25, No. 1 (Spring 1987), © 1987 by West Virginia University. Reprinted by permission.

"The Case of Colonialism in *The Tempest*" (originally titled "Discourse and the Individual: The Case of Colonialism in *The Tempest*") by Meredith Anne Skura from *Shakespeare Quarterly* 40, No. 1 (Spring 1989), © 1989 by The Folger Shakespeare Library. Reprinted by permission of *Shakespeare Quarterly*.

INDEX